Schnitt-A.B.C.D.

Dezember 2012

Lieber Steffen, wir wünschen Ihnen für die

Das Richard Wagner Festspielhaus Bayreuth
The Richard Wagner Festival Theatre Bayreuth

Zukunft Alles Gute und werden Sie vermissen.

Beste Wünsche
Ihre
Eva Wagner-Pasquier
Irene Neesse
Waltraud Seuar

Impressum Imprint

Das Richard Wagner Festspielhaus Bayreuth
The Richard Wagner Festival Theatre Bayreuth

Herausgeber Editor
Markus Kiesel, Ludwigsburg

Text Text
Dietmar Schuth, Heidelberg

Fotografie und Lithografie Photography and Lithography
Jens Willebrand, Köln
www.willebrand.com

Gestaltung Graphic Design
Joachim Mildner, Düsseldorf
www.joachimmildner.com

Redaktion Assistant editor
Hannelore Ostfeld, Köln

Korrektur Proofreading
Sabine Rochlitz, Riehen

Übersetzung Translation
K. Scott Witmer, Düsseldorf / New York

Besonderer Dank an Special thanks to Wolfgang Wagner und die Leitung der Bayreuther Festspiele, Peter Emmerich, Stephan Jöris, Karl-Heinz Matitschka, Norbert Kessler, Helmut Jahn; Gesellschaft der Freunde von Bayreuth e. V., Karl Gerhard Schmidt, Georg Freiherr von Waldenfels, Hans-Ludwig Grüschow, Heribert Johann, Ina Besser-Eichler; Nationalarchiv der Richard-Wagner-Stiftung Bayreuth Haus Wahnfried, Sven Friedrich, Gudrun Föttinger; Richard Wagner Museum Luzern, Katja Fleischer; Richard Wagner Verband International, Josef Lienhart; sowie Bill Birge, Bobby Christian, Hedel Enders, Claus J. Frankl, Lilo Heuberger, Bettina Munzer, Ludovicus Schmitz, Dieter Senft, Marilyn Tucker, Stefan Walter, Yolexis Willebrand

Herstellung und Vertrieb Production and Distribution
nettpress
Kuenstr. 13
50733 Köln / Germany
www.bayreuthbuch.de www.nettpress.de

Druck Printing
farbo print + media, Köln
www.farbo.de

Bindung Binding
Thomas Müntzer, Bad Langensalza
www.dhtm.de

ISBN 978-3-00-020809-6

Bibliografische Information der Deutschen Bibliothek
Die Deutsche Bibliothek verzeichnet diese Publikation in der Deutschen Nationalbibliografie; detaillierte bibliografische Daten sind im Internet über <http://dnb.ddb.de> abrufbar.

Dieses Werk ist urheberrechtlich geschützt. Die dadurch begründeten Rechte, insbesondere die der Übersetzung, des Nachdrucks, des Vortrags, der Entnahme von Abbildungen, der Funksendung, der Mikroverfilmung oder der Vervielfältigung auf anderen Wegen und der Speicherung in Datenverarbeitungsanlagen, bleiben, auch bei nur auszugsweiser Verwertung, vorbehalten. Eine Vervielfältigung dieses Werks oder von Teilen dieses Werks ist auch im Einzelfall nur in den Grenzen der gesetzlichen Bestimmungen des Urheberrechtsgesetzes in der jeweils geltenden Fassung zulässig. Sie ist grundsätzlich vergütungspflichtig. Zuwiderhandlungen unterliegen den Strafbestimmungen des Urheberrechts.

Wir haben uns intensiv bemüht, die Rechte für die einzelnen Abbildungen zu verfolgen und zu wahren. Sollte es trotzdem zu unbeabsichtigten Versäumnissen gekommen sein, entschuldigen wir uns bei Fotografen und Organisationen im Voraus und würden uns freuen, die passende Anerkennung in einer folgenden Ausgabe einzusetzen.

© 2007 nettpress und die Text- und Bildautoren
Gedruckt auf säurefreiem Papier, hergestellt aus chlorfrei gebleichtem Zellstoff.

Gedruckt in Europa / Deutschland

Bibliographic information published by the Deutsche Nationalbibliothek
The Deutsche Nationalbibliothek lists this publication in the Deutsche Nationalbibliografie; detailed bibliographic data is available in the Internet at <http://dnb.ddb.de>.

This work is subject to copyright. All rights are reserved, whether the whole or part of the material is concerned, specifically the rights of translation, reprinting, reuse of illustrations, recitation, broadcasting, reproduction on microfilms or in other ways, and storage in data banks. For any kind of use, permission of the copyright owner must be obtained.

Every effort has been made to trace the copyright holders, and we apologise in advance for any unintentional omission and would be pleased to insert the appropriate acknowledgement in any subsequent edition.

© 2007 nettpress and the text and image authors
Printed on acid-free paper produced from chlorine-free pulp.

Printed in Europe / Germany

Das Richard Wagner Festspielhaus Bayreuth
The Richard Wagner Festival Theatre Bayreuth
Herausgegeben von edited by **Markus Kiesel**

nettpress

Inhalt Content

- 8 — Wolfgang Wagner: *"Haus und Hof" für die Zukunft bestellen* Keeping "house and home" up and running for the future
- 10 — Markus Kiesel: *Ein Gedankengebäude* A thought construction
- 14 — Lageplan Orientation plan
- 16 — Dietmar Schuth: *Was für ein Theater?* What kind of theater?

Wagner und die Architektur Wagner and the architecture

- 20 — Wagners Bühnenarchitektur Wagner's stage architecture
- 26 — Was geht mich alle Baukunst der Welt an! What do I care about all the architecture in the world!
- 30 — Wagner und die Architektur des Nordens Wagner and the architecture of the north
  Gotik und Romanik Gothic and Romanesque Style
- 35 — Wagner und die Architektur des Südens Wagner and the architecture of the south
  Italienische Gotik und Byzantinik Italian Gothic and Byzantinic
- 36 — Renaissance Renaissance
- 38 — Barock und Rokoko Baroque and Rococo
- 39 — Klassizismus Classicism
- 40 — Historismus Historicism
- 42 — Wagner und die antike Architektur Wagner and antique architecture

Visionen eines idealen Theaters Visions for an ideal theater

- 46 — Wagners Theater der Zukunft Wagner's theater of the future
- 51 — Eine Vision konkretisiert sich A vision takes concrete form
- 54 — Gescheiterte Visionen für München Failed visions for Munich
- 55 — Entscheidung für Bayreuth Decision to build in Bayreuth

DAS BAYREUTHER FESTSPIELHAUS THE BAYREUTH FESTSPIELHAUS

Die Baugeschichte Construction history

- 56 — Bezaubernd ist dieser Punkt Enchanting – this spot is magical
- 58 — Tu Geld in deinen Beutel! Put money in your pocket!
- 59 — Wie heißt eigentlich der Architekt? What was the architect's name, anyway?
- 63 — Der Grundstein wird gelegt The cornerstone gets laid
- 64 — Otto Brückwalds Aufgabenstellung Otto Brückwald's job definition
- 70 — Vision von einer deutschen Architektur Vision of a German architecture
- 72 — Architektonische Zukunftsmusik Architectural dreams of the future
- 75 — Die Fundamente The foundations
- 78 — Das Richtfest The topping-out ceremony
- 81 — Bewahr es Gott vor Sturz und Krach! May God shield it from storms and collapse!
  Vollendet das ewige Werk The eternal work is complete
- 84 — Der liebliche Hügel The pleasant hill

DER AUSSENBAU THE EXTERIOR

Der Fachwerkbau The half-timbered building

- 88 — Theater-Scheune auf dem Hügel The theater barn on the hill
- 92 — Nordisches Fachwerk in Oberfranken Nordic timber framing in Upper Franconia
  Eine altertümliche Skelettbauweise A traditional skeletal architecture
- 94 — Andreaskreuze und Wilde Männer St. Andrew's cross and wild men
- 96 — Potemkinsches Theater Smokescreen theater
- 98 — Asketische Architektur Ascetic architecture

Der Backsteinbau Brick building

- 100 — Zur Not auch Backstein If need be, even brick
- 102 — Marienburg, Manchester und der Maurerstil Marienburg, Manchester and masonry style
- 106 — Bunte Backsteine Colorful bricks
- 108 — Ein Theater als Fabrik A theater as a factory

Antikensehnsucht Longing for the antique
112 Römische Schwitzbadfenster Roman sweat bath windows
114 Blaue Fenster, blaue Türen Blue windows, blue doors
116 Griechischer Tempel im Industriezeitalter A Greek temple in the industrial age
118 Voluten, Palmetten, Akroterien Volutes, palmettes, acroteria

Die Eckpavillons The corner pavilions
120 Neorenaissance mit Natursteinen Neo-Renaissance with natural stone
122 Theatermotiv mit Tympanon Theater motif with tympanum

Der Königsbau The Königsbau
125 Königsbau ohne König Königsbau without a king
127 Portikus plus preußische Kappen Portico with Prussian barrel vaults
128 Laternen mit Lindwürmern Lanterns with lindworms

Architektur für ein neues Publikum Architecture for a new audience
130 Garantiert und gratis Guaranteed and free
Polarisiertes Publikum Polarized audience
134 Besinnlichkeit der blauen Stunde The sensuality of twilight
Erholung und Entspannung Rest and relaxation
136 Bier und Bratwurst Beer and bratwurst
138 Lüftungslaterne und leichte Kleidung Ventilation lantern and light clothing

DER INNENBAU THE INTERIOR

Vor dem Zuschauerraum Leading up to the auditorium
140 Sonnige Scheinarchitektur Sunny illusionistic architecture
142 Salons und Studios Salons and studios
143 Gedenkstein gleich Grabstein Memorial stone and gravestone in one
144 Pompejanische Polychromie Pompeian polychromy

Der Zuschauerraum The auditorium
150 Eine völlige Schmucklosigkeit? A complete lack of decoration?
156 Das Zeltdach der Sommerbühne The tented roof of the summer stage
164 Anordnung des antiken Amphitheaters Arrangement of an ancient amphitheater
167 Die Bestuhlung The seating
170 Die Illusionswände Walls of illusion

174 Karlheinz Müller: *Die Demokratisierung der Akustik* The democratization of acoustics

181 Der mystische Abgrund The mystical abyss
182 Der Vorhang The curtain
183 Die Beleuchtung Lighting
190 Das versenkte Orchester The sunken orchestra

198 Pierre Boulez: „*Ein einzigartiges Objekt und Modell*" "A unique object and a model"

Die Bühne The stage
204 Die Bühnentechnik Stage technology
212 Die Bühnenbeleuchtung Stage lighting
214 Der Brandschutz Fire protection

216 Harry Kupfer: „*Man geht herum, man ist inspiriert und bekommt Ideen*"
"You walk around and it's totally inspiring, you get ideas"

222 **Biografien** Biographies
223 **Anmerkungen – Literaturverzeichnis – Bildnachweis**

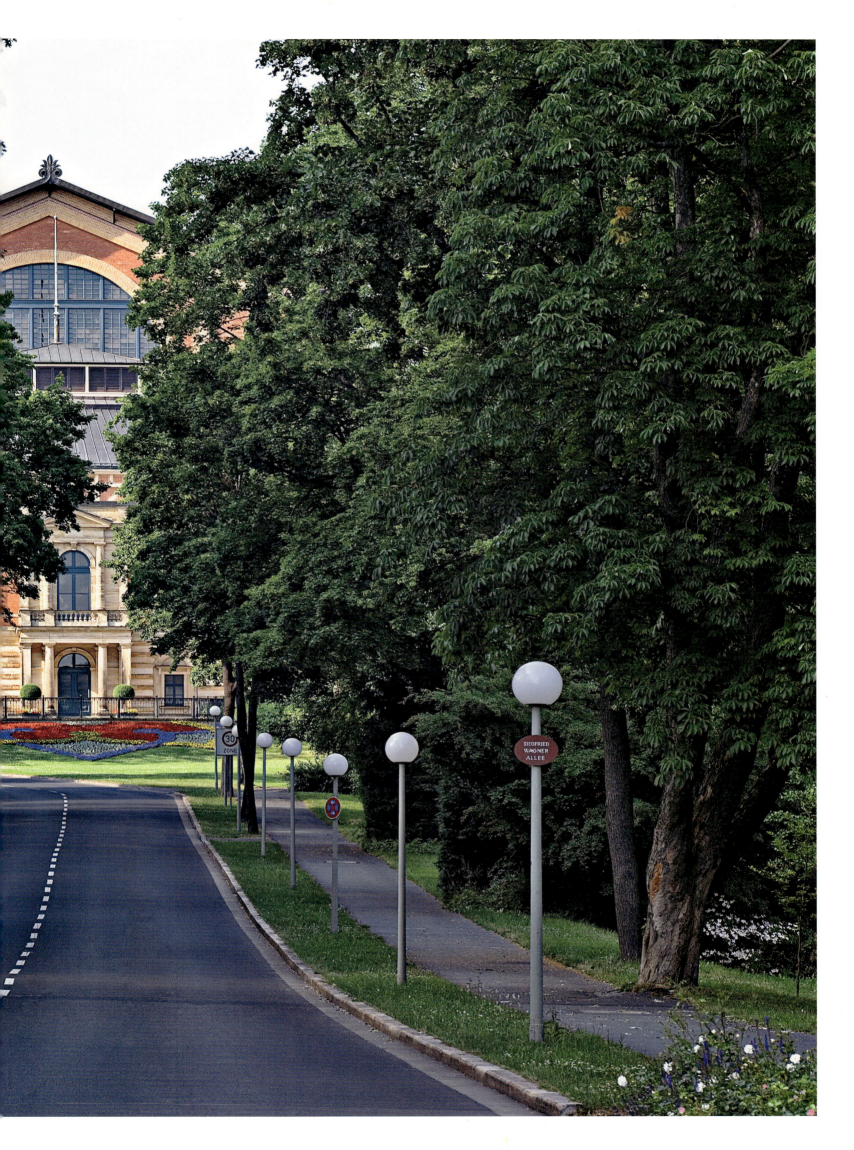

Wolfgang Wagner
„Haus und Hof" für die Zukunft bestellen

Die Flut der Literatur jedweden Genres, auch der Tondokumente und audiovisuellen Beiträge über Richard Wagner und sein Werk, über die Bayreuther Festspiele, einzelne Aufführungen, die verschiedensten Teilaspekte und so weiter und so fort, ist kaum noch überschaubar. Jahr für Jahr wird Neues in erstaunlicher Zahl veröffentlicht. Und so mag sich denn mancher fragen, ob dieses hier vorliegende Buch notwendig sei? Meine Antwort darauf ist ein ganz klares Ja!

Ungeachtet der enormen Publikationsfülle klafft seit Jahrzehnten eine auffällige Lücke in Bezug auf das Festspielhaus und dessen Inneres selbst, welches ja immerhin nach wie vor das ebenso unverändert-markante, weithin erkennbare und traditionsreiche wie zugleich ständig in einer Metamorphose befindliche Gehäuse bildet für jede Aufführung, jede künstlerische Entwicklung, eben für jene „ersichtlich gewordenen Taten der Musik", wie Wagner sein Schaffen einmal kennzeichnete. Wer in Bayreuths Festspielhaus etwa allein den Geist des Historismus suchen würde, wer ernsthaft glaubte, der einzigartige Giebel und so manch anderes Detail bewahre und verbürge getreulich das Überlieferte, der irrte gründlich. Wer gar aus der Beibehaltung diverser äußerer Bräuche und Strukturen schließen würde, in solch Archaischem würde eine gleichsam ewige Treue zu allem Ererbtem gewährleistet, der ginge völlig fehl. Das Festspielhaus war nie bestimmt zu einem Tempel oder irgendeiner Ersatzkirche, seine Mauern und Einrichtungen sollten zu keiner Zeit den Erfordernissen der Zeit widerstehen, vielmehr war und ist es eine der vornehmsten Aufgaben der Festspielleitung, „Haus und Hof" nicht allein in Ordnung zu halten, sondern für die Zukunft zu bestellen. Jeder, der bisher diese Verantwortung trug, war sich dessen bewusst und tat dies. Zwar in verschiedenem Maße und Umfang – nicht zuletzt, weil in voneinander sehr getrennte Zeitverhältnisse gestellt –, gleichwohl in der Erkenntnis, dass das generell Schützenswerte einen dauernden Bund mit dem temporär Veränderlichen eingehen müsse.

Wenn sich während der Phase gemeinschaftlicher Leitung durch meinen früh verstorbenen Bruder und mich sowie in der daran anschließenden Zeit meiner alleinigen Führung der Festspiele die allgemeine Bautätigkeit und zahlreiche Veränderungen ungemein verstärkten, so war und ist dies unterschiedlichen Gegebenheiten geschuldet: Zum einen galt es, die Substanz des Festspielhauses zu erhalten und baulich den Bedürfnissen der künstlerischen Arbeit sukzessive anzupassen, zum anderen musste der zunehmend rasanten Entwicklung innerhalb von Technik und Beleuchtung und auch der Entwicklung innerhalb ästhetisch-künstlerischer Aneignungs- und Wiedergabeprozesse adäquat Rechnung getragen werden.

Die Bayreuther Festspiele, die sich alljährlich sommers im Festspielhaus manifestieren, sind etwas ungemein Lebendiges – sie bieten Rahmenbedingungen, wie sie vergleichsweise kaum ein anderes Theater so offerieren kann. Selbstverständlich kommt es jeweils darauf an, wie intensiv und fantasievoll die einzelnen Teams der Inszenierungen unsere Angebote und Möglichkeiten nutzen, denn wir schaffen Voraussetzungen, Anreize zur Kreativität. Daraufhin gerichtet sind alle Bemühungen, daraus resultiert die enorme Zweckmäßigkeit sowohl des Haupthauses als auch die all seiner Nebengebäude.

Wolfgang Wagner
Keeping "house and home" up and running for the future

The flood of literature of every imaginable genre and tonal documents and audiovisual material about Richard Wagner, his oeuvre, the Bayreuth Festival, individual productions, various subtopics, etc. etc. can hardly be grasped. Every year an astonishing volume of new material is published. One might question whether this book is necessary at all. My answer to this question is a resounding Yes!

Despite the enormous number of publications, there has been a noticeable gap of materials over the past decades related to the Festspielhaus and its interior, even though it continues to provide the supporting framework for every production and every artistic development – that is, for every *"visual manifestation of the musical act,"* as Wagner liked to describe his creative output. Through all this, the theater remains striking, recognizable and traditional, yet is nonetheless in a state of constant metamorphosis. If one were only to seek the spirit of Historicism in the Bayreuth Festspielhaus, believing in all seriousness that the unique gable roof and some other notable details contain and bear true witness to the legacy, one would be gravely in error. If one would conclude that maintaining various outward traditions and structures implies that these archaisms are a sort of guarantee for eternal loyalty to that which was inherited, one would be on the wrong track completely. The Festspielhaus was never intended to be treated as a temple or as a church substitute. Its walls and apparatus were never supposed to resist the changing requirements over time. Rather, one of the most important duties of the Festspielhaus was and still is not only to keep *"house and home"* up and running, but to provide for the future as well. Everyone who has ever held this responsibility understood and fulfilled this duty to a greater or lesser degree, mainly because they were facing very different times, while realizing at the same time that the features generally worth protecting have to enter a constant alliance with those that change over time.

The great increase in the volume of building activity and changes that took place during the period when my brother, before his early death, and I jointly managed the Festival, as well as during the period when I have been managing it alone, was and still is attributable to various factors. First, we had to substantively fortify and successively adapt the Festspielhaus to changing artistic needs. Second, we had to seize on rapid technological and lighting developments and respond adequately to developments in the aesthetic-artistic process of appropriation and rendition.

In short, the Bayreuth Festival that takes place every summer in the Festspielhaus is incredibly vital. It offers conditions incomparable to almost any other theater. Naturally it depends to what degree and how creatively the individual production teams avail themselves of the opportunities we offer – we provide what it takes to ignite creativity. All of our efforts are focused in this direction, which explains the extreme degree of utility not only of the main theater, but of all of the supporting buildings as well.

Ich freue mich sehr, dass es den Autoren dieses Buches gelungen ist, eine umfangreiche und eingehende, eine sachgerechte und einfühlsame Beschreibung und Darstellung der besonderen Architektur des Festspielhauses zu geben, die ja von Anfang an einen Kompromiss fand zwischen heiterer Festlichkeit und scheunenartig empfundener Nüchternheit, auch zwischen äußerer Armut und innerem Reichtum – etwas, das bis heute die Besucher aus aller Welt ungemein fasziniert. Und ich freue mich, dass es den Autoren in gleicher Weise gelang, die meist vernachlässigte Bühnentechnik in ihren Facetten und Möglichkeiten eindrucksvoll miterlebbar zu machen. „Prospekte und Maschinen" sind ja, wie Goethes Theaterdirektor weiß, ein wichtiger Teil jenes wunderbaren Zaubers, der sich des Publikums bemächtigt.

Dieses Buch wird seinen Weg in eine breite Öffentlichkeit finden und seine Wirkung entfalten. Es berichtet von unserer Arbeit, eine der vermutlich schönsten, die Menschen ausüben dürfen. Ich wünsche ihm Glück und Erfolg.

Bayreuth, im Winter 2007

I am very pleased that the authors of this book succeeded in providing a broad and detailed, a technically accurate and perceptive description and representation of the unique architecture of the Festspielhaus, which itself strikes a compromise from the start between celebratory festivity and what some experience as barn-like sobriety, between poverty on the outside and wealth on the inside, something that fascinates visitors from all over the world to this day. I am also pleased that the authors likewise succeeded in making the details and potential of the stage technology tangible for the reader. It is usually ignored. As Goethe's theater director knows, "backdrops and machines" are an important part of the wonderful magic that washes over an audience.

This book will find its way to a broad public and grow in its effect. It bears witness to our work, presumably one of the best types of work a person could have. I wish the book much luck and success.

Bayreuth, winter of 2007

Markus Kiesel
Ein Gedankengebäude

Jedes Jahr besuchen Tausende Menschen das Festspielhaus Bayreuth. Zu den Vorstellungen der seit 1876 regelmäßig (seit 1951 alljährlich) im Sommer stattfindenden festlichen Aufführungen der Werke Richard Wagners reisen zirka 60000 Besucher nach Bayreuth. Zahlreiche Touristen erleben – außerhalb der Probenzeit – eine der Führungen durch das Theater. Hinzu kommen die Mitarbeiter der Festspiele, wovon sechsundfünfzig ganzjährig und über achthundert Künstler und Zeitkräfte im Sommer ab Mitte April bis Ende August nicht nur den Hügel, sondern auch Stadt und Umgebung Bayreuths bevölkern.

Dieses lebendige Theater, das mit seinen Künstlern, Mitarbeitern, Besuchern und Fans nun mehr als einhundertdreißig Jahre fasziniert, ist wie sein Erschaffer Richard Wagner aus der Musik- und Theatergeschichte nicht mehr wegzudenken. Aber eine genauso große Rolle spielen die Festspiele als Standortfaktor in Stadt und Umgebung Bayreuths: Jedem Besucher begegnen Werke und Helden des Meisters nicht nur in den Straßennamen, sondern auch in der Namensgebung zahlreicher Betriebe des Einzelhandels, wobei die eine oder andere Kuriosität zu entdecken ist, von den Auslagen in den Geschäften ganz zu schweigen, wo die überbordende Fantasie der Geschäftsleute den Vergleich mit der theatralischen Kraft des Verursachers oftmals nicht zu scheuen braucht ...

Es ist viel über die Werke und das Leben Richard Wagners sowie über die Geschichte der Bayreuther Festspiele geschrieben worden, und niemand wird sich der Wirkung und geballten Kraft der künstlerischen, aber auch familiären Tradition dieses ältesten Festspiels der neueren Welt entziehen können. Und dennoch: Was dem Besucher auf den ersten Blick als historisches Theatergebäude aus dem 19. Jahrhundert so authentisch daherkommt, ist in Wahrheit und bei näherem Hinschauen ein Paradoxon aus Tradition und lebendigster Theatergeschichte. Modernste Theatertechnik paart sich mit uralt Bewährtem. Was ursprünglich nur für die musterhafte Aufführung des RING DES NIBELUNGEN geplant war, wurde über die Zeit zu einem Ort lebendigster Theatergeschichte. Aus einem Provisorium wurde ein perfekter Theaterbetrieb, der nicht nur in seiner modernen und zeitgemäßen Betriebsstruktur grundsolide und stabil für die Zukunft gesichert ist, sondern auch als reale Immobilie funktions- und aufgabengerecht ausgebaut wurde und so für spätere Generationen zur Verfügung steht. Kaum ein ursprünglicher Stein steht mehr auf dem anderen, und dennoch hat sich der Charakter des Hauses kaum verändert, im Gegenteil: Mit dem Ausbau des Festspielhauses wurde und wird nichts anderes versucht, als der Idee seines Schöpfers auf immer perfektere Weise näher zu kommen. Im wahrsten Sinne des Wortes ein „Gedankengebäude".

Richard Wagner, am 22. Mai 1813 in Leipzig geboren, kam als Kapellmeister in Würzburg (1833), Magdeburg (1834), Königsberg (1836) und Riga (1837) schon früh mit verschiedensten Theaterbetrieben und -bauten in Berührung. Auch während seines denk-

Markus Kiesel
A thought construction

Every year, thousands of people visit the Bayreuth Festspielhaus. Around 60,000 visitors travel to Bayreuth every summer to attend the festive performances of Richard Wagner's works, a regular tradition that dates back to 1876 (annually since 1951). In addition, many tourists take a tour of the theater when rehearsals are note in session. Add to that the festival employees, including fifty-six full-time employees and over eight hundred artists and part-time employees who populate not only the hill, but also the city of Bayreuth and its surroundings from the middle of April through the end of August.

This living theater, its artists, employees, visitors, and fans, has been a point of fascination for over one hundred and thirty years and, like its creator Richard Wagner, is a landmark of musical and theater history. The festival has also left its mark on the city of Bayreuth and its surroundings. Visitors will recognize the names of the maestro's compositions and heroes not only in the street names, but also in the names of numerous shops. The city is full of curiosities – to say nothing of the shop displays by business owners, whose over-the-top fantasies are easily on a par with the theatrical power of the original creative spirit behind it all ...

Much has been written about Richard Wagner's works, his life, and about the history of the Bayreuth Festival. No one would deny the impact and the collective energy that this artistic and family tradition, the oldest festival in the modern world has had to date. And yet, what visitors perceive at first glance to be an authentic historical theater from the 19th century, reveals itself upon closer inspection to be a paradox of tradition and vital living theater history. The most modern theater technology complements elements that have proven themselves since ancient times. Over time, this theater originally intended only to house an exemplary performance of DER RING DES NIBELUNGEN, gradually became a center for vital living theater history. A provisional construction thus evolved into a perfect theater machinery boasting not only a rock solid modern festival production structure stable enough to last into the future, but also a real physical structure expanded to meet the new functional and artistic demands of this and future generations. Almost nothing remains of the original building blocks, and yet the building's character has hardly changed at all. In fact, just the opposite is true. The sole intention behind expanding the Festspielhaus was, and will continue to be, to attempt to hone in on its creator's concept more and more perfectly. It is, in the true sense of the word, a "thought construction."

Richard Wagner was born on May 22, 1813 in Leipzig. As musical director in Würzburg (1833), Magdeburg (1834), Königsberg (1836), and Riga (1837), he came in contact with various theater operations and buildings. During his memorable time in Paris, he also had a critical view of theater as a site of public art. His friendship with the influential architect Gottfried Semper (1803 – 1879) while Wagner was the musical director in Dresden (1843 to 1849: RIENZI, 1842, DER FLIEGENDE HOLLÄNDER, 1843, TANNHÄUSER, 1845) influenced him greatly. After his involvement in the Dresdner Revolution (1849), Wagner went into

würdigen Aufenthalts in Paris nahm er Theater als Ort öffentlichen Kunstwesens durchaus kritisch wahr. Prägend wurde seine Freundschaft mit dem bedeutenden Architekten Gottfried Semper (1803 – 1879) in seiner Zeit als Musikdirektor in Dresden (1843 bis 1849; RIENZI, 1842, HOLLÄNDER, 1843, TANNHÄUSER, 1845). Nach seinen Verstrickungen in die Dresdner Revolution (1849) lebte Wagner unter anderem im Schweizer Exil, bereiste halb Europa und entwickelte aus seinen biografischen Erfahrungen heraus nicht nur seine theoretischen Ideen einer neuen Kunst, sondern auch seine musikdramatischen Hauptwerke (LOHENGRIN 1850, DER RING DES NIBELUNGEN 1848 – 1876, TRISTAN UND ISOLDE 1859). Die Begegnung mit König Ludwig I. von Bayern (1864) garantierte Wagner eine gesicherte Existenz und ermöglichte – nicht ohne Komplikationen und emotionale Verwerfungen – die Verwirklichung seiner wesentlichen Kunstideen (Uraufführung TRISTAN 1865, MEISTERSINGER 1868), insbesondere die Begründung der Bayreuther Festspiele mit der Uraufführung des RING (1876) und des PARSIFAL (1882).

Das Festspielhaus war Privatbesitz Richard Wagners. Er hinterließ nach seinem Tode am 13. Februar 1883 kein Testament, jedoch leitete seine Gattin Cosima (1837 – 1930) als Vorerbin des gemeinsamen Sohnes Siegfried (1869 – 1930) unter der Vormundschaft des Geheimrats Adolf von Groß bis 1906 das Unternehmen. Seit 1906 war das Defizit von 1874 und 1878 entschuldet, und bis 1914 blickte die Familie auf ein millionenschweres Vermögen. Dennoch wurde in dieser Zeit am Festspielhaus kaum gebaut. Auch der von Richard Wagner auf spätere Generationen verschobene monumentale Ausbau in einem noch zu findenden „deutschen Stil" wurde in dieser einzigen Phase pekuniärer Entspanntheit erstaunlicherweise nicht geleistet. Von 1908 bis 1930 leitete Siegfried Wagner die Festspiele. Erst in die Zeit nach dem Ersten Weltkrieg fallen der große Anbau an der Hinterbühne, einiges an Nebengebäuden und der Einbau des Balkons im Zuschauerraum. Winifred Wagner machte sich ab 1930 an einige Pläne, von denen unter anderem der Verwaltungstrakt an der Westseite (heute Verwaltung, Festspielleitung und Kartenbüro) und die Sanierung der Foyers realisiert wurden. Auch einige Nebengebäude auf der Westseite, die heute noch erhalten sind (wie das Sanitäts- und Polizeihäuschen und der ehemalige Gästedienst, heute Post und Buchhandlung) stammen aus dieser Zeit. Nach Unwetterschäden 1939 kam es zu einem großen Plan von Emil Mewes, das Festspielhaus im monumentalen Stil der Nazis auszubauen.

Die Zeitläufe erledigten diese Pläne von selbst. 1945 wurde das Gebäude von den Amerikanern beschlagnahmt und für diverse Zwecke, Gottesdienste, Konzerte und theatralische Veranstaltungen der verschiedensten Art genutzt. Durch die Erklärung Winifred Wagners vom 21. Januar 1949, sich „jedweder Mitwirkung an der Organisation, Verwaltung und Leitung der Bayreuther Festspiele zu enthalten", wurde es möglich, das beschlagnahmte Gebäude am 28. Februar 1949 freizubekommen und an Wieland und Wolfgang Wagner als Mietsache zu übergeben. Das Haus war in einem baulich desolaten Zustand und die Frage nach der Wiedereröffnung der Festspiele mehr als offen.

exile in Switzerland and other places and traveled across half of Europe. These life experiences led to the development not only of his theoretical ideas about a new art, but also to his main works of musical drama (LOHENGRIN, 1850, DER RING DES NIBELUNGEN, 1848 to 1876, TRISTAN UND ISOLDE, 1859). Wagner's contact with King Ludwig I of Bavaria (1864) guaranteed his existence and, despite complications and emotional rejection, enabled him to bring his core artistic ideas to fruition (premiere of TRISTAN UND ISOLDE, 1865, DIE MEISTERSINGER, 1868), especially in founding the Bayreuth Festival with the premiere of DER RING DES NIBELUNGEN (1876) and PARSIFAL (1882).

The Festspielhaus was privately owned by Richard Wagner. Although not stipulated in a will after Richard's death (Februar 13, 1883), his wife Cosima (1837 – 1930) ran the business until 1906 as a pre-inheritor for their son Siegfried (1869 – 1930) under the guardianship of Privy Councillor, Adolf von Groß. The debts accumulated between 1874 and 1878 were paid off by 1906, and by 1914 the family possessed an asset valuing millions. Nonetheless, little work was done on the Festspielhaus during these years. Astonishingly, not even the monumental expansion in a not-yet discovered "German style" that Richard Wagner had assigned to later generations was undertaken in this unique phase of pecuniary relaxation. Siegfried Wagner led the festival between 1908 and 1930. The large addition to the backstage, several additional buildings and the balcony addition in the auditorium were not built until after the First World War. Starting in 1930, Winifred Wagner developed her own designs to build the administrative tract on the west side (which currently houses the administration, festival direction and ticket office), to refurbish the foyer, etc. Several additional buildings on the west side that are still standing today (such as the small medical and police houses and the former guest relation service, now post office and bookshop) were also built during this time. Following storm damage in 1939, Emil Mewes submitted a grand plan to expand the Festspielhaus in monumental Nazi style.

The march of time disposed of these plans on its own. In 1945 the Americans took possession of the building and used it for diverse purposes, such as church services, concerts, and theatrical productions of all sorts. Winifried Wagner's agreement on January 21, 1949 to "forfeit any and all participation in the organization, the management and the leadership of the Bayreuth Festival" made it possible to repossess the building from the Americans on February 28, 1949 and establish Wieland and Wolfgang Wagner as renters. The theater was in a desolate physical condition and it was far from clear whether the festival would resume.

During this turbulent time of great and speculative discussions about re-organizing and establishing a new direction for the festival, the "Society of Friends of Bayreuth" was founded in 1949. This organization not only raised start-up capital for the first post-war festival productions (thereby shielding the festival from 3rd-party influences, including the state), but also adopted the continuing special role of supporting and, since 1990 solely, financing physical plant maintenance and construction endeavors. A plaque on a middle class house in Bayreuth (Münzgasse 7) states it well: "It is a lot more fun to renovate an old house than to build a new one – and it costs barely twice as much." Between 1997 and 2004 alone, the "Society of Friends of Bayreuth" raised seventeen million Euro.

Wolfgang Wagner und die Mannen der Festspiele (Peter Emmerich, Stephan Jöris, Karl-Heinz Matitschka) sowie Markus Kiesel und Dietmar Schuth vom Buch-Team im improvisierten Büro im Festspielhaus
Wolfgang Wagner and the festival men (Peter Emmerich, Stephan Jöris and Karl-Heinz Matitschka) with Markus Kiesel and Dietmar Schuth from the book team in their improvised office in the Festspielhaus

In diese Zeit der vielen – auch spekulativen – Diskussionen um eine Neuorganisation und -ausrichtung der Festspiele fiel 1949 die Gründung der „Gesellschaft der Freunde Bayreuths", die zunächst nicht nur das Startkapital für die ersten Nachkriegsfestspiele zusammenbrachte (und damit die Festspiele vor äußerer – auch staatlicher – Einflussnahme schützte!), sondern es sich seither zur besonderen Aufgabe gemacht hat, die baulichen Maßnahmen an der Immobilie zu unterstützen und – seit 1990 ausschließlich – zu finanzieren. Wie eine Inschrift in einem Bürgerhaus in Bayreuth (Münzgasse 7) besagt, macht es „viel mehr Spaß, ein altes Haus zu renovieren als ein neues zu bauen – und kostet kaum das Doppelte". Allein in der jüngsten Zeit zwischen 1997 und 2004 hat die „Gesellschaft der Freunde Bayreuths" über siebzehn Millionen Euro aufgebracht.

Mit großer Weitsicht garantierte die Familie Wagner mit der Überführung des Festspielhauses und seiner Nebengebäude in die Richard-Wagner-Stiftung Bayreuth (1973) die Zukunft der Bayreuther Festspiele auf einer soliden ökonomischen und organisatorischen Basis. Seit 1973 gehört das Bayreuther Festspielhaus demnach „dem Volk". (Der Geschäftsführer des Festspielunternehmens – seit den 1980er Jahren eine GmbH – als Veranstalter der Festspiele tritt als Mieter auf.)

Seit 1951 leitet Wolfgang Wagner (bis 1966 zusammen mit seinem Bruder Wieland) mit einer in der Theatergeschichte einmaligen Kontinuität künstlerischer und unternehmerischer Beharrlichkeit die Festspiele. In „seine Zeit", 1958 bis heute, fallen die größten Neu-, Umbau- und Restaurierungsmaßnahmen der Gesamtanlage. Das Bayreuther Festspielhaus ist auch das Stein gewordene Denkmal des Bauherrn Wolfgang Wagner.

Damit dieses Buch entstehen konnte, wurden von dem Fotografen Jens Willebrand zuweilen bei beißender Kälte in den Wintermonaten 2005/06 über 900 Aufnahmen gemacht, von denen etwa 200 für dieses Werk ausgewählt wurden, der Kunsthistoriker Dietmar Schuth vertiefte sich in die Quellen zum Festspielhaus und in die zirka 50 000 Seiten Schrifttum von Wagners Gedankenwelt, um ein Destillat dessen, was Wagner unter „Architektur" verstanden haben könnte und wie er sein ideales Theater erbaut haben wollte, zu gewinnen. Joachim Mildner, der die Idee zu diesem Buch hatte, entwickelte das Design und war zusammen mit Hannelore Ostfeld für die Produktion verantwortlich.

Gemeinsam hat dieses Team Tausende Fotos der Bautagebücher der Jahre 1962 bis 2005 und unzählige Originalpläne aus dem Festspielarchiv gesichtet. Stundenlang durften wir bei Gudrun Föttinger im Richard-Wagner-Bildarchiv stöbern. Es gab wunderbare und wundersame Gespräche und Begegnungen. In Berlin mit Harry Kupfer, in Salzburg mit Pierre Boulez. Und immer wieder in Bayreuth selbst mit den Mannen der Festspiele und bei überraschenden Besuchen Wolfgang Wagners in unserem improvisierten Büro. Das große Interesse und die offenherzig-großzügige Unterstützung der Festspielleitung und des Teams um Peter Emmerich (Leiter der Abteilung Medien und Publikationen),

The Wagner family had the foresight to transfer the Festspielhaus and the surrounding buildings to the Richard Wagner Foundation (1973), guaranteeing the future economic and organizational stability of the Bayreuth Festival. Accordingly, the Bayreuth Festspielhaus has belonged to "the people" since 1973. (As festival host, the business director of the festival company, which has been incorporated since the 1980s, officially rents the building complex.)

Wolfgang Wagner (together with his brother until 1966) has been managing the festival since 1951, providing a continuity of artistic and business dedication unrivalled in theater history. The largest new construction, alteration and restoration projects on the entire complex have taken place during "his years" 1958 until today. In this light, the Bayreuth Festspielhaus is also a physical monument to the builder Wolfgang Wagner.

To make this book possible, photographer Jens Willebrand braved the sometimes bitter cold during the winter months of 2005/2006 to take over 900 photographs, including the approximately 200 selected for the book. Art historian Dietmar Schuth submerged himself in primary and secondary source material about the Festspielhaus and in around 50,000 pages of written evidence of Wagner's thoughts to distill Wagner's understanding of "architecture" and how he wanted his ideal theater to be built. Joachim Mildner, who had the idea for this book, created its design and managed together with Hannelore Ostfeld its production.

Our team viewed thousands of photographs from construction records from 1962 to 2005 and countless original plans from the festival archives. We were given the chance to peruse archivist Gudrun Föttinger's Richard Wagner photograph archive. We also had wonderful and wondrous discussions and encounters – with Harry Kupfer in Berlin, with Pierre Boulez in Salzburg, and time and again with festival personnel and in surprising visits from Wolfgang Wagner in our improvised office in Bayreuth. The great interest and the warm and generous support shown by festival management and Peter Emmerich (director of the media and publication department) and his team, Stephan Jöris (artistic-organizational member of festival management) and Karl-Heinz Matitschka (technical director), was trumped only by the team's immense patience for us and our never-ending requests for over a year. After all, in the time it took to create this book, not only was the substage machinery completely modernized, but a new RING was staged and the 2007 production of DIE MEISTERSINGER VON NÜRNBERG was rehearsed.

We were extremely fortunate to have had the chance to consult with Bayreuth architect Helmut Jahn, who displayed extraordinary attention to detail and love for the theater as overseer of the general overhaul in the 1960s and also during the restoration efforts in the 1990s.

This book's photographs and text offer a detailed description and a new interpretation of the current appearance of the Festspielhaus and its art historical value. In addition, the at times uncommon perspectives, poetical impressions and associative comments revealing openly subjective views invite the observer to look more closely and discover the history and the stories behind the facade and the first impression. It is

Stephan Jöris (künstlerisch-organisatorischer Mitarbeiter der Festspielleitung) und Karl-Heinz Matitschka (Technische Leitung) wurde nur übertroffen von der Engelsgeduld, mit der dieses Team uns und unsere dauernden Anfragen über ein Jahr ertragen hat. Immerhin wurde, während dieses Buch entstanden ist, nicht nur die Unterbühnenmaschinerie komplett modernisiert, sondern auch ein neuer RING gestemmt und die MEISTERSINGER für 2007 vorbereitet.

Ein großes Glück war es, den Bayreuther Architekten Helmut Jahn als Gesprächspartner zu haben, der nicht nur die Grundsanierung der 1960er Jahre, sondern auch und vor allem die Restaurierung der 1990er Jahre mit einer gleichermaßen großen Detailbesessenheit und Liebe zu dem Bau betreut hat.

Dieses Buch möchte mit seinen Bildern und Texten das Festspielhaus ausführlich in seiner realen Erscheinung wie auch kunsthistorischen Bedeutung beschreiben und neu bewerten. Mit den manchmal ungewöhnlichen Perspektiven, poetischen Blicken und assoziativen Kommentaren sollen darüber hinaus durchaus subjektive „An-Sichten" den Betrachter einladen, genauer hinzuschauen und Geschichte und Geschichten hinter der Fassade und dem ersten Augenschein zu entdecken. Es wendet sich an den Festspielbesucher ebenso wie an den Reisenden, an den Kunst- und Kulturinteressierten ebenso wie an den angehenden Architekturstudenten, dessen Aufgabe es vielleicht einmal sein wird, ein Theater oder Konzerthaus bauen zu dürfen.

Uns allen steht hier ein Bau der Theatergeschichte vor Augen, der in seiner Art, wie er erdacht wurde, was er durch die Zeit war, was er kann und was er in der Zukunft leisten muss, ein Meilenstein in der Gattungsgeschichte der Theaterarchitektur ist. Darüber hinaus gibt es Auskunft darüber, was „Architektur" Richard Wagner selbst bedeutet hat, wie er in Theorie und Alltag, zu Hause und auf Reisen über Gebäude dachte, was er sah (und was er – nicht! – sehen wollte), wie er in seiner so widersprüchlichen Existenz Architektur als Vision und Wirklichkeit erlebt hat.

meant for festival visitors and passers-by alike, for anyone interested in art and culture, and for beginning architectural students, who may themselves one day be commissioned with building a theater or a concert hall.

We all find ourselves facing a building out of theater history. Its underlying concepts, its status throughout time, what it is capable of, and what will be expected of it in the future make it a milestone in the history of theater architecture. Finally, this book informs the reader about what "architecture" meant to Richard Wagner himself, what he thought about buildings in theory and in practice, at home and in his travels, what he saw (and what he wanted – or didn't want! – to see), and how he, in his contradictory existence, experienced architecture as vision and reality.

Sichtung der Bautagebücher mit dem Bayreuther Architekten Helmut Jahn, der die Sanierungen und Umbauten im und am Festspielhaus seit Jahrzehnten begleitet
Looking through the construction records with Bayreuth architect Helmut Jahn, who has been in charge of the renovations and rebuilding on the interior and the exterior of the Festspielhaus for decades

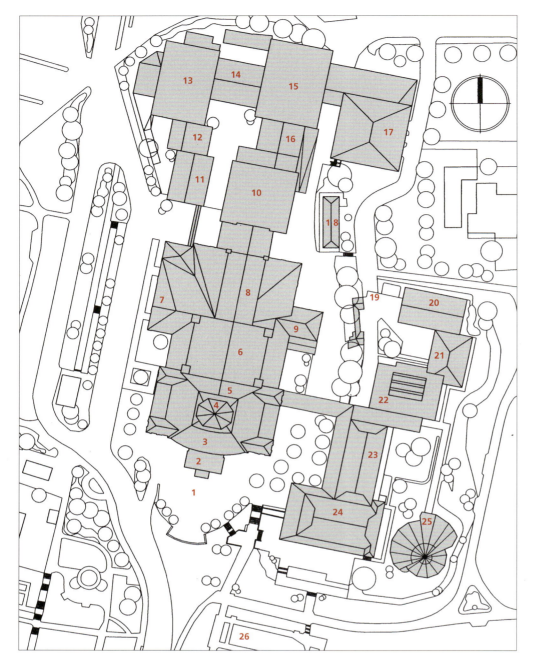

1. **Vorplatz** Forecourt
2. **Königsbau** Königsbau (King's extension)
3. **Südliches Foyer / Wandelhalle** South foyer / foyer
4. **Zuschauerraum** Auditorium
5. **Orchestergraben** Orchestra pit
6. **Hauptbühne** Main stage
7. **Verwaltung** Administration
8. **Hinterbühne** Backstage
9. **Probebühne I (Garderoben / Kostümwerkstätten)** Rehearsal stage I (dressing rooms / costume workshops)
10. **Probebühne III** Rehearsal stage III
11. **Probebühne II (Ballettsaal / Garderoben)** Rehearsal stage II (ballet rehearsal hall / dressing rooms)
12. **Schlosserei** Metal shop
13. **Probebühne V** Rehearsal stage V (o. Abb. / no picture)
14. **Fotoabteilung** Photo department
15. **Probebühne VI** Rehearsal stage VI (**Malersaal** Painting room)
16. **Schreinerei** Carpentry shop
17. **Probebühne VII** Rehearsal stage VII
18. **Maschinenhaus** Engine house
19. **Bühneneingang** Stage entrance
20. **Probebühne IV** Rehearsal stage IV
21. **Regisseure / Assistenten (o. Abb.)** Directors / assistants (no picture)
22. **Orchestergebäude** Orchestra pit (**Stimmzimmer / Repititionsräume**) (Tuning room / Rehearsal pianist rooms)
23. **Selbstbedienungsrestaurant / Proberaum** Self-service restaurant / Rehearsal room
24. **Festspielrestaurant** Festival restaurant (**Orchesterproberaum** Orchestra rehearsal room)
25. **Chorprobensaal** Chorus rehearsal hall
26. **Park mit Wagner-Büste** Park with Wagner bust

Dietmar Schuth
Was für ein Theater?

Viele, die zum ersten Mal nach Bayreuth kommen und das Festspielhaus nach langen Jahren des Wartens und einer manchmal etwas umständlichen Anreise erstmals erblicken, sind ein wenig enttäuscht. Denn schön ist dieses Gebäude nicht! Wie prächtig dagegen das nahe Markgräfliche Opernhaus, das in seinem prunkvollen Rokoko die fürstlichen Hoftheater des 18. Jahrhunderts repräsentiert. Noch prachtvoller sind die meisten Musentempel der (großbürgerlichen) Gründerzeit im späten 19. Jahrhundert. Dieses Bayreuther Festspielhaus dagegen erinnert in seiner kruden Architektur aus einfachen Backsteinen mit hölzernem Fachwerk eher an einen profanen Nutzbau. Oft wurde es gar als Scheune beschimpft oder als Stall für ein besonders großes grünes Fabeltier angesehen.

Das mit Backsteinen gefüllte Fachwerk hat vor allem in Norddeutschland eine jahrhundertealte Tradition. Aber wir sind hier im bayerischen Oberfranken, wo es ein ganz anderes Fachwerk gibt und ein schöner gelber Sandstein typisch ist, der den Barock der Städte prägt. Das Bayreuther Festspielhaus wirkt hier sehr fremd. Aber vielleicht wollte Wagner ja mit einer so „nordischen", so altertümlich und ländlich anmutenden Architektur den passenden Rahmen für seine (mittelalterlichen und mythischen) Bühnenstoffe schaffen. Wilder Wein wuchert um das alte Gemäuer wie beim Dornröschenschloss. Handelt es sich vielleicht um eine „romantische" Architektur in der Nachfolge Karl Friedrich Schinkels (1781 – 1841), der den Backsteinbau – in Anlehnung an die Backsteingotik des Nordens – als eine deutsche Neogotik etabliert hatte? Doch wenn man so deutsch, so romantisch bauen wollte, warum hat der Architekt dann auf gotische Spitzbögen, Maßwerk und Wimpergen verzichtet?

Gegen die These einer „romantischen" Architektur sprechen freilich einige merkwürdige Schmuckelemente, die weniger mit deutschem Mittelalter als vielmehr mit einer mittelmeerischen Antike zu tun haben. Das Dach des Bühnenturms gleicht einem griechischen Tempeldach mit einer Palmette obenauf, wie auf dem Parthenon in Athen. Es wird von feinen Konsolen getragen, die an den antikisierenden Stil des Biedermeier erinnern. Das große Fenster darunter scheint aus der (römischen) Antike bekannt. Dazu kommen die Voluten am Tempeldach und einige Akroterien auf den anderen Dächern. Ebenfalls der Antike verpflichtet sind die Hausteinelemente in jenem gelben Sandstein, die an den vier Eckbauten am Zuschauerraum und am sogenannten Königsbau toskanische Säulen und Pfeiler mit Kapitellen erkennen lassen. Kenner wie Heinrich Habel[1] beschreiben hier eine Neorenaissance, die freilich eine sehr lakonische ist.

Jener Königsbau ist der schmuckvollste Teil der gesamten Außenarchitektur. Er kontrastiert mit dem Fachwerk der konvexen Rückwand des Zuschauerraums und muss ganz allein – viel zu niedrig und zu einfach – den Mittelrisalit dieser Fassade markieren. Trotzdem treffen sich vor dem Königsbau immer wieder neue Besucher, die hier den schönen Haupteingang suchen, da sie gewohnt sind, diesen in der symmetrischen Mitte einer Fassade zu finden. Doch dieses Festspielhaus hat keine repräsentative Schaufront, die zum Eintreten einlädt. Stattdessen werden die meisten Besucher auf die Seite umgelenkt, wie Lieferanten, die man zum Boteneingang schickt.

Tritt man endlich in das Gebäude, ließe sich wenigstens ein prächtiges Foyer erwarten, in dessen Spiegeln und Lampen sich der Glanz eines glamourösen Festspielabends widerspiegeln könnte. Stattdessen wird man von einem eher depressiven Violett an Wänden und Türen empfangen. Auch die einfache „altdeutsche" Holzarchitektur wirkt sehr nüchtern, sodass Damen in teuren Abendkleidern und Herren im Smoking etwas overdressed erscheinen. Diese Architektur erinnert an eine ärmliche Trinkhalle

Dietmar Schuth
What kind of theater?

After years of waiting and an often complicated journey, many first-time visitors to Bayreuth are disappointed by their first glimpse of the Festspielhaus. The building is simply not beautiful. In comparison, the nearby Margravial Opera House is a gem, its decorative Rococo architecture representative of the 18th century princely court theater. Most theaters from the (bourgeois) Wilhelminian era at the end of the 19th century are even more decorative. In contrast, the crude architecture, simple bricks and timber framing of the Bayreuth Festspielhaus brings a profane functional building to mind. Critics even often mockingly call it a barn or a stable for an especially large green mythical animal.

The tradition of brick-inlayed timber framing goes back centuries, especially in northern Germany. But we are here in Bavarian Upper Franconia, where a completely different timber framing style and the beautiful yellow sandstone dominating the city's baroque buildings are typical. The Bayreuth Festspielhaus appears quite out of place in this setting. But perhaps Wagner's intention was to use this "Nordic," old-fashioned and rural-seeming architecture to create the appropriate setting for his stage material (set in medieval and mythical times). Wild grape vines engulf the old walls like Sleeping Beauty's castle. Is this perhaps an example of "romantic" architecture in the tradition of Karl Friedrich Schinkel (1781 – 1841) that picks up on the northern brick Gothic style to establish brick buildings as a German neo-Gothic style? But if the intention was to build in such a strongly German, Romantic style, why did the architect forgo Gothic pointed arches, tracery and openwork gablets?

Clearly, several odd decorative elements have less to do with medieval Germany than Mediterranean antiquity and weaken the "Romantic" architecture thesis. The roof of the stage tower looks like a Greek temple roof topped with a palmette, just like the Parthenon in Athens. It is supported by delicate corbels reminiscent of the classical Biedermeier style. The large window below it seems familiar from (Roman) antiquity. Then there are the scrolls along the temple roof and several acroteria on top of the other roofs. The hewn stone elements of yellow sandstone on the four corner constructions of the auditorium and the so-called Königsbau resembling Tuscan pillars and piers with capitals are likewise straight out of antiquity. Experts such as Heinrich Habel consider it neo-Renaissance, though clearly in highly laconic form.

The Königsbau (King's extension) is the most decorative part of the entire exterior architecture. It contrasts with the timber frame of the convex rear wall of the auditorium and, although it is far too short and simple, it is the only element marking the center projection of this facade. Still, first-time visitors always seem to congregate in front of the Königsbau in search of the beautiful main entrance they are used to finding in the symmetrical center of a facade. However, this Festspielhaus lacks a representative frontispiece inviting entry. Instead, most visitors are directed to the side like a delivery service sent to the service entrance.

Once you enter the building, you expect at the very least a fancy foyer full of mirrors and lights mirroring the sparkle of a glamorous festival evening. Instead, you are greeted by rather depressing violet walls and doors. Even the simple "old-German" wooden architecture is sobering, causing ladies dressed in costly evening gowns and gentlemen in tuxedos to appear somewhat overdressed. This architecture brings to mind the simple drinking hall in a not especially mundane spa or a railroad station from the colonial times. Just like in a railway station, there is the pull to quickly locate the track – and the entry to the auditorium. Representative foyers and vestibules for seeing and being seen are nowhere to be found. Despite its name, even the Königsbau (King's building) is not an exception. It appears more bourgeois than feudal, is narrow and very plain, and its marble is faux. For better or worse, guests have little choice but to go outside into the odor of bratwurst – as at a farmer's wedding party – before and after the performances and during the intermissions.

eines nicht sehr mondänen Kurbads oder an einen Bahnhof des Kolonialzeitalters. Wie in einem solchen sucht man sich nun – ganz unvermittelt – seinen Bahnsteig und den Zutritt zum Zuschauerraum. Repräsentative Foyers und Vestibüle zum Flanieren sind einfach nicht vorhanden. Ja, selbst der Königsbau bildet hier – trotz des Namens – keine Ausnahme. Er erscheint eher bürgerlich als feudal, ist eng und sehr schlicht, der Marmor nur aufgemalt. Vor und nach den Vorstellungen und in den Pausen muss sich der Gast wohl oder übel im Freien aufhalten, wo es nach Bratwurst duftet – wie auf einer Bauernhochzeit.

Der Zuschauerraum aber, stellt man erleichtert fest, versöhnt, ist er doch der schönste Teil des Ganzen. Golden glänzen hier korinthische Säulen, prunkvolle Kandelaber erzeugen ein festliches Licht, roter (allerdings nur aufgemalter) Samt in den rückwärtigen Logen erwärmt das sinnliche Gemüt. Ein elegant geschwungenes und sanft ansteigendes Theater öffnet sich dem Besucher wie in den Theatern des alten Griechenland. Das verspricht eine gute Sicht und eine hervorragende Akustik. Für Letzteres steht sicherlich auch der schwingende Holzboden, der sich beim Einlass des Publikums mit einem großen Poltern bemerkbar macht.

Alles scheint hier aus Holz – und man denkt daran, wie viele Theaterbauten in der Geschichte gerade deshalb schon abgebrannt sind. Selbst die Mauern, die sich als Scherwände wie Kulissen in den Zuschauerraum hineinrücken, sind – wenn man daran klopft – hörbar aus Gips und Holz, ihr Mauerwerk ist nicht echt. Aber was sind das eigentlich für merkwürdige „Mauern"? Sie ersetzen die klassischen Seitenlogen und -balkons, von denen man anderenorts so schön die Dekolletés und die schreienden Krawatten der Besucher studieren kann. Kein anderes Theater dieser Welt hat solche Scherwände. Mit korinthischen Säulen und Pfeilern versehen, tragen sie ein Gebälk, doch darüber stemmen sie nichts, allenfalls eine schwere oberfränkische Sommerluft. Sie scheinen vollkommen sinnlos. Oder haben sie eine akustische Funktion, vielleicht auch eine optische?

Immerhin tragen sie die Beleuchtung des Zuschauerraums, keine Kristallüster, so doch durchaus prunkvolle Kandelaber, die den zentralen Kronleuchter ersetzen, der ebenfalls in jedem „normalen" Theater des 19. Jahrhunderts zur repräsentativen Grundausstattung gehört. Stattdessen erkennt man ein sogenanntes Velarium, die gemalte Imitation eines antiken Zeltdachs. Für den Bruchteil einer Sekunde mag man an den zu Hause liegenden Regenschirm denken, doch dieses Zeltdach ist ja nicht echt, die Decke darüber in Wahrheit solide. Es erinnert an ein luftiges Zirkusdach und suggeriert dem Zuschauer einen Hauch von Open-Air-Feeling. Tatsächlich fragen besorgte Erstbesucher zuweilen im Kartenbüro nach, ob Bayreuth, diese „oberfränkische Sommerbühne", denn überdacht sei.

Langsam nähert sich der Beginn der Vorstellung; Zeit sich weiter umzuschauen. Auf jenem Velarium findet sich endlich auch ein bisschen Dekor fürs Auge: Dieses Zelt ist im Gegensatz zu allen anderen Wand- und Mauerflächen des Festspielhauses dekorativ bemalt, doch bedarf es schon eines etwas abgelenkten Opernglases, um die floralen, pompejanisch anmutenden Ornamente und Arabesken anzuschauen.

Schließlich beginnt die Vorstellung, doch auch hier erwartet manchen neuen Besucher eine Enttäuschung. Die Sicht ist zwar sehr gut, doch wo ist das Orchester? Der sonst so beliebte Blickfang mit romantischer Repoussoirfigur in rabenschwarzer Robe (gemeint ist der Dirigent) fehlt. Ganz gedämpft, fast leise ertönt die Musik des Meisters, die man fast immer und fast überall viel zu laut zu hören gewohnt ist. In Bayreuth herrscht für das Orchester und seinen Dirigenten ein echtes Understatement: Beide sind vor der Bühne im Proszenium versenkt und sogar unter einem wulstigen Überbau verborgen.

To the guest's relief, the disappointment doesn't continue in the auditorium. It is the most beautiful part of the whole theater. Corinthian pillars shimmer in gold, elaborate candelabras cast a festive light, the red (only faux painted) velvet in the rear loges warms the senses. An elegantly curved and gracefully sloped theater spreads before the visitor like the ancient Greek theaters, promising a good view and excellent acoustics. The sprung wood floor that resonates loudly when the audience is admitted surely also provides acoustical benefits.

Everything appears to be made of wood, causing one to recall how many historical theaters have already burned down for that very reason. If you knock on the shear walls jutting into the auditorium like flats, you will hear that they are made of plaster and wood. Their solid wall appearance is only an illusion. But what is the purpose of these strange "walls," anyway? They take the place of traditional side loges and balconies that, in other theaters, provide the ideal vantage points from which to study other guests' beautiful décolletés and shrill ties. No other theater in the world has shear walls like these. They have Corinthian pillars and piers and support a beam, but nothing on top of that, except perhaps the heavy Upper Franconian summer air. They appear to have no purpose. Or do they have an acoustical function, perhaps an optical one as well?

At the very least they bear the auditorium lighting, not crystal chandeliers, but at least decorative candelabras that take the place of the central crystal chandelier that belongs to the basic representational inventory of every "normal" 19th century theater. Instead you will recognize a so-called velarium on the ceiling, a painted imitation of a tent roof. For a split second your mind may wander to the umbrella you left at home, but not to worry, this tent roof is not real. The ceiling above you is actually solid. It evokes an airy circus tent and creates a touch of open-air feeling for the audience. In fact, concerned first-timers occasionally inquire in the ticket office whether the "Upper Franconian summer stage" in Bayreuth has a roof.

The start of the performance is gradually approaching, but there is still time for another look around. A closer look at the velarium reveals a bit of décor for the eye, finally. Unlike the other wall surfaces in the Festspielhaus, this tent is decoratively painted. You may, however, need to divert your opera glass a bit to appreciate the Pompeii-style floral ornaments and arabesques.

The performance is about to begin, and some first-timers are in for yet another disappointment. The view is indeed good, but where is the orchestra? The eye-catching repoussoir figure dressed in pitch black we normally love to watch (that is, the conductor) is nowhere to be seen. The maestro's music we have grown accustomed to hearing much too loudly almost everywhere we go rises up muffled, almost quietly. The orchestra and its conductor in Bayreuth truly embody the word understatement. Both are not only sunk down into the proscenium, but also hidden by a bulging lid.

The lights slowly dim. There is no turning back now. The narrow seats form endless rows without a center corridor, squelching any hope of spontaneous escape. You are physically and sensually trapped. Some may recollect poor Fontane or Stravinsky, who suffered truly hellish torment here. But the good view and the subtle acoustics also have their merits. They draw the audience in, one might even say suggestively, removing all obstacles to experiencing the performance directly. Nothing gets in the way of concentrating. The focus is on the singers and the stage, and nothing more.

The hours pass. In addition to adoring the music and the drama, many gradually grow aware of their bodies. This theater is not only Greek, it's downright Spartan! The chairs are as undeniably hard as the "wood class" in a Wilhelminian express train. But at some point, it draws to a close, an acoustically and optically memorable evening in an admittedly somewhat strange building.

But how can all of these architectural anomalies and inhospitable features be explained? Did Wagner want to provoke his audiences, or

Langsam geht das Licht aus, nun gibt es kein Entrinnen mehr. Man sitzt meist eng in einer endlosen Reihe ohne Mittelgang, die jede spontane Flucht unmöglich macht. Man ist gefangen, körperlich wie sinnlich. Mancher mag an den armen Fontane oder an Strawinsky[1] denken, die hier echte Höllenqualen erlitten. Die gute Sicht und die subtile Akustik jedoch bannen den Zuschauer geradezu suggestiv, lassen das Bühnengeschehen ganz unvermittelt erleben, nichts stört die Konzentration, der ganze Blick gehört den Sängern und ihrer Bühne.

Stunde um Stunde vergeht. Und allmählich spüren viele neben aller Begeisterung für die Musik und das Drama allmählich wieder ihren Körper. Dieses Theater ist nämlich nicht nur ein griechisches, sondern namentlich ein spartanisches, die Stühle ausgesprochen hart wie in der Holzklasse eines gründerzeitlichen D-Zugs. Doch dann ist irgendwann alles vorbei, ein akustisch wie optisch im wahrsten Sinne des Wortes denkwürdiger Abend in einem freilich etwas merkwürdigen Gebäude.

Aber wie erklären sich all diese architektonischen Sonder- und Ungastlichkeiten? Wollte Wagner sein Publikum provozieren oder ist vieles von unfähigen Architekten einfach nicht recht bedacht worden? Ist alles, was wir heute sehen, überhaupt original und im Sinne des Erfinders? Wer war eigentlich der Architekt, den man zur Rechenschaft ziehen möchte? Oder steckt Wagner selbst dahinter? War diese Architektur wirklich als adäquates ästhetisches Ambiente zu seinen Bühnenwerken konzipiert? Was hat Wagner selbst zu seinen Intentionen und zur konkreten Architektur des Festspielhauses gesagt, was zur Architektur überhaupt, wenn überhaupt?

Wie erklären sich dieser profane Außenbau und die nüchternen Foyers? War es einfach nur das – bei Wagner stets – fehlende Geld, das den Bauherrn zu all den billigen Baumaterialien, den harten Stühlen, dem Holz, dem Backstein und den aufgemalten Imitationen gezwungen hat? Ist er mit seinem Bau vielleicht gar nicht fertig geworden? Wie jedoch erklären sich dann die antikisierenden Schmuckelemente, die außen wie innen teuer gewesen sein müssen? Sie wirken irgendwie beschönigend und entsprechen einer Antikenmode, die man eher vom Klassizismus um 1800 und vom Biedermeier kennt. Man fühlt sich an die „hellenistischen" Bauten des bayerischen Königs Ludwig I. erinnert. Seinem Enkel Ludwig II., Wagners größtem Gönner, kann das Festspielhaus damals sicherlich nicht gefallen haben. In diesem Sinne wäre das Bayreuther Festspielhaus ein geradezu altmodischer, nostalgischer Bau.

Oder ist das Festspielhaus im Gegenteil ein revolutionärer, ein damals fast futuristischer Bau, der die Funktionalität der Industriearchitektur als einer der ersten auf einen Musentempel übertrug? Mag hier Wagners revolutionäre Vergangenheit eine Rolle gespielt haben? Man könnte sogar nach Elementen der Revolutionsarchitektur vor 1800 suchen, die dieses Festspielhaus unversehens als eine politische Architektur erscheinen ließen. Ist dieses Bayreuther Festspielhaus wirklich nur ein Monument mit manch merkwürdigen Mauern und Motiven, ein widersprüchliches Unikum, oder ist es vielleicht doch ein ästhetisch gelungenes Gebäude?

did incompetent architects simply fail to think through a lot of things well enough? Is everything we see today original and as the inventor intended? Who was the architect one would like to hold responsible? Or was Wagner himself behind it all? Was this architecture really conceptualized to create an appropriate aesthetic atmosphere for his stage works? What did Wagner himself say about his intentions and about the architecture of the Festspielhaus specifically? What, if anything, did he say about architecture in general?

How can the profane exterior and the plain foyers be explained? Was it simply lack of money, as was so often the case with Wagner, that was driving the builder to choose the cheap construction materials, the hard chairs, the wood, the bricks and the painted imitations? Or did he perhaps not even finish the building? But then how can the classical elements be explained? They must have been costly, both outside and inside. To a degree, they add beauty and seem in line with the preference for the antique more in fashion in the classicistic era around 1800 and from Biedermeier times. They bring to mind the Bavarian King Ludwig I's "Hellenistic" structures. Surely his grandson Ludwig II, Wagner's largest benefactor, couldn't have liked the Festspielhaus. From this perspective, one might even call the Bayreuth Festspielhaus an old-fashioned, nostalgic building.

Or is just the opposite true? Was the Festspielhaus revolutionary, for its time almost futuristic, one of the forerunners in applying the functionality of industrial architecture to a theater? Could Wagner's revolutionary background have played a role here? One could even look for elements of pre-1800 revolutionary architecture that suddenly cast a political light on the Festspielhaus. Is the Bayreuth Festspielhaus nothing more than a monument with a few strange walls and motives, a contradictory one-of-a-kind? Or is it an aesthetically successful building after all?

Hinterbühnentür
Backstage door

„Hier schliess' ich ein Geheimnis ein, da ruh' es viele hundert Jahr':
so lange es verwahrt der Stein, macht es der Welt sich offenbar."[1]

"A secret I do bury here for centuries, may it be:
doth the stone yet persevere, its truth the world shall see."

Richard Wagner (1872)
Sinnspruch der Grundsteinlegung
Motto of the cornerstone laying ceremony

Wagner und die Architektur

Wagners Bühnenarchitektur

Wagner war Komponist und Dichter, kein Architekt. Doch jeder, der Stücke für eine Theaterbühne schreibt, muss auch an Bühnenbilder denken. Und diese sind – nicht nur bei Wagner – meist architektonische Visionen: ein von Mauern umgrenzter Handlungsort, ein Interieur, ein Straßenzug, ein Platz und so weiter. Wagner nutzt in seinen Werken bisweilen historisch-reale Kulissen (wie die Wartburg) oder benennt die Gebäude lediglich als (fiktive) Burg, Palast, Wohnhaus oder Kirche. Sehr genau ist Wagner selten, sodass die Architektur durch allgemeine Zeit- und Ortsangaben der Textbücher rekonstruiert beziehungsweise hypostasiert werden kann. Moderne Inszenierungen kümmern sich selten um solche Wissenschaft und verwandeln die Burg „Walhall" in ein Kernkraftwerk oder das Brautgemach im LOHENGRIN in eine 1960er-Jahre-Einbauküche. Jüngere Wagnerianer können den „Bühnenarchitekten" Wagner nur kennen lernen, wenn sie im Textbuch und in den Regieanweisungen nachlesen.

Häufig sind natürliche Architekturen in den Bühnenbildern Wagners, sprich Höhlen wie im TANNHÄUSER oder Mimes und Fafners Höhle im RING. Hundings Hütte in DIE WALKÜRE, eine Art Baumhaus, kann als Ur-Architektur angesprochen werden, wie sie einst der römische Architekturtheoretiker Vitruv an den Beginn der Architekturgeschichte stellte. DER RING DES NIBELUNGEN spielt in der Tat in einer prähistorischen Zeit und ist, wie andere Stücke Wagners, einem Mythenreich zuzuordnen. Die darin erscheinende Architektur hat keine realen Vorbilder, weil Germanien keinen Palast von Knossos, keine Burg von Mykene aufweisen kann. Sie ist „irgendwie" alt und in einer archaischen Phantastik vorzustellen. Alle anderen Stücke Wagners spielen im Mittelalter und lassen sich mit realen historischen Bauwerken vergleichen, auch wenn Wagner stilkundliche Begriffe wie „romanisch", „gotisch" oder „normannisch" vermissen lässt und seine Bühnenbilder immer nur skizzenhaft andeutet.

Die in Wagners Werken häufigste Architekturform ist die (mittelalterliche) Burg, seit der Romantik das Sinnbild des Mittelalters schlechthin, eine Kulisse, die Wagner schon als Kind geliebt hat. In „Mein Leben"[1] beschreibt er sich selbst als fantasiebegabten Knaben, der in seinen Tag- und Nachtträumen von Gespenstern heimgesucht wurde. Alles Fantastische zog ihn an und schreckte ihn zugleich; in seinen Spielen zog es ihn immer wieder in die schaurige Welt des Mittelalters. Sein allererstes selbst gedichtetes und inszeniertes Theaterstück war ein rauflustiges Ritterstück und wurde in Loschwitz auf dem Burgberg vom kleinen Richard in einem Puppentheater auf-, und trotz Gewitters unter Tränen auch zu Ende ausgeführt.[2] Burgen, nicht Kirchen oder Schlösser, waren also die ersten Architekturen, die Wagner faszinierten, was selbst für normale Jungen nichts Außergewöhnliches ist. Hier in der Kindheit prägten sich letztlich seine architektonischen Idealbilder ein.

Wagner and the architecture

Wagner's stage architecture

Wagner was a composer and poet, but not an architect. But anyone who writes for the theater stage has to give some thought to set design. In most cases, and not only for Wagner, sets are architectural visions: a walled-in area where something takes place, an interior, a streetscape, a square. Wagner sometimes uses real historical settings (like Wartburg) and sometimes only refers to buildings as (fictional) fortresses, palaces, houses or churches. Wagner's references to time and location in the libretto are rarely precise enough for us to be able to reconstruct or hypostatize the architecture. Modern productions rarely concern themselves with such research and freely transform the fortress "Walhall" into a nuclear power generation plant or the bridal chamber in LOHENGRIN into a fitted kitchen from the 1960s. The only way younger Wagnerians can become familiar with the "stage architect" Wagner is to read his libretto and stage directions.

Wager's sets frequently include natural architectures, such as caves in TANNHÄUSER or Mime's and Fafner's cave in the RING. Hunding's hut in DIE WALKÜRE, akin to a tree house, can be considered ur-architecture, following the Roman architectural theoretician Vitruv's lead, who positioned it at the beginning of architectural history. DER RING DES NIBELUNGEN actually takes place in a prehistoric time and, like other works by Wagner, falls into the mythical world category. Its architecture has no real models, since there is no Palace of Knossos and no Fortress of Mykene in Germania. It is supposed to be "somehow" old, belonging to a fantastical archaic world. Wagner's remaining works take place in the Middle Ages in settings comparable to real historical constructions, even though Wagner does not use stylistic terms such as "Romanesque," "Gothic" or "Norman" and only briefly sketches the sets.

The most common architectural form in Wagner's works is the (medieval) fortress, considered the epitome of the Middle Ages since the Romantic era. Wagner loved the medieval setting even as a child. In "My Life," he recounts having had an exceptionally vivid fantasy and having been haunted by ghosts in his daydreams and nightmares as a boy. He felt drawn to and simultaneously frightened by the fantastical. Time and again, his playtime would lure him into the eerie world of the Middle Ages. According to his account, the very first play he wrote and produced himself involved plenty of fighting knights. Young Richard performed his play in a puppet theater in Löschwitz on the fortress hill and tearfully saw it through to the end despite a thunderstorm. So the first architectural structures that fascinated Wagner were fortresses, not churches or castles, which is nothing unusual even for normal boys. In the end, his architectural ideals took form during childhood.

DER FLIEGENDE HOLLÄNDER (1843) ist ohne Zeitangabe (und ohne markante Architektur im Bühnenbild, Dalands Haus bleibt unbestimmt) wiederum in einem zeitlosen Sagenreich anzusiedeln, wobei der „*Großvaterstuhle*"[1] im ersten Aufzug allerdings, wie die Wanduhr in Novalis' „Heinrich von Ofterdingen", einen kleinen Anachronismus darstellt, da Polstermöbel erst aus der Neuzeit bekannt sind.

Mit dem TANNHÄUSER (1845) entscheidet sich Wagner für einen historischen Stoff der Minnesängerzeit, den er Anfang des 13. Jahrhunderts und auf seiner Lieblingsburg, der Wartburg mit ihrer (romanischen) Sängerhalle, ansetzt. Für die deutsche Theaterlandschaft war das neu und sehr modern nach französischem Vorbild. Wagner hatte diesen exakten Historismus in Paris kennen gelernt, wo er an der Grand Opéra vorbildlich gepflegt wurde, während man an deutschen Stadttheatern nur einfache Standardkulissen besaß, die für alle möglichen Stücke benutzt wurden. Das Original der Wartburg wurde von Wagner mehrfach im ursprünglichen und im (neoromanisch) restaurierten Zustand besucht. 1842 sieht er sie zum ersten Mal: „*Der Anblick des Bergschlosses, […], regte mich ungemein warm an. Einen seitab von ihr gelegenen ferneren Bergrücken stempelte ich sogleich zum ‚Hörselberg' und konstruierte mir so, in dem Tal dahinfahrend, die Szene zum dritten Akte meines TANNHÄUSER, wie ich sie seitdem als Bild in mir festhielt […]*"[2]

Der LOHENGRIN (1850) spielt in Antwerpen, in der ersten Hälfte des 10. Jahrhunderts: „*In der Burg von Antwerpen. In der Mitte des Hintergrundes der Palas (Ritterwohnung), die Kemenate (Frauenwohnung) im Vordergrunde links; rechts im Vordergrunde die Pforte des Münsters; ebenda im Hintergrunde das Turmtor.*"[3] 1860, zehn Jahre nach der Uraufführung, besuchte Wagner das Original, gemeint ist der sogenannte Steen, die alte Burg im Zentrum der Stadt (Zitadelle), die tatsächlich auf das 10. Jahrhundert zurückgeht. Wagner aber ist von der Realität etwas enttäuscht: „*Ich hatte zugunsten der Szene des ersten Aktes meines LOHENGRIN angenommen, diese Zitadelle, welche ich mir als die alte Burg von Antwerpen dachte, böte jenseits der Schelde einen irgendwie hervorragenden Punkt dar; stattdessen nun nichts als eine unterschiedslose Fläche mit in die Erde eingegrabenen Befestigungen zu erkennen war. Bei späteren Aufführungen des LOHENGRIN, welchen ich beiwohnte, musste ich nun gewöhnlich über die auf stattlichem Berge im Hintergrunde sich erhebende Burg des Theaterdekorateurs lächeln.*"[4]

TRISTAN UND ISOLDE (1859) ist, im Textbuch ohne Orts- und Zeitangabe, wiederum ein Sagenstoff. Der zweite Aufzug zeigt einen „*Garten mit hohen Bäumen vor dem Gemache Isoldes, zu welchem, seitwärts gelegen, Stufen hinaufführen*", der dritte Aufzug einen „*Burggarten. Zur einen Seite hohe Burggebäude, zur anderen eine niedrige Mauerbrüstung, von einer Warte unterbrochen; im Hintergrunde das Burgtor. Die Lage ist auf felsiger Höhe anzunehmen*".[5] Auf dem Theaterzettel zur Bayreuther Erstaufführung 1886 wurde allerdings (posthum) Näheres hinzugefügt: „*Zweiter Aufzug: In der königlichen Burg Markes in Kornwall*" und „*Dritter Aufzug: Tristans Burg in der Bretagne.*" In Wagners Textbuch wird immerhin ein pittoreskes Bild der Architektur gezeichnet: „*Das Ganze macht einen Eindruck der Herrenlosigkeit, übel gepflegt, hie und da schadhaft und bewachsen.*"[6]

DER FLIEGENDE HOLLÄNDER (1843) is not set in a specific time (and its sets lack striking architecture – Daland's house lacks description). It, too belongs in the mythical world category. It is noteworthy, however, that the "wing chair" in Act I, like the wall clock in Novalis' "Heinrich von Ofterdingen" is a small anachronism, since upholstered furniture was only developed after the Middle Ages.

Wagner chose historical material from the Minnesinger period for TANNHÄUSER (1845), and set the scene in his *"favorite fortress,"* the Wartburg, and its (Romanic) hall. This was new and quite modern for the German theater landscape and followed the French model. Wagner had been exposed to precisely this flavor of historicism in Paris, where the Grand Opéra was applying it in exemplary fashion. In contrast, German state theaters only owned simple standard backdrops and used them for operas of all sorts. Wagner visited the original Wartburg several times before and after its (neo-Romantic) restoration. He recalls seeing it for the first time in 1842, writing *"The sight the castle on the mountaintop […] warmed me with incredible excitement. I immediately nicknamed a distant mountain chain off to the side 'Hörsel Mountain' and so conceived the scene for the third act of my TANNHÄUSER as I approached it in the valley. That image has stuck with me every since."*

LOHENGRIN (1850) is set in Antwerp in the first half of the 10th century. *"In the fortress of Antwerp. In the middle of the background the palace (knights' quarters), the Kemenate (women's chamber) in the foreground left, right in the foreground the doors of the cloister; the tower gates in the background there as well."* Ten years after the debut, in 1860, Wagner visited the original so-called Steen, the old fortress in the city center (citadel), that indeed dates back to the 10th century. Wagner found reality somewhat disappointing: *"For the sake of the scene in the first act of my LOHENGRIN I had assumed that this citadel, which I had taken to be the old fortress of Antwerp, would offer some point of elevation that side of the Schelde. Instead, I saw nothing but a monotonous flat expanse with supports dug down into the earth. When I later saw LOHENGRIN productions I had to smile at the set decorator's fortress atop a sizeable mountain in the background."*

TRISTAN UND ISOLDE (1859) also lacks location and time specifications, and is mythic. The second act takes place in a *"garden with tall trees in front of Isolde's bed chamber with steps leading up to it off to the side,"* and the third act takes place in a *"fortress garden. To one side tall fortress building, to the other side a low wall ledge with a lookout; in the background the fortress gate. The location is presumably set high among cliffs."* It is noteworthy, however, that further details were found (posthumously) on the playbill from the Bayreuth premiere in 1886: *"Act 2: in the Royal Fortress in Cornwall"* and *"Act 3: Tristan's fortress in Brittany"*. Wagner's libretto gives a picturesque image of the architecture: *"The overall effect is one of abandonment, not well cared for, here and there damaged and grown over with plants."*

Wagners eigenhändige Skizze zum LOHENGRIN (mit gotischer Tür rechts) für das Brautgemach des 3. Aufzugs für die Uraufführung in Weimar 1850[7]
Wagner's own sketch for LOHENGRIN with Gothic door (right) to the bridal chamber in the third act in scenic designs for the premiere in Weimar, 1850

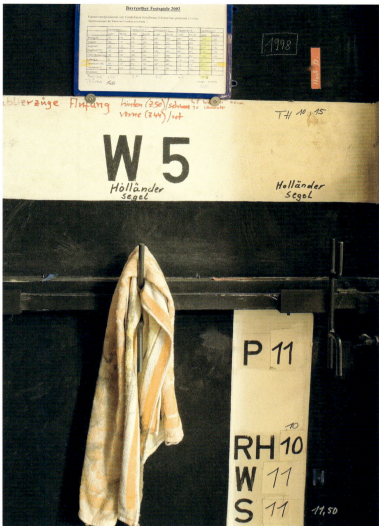

Wohlsortierte Stellage im Prospektlager
Well-organized shelving in backdrop storage

Ritterrüstungen aus der LOHENGRIN-Inszenierung
von Keith Warner, zur Entsorgung abgestellt
Knight costumes from Keith Warner's LOHENGRIN
production, laid aside for disposal.

Arbeitsgalerie der Bühnentechnik mit Markierungen für Fahrten und Stände beweglicher Teile (Schwan, Segel)
Stage technology work gallery with signage for moveable pieces (swan, sails)
P = PARSIFAL, RH = RHEINGOLD, W = WALKÜRE, S = SIEGFRIED

Bild von Wieland Wagners LOHENGRIN-Inszenierung 1958 in der Requisite
Photo from Wieland Wagner's LOHENGRIN production 1958 in landing storage

Probendekoration von Christoph Schlingensiefs PARSIFAL-Inszenierung 2004
Rehearsal decoration from Christoph Schlingensief's 2004 PARSIFAL staging

Dekorationsteile der RING-Inszenierung von Tankred Dorst 2006
Set design from Tankred Dorst's 2006 RING staging

DIE MEISTERSINGER VON NÜRNBERG (1868) sind ins 16. Jahrhundert gerückt, an die Wende des Mittelalters zur Renaissance und durch die historische Figur des Hans Sachs wiederum ein historistischer Stoff. Der erste Aufzug spielt in der (heute ruinösen) Katharinenkirche, ohne dass Wagner ihre gotische Erscheinung beschreiben würde. Auch das mittelalterliche Stadtbild im zweiten Aufzug wird mit „schmale Gasse, nach dem Hintergrund zu krumm abbiegend"[1] nur angedeutet. Das von Wagner mehrfach besuchte, reale Nürnberg, das in seinem mittelalterlichen Stadtbild noch heute beeindruckt, kommentiert Wagner lediglich einmal in einem Brief an Mathilde Wesendonck am 21. Dezember 1861 mit. „Da ist viel Hübsches zu sehen."[2]

PARSIFAL (1882) spielt im „gotischen Spanien"[3], wobei gotisch (leider) nicht als architekturhistorischer Begriff gebraucht wird, sondern die Zeit der Völkerwanderung benennt und damit (heute) zwischen dem 5. und 8. Jahrhundert anzusiedeln wäre. Ort ist wiederum eine burgähnliche Anlage, das Kloster „Monsalvat", das allgemein mit dem Kloster Montserrat bei Barcelona gleichgesetzt wird. Dieses wurde freilich – der Sage nach – erst im 9. Jahrhundert begründet. Dazu kommt Klingsors Zauberschloss als architektonische Kulisse im „arabischen reichen Stile"[4], dessen Vorbild Wagner bei seinem Besuch im italienischen Ravello am 26. Mai 1880 in der sarazenischen Villa Rufolo des 11. Jahrhunderts fand. Ins Gästebuch schrieb er: „Klingsors Zaubergarten ist gefunden!"[5] Als dritte architektonische Kulisse im PARSIFAL erscheint die Gralsburg, für die ihn nachweislich der gotische Dom von Siena aus dem 12./13. Jahrhundert inspirierte. Der PARSIFAL macht deutlich, dass Wagner es mit der Kunstgeschichte nicht so genau nahm und gotische Kirchen, sarazenische Paläste und noch gar nicht gebaute Klöster in die Völkerwanderungszeit rückte. Mitte des 19. Jahrhunderts war die Kunstgeschichte als eigene Wissenschaft allerdings noch gar nicht geboren (die erst von Männern wie Wagners Stiefschwiegersohn Henry Thode mit seinem Lehrstuhl in Heidelberg begründet wurde).

DIE MEISTERSINGER VON NÜRNBERG (1868) takes place in the 16th century, at the transition from the Middle Ages to the Renaissance. The historical figure of Hans Sachs marks it as historical material. The first act takes place in the St. Catherine's Church (today in ruins), though Wagner does not describe its Gothic appearance. Wagner only alludes to the city's medieval appearance "with narrow lanes turning too sharply toward the background." After Wagner visited Nurnberg, which still maintains an impressive medieval appearance, his only comment was in a letter on December 21, 1861 to Mathilde Wesendonck: "The city has a lot of beauty to offer."

PARSIFAL (1882) takes place in "Gothic Spain," whereby Gothic is (unfortunately) not used as an architectural historical term, but rather identifies the migration period, which we would (today) place between the 5th and 8th centuries. The location is once again a fortress-like complex, the "Monsalvat" monastery that most people equate with the Monserrat Monastery in Barcelona. According to legend, it was first founded in the 9th century. Wagner discovered a model for another architectural backdrop, Klingsor's magical castle in "wealthy Arabian style," during a trip to Ravello, Italy, where he visited the Saracenic Rufolo Villa built in the 11th Century. On May 26, 1880 he noted in his diary: "I have found Klingsor's magical garden!" The third architectural setting in PARSIFAL is the Grail Fortress. Research has proven that the Gothic Siena Cathedral from the 12th/13th centuries inspired this setting. PARSIFAL demonstrates that Wagner is by no means exact when it comes to art history, placing Gothic churches, Saracenic palaces and not-yet built monasteries into the migration period. It is only fair to note that art history had not even been born as a science in the middle of the 19th century. (It would be founded much later by by men such as Wagner's step son-in-law Henry Thode, who held a faculty appointment in it in Heidelberg.)

Probentafel der Schlingensief-Inszenierung PARSIFAL
Rehearsal board from Schlingensief's PARSIFAL staging

Uraufführungsdekoration PARSIFAL mit Bühnenbild des Gralstempels von Paul von Joukowsky (1845 – 1912), 1882
Scenery from premiere of PARSIFAL with set design for Grail Temple by Paul von Joukowsky (1845 – 1912) from 1882

Die Architektur im RING DES NIBELUNGEN (1876) lässt sich keinem romanischen, normannischen oder gotischen Mittelalter zuordnen. Auch hier spielen die von Wagner so geliebten Burgen eine zentrale Rolle, obgleich Burgen in Mitteleuropa erst seit dem 11. Jahrhundert häufig werden. Dessen ungeachtet wurde für „Gibichungenhalle" und „Walhall" eine (archäologisch damals noch kaum dokumentierte) germanische Frühzeit bemüht. Man orientierte sich schon bei der Uraufführung in Bayreuth für die Bauten gerne an skandinavischer Holzarchitektur, wie in den (nicht ausgeführten) Bühnenbildentwürfen Josef Hoffmanns, die – lange verschollen – 1993 in Worms wiederentdeckt wurden.

Cosima Wagner sollte mit dem Ring 1896 einen geradezu wissenschaftlichen „Germanenkult" treiben und ließ sich für Bühnenbild und Ausstattung von akademischen Historikern beraten. Einige dieser Relikte sind im Festspielhaus noch erhalten. Allzu historische Bühnenbilder lehnte Wagner allerdings kategorisch ab, wie eine (unbekannte, scheinbar gotische oder romanische) Architekturskizze zu Walhall der Hoftheatermaler im RHEINGOLD für die Münchner Uraufführung 1869: *„Fasolt und Fafner wussten von diesem Baustil noch nichts!"*[1] Schon 1861 hatte sich Wagner gegen das Titelblatt zur Herausgabe des RHEINGOLD beim Verlag der Gebrüder Schott gewehrt: *„Die ganze gotische Einfassung hat nicht den mindesten Sinn. Ich ersuche Sie auf das dringendste, dies Blatt durchaus zurückziehen zu lassen, und lieber den Titel, wie er da steht, in einem einfachen Rahmen hinzustellen, in welchem ich den gotischen Stil am wenigsten beachtet wissen wollte."*[2] Beide Zitate verraten, dass Wagner die von ihm in den Textbüchern vermiedenen Stilbegriffe durchaus kannte und seinen RING ganz bewusst als einen zeitlosen Mythos verstand. Die architektonische Welt der Nibelungen ließ und lässt sich nicht mit bekannten Architekturstilen illustrieren und muss stets neu fantasiert werden.

Fazit

Alle Bühnenwerke Wagners spielen also im Mittelalter oder in einer mythischen Vorzeit. Nur die Zitate zum TANNHÄUSER legen nahe, dass er hier eine gewisse historische Authentizität nach Pariser Vorbild anstrebte. Andererseits skizziert er seine Bühnenbilder nur, sodass damals die Standardkulissen benutzt werden konnten und heutige Bühnenbildner ihre Fantasie bemühen müssen. So zeigen fast alle Inszenierungen der Stücke Wagners seit dem 19. Jahrhundert Bühnenbilder, in denen reichlich Fachwerk und auch Backsteine vorkommen sowie „germanisches", romanisches und gotisches Formenrepertoire, freilich ohne echte „Legitimation" des Komponisten, der die Architektur einfach nicht näher bestimmen wollte und damit allen modernen Interpretationen Raum gibt. Warum? Vielleicht weil man die Handlungsorte seiner Stücke nicht zu veristisch, zu historistisch betrachten sollte, sondern als abstrakte, als psychologische oder philosophische Räume.

The architecture in DER RING DES NIBELUNGEN (1876) does not fit a Romanesque, Norman or Gothic medieval category. Here again, the fortresses Wagner loves so much play a pivotal role, even though fortresses weren't commonplace in central Europe until the 11th century. Despite this historical fact, Wagner attempted to tap into an ur-Germanic period (which at that point had hardly been archeologically documented) for his "Gibichung Hall" and "Walhall." Even the set for the premiere in Bayreuth was orientated toward Scandinavian wooden architecture, as evidenced by Josef Hoffmann's (unrealized) set designs, which had vanished for many years and were rediscovered in Worms in 1993.

In 1896, Cosima Wagner led an almost scientific "Germanic tribe cult," calling in academic historians to advise her on stage design and props. Some of these relics still exist to this day. However, Wagner categorically rejected overly historical set designs, such as the (unknown, but likely Gothic or Romanesque) architectural sketches for Walhall by court theater painters in the Munich premiere of RHEINGOLD in 1869: *"Fasolt and Fafner knew nothing of this architecture!"* As early as 1861, Wagner reacted negatively to the Gebrüder Schott publishing house's title page for their RHEINGOLD edition: *"The whole Gothic look is completely out of place. I urgently request you to remove this page entirely and to set the title as it stands now in a simple frame, preferably making use of as little Gothic as possible."* Both quotations reveal that Wagner was indeed familiar with the stylistic terminology he avoids in his librettos and quite consciously conceived his RING as a timeless myth. It was and is not possible to illustrate the architectural world of the Nibelungen using familiar architectural styles. Rather, it must always be fantasized anew.

Summary

All of Wagner's stage works take place in medieval or mythical timelessness. Only Wagner's remarks about TANNHÄUSER lead to the conclusion that, in this case, he attempted a certain degree of historical authenticity following the Parisian model. However, he only barely sketched his set designs, making it possible to use standard backdrops back then, and requiring modern designers to rely on their own fantasy. Almost all productions of Wagner's works since the 19th century have set designs full of timber framing and bricks that quote "Germanic," Romanesque and Gothic form repertoire. Needless to say, the composer never legitimized these elements, but rather simply chose not to identify the architecture more precisely, thus leaving the door open for all modern interpretations. Why? Perhaps he didn't want the locations in his works to be understood too literally or historically, but rather as abstract, psychological or philosophical spaces.

Heiliger Gral im Beleuchtungsfundus
Holy Grail in lighting storage

Rheintochter-Kostüm 1896 nach Entwurf von Hans Thoma
1896 costume for Rhine daughter designed by Hans Thoma

Germanische Lure
Germanic lure

Was geht mich alle Baukunst der Welt an![1]

Die Bühnenarchitektur Wagners offenbart eine große Liebe zum Mittelalter, sodass die These, Wagner habe mit seinem Festspielhaus insgeheim eine romantische Kulisse für seine Stücke gewollt, nach wie vor als Hypothese berechtigt ist. Doch wie hätte ein reicher Richard Wagner gebaut? Vielleicht hätte er sich dann doch für ein prächtiges Gebäude entschieden, das ihm und seinem Werk ein gebührendes Denkmal gesetzt hätte. Vielleicht hat er sich im Stillen das schönste Theater dieser Welt gewünscht, das womöglich im edelsten Renaissancestil oder gar im üppigsten Neobarock zu errichten gewesen wäre. Schließlich hat er sich für die Uraufführung seines RING DES NIBELUNGEN das Markgräfliche Opernhaus in Bayreuth angeschaut und dieses aus technischen Gründen als zu klein abgelehnt, ohne Anstoß an seinem verschwenderischen Rokoko zu nehmen.

Eine ganz grundsätzliche Recherche zu Wagners Verhältnis zur Architektur scheint also nötig. Doch leider geben nur sehr wenige Stellen in Wagners biografischen und theoretischen Schriften Auskunft darüber. Schnell vermittelt sich der Eindruck, dass die Architektur Wagner nicht sonderlich interessiert und kaum zu intellektuellen Betrachtungen angeregt hat, was im Übrigen auch für andere Bereiche der bildenden Kunst gilt, für die Malerei und die Plastik. Das bisher kaum untersuchte Verhältnis von Wagner zur Architektur kann also fast nur in den Primärquellen recherchiert werden und ist auf den ersten Blick nicht sehr ergiebig. Leichter wären Themen wie Wagner und die Hunde, Wagner und die Papageien oder Wagner und die Eisenbahn.

Sehr sympathisch ist das körperliche, ja sogar akrobatische Verhältnis Wagners zur Architektur, wie etwa jene Geschichte aus dem Jahr 1834 in Prag belegt, als der junge Komponist im beziehungsweise auf einem Gasthof Unfug trieb: *„Dass ich … beim Auskleiden dann auf den äußeren Mauersimsen von einem Fenster zum andern des zweiten Stockes kletterte, erschien natürlich denjenigen entsetzlich, die meine in frühester Knabenzeit ausgebildete Neigung zu akrobatischen Übungen nicht kannten."*[2] Im gleichen Jahr bahnte sich das Verhältnis zu Minna Planer an, zu der er im wahrsten Sinne des Wortes fensterlte: *„Als ich eines Abends spät in mein Parterre-Zimmer, weil ich den Hausschlüssel nicht mit mir führte, durch das Fenster zurückkehrte, zog das Geräusch dieses Einbruches Minna an ihr über dem meinigen gelegenes Fenster; ich bat sie, immer auf meinem Fenstersims stehend, mir zu erlauben, ihr noch gute Nacht zu sagen."*[3]

Diese Sportlichkeit verrät einen impulsiven Menschen, der lieber turnte, wanderte oder spazieren ging, als sich hinter gelehrten Büchern zu vergraben. Er liebte die Natur, die Berge, wie viele Schilderungen seiner oft abenteuerlichen und gefährlichen Klettertouren und Gletscherwanderungen belegen. In den Städten mit ihrer steinernen Architektur fühlte er sich eher gefangen und suchte – selbst im Häusermeer von Venedig oder Paris – immer die Parks und die freien Plätze auf. Um Museen, Kirchen und andere Sehenswürdigkeiten machte er normalerweise einen großen Bogen, wie zum Beispiel 1858 in Venedig: *„Während ich von Ritter nur sehr schwierig zu bewegen war, … eine Galerie oder eine Kirche mir anzusehen, obgleich auf jeder nötigen Wanderung durch die Stadt die namenlos mannigfaltigen architektonischen Eigentümlichkeiten und Schönheiten derselben stets von neuem mich entzückten, boten fast die ganze Dauer meines Aufenthaltes in Venedig über häufige Gondelfahrten nach dem Lido mir die Hauptgenüsse."*[4]

Wagner war für poetische Eindrücke eines schönen Stadtbilds (wie in Venedig) und eine emotionale Wahrnehmung von Architektur durchaus nicht unempfänglich – insbesondere in Italien (wo sonst). Doch Wagner war grundsätzlich kein Augenmensch. *„Er ermüdete schnell an allem Äußeren, innere Bilder bedrängten ihn mehr, und je älter er wurde, um so weniger bedeuteten ihm*

What do I care about all the architecture in the world!

Wagner's stage architecture reveals his great love for the Middle Ages, giving some credence to the thesis that Wagner secretly desired a Festspielhaus to create a romantic backdrop for his works. But what would a wealthy Richard Wagner's theater have looked like? Perhaps he would have opted for an elaborate building after all, as a fitting memorial to himself and his works. Perhaps his secret inner wish was to build the most beautiful theater in the world in finest Renaissance or even in gushing neo-Baroque style. After all, he considered premiering DER RING DES NIBELUNGEN in the Margravial Opera House in Bayreuth but rejected it because it was too small to meet his technical needs, apparently without being bothered by its wasteful Rococo.

A thorough study of Wagner's relationship to architecture appears necessary. Unfortunately, only very few passages in Wagner's biographical and theoretical writings refer to architecture. One could quickly get the impression that Wagner was not very interested in architecture and that it provided him with little intellectual stimulus. In fact, this was indeed the case for other forms of visual arts, such as painting and sculpturing. Wagner's relationship to architecture has hardly been investigated. At first glance, the primary sources forming the basis of such a study do not appear to offer much substance. It would be easier to investigate other topics, such as Wagner and dogs, Wagner and parrots, or Wagner and the railroad.

Wagner's physical, even acrobatic, relationship to architecture is very sympathetic. Consider this story, for example, from 1834 in Prague, when the young composer got carried away in – and on – a boarding house: *"Of course, people not familiar with my knack for acrobatics developed in early childhood were horrified to see me climbing from one window to the other on the outer wall cornices while getting undressed."* That same year, Wagner and Minna Planer started to get closer, and he regularly (quite literally) courted her through her window: *"One evening, when I didn't have my key and was climbing into my room on the ground floor through the window, the sound of my breaking in drew Minna to her window above mine. I asked her, still standing on my wall cornice, to permit me to bid her good night."*

This athleticism portrays an impulsive person who would rather play sports, go for a hike or go for a walk than submerge himself in learned books. Descriptions of many often adventurous and dangerous climbing and glacier tours attest that he loved nature and the mountains. He felt rather trapped amid the stone architecture of the city and was always drawn to the parks and open areas, even in the middle of a sea of houses in Venice or Paris. He typically steered clear of museums, churches and other points of interest. For example, in 1858 he writes about Venice: *"Whereas Mr. Ritter had difficulty convincing me to have a look at a gallery or a church, even though their nameless bounty of architectural qualities and beauty delighted me time and again whenever a stroll through the city was necessary, frequent gondola rides to the beach were my main pleasure during the majority of my stay in Venice."*

Wagner was by no means immune to the poetic impressions emanating from a beautiful city (such as in Venice) and to experiencing architecture emotionally – especially in Italy (where else). But Wagner was not fundamentally a visual person. *"Outside impulses tired him out quickly and he was more moved by internal images. The older he got, the less he valued natural phenomena, art collections or relics – the normal feast for tourists' eyes."*

Wagner, the unsettled nomad, always in exile, spent his entire life searching for a place he could call home. A cozy feeling of homliness was important to him. As a result, he readily describes the furniture, carpets and draperies in his dwellings, but hardly mentions the exteriors of most of his houses, as if he never even "saw" their facade. The same applies to the architectural sights during his extensive travels. Once in a while he mentions impressive buildings, but he never really studies them, not to mention analyzing them. He doesn't even mention the

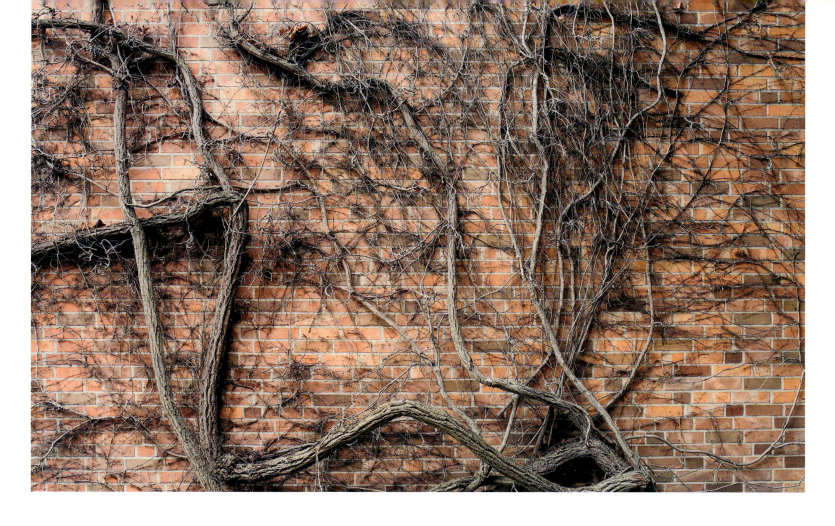

„Mein Herz kann sich an Steinen und Menschen nicht erlaben – ich will Natur – und Freunde."[1]
"My heart finds no refreshment in stone and people – I want nature – and friends."

Richard Wagner (1842)

Naturschauspiele, Kunstsammlungen oder Altertümer, der Augenschmaus der Touristen."[2]

Wagner, der Exilant, der ruhelose Wanderer, war zeitlebens auf der Suche nach einem bleibenden Zuhause, denn eine gemütliche Häuslichkeit war ihm wichtig. Hier beschreibt er gerne die Möbel, Tapeten und Vorhänge seiner Wohnungen, doch von außen bleiben fast alle seiner Häuser unbeachtet, als habe er ihre Fassaden gar nicht „gesehen". Gleiches gilt für die architektonischen Sehenswürdigkeiten seiner vielen Reisen. Hin und wieder werden imposante Bauwerke genannt, doch nie wirklich studiert oder gar analysiert. Selbst die vielen Theaterbauten, die er privat oder beruflich kennenlernen sollte, bleiben in ihrer Architektur meist unbeachtet.

Wagner fehlte es im Bereich der bildenden Kunst und der Architektur etwas an der nötigen Bildung, wie er einmal selbst eingestand. So schreibt Cosima am 16. November 1879: *„Die Freunde beschreiben Paestum und vieles noch, worauf R. sich zu mir wendet: ,Gott, wie ungebildet sind wir – die kennen schon alles, wir gar nicht'."*[3] Wagner war kein Goethe und kein Universalgelehrter, kein Adelsspross, kein Großbürgersohn, dem das Privileg einer umfassenden Bildung und Ausbildung gewährt worden ist. Er war in vielem ein Autodidakt und speziell in Fragen der Architektur alles andere als ein belesener Bildungsbürger. Ihn interessierte seine eigene Kunst. Andere Künste waren ihm nicht wichtig. Seine eher sekundäre Beziehung zur Architektur gipfelt in einem Ausspruch von 1865 (als ihn das Gerangel um sein Festspielhaus zunehmend verärgerte): *„Was geht mich alle Baukunst der Welt an!"*

architecture of the many theaters he has personal or professional contact to.

As Wagner once admitted himself, he lacked a certain amount of education in the visual arts and architecture. On November 16, 1879, Cosima writes: *"Our friends were talking about Paestum and other things when R. turned to me and said, 'God, we are so uneducated – they've already seen everything and we haven't seen a thing.'"* Wagner was not like Goethe, he was not universally well educated, he was not the son of nobility, nor was he born into the haute bourgeoisie. Rather, he was never given the privilege of receiving a well-rounded education and training. He taught himself many things, and, when it came to architecture in particular, was anything but a well-read bourgeois citizen. He was interested in his own art. Other art forms weren't important to him. A statement he made in 1865 (when the bickering about his Festspielhaus was increasingly irritating him) brings the clearly secondary nature of his relationship to architecture into sharp focus: *"What do I care about all the architecture in the world."*

Wagner und die Architektur des Nordens

Wagner liebte das Mittelalter nicht nur in seinen Bühnenwerken. Schon als Kind träumte er von Burgen und Rittern. Diese kindlich-romantische Sichtweise projizierte Wagner gerne auf alte Städte und Häuser, die er in „Mein Leben" als schöne Erinnerungen verklärt. Nach dem frühen Tod des Vaters verbrachte Wagner eine eher unruhige Jugend mit vielen Wohnsitzwechseln, von denen er die schönsten Orte näher erwähnt: So klagt er zum Beispiel über das Pfarrhaus in Possendorf, wo er als Knabe in Pflege war und das er später wieder besuchte: *„Es ergriff mich sehr, das alte Pfarrhaus nicht mehr zu finden, dafür einen reichlichern modernen Aufbau, der mich so gegen den Ort verstimmte, dass ich späterhin meine Ausflüge nie wieder in diese Gegend richtete."*[1] Ähnlich sentimentale Schwärmereien finden sich über *„die kleine altertümliche Stadt"*[2] Eisleben, wo er 1822 eine Privatschule besuchte, und über *„die altertümliche Pracht und Schönheit der unvergleichlichen Stadt Prag"*[3], die *„auf meine Phantasie einen unerlöschlichen Eindruck"* machte.

Gotik und Romanik

„Altertümlich" bedeutet für Wagner hier wohl mittelalterlich und in die Sprache der Architektur übersetzt: gotisch, romanisch, ohne dass er diese Worte benutzen würde. Der Begriff der Romanik erscheint in seinen Schriften nirgendwo als architektonischer Stilbegriff (sondern nur als „romanisch" im Sinne von „welsch" als kultureller oder ethnischer Begriff). Der Begriff der „Gotik", der seit Jablonskis „Allgemeinem Lexikon der Künste und Wissenschaften" (1721) im Deutschen als Bezeichnung der mittelalterlichen Bauart eingebürgert war, war Wagner jedoch vertraut.

Zu jener altertümlichen Architektur im romantischen Geiste Wagners gehörte auch die reiche Fachwerkarchitektur, die in der ersten Hälfte des 19. Jahrhunderts fast jede deutsche Stadt prägte. Auch im barocken 18. Jahrhundert wurden überall noch Fachwerkbauten errichtet, doch gehören sie in ihrer pittoresken Erscheinung ursprünglich ins Mittelalter. Spätestens seit den romantischen Malern und dem Zeitgenossen Wagners Carl Spitzweg waren diese „Altertümlichkeiten" in ihrer malerischen Schönheit erkannt worden. Wagner wohnte 1846 in Groß-Graupa sogar selbst in einem Fachwerkbau. 1855 fragt er in einem Brief an Xaver Aufdermaur in Brunnen, Zürich, an, ob dieser ein *„hübsches Wohnhäuschen, nach Schweizer Bauart in Holz"*[4] vermieten wolle. Später sollte er tatsächlich in Zürich-Enge in einem alten Fachwerkhaus, einem Gartenhaus der Villa Wesendonck, ein romantisches Domizil finden.

Wagners Liebe zur altertümlichen (Holz-)Architektur des Mittelalters ist eine genuin romantische Grundhaltung, wie sie von einer Generation vor Wagner ersonnen worden war. Goethe war der Erste, der 1773 in „Von deutscher Baukunst" bei seiner Beschreibung des Straßburger Münsters die gotische – damals noch als genuin deutsch geltende – Baukunst zu würdigen wusste, die bis

Wagner and the architecture of the north

Wagner didn't only love the Middle Ages in his stage works. Even as a child he dreamt about fortresses and knights. He often projected this childlike, romantic perspective onto old cities and houses that he later idealized as fond memories in "My Life." Following his father's early death, Wagner's youth was unsettled and he moved many times. He later mentions a few of the most beautiful locations. For example, he was cared for in the rectory in Possendorf as a young boy. When he later visits the house, he complains: *"It saddened me greatly not to find the old rectory. In its place stood a larger, modern, expanded building that turned me off to the town so much that I never again took an excursion to the area."* Similar sentimental swooning can be found about *"the small ancient city"* of Eisleben, where he attended a private school in 1822, and about *"the ancient splendor and beauty of the unforgettable city of Prague"* that *"left an indelible mark on my fantasy."*

Gothic and Romanesque Style

By *"ancient,"* Wagner apparently meant medieval, translated into architectural terms: Gothic or Romanesque, even though he would not use these terms. His writings never include the term Romanesque as an architectural style term (but rather only "Romanic," referring to "Welsh" as a cultural or ethnic term). Wagner was, however, familiar with the German term "Gothic" standardized by Jablonski in his "Allgemeines Lexikon der Künste und Wissenschaften" (General Lexicon of the Arts and the Sciences, 1721) in reference to medieval architecture.

For Wagner's romantic spirit, the rich timber-framed buildings that still characterized almost every German city in the first half of the 19th century also belong to the category of ancient architecture. Half-timbered buildings were still being constructed everywhere in the Baroque 18th century, yet their picturesque appearance roots them originally in the Middle Ages. Romantic painters and Wagner's contemporary Carl Spitzweg were well aware of the picturesque beauty of these "ancient elements." Wagner even lived in a half-timbered house in Groß-Graupa in 1846. In a letter to Xaver Aufdermaur in Brunnen, Zurich, dated 1855, Wagner asks him whether he would like to rent out a *"cute little house built in wooden Swiss style"*. Actually he would later find a romantic domicile in an old half-timbered house in Zurich Enge, the Wesendonck Villa's garden house.

Wagner's love for ancient (wood) architecture from the Middle Ages is typical of the genuinely romantic attitude that had been adopted by the previous generation. In his essay on the Strasburg Cathedral "On German Architecture" from 1773, Goethe was the first to honor the Gothic as a genuinely German architectural style. Up until then, the classically educated world had considered this architecture barbaric and ugly. Wagner was also *"captivated and moved"* by the Strasburg Cathedral.

The Romantics after Goethe would come to view the Gothic as a symbol of German identity. The Gothic, called "maniera tedesca" in Italy, was –

Altes Landhaus im Park der Wesendonck-Villa in Zürich
Old country house in the Wesendonck villa park in Zürich

Malersaal (von 1872) am Festspielhaus, 1978 abgerissen
1872 paint shop at the Festspielhaus, torn down in 1978

dahin der klassisch gebildeten Welt als barbarisch und hässlich galt. Auch Wagner war vom Straßburger Münster „*gefesselt und ergriffen*"[1].

Die Romantiker nach Goethe erkannten in der Gotik schließlich ein Symbol deutscher Identität. Galt die Gotik, die in Italien als „maniera tedesca" bezeichnet wurde, noch lange nach Goethe – fälschlicherweise – als urdeutsche Baukunst. Cosima überliefert Wagners Wissensstand im Jahre 1880: Er wusste, „*dass die Bezeichnung gotisch aus Spanien käme, dass der gotische Stil in den nordischen, gotischen Reichen durch Berührung mit den Arabern entstanden sei, von da nach Frankreich, schließlich nach Deutschland sich verbreitet hätte und die traditionelle Benennung die Herkunft dieses Baustiles demnach ganz richtig bezeichne*"[2].

Die bereits Ende des 18. Jahrhunderts (in England) aufkommende und dann ab der Mitte des 19. Jahrhunderts auch in Deutschland sehr populäre Neugotik wird häufig als „romantische Architektur" bezeichnet. Wagner war also prinzipiell ein Spätromantiker! Der Romantiker E. T. A. Hoffmann war in jungen Jahren Wagners Lieblingsautor, der romantische „Freischütz" von Weber seine Lieblingsoper. Diese jugendliche Romantik ging Wagner in späteren Jahren nicht verloren, wie jene Geschichte aus dem Jahr 1842 im Böhmischen Wald beweisen mag, eine Szene, die ein Caspar David Friedrich oder ein Novalis kaum schöner hätte erfinden können: Wagner wanderte beim – wie er selbst formulierte – „romantischen" Schreckenstein, der ihn für seinen TANNHÄUSER inspirierte: „*… und die phantastische Einsamkeit regte meinen Jugendmut in der Art wieder auf, dass ich eine volle Mondnacht, in das bloße Bettuch gewickelt, auf den Ruinen des Schreckensteins herumkletterte, um mir so selbst zur fehlenden Gespenstererscheinung zu werden.*"[3]

Selbst für sein eigenes Wohnhaus sehnte sich Wagner nach einer romantischen Burgruine: Im Biebricher Schlosspark findet er 1862 „*an einem Teiche ein altertümlich aussehendes kleines Schlösschen, welches in dem Sinne einer pittoresken Ruine verwendet war und zur Zeit einem Bildhauer als Atelier diente. Es regte sich in mir der kühne Wunsch, dieses kleine, halb verwitterte Gebäude mir für Lebenszeit zugeteilt wissen zu können.*" Man rät ihm jedoch davon ab, wegen zu hoher Feuchtigkeit des Gemäuers. „*Im Übrigen ließ ich mich jedoch nicht davon abhalten, immer wieder zum Aufsuchen des von mir ersehnten einsamen kleinen Häuschens mit Garten mich aufzumachen.*" Auf der Suche nach einem „kleinen Zukunftsschlösschen" findet er in Bingen „*den berühmten alten Turmbau, in welchem dereinst Kaiser Heinrich IV. gefangen gehalten worden war*". „*Nachdem man eine ziemliche Felsenhöhe zu besteigen gehabt, auf welcher der Turm lag, gerieten wir in dessen viertem Stockwerke auf einen das ganze Quadrat des Gebäudes einnehmenden Raum, von welchem ein einziges Erkerfenster auf den Rhein hinausging. Ich erkannte diesen als das Ideal aller meiner Vorstellungen einer Wohnung für mich.*" Und ein für alle Zeiten „*herrliches Asyl*"[4]. Aber auch dieses Projekt blieb Träumerei.

inaccurately – considered an ur-German architecture for a long time after Goethe. Cosima documents Wagner's understanding of the matter in 1880: He knew "*that the term Gothic comes from Spain, that the Gothic style developed in the Nordic Gothic kingdoms through contact with the Arabs, that it spread from there to France and, finally, to Germany, and that the traditional term therefore correctly reflects the origin of this architectural style.*"

The neo-Gothic, which arose in the end of the 18th century in England and was very popular in Germany as well starting in the middle of the 19th century, is frequently referred to as "romantic architecture." In this regard, Wagner was principally a late Romantic. The Romantic author E. T. A. Hoffmann was Wagner's favorite author when he was young, and Weber's Romantic opera „Freischütz" was his favorite opera. As the following story seems to prove, Wagner did not lose his youthful preference for the Romantic as he got older. The likes of Caspar David Friedrich or Novalis could hardly have topped Wagner's account of an experience in the Bohemian Forest in 1842. Wagner was hiking near – as he himself calls it – "romantic" Schreckenstein, the fortress that inspired his TANNHÄUSER "*… and the fantastic loneliness stirred my youthful courage so much that I climbed around in the Schreckenstein ruins by the full moon draped in a plain sheet, so that I myself might become the ghostly appearance that was lacking.*"

Wagner even longed to dwell in a romantic fortress ruin. In 1862 in the Biebrich Castle park, he discovered "*a small, ancient-looking castle, built to be a picturesque ruin, which a sculptor was using as an atelier. I felt the brazen wish rise inside myself to be able to call this small, half-weathered building my own for the rest of my life.*" He was advised against it because the walls were too humid. "*But that didn't stop me from going over regularly to visit the small house and garden I so desired.*" His continued his search for a "*small castle for the future*" in Bingen, where he found "*the famous old tower where Kaiser Heinrich IV had once been held captive.*" "*After climbing up the sizeable peak on which the tower stood, we ascended to the fourth floor of the tower to a room with the same floor area as the building with a single oriel window overlooking the Rhine. I recognized this as the best imaginable place for me to live.*" And a "*wonderful asylum*" for all times. Alas, this project also remained only a dream.

Wagner was fascinated by medieval buildings during his travels as well. If a building is even named and thereby emphasized in his writings or in Cosima's diaries, it is almost always from the Middle Ages. For example, the first attraction outside of Saxony he mentions in "My Life" is the old Hamlet Castle in Helsingör (during his trip to London), which he calls "*beautiful.*" The few churches he notices were also almost all medieval, even though the revolutionary and anarchistic Wagner was fundamentally suspicious of churches. He only starts paying attention to sacred architecture during his relationship with and for the sake of Cosima, of noble birth and very well educated. She shows him many churches of art historical importance, such as the Gothic Kilian Church in Heilbronn or the cathedrals in Bremen, Bamberg, Regensburg and Magdeburg.

However, Wagner doesn't say a thing about the (Romanesque) Worms Cathedral, which was, after all, where Luther, whom Wagner still

Spitze Türen am Zuschauerhaus muten gotisch an
Pointed arches at the auditorium building give a Gothic feel

Hausmeisterwohnung am Festspielhaus (Neubau 1982)
New Festspielhaus caretaker's apartment (built 1982)

Wagners Traumvilla – die Moosburg im Biebricher Schlosspark
Wagner's dream villa – Moosburg in the Biebrich Castle park

Mittelalterliche Bauten faszinierten Wagner auch auf seinen Reisen. Wenn einmal eine Architektur in seinen eigenen Schriften oder in Cosimas Tagebüchern genannt und damit hervorgehoben wird, ist es fast immer eine mittelalterliche, wie zum Beispiel die erste von ihm in „Mein Leben" erwähnte Sehenswürdigkeit außerhalb Sachsens, das alte Hamletschloss in Helsingör (auf seiner Reise nach London), das er als „schön"[1] bezeichnet. Die (wenigen) von ihm wahrgenommenen Kirchen waren ebenfalls fast immer mittelalterlich, obwohl dem Revolutionär und Anarchisten Wagner Kirchen grundsätzlich suspekt waren. Erst in der Beziehung zur adligen und hochgebildeten Cosima näherte er sich – ihr zuliebe – sakraler Architektur. Sie zeigte ihm viele kunsthistorisch bedeutende Kirchen, wie etwa die gotische Kilianskirche in Heilbronn oder die Dome in Bremen, Bamberg, Regensburg und Magdeburg.

Über den (romanischen) Wormser Dom jedoch, immerhin Wirkungsstätte des von ihm in Eisenach hochverehrten Luther und nebenbei sagenhafter Spielort des Nibelungenstoffs, verliert Wagner kein Wort. „Während ich tags darauf (nach einem Besuch von Freunden im rheinhessischen Osthofen), anderen Gründen der Verstimmung über meine Lebenslage nachhängend, mich zur Rückkehr anschickte, bewog Cosima, Zerstreuung und Erheiterung in der Aufsuchung des dortigen alten Domes suchend, Hans zu einer Weiterfahrt nach Worms, von wo aus sie mir später nach Biebrich nachfolgten."[2] Der nicht immer zuverlässige Wendelin Weißheimer allerdings behauptet, „Wagner und ich begleiteten sie dorthin"[3], und will die Freunde alle durch die Stadt Worms geführt haben.

Erneut stellt sich die Frage, warum Wagner sein Bayreuther Festspielhaus nicht im Stil einer romanischen oder gotischen Burg erbauen ließ, so wie ein anderer großer Spätromantiker seiner Zeit, sein Freund Ludwig II. von Bayern, sich sein Hohenschwangau und Neuschwanstein errichtete: „Ich habe die Absicht, die alte Burgruine Hohenschwangau bei der Pöllatschlucht neu aufbauen zu lassen im echten Styl der alten deutschen Ritterburgen, und muss Ihnen gestehen, dass ich mich sehr darauf freue, dort einst (in 3 Jahren) zu hausen; [...] Sie kennen Ihn, den angebeteten Gast, den ich dort beherbergen möchte; der Punkt ist einer der schönsten, die zu finden sind, heilig und unnahbar, ein würdiger Tempel für den göttlichen Freund, durch den einzig Heil und wahrer Segen der Welt erblühte. Auch Reminiszenzen aus TANNHÄUSER (Sängersaal mit Aussicht auf die Burg im Hintergrunde), aus LOHENGRIN (Burghof, offener Gang, Weg zur Kapelle), werden Sie dort finden."[4]

Ludwig schwärmte in seinen Briefen immer wieder von der Gotik, vom (neu rekonstruierten) Kölner Dom zum Beispiel, doch ließ sich Wagner davon – merkwürdigerweise – nie inspirieren. Schon Ludwigs Vorgänger König Maximilian hatte mit dem gotisch beeinflussten sogenannten Maximiliansstil eine romantische Architektur gefördert. Wagner lobte sogar die Baukunst, die in München unter Maximilian errichtet wurde, den er als „Wiedererwecker der deutschen bildenden Kunst"[5] preist. Doch die Neugotik, die vor allem nach der Reichsgründung 1871 ganze Straßenzüge und Stadtviertel der Gründerzeit beherrschte, ließ Wagner unberührt.

Die theoretischen Schriften Wagners sind erfüllt von der Sehnsucht, einen deutschen Stil für die Musik und das Theater zu finden, einen deutschen Gesangsstil, einen deutschen Opernstil, ein deutsches Nationaltheater. Gerne hätte Wagner auch für die Architektur einen „deutschen" Stil protegiert und hat diesen später für sein Bayreuther Festspielhaus auch verlangt.

Doch fast alle Länder Europas waren zu dieser Zeit auf der Suche nach einem Nationalstil, selbst die Juden in aller Welt, die sich mit orientalischen Stilelementen an ihren Synagogen eine architektonische Identität geben wollten. In der deutschen Architektur-

admired in Eisenach, wielded his influence and, moreover, which was the legendary setting for the Nibelungen material. *"A few days later (after visiting with friends in Osthofen in Rhine-Hessen), I was still possessed by other reasons for feeling negative about my life situation and was just ready to embark on my return. Cosima gave Hans instructions to continue on to Worms so she could distract herself and improve her mood by visiting the old cathedral there. She later traveled from there to join me in Biebrich."* The not always completely reliable Wendelin Weißheimer maintains, however, that *"Wagner and I accompanied her there"* and claims to have shown the group of friends around the city of Worms.

The question again arises as to why Wagner didn't have his Bayreuth Festspielhaus built in the style of a Romanesque or Gothic fortress, as another important late Romantic of his time did, his friend Ludwig II of Bavaria when he built Hohenschwangau and Neuschwanstein: *"I intend to have the old Hohenschwangau fortress ruin near the Pöllat Ravine rebuilt in the authentic style of the fortresses of the old German knights. I must admit, that I so look forward to living there one day (in three years). [...] You know this person, the honored guest I would like to put up there. It is one of the most beautiful spots one can find, holy and removed, a worthy temple for my godly friend, through whom only joy and true blessing of the world comes to fruition. You will also discover reminiscences from TANNHÄUSER (hall with a view of the fortress in the background) and from LOHENGRIN (fortress court, open passageway, path to the chapel)."*

In his letters, Ludwig repeatedly raves about the Gothic, for example, in the (newly reconstructed) Cologne Cathedral, but – strangely – Wagner was never inspired by it. Even Ludwig's predecessor King Maximilian's so-called Maximilianic style, influenced by the Gothic, had advanced Romantic architecture. Wagner even praised the architecture of the buildings in Munich Maximilian had built, calling Maximilian *"the rediscoverer of German visual arts."* But Wagner remained uninterested in the Neo-Gothic, which dominated entire Wilhelminian streetscapes and city districts especially after the founding of the German Reich in 1871.

Wagner's theoretical writings are full of the longing to find a German style of music and theater, a German style of singing, a German operatic style, a German national theater. Wagner would have liked to have contributed to a "German" architectural style, as well, and did demand that later for his Bayreuth Festspielhaus.

But at the time, nearly all European countries were searching for a national style. Even the Jews all over the world sought to give their synagogues architectural identity by adding oriental stylistic elements. Back then, however, hardly anything genuinely "German" could be found in architectural history. In essence, all architectural styles developed through the 19th century were receptions of classical Greek and Roman antiquity. France and Italy were models for German architecture for centuries and the Gothic – as mentioned – was not actually German.

Modern art historians are now aware that the Romanesque of the German imperial cathedrals, such as in Worms, the brick Gothic (with influence in the Scandinavian and Baltic regions), and the late Gothic in southern Germany are held to be "German" contributions, even though such nationalistic categories have been obsolete for a long time. The same holds true for the so-called German Renaissance. What began as a reception of the Italian Renaissance following Dutch models reached Germany through indirect channels in the late 16th century and came to full bloom in the north as the Weser Renaissance and took hold in the south as well, remaining prevalent into the 17th century. Starting in the Wilhelminian Era in 1871 it underwent a revival in exterior and interior building decoration styles as an expression of a patriotic neo-Renaissance.

But someone who associates a city as important as Worms only with Luther and beer can't have suspected any of that: *"In Worms a mug of Einbecker beer, / that quenches Luther's thirst: / heroi Lohengrin after the tourney, / in Braunschweig feasts on wurst."*

„In einem hinteren Teile [des] Parkes stand an einem Teiche ein altertümlich aussehendes kleines Schlösschen, welches in dem Sinne einer pittoresken Ruine verwendet war […]. Es regte sich in mir der kühne Wunsch, dieses kleine, halb verwitterte Gebäude mir für Lebenszeit zugeteilt wissen zu können."

"In the back part of the park there was a small, ancient-looking castle beside a pond, built to be a picturesque ruin [...]. I felt the brazen wish rise inside myself to be able to call this small, half-weathered building my own for the rest of my life."

Richard Wagner, „Mein Leben" (1861 – 1864)

geschichte fand sich damals aber kaum etwas genuin „Deutsches". Alle bis ins 19. Jahrhundert entwickelten Architekturstile rezipierten letztlich die griechisch-römische Antike, Frankreich und Italien waren jahrhundertelang Vorbild für die deutsche Architektur, und die Gotik war – wie gesagt – nicht wirklich deutsch.

Heutige Kunsthistoriker wissen, dass die Romanik der deutschen Kaiserdome wie in Worms, wie auch die Backsteingotik (mit ihren Auswirkungen nach Skandinavien und das Baltikum) und die süddeutsche Spätgotik durchaus als „eigene" Leistungen der deutschen Architektur gelten, wobei solche Nationalismen längst obsolet geworden sind. Gleiches gilt für die sogenannte deutsche Renaissance. Ursprünglich eine Rezeption der italienischen Renaissance nach niederländischen Vorbildern, gelangte sie im späten 16. Jahrhundert auf indirektem Weg nach Deutschland, blühte im Norden als Weserrenaissance, aber auch im Süden, und war bis in das 17. Jahrhundert verbreitet. In der Gründerzeit ab 1871 erfuhr sie im Außen- wie im Innenbau als Dekorationsstil eine Wiederbelebung als patriotische Neorenaissance.

Doch wer eine architektonisch so bedeutende Stadt wie Worms lediglich mit Luther und Bier in Verbindung bringt, kann von alledem nichts ahnen: *„Zu Worms ein Krug Einbecker Bier, / der labte Luthers Durst / Held Lohengrin, nach dem Turnier, / zu Braunschweig stärkt ihn Wurst."*[1] (Richard Wagner 1870).

Susanne Schinkel, 1876, idealisiert das Festspielhaus als romantische Burg in der Abendsonne
Susanne Schinkel, 1876, idealizes the Festspielhaus as a romantic fortress lit up by the late afternoon sun

„Auf Berges Gipfel die Götter-Burg, prachtvoll prahlt der prangende Bau! Wie im Traume ich ihn trug, wie mein Wille ihn wies, stark und schön steht er zur Schau: hehrer, herrlicher Bau!"

Wotan in DAS RHEINGOLD

Wagner und die Architektur des Südens

Italienische Gotik und Byzantinik

Selbst in Italien, das eigentlich durch seine antiken Ruinen und durch seine Renaissance- und Barockarchitektur berühmt war und ist, interessierten Wagner die dort eher seltenen Beispiele der Gotik. Allzu gerne verstand er sie sogar als eine „germanische" Architektur, so in einem Brief an Ludwig II.: *„Ich kenne nichts [so] ernst Erhabenes wie die Werke der Normannen in Sizilien, der Hohenstaufen und ihres Geistes, der noch jüngst durch König Ludwig I von Bayern, durch die Wiederherstellung beschädigter Teile der Kathedrale von Monreale, sich bewährt hat."*[1]

Von Mailand berichtet er 1859 seiner Minna: *„In Mailand war ich ein Paar Tag, habe herrliche Bilder und Kunstwerke besucht, und bin auf dem kolossalen, bis zur Langweiligkeit großartigen und reichen Weißen-Marmor-Dom herumgeklettert."*[2] Dieser ist bekanntlich der größte und prächtigste, in jener „maniera tedesca" errichtete gotische Dom Italiens. Zu seinen Lieblingskirchen gehörte er freilich nicht. Für Italien fasst Wagner 1882 diese wie folgt zusammen: *„Ich habe"*, sagte er, *„meine drei Kirchen: den Dom von Siena, von Pisa und San Marco (Venedig)."*[3] Alle drei sind mittelalterlich!

Der Dom von Siena sollte ihn bekanntlich zum Gralstempel für den PARSIFAL inspirieren. Sein Biograf Carl Friedrich Glasenapp berichtet: *„Mehr als alles aber sprach zu ihm, gleich am Tage seiner Ankunft, der gewaltige Dom, dieses gotische Wunderwerk auf dem obersten Plateau der östlichen Höhe der Stadt. Das Innere des erhabenen Baues mit seiner ernsten ungeheuren Kuppel versetzte ihn gleich beim allerersten Betreten in eine förmliche Entzückung: bis zu Tränen hingerissen, erklärte er, es sei der größte Eindruck, den er je von einem Gebäude gehabt."*[4] Ein erstaunliches Zitat.

In Italien kommt ein weiterer Stilbegriff der mittelalterlichen Architektur ins Spiel, der des Byzantinischen. Dieser ist in Venedig (und Ravenna) zu finden und zeigte sich Wagner in seiner Lieblingskirche in Venedig, dem Markusdom aus dem 11. Jahrhundert. Die byzantinische Baukunst steht der Romanik näher als der Gotik und beeindruckte Wagner sicherlich in ihrer ehrwürdigen Altertümlichkeit. Cosima berichtet über den Besuch von Santa Maria della Salute in Venedig, einer der schönsten Barockkirchen der Lagunenstadt (von Longhena, 1681), *„deren kaltes Innere R. völlig anwidert! – Er begreift nicht, wie man den warmen Stil der byzantinischen Kirche für diese antikisierende Weißlichkeit aufgeben konnte."*[5]

Das Byzantinische findet sich überraschend – als einzige Stilbezeichnung in sämtlichen Bühnenwerken Wagners – in den *„Szenischen Vorschriften für die Aufführungen des LOHENGRINS"*, zweiter Aufzug, wo Wagner das Portal des Münsters als *„byzantinisch"*[6] angibt. Es ist nicht ganz klar, was Wagner unter jenem Münster versteht, wahrscheinlich die – bei seinem Besuch in Antwerpen ignorierte – gotische Kathedrale, die Onze-Lieve-Vrouwkathedraal aus dem 14. Jahrhundert, doch findet sich in der Architektur Flanderns kein byzantinischer Einfluss. Das hat Wagner vielleicht selbst erkannt und den Begriff im endgültigen Textbuch gestrichen.

Doch niemand fuhr und fährt nach Italien, um dort allein gotische oder (byzantinische) Architektur zu bestaunen. Frankreich wäre da viel lohnender, gerade Paris und die Ile de France mit ihren hochgotischen Kathedralen, die der mehrmals und lange in Paris lebende Wagner jedoch offensichtlich ignorierte und – den Quellen nach – vielleicht gar nie besucht hat.

Wagner and the architecture of the south

Italian Gothic and Byzantinic

Even in Italy, which was and is famous for its antique ruins and its Renaissance and Baroque architecture, Wagner was interested in the rare examples of buildings in Gothic style. As this letter to Ludwig II illustrates, he was only too happy to identify this as "Germanic" architecture: *"I know of nothing [as] seriously sublime as the works of the Normans in Sicily by the Hohenstaufen and their spirit, that most recently proved itself when King Ludwig I of Bavaria had damaged parts of the Monreale Cathedral restored."*

In 1859 he writes to Minna about Milan: *"I spent a few days in Milan and saw wonderful paintings and artworks and climbed around the colossal, boringly tremendous and rich white marble cathedral."* This is, of course, the largest and most elaborate cathedral in Italy built in the so-called "maniera tedesca" Gothic style. It was clearly not one his favorite churches. In 1882 Wagner recaps his view on Italian churches: *"I have my three churches: the cathedrals in Siena, Pisa and San Marco (Venice)."* All three are medieval!

The Siena Cathedral would later serve as the inspiration for the Grail Temple in PARSIFAL. His biographer Carl Friedrich Glasenapp reports: *"It was the enormous cathedral that appealed to him right from the first day of his arrival, that Gothic wonder on top of the highest plateau of the eastern city hill. He trembled with delight when he first entered and saw the interior of the building with its foreboding dome. Moved to tears, he explained that this was the most powerful impression a building had ever made on him."* A remarkable quotation.

Another style term from medieval architecture that applies to Italy as well is Byzantine. This can be found in Venice (and Ravenna). Wagner encountered it in his favorite church in Venice, St. Mark's Cathedral, built in the 11th century. Byzantine architecture is closer to the Romanesque than to the Gothic. Its ancient respectability surely impressed Wagner. Cosima describes a visit to Santa Maria della Salute in Venice, one of the most beautiful Baroque churches in the lagoon city (by Longhena, 1681), *"R. was completely revolted by its cold interior! – He doesn't understand how the warm style of the Byzantine church could give way to this classical whiteness."*

Surprisingly, "Byzantine" is the only stylistic term found in all of Wagner's stage works. Wagner identifies the portal of the cathedral as *"Byzantine"* in the *"Scenic directions for performing LOHENGRIN,"* Act 2. It is not completely clear what this cathedral means for Wagner. It is likely to be the Gothic cathedral he ignored on his visit to Antwerp, the Onze Lieve Vrouwkathedraal from the 14th century, even though there is no evidence of Byzantine influence in the architecture of Flanders. Perhaps Wagner realized this, too, and struck the term from his final libretto.

But no one traveled or travels to Italy just to gaze at the Gothic (or Byzantine) architecture. France is a much more lucrative destination in this regard, especially Paris and the Isle of France with its High Gothic cathedrals. But it would seem that Wagner, who lived in Paris for a long time and on several occasions, ignored these cathedrals and, according to the sources, may not even have visited them.

Renaissance

Die Renaissance, die als erste Epoche nach der Antike steinerne Theater errichtete, hätte Wagner als Theatermann besonders interessieren müssen, was in seinen kulturhistorischen Schriften auch geschah. Denn das Mittelalter und die Gotik kannten keine feststehenden Theater, nur Bretterbühnen. Wagner las sogar die „Geschichte der Renaissance in Italien" (1867) von Jacob Burckhardt und Vasaris Biografie berühmter Renaissancekünstler. Wagner begriff die Renaissance durchaus richtig als Wiedergeburt der Antike, die von den romanischen Völkern jedoch nie wirklich und wahrhaft verstanden worden sei, wie er schon 1849 schreibt: *„Die eigentliche wirkliche Kunst ist aber durch und seit der Renaissance noch nicht wiedergeboren worden."*[1]

In seinen zunehmend chauvinistischen Ansichten betrachtet er die Renaissance Frankreichs und Italiens sogar ausgesprochen feindlich als *„undeutsch"*, wie Cosima am 2. April 1872 berichtet: *„Zu Tisch eifert er gegen die Renaissance, von der er behauptet, dass sie der germanischen Entwicklung ungeheuer geschadet hätte, diese Zeit habe die Antike ebenso wenig wie das Christentum ernst genommen und verstanden, [...] und wie stets habe der naive Deutsche sich von der fremden Kultur so imponieren lassen, dass sein eignes Gefühl beinahe zu Grund gegangen sei."*[2]

Ebenso kritisch betrachtet Wagner die reale Architektur der Renaissance: Den Palazzo Pitti in Florenz, einen der berühmtesten Renaissancebauten der Kunstgeschichte, bezeichnet Wagner 1880 als *„langweiligen Palast"*[3]. Über die nicht minder berühmten Prokuratien in Venedig, dreistöckige Renaissancepaläste am Markusplatz, heißt es 1883: *„Von der Stube aus hatte er die Fassade der Prokuratien angesehen und erklärt, wie langweilig, phantasie- und erfindungslos er sie fände, wie [...] anders ein gotischer Dom zu ihm spräche als diese nachgebildete Monotonie."*[4] Und 1882: *„Den Dogen-Palast betrachtend, rühmt er die mittelalterliche Baukunst und sagt, mit ihr sei alle Phantasie, alles Leben und Erfinden erloschen. Die ganze Renaissance ist ihm kalt."*[5]

Ja, selbst den von Bramante, Raffael, Sangallo und Michelangelo gebauten Petersdom in Rom, die *„eindrucksvollste Kirche der Christenheit"* (Baedeker), findet Wagner abschreckend, wie Cosima berichtet: *„Grauenhafter Eindruck in St. Peter, alles, was Unmusik ist, drückt sich darin aus. In der Seele von Dr. Luther mitempfunden."* Und etwas später: *„‚Ein verfehlter Cäsarenpalast', sagt R."*[6]

All diese (erschütternden) Sätze machen deutlich, dass Wagner die Renaissance in ihrer *„Monotonie"* und *„antikisierenden Weißlichkeit"* nicht als echte Wiederbelebung der Antike gelten ließ. Die in seiner Zeit aufkommende Neorenaissance, der Stil, mit dem sein einziger Architektenfreund Gottfried Semper erfolgreich war, muss Wagner demnach ebenso negativ begegnet sein. Kein Wunder also, dass er den von Semper geschaffenen ersten Entwurf für ein Münchner Festspielhausprojekt – wovon noch die Rede sein wird – ablehnen musste. Auch die stilistische Einordnung des Bayreuther Festspielhauses von Heinrich Habel als Bau der Neorenaissance offenbart einen Widerspruch. Dabei hätte Wagner in der Renaissance durchaus beispielhafte Theaterbauten finden können, die sehr um die griechisch-antiken Vorbilder bemüht waren, wie jene in Parma und Vicenza, doch hat er diese – obwohl mehrfach in ihrer Nähe – den Quellen nach nie besucht.

Renaissance

As a theater specialist, one would expect Wagner to have been especially interested in the Renaissance, the first era since the Antique to build stone theaters. And that is the case in his cultural historical writings. The Middle Ages and the Gothic did not produce solid theaters, but rather wooden board stages. Wagner even read Jacob Burckhardt's "History of the Renaissance in Italy" (1867) and Vasari's biography of famous Renaissance artists. Wagner correctly understood the Renaissance as the rebirth of the Antique, but claims that the Romanic peoples never truly and fully understood the Antique. For example, in 1849 he writes: *"The actual real art wasn't and still hasn't been reborn through the Renaissance."*

In his increasing chauvinism, he even looks down on the Renaissance in France and Italy with downright hostility as *"un-German."* On April 2, 1872 Cosima notes: *"At the table he raved against the Renaissance, which he claims greatly slowed Germanic development. He claims this period misunderstood and failed to take antiquity seriously, as he thinks is the case with Christianity as well. [...] and that the naive Germans always let themselves be so impressed by foreign culture that their own feelings very nearly shriveled up."*

Wagner was just as critical of the real architecture of the Renaissance. In 1880 he calls the Palazzo Pitti in Florence, one of the most famous Renaissance buildings in art history, a *"boring palace."* His opinion about the no less famous Procurators' Offices in Venice, three-story Renaissance palaces on St. Mark's Square, was little better: *"He saw the facade of the Procurators' Offices from the room and exclaimed how boring, unimaginative and uncreative he finds them and how [...] much more appealing he finds a Gothic cathedral over this mimicked monotony."* And in 1882: *"Viewing the Doge's Palace, he praised the medieval architecture, claiming all fantasy, life and creativity was extinguished when it passed. He finds the entire Renaissance cold."*

Even St. Peter's Cathedral in Rome built by Bramante, Raphael, Sangallo and Michelangelo, the *"most impressive church in Christendom"* (Baedeker), is dreadful in Wagner's eyes. Cosima writes: *"Horrible impression in St. Peter's. It expresses everything unmusical. I empathize with Dr. Luther's soul."* And somewhat later: *"R. calls it a failed Cesar's palace."*

These (disturbing) sentences make it clear that Wagner did not consider the Renaissance, with its "monotony" and "classical whiteness," the true rebirth of antiquity. Accordingly, he must have been just as critical of the neo-Renaissance, which grew in popularity during his lifetime, and in which his only architect friend, Gottfried Semper, found much success. It therefore comes as no surprise that he rejected Semper's first design for a Festspielhaus project in Munich, which will be discussed in more detail below. The stylistic categorization by Heinrich Habel of the Bayreuth Festspielhaus as neo-Renaissance also reveals a contradiction. Wagner could have found exemplary theaters in the Renaissance that were strongly oriented toward models from Greek antiquity, such as the theaters in Parma and Vicenza. However, although he was near them several times, the sources make no reference of him having visited them.

Ein Renaissancepalast in Oberfranken?
Kutschenauffahrt Königsbau

A Renaissance palace in Upper Franconia?
Königsbau carriage ramp

Barock und Rokoko

Wie stand Wagner zur Architektur des 17. und 18. Jahrhunderts? Er begriff den Barock und das Rokoko mit ihrem weiterhin antiken Formenrepertoire – wie schon die Renaissance – als eine falsch verstandene Antikenrezeption. So berichtet Glasenapp von Wagner in Palermo: *„Abstoßend und anwidernd wirkte dagegen auf ihn die Zopfkirche San Domenico […], dahin führte die Renaissance! rief er aus. Die griechische Kunst habe noch lange nach ihrem Untergange die Welt beeinflusst; aber mit dieser Beflissenheit, es schön zu machen, das Herbe zu meiden, wäre man bis zum Rokoko gekommen."*[1]

Jene Kirche San Domenico ist eindeutig ein Bau des Barocks des 17. Jahrhunderts, sodass die Zuordnung zum (späteren) Zopfstil unrichtig ist. Also auch der Barock wurde von Wagner als falsch und als zu dekorativ verstanden. In Rom kritisiert Wagner (1870) die barocke Architektur der Gegenreformation: *„So verdeckt der gleiche jesuitische Baustil der zwei letzten Jahrhunderte dem sinnvollen Beschauer das ehrwürdig edle Rom."*[2]

„Zopfstil" und „jesuitischer Stil" verraten, dass Wagner den Begriff „Barock" nicht kennt, zumindest nicht in der Architektur, sondern ausschließlich als Bezeichnung für die Musik (Bachs zum Beispiel). In der Kunstgeschichte war der Begriff Barock als Stilepoche damals noch nicht sehr lange gefestigt und bezeichnete generell alles „Schwülstige" und „Absonderliche". Trotzdem sah und erlebte Wagner viele barocke Bauten, auch wenn er sie nicht „barock" nannte, schließlich verkehrte er in den höchsten adeligen Kreisen, doch kein einziges Schloss wird irgendwie und sei es nur als schön oder prächtig kommentiert. Am Biebricher Barockschloss zum Beispiel interessierte ihn – wie zitiert – die verfallene Burgruine im Park.

Selbst die eigenen barocken Wohnadressen werden von Wagner nicht in ihrer äußeren Erscheinung besprochen, wie sein barockes Geburtshaus in Leipzig, sein Wohnhaus in Meudon bei Paris oder sein Dresdner Domizil als Kapellmeister; *„eine geräumige, hübsch gelegene Wohnung an der Ostra-Allee mit der Aussicht auf den Zwinger."*[3] Immerhin verschließt Wagner seine Augen nicht vor dem berühmtesten Barockbau Dresdens, dem damals schon weltberühmten Zwinger, und attestiert ihm an anderer Stelle eine *„schöne Wirkung"*[4].

Das „Rokoko", die Spätform des Barock, aber war Wagner – im Gegensatz zum Barock – als Architekturstil und Begriff geläufig. Das Rokoko verbindet sich in „Mein Leben" sogar mit einem nahezu traumatischen Kindheitserlebnis. In Leipzig wohnte er bei der altjüngferlichen Tante Jeanette Thomé, der Mitbesitzerin eines großen Hauses am Markte, in welchem die sächsische Königsfamilie die zwei Hauptstockwerke als eine Art Stadtpalais gemietet und eingerichtet hatte. *„Und in einem dieser Prunkgemächer war es denn auch, wo mir meine Schlafstelle angewiesen wurde. Die Einrichtung dieser Räume war noch aus den Zeiten Augusts des Starken; prächtig aus schweren Seidenstoffen mit*

Baroque and Rococo

What did Wagner think about the architecture of the 17th and 18th centuries? He considered the Baroque and the Rococo, that continued to use antique form repertoire, an incorrect reception of antiquity, just like the Renaissance. For example, Glasenapp comments about Wagner in Palermo: *"He found the Louis-seize church San Domenico horrible and repulsive. [...] He cried out 'That's where the Renaissance leads!' He remarked that Greek art influenced the world long after the fall of their civilization, but that this zealous attempt to make things beautiful and to avoid harshness led right up to the Rococo."*

San Domenico Church was clearly built in the 17th century Baroque style, so classifying it as (late Rococo) Louis-seize style is incorrect. It seems Wagner considered the Baroque dishonest and too decorative as well. In 1870 Wagner criticizes the Baroque architecture of the Counter-Reformation: *"The same Jesuit architectural style from the past two centuries prevents worthy Rome from being properly admired."*

Wagner's misuse of "Louis-seize style" and "Jesuit style" betrays that he was not familiar with the term "Baroque," at least in terms of architecture, but rather exclusively as a musical period (during which Bach was composing, for example). In art history, the term Baroque had not yet long been narrowed, and was generally used to describe anything "bombastic" and "strange." Nonetheless, Wagner saw and experienced many Baroque buildings, even though he didn't label them "Baroque." After all, he mixed in the best noble circles. Still, he doesn't comment on a single castle at all, even as being beautiful or grand. As quoted, only the dilapidated fortress ruins in the Baroque Biebrich Castle park interested him.

Wagner doesn't even mention the exterior appearance of his own Baroque residences, such as his Baroque birthplace in Leipzig, his residence in Meudon near Paris, or his domicile while chapel master in Dresden. *"A spacious apartment well located in Ostra Allee with a view of the Zwinger."* At least Wagner doesn't avert his eyes from Dresden's most famous Baroque building, the even then world renowned Zwinger, and elsewhere remarks on the *"beautiful impression"* it makes.

Unlike the term Baroque, the term and architectural style "Rococo", the late form of the Baroque, was familiar to Wagner. In fact, in "My Life," Wagner associates Rococo with a nearly traumatic childhood experience. While in Leipzig, Wagner lived with his unmarried elderly aunt Jeanette Thomé, co-owner of a large house on the market square. The Saxon royal family rented out the two main floors and had decorated them as something of a city palace. *"And my sleeping quarters were in one of these decorative rooms. The room's furnishings were still from August the Strong's era; ornamental with heavy silk fabric and rich Rococo furniture, all heavily worn with age. […] Not a night passed when I wasn't soaked in sweat, plagued by the most horrible visions of ghosts."*

Later in life he again uses the architectural term Rococo to identify the Margravial Opera House in Bayreuth in his speech at the laying the cornerstone of the Festspielhaus in 1872: *"With this large opera house, an Italian constructed one of the most fantastical monuments to the*

Wagners Geburtshaus in Leipzig
Wagner's birthplace in Leipzig

Markgräfliches Opernhaus Bayreuth mit seinem *„wunderlichen Rokoko-Saale"*
Margravial Opera House in Bayreuth with its *"wondrous Rococo hall"*

reichen Rokoko-Möbeln, alles bereits vom Alter stark abgenutzt."
Hier „... verging nie eine Nacht, ohne dass ich in Angstschweiß
gebadet den schrecklichsten Gespenster-Visionen ausgesetzt war".[1]

In späten Jahren findet sich der architektonische Begriff des
Rokoko noch einmal bei der Nennung des Markgräflichen Opernhauses zu Bayreuth in seiner Rede zur Grundsteinlegung des
Festspielhauses 1872: „Ein Italiener erbaute mit einem großen
Opernhause eines der phantasievollsten Denkmäler des Rokokostiles" mit einem „wunderlichen Rokoko-Saale"[2]. Eine negative
Bewertung ist hier nicht zu erkennen, eher eine höfliche Reverenz
dem von ihm als Wohnort gewählten Bayreuth gegenüber, doch
zeigt die so seltene Beachtung von Bauten des 17. und 18. Jahrhunderts, dass diese ihn nicht interessierten. Weil er sie als rein
dekorative Rezeption antiker Formensprache nicht gelten ließ?
Weil er ihren katholischen Pomp nicht mochte? Weil er sie als
„welschen", sprich italienischen oder französischen Import mit
großem Misstrauen belegte? Weil er, der einstige Revolutionär, sie
als Ausdruck des politischen Absolutismus insgeheim verachtete?

Klassizismus

Wagners Kritik am falschen Antikenverständnis war nicht neu. Im
Laufe der Architektur- und Kunstgeschichte wurde mehrfach um
eine wahrhafte Rezeption der Antike gerungen, so auch im
Klassizismus um 1800. Der Begriff fehlt ebenfalls im Vokabular
Wagners. Wagner, der lange in München lebte, kannte natürlich
die dort vor allem unter Ludwig I. errichteten Bauten im Stil des
Klassizismus, referiert darüber (1861) aber nur indirekt und kommentarlos in „Mein Leben": Sein Schwager Ollivier in München
fand, „dass der antikisierende Stil, in welchem namentlich die von
König Ludwig I. ausgeführten Kunstgebäude sich darstellten,
höchst vorteilhaft gegen die Gebäude sich auszeichnete, mit welchen Louis Napoleon zu Olliviers größtem Ärger Paris anzufüllen
beliebt hatte."[3] Wagner selbst besuchte am 15. März 1875 die
Walhalla bei Regensburg, das Hauptwerk der Bauten Ludwigs I.,
1830 bis 1842 von Leo von Klenze im Stil eines antiken Tempels
errichtet. Cosima berichtet: „Um 6 Uhr früh in Regensburg, [...]
besuchen wir den [gotischen] Dom und machen eine Spazierfahrt
bis dem Walhall gegenüber. Der Dom macht einen großen
Eindruck, allein das Walhall einen sehr geringen."[4]

Schon 1847 hätte Wagner in Berlin, wo er am Gendarmenmarkt
wohnte, mit dem Schauspielhaus von Karl Friedrich Schinkel einen
der wichtigsten klassizistischen Bauten eines der bedeutendsten
klassizistischen Architekten bestaunen können, findet den ganzen
Platz aber uninteressant. Selbst das berühmteste klassizistische
Theater in (Bad) Lauchstädt, das er 1834 am Anfang seiner
Karriere intensiv kennenlernte, wird von ihm in seiner so sehr um
antike Klassizität bemühten Architektur nicht gewürdigt. Er sagt
lediglich: „Das aus Holz errichtete Theater war nach Goethes Plan
ausgeführt."[5]

Rococo style" with a "wondrous Rococo hall". No negative critique is
audible in these words, but rather a polite reverence for the city of
Bayreuth, which he had chosen as his residence. However, the fact that
he so seldom comments on buildings from the 17th and 18th centuries
illustrates that he has no interest in them. Is that because he does not
accept them as a purely decorative reception of the language of form
from the Antique? Because he didn't like their Catholic pomp? Because
he greatly mistrusted them as a "Welsh" (i. e., Italian or French) import?
Or because he, the former revolutionary, secretly despised them as
expressions of political absolutism?

Classicism

Wagner's critique of an incorrect interpretation of antiquity was nothing
new. Throughout architectural and art history, people struggled repeatedly to find a veritable reception of antiquity, and the Classicism around
1800 was another attempt. This term is also not in Wagner's vocabulary.
Having lived in Munich for many years, Wagner was naturally familiar
with the Classicist buildings there, especially those constructed under
Ludwig I, but he only mentions them (1861) indirectly and without comment in "My Life." He remarks that his brother-in-law considers "the
classical style used in the art buildings commissioned by King Ludwig, in
particular, has proven quite advantageous over those that Louis
Napoleon preferred to fill Paris with, much to Ollivier's consternation."
On March 15, 1875, Wagner himself visited Walhalla near Regensburg,
Ludwig I's most well-known building, which was built by Leo von Klenze
between 1830 and 1842 in the style of an antique temple. Cosima
writes: "6:00 in the morning in Regensburg [...] we visited the [Gothic]
cathedral and went for a ride toward Walhall. The cathedral is quite
impressive. Walhall, on the contrary, isn't."

In 1847, when Wagner was living on Gendarmenmarkt in Berlin, he
could have admired one of the most important Classicistic buildings,
Karl Friedrich Schinkel's theater. Instead, he considers the square uninteresting. He doesn't even mention the most famous Classicistic
theater in (Bad) Lauchstädt, which he got to know intensively at the
beginning of his career in 1834, even though this theater's architecture
pays great tribute to antique classicality. He writes only: "The wooden
theater was built according to Goethe's plan."

Die gusseisernen Blumenkästen
vor dem Königsbau gehören der
Stadt Bayreuth und zeigen ein
im Sinne Wagners vollkommen
unpassendes Rokoko-Dekor
The cast iron flower boxes in front
belong to the city of Bayreuth and
are of Rococo décor, which contradicts Wagner's concept completely

Villa Wahnfried, Wagner's
Wohnhaus in Bayreuth
Wahnfried Villa, Wagner's home
in Bayreuth

Sein eigenes Haus immerhin, die Villa Wahnfried, ließ er in einem strengen antikisierenden Stil errichten, den man einem Neoklassizismus oder einer Art palladianischer Neorenaissance zuordnen könnte. Palladio, den wichtigsten Baumeister der italienischen Renaissance, kannte Wagner, wie eine einzige Stelle belegt: „*Ich las in [Heinrich] Laube, von Verona – von Vicenza u. seinem Palladio.*"[1] Doch warum bekennt sich Wagner zur eigentlich verhassten italienischen Renaissance und warum baute er sich keinen romantischen, neogotischen Wohnturm, den er doch als Ideal einer Wohnung einst fantasiert hatte?

Historismus

Damit haben wir den Historismus erreicht. Er selbst wohnte zum Beispiel in Biebrich in einer englischen Landhausvilla mit neogotischen Elementen, in Zürich war er oft Gast in der Wesendonck-Villa, einem Palast der Neorenaissance, und in München in einer neobarocken Villa, um nur einige historistische Adressen anzuführen. Doch wie zu erwarten, betrachtete er diese damals moderne Architektur sehr kritisch. Er beklagt 1870 den allein von Modelaunen getriebenen Eklektizismus seiner Zeit sehr spöttisch: „*Das Originelle derselben ist ihre gänzliche Originalitätslosigkeit, und ihr unermesslicher Gewinn besteht in dem Umsatz aller Kunststile, welche [...] nach beliebigem Geschmack für Jeden verwendbar geworden sind.*" Und: „*Jetzt wechseln Antike und Rokoko, Gotik und Renaissance unter sich ab.*"[2]

Schon 1849 im „Kunstwerk der Zukunft" karikierte er den Historismus als Ausverkauf der (griechischen) Antike: „*Die eigentlichen Tempel unserer modernen Religion, die Börsengebäude, werden zwar sehr sinnreich wieder auf griechische Säulen konstruiert; griechische Giebelfelder laden zu Eisenbahnfahrten ein, und aus dem athenischen Parthenon schreitet uns die abgelöste Militärwache entgegen.*"[3] Wagner vermisst den rechten Sinn dieses meist auf Prunk und Pracht hin orientierten Eklektizismus und kritisiert, wie „*alle nationalen Baustile der Welt zu unzusammenhängenden, scheckigen Gestaltungen*"[4] vermengt würden. 1879 entsetzt ihn in seiner Schrift „Wollen wir hoffen?" der Neubau der Synagoge in Nürnberg im „*reinsten orientalischen Stile*"[5], den man ausgerechnet dem, von ihm selbst geförderten, Denkmal seines deutschen Helden Hans Sachs gegenübergestellt habe.

Fazit

Wie schwer muss es für den so kritischen Wagner gewesen sein, einen passenden Stil für sein Festspielhaus zu finden. Die Gotik, der eigentlich sein Herz gehörte, kam wegen fehlender Theatertradition nicht in Frage. Oder sind die Fachwerk- und Backsteinelemente des ausgeführten Festspielbaus doch als gotischmittelalterliche Elemente aufzufassen? Doch wie beschrieben, zeigt das Festspielhaus zahlreiche antikisierende Stilmerkmale. Der verhassten Renaissance sollten diese eigentlich nicht entliehen sein, ebenso wenig dem Barock und dem Rokoko. Eigentlich hätte Wagner einen klassizistischen Bau betreiben müssen, doch wird dieser Stil von ihm an keiner Stelle reflektiert. Warum lässt er ihn als adäquate Rezeption der von ihm so verehrten Antike nicht gelten?

At least he had his own home, the Wahnfried Villa, built in strict classical style categorized as neo-Classical or a type of Palladian neo-Renaissance style. Wagner was familiar with Palladio, the most important builder of the Italian Renaissance, as evidenced by a single passage: "*In the book by [Heinrich] Laube I read of Verona – of Vicenza and his Palladio.*" But why would Wagner associate himself with the Renaissance, which he actually despised, and why didn't he build himself the Romantic, neo-Gothic tower to live in that he had once so fantasized as his ideal living space?

Historicism

That brings us to Historicism. In Biebrich, Wagner himself lived in an English country villa with neo-Gothic elements, in Zurich he was frequently a guest in the Wesendonck Villa, a neo-Renaissance palace, and in Munich he often stayed in a neo-Baroque villa – to name just a few historistic addresses. But, as expected, he was highly critical of this then modern architecture. In 1870 he makes fun of the eclecticism of his time as being driven solely by fashion whims: "*The only thing original about it is its complete lack of originality. Its immeasurable profit comes from turning over all artistic styles, which [...] have become available for anyone however their tastes dictate.*" And "*Antique and Rococo, Gothic and Renaissance are all taking turns.*"

In his 1849 essay, "The Artwork of the Future," Wagner caricatures Historicism as a sellout of (Greek) antiquity. "*The actual temples of our modern religion, the stock market buildings, have been meaningfully built with Greek pillars, Greek tympana invite us to ride the train, and the relieved military guard strides toward us from the Parthenon in Athens.*" Wagner sees no true meaning behind an eclecticism oriented mainly toward show and glamour, criticizing how "*all the national architectures of the world*" are combined to form a "*disjointed, checkered appearance.*" In his 1879 essay "Shall We Hope?," he expresses his horror over the new Synagogue being built in Nurnberg "*in the most pure oriental style*" directly across from the monument to his German hero Hans Sachs, of all places, which he himself had so avidly supported erecting.

Summary

How difficult it must have been for the so critical Wagner to find an appropriate style for his Festspielhaus. Gothic, to whom his heart really belonged, was out of the question because of the lack of theater tradition. Or are timber framing and brick elements of the Festspielhaus really meant to signal the medieval Gothic? But, as described, the Festspielhaus has many classical stylistic elements, which actually shouldn't have been borrowed from the despised Renaissance, or from the Baroque or the Rococo, for that matter. Wagner really should have built in the Classicist style, but he does not reflect on this style anywhere. Why doesn't he embrace it as a plausible reception of the antique he so admires?

Die Bürgerreuther Straße in Bayreuth mit historistischen Villen des 19. Jahrhunderts (Postkarte von 1924)
Bürgerreuther Straße in Bayreuth with historicist villas from the 19th century (postcard from 1924)

Wagner and antique architecture

Ever since childhood, Wagner loved not only the Middle Ages, but Greek antiquity as well. Glasenapp quotes him: *"I don't think there could have been any boy more enthralled with classical antiquity as I was when I attended the Dresden Kreuzschule. I was drawn especially to Greek mythology and history, but above all I wanted to study the Greek language, avoiding Latin as much as possible, almost to the point of having disciplinary problems."* Even as a boy, Wagner read Homer in the original and – like many other pan-Hellenists of the time – supported the Greeks in their fight for liberty from the Ottoman Empire. It would be possible to find many more indices for Wagner's fondness for Greece. As was already true for Latin lessons, however, he was critical of Roman antiquity.

Clearly, Wagner viewed his high esteem for antiquity through a patriotic lens. *"Hail to thee, Winckelmann and Lessing, for tracing back beyond the centuries of German greatness to recognize the once-related godly Hellene, the pure ideal of human beauty [...]"* Wagner confirms this interpretation elsewhere: *"It can be argued that the concept of antiquity has only existed since the middle of the last century, that is, since Winckelmann and Lessing."* Wedding the Greek ideal with the German spirit is one of the fundamental principles of Wagner's thinking – in his theoretical writings about theater as well! In fact, Winckelmann and Lessing paved the way for a Classicism valid for all of Europe half a century before Wagner's writings. It was here, in German Classicism, that Wagner saw the one true comprehensible reinvigoration of antiquity, which he denies the "Romanic Renaissance" and all of the epochs that followed. Strangely, Wagner never took notice of Classicistic architecture.

How did Wagner's theoretical understanding of antiquity, that is, in terms of the history of ideas, apply to actual antique architecture? In his works, the only allusion is in RIENZI to *"the broken remains of pillars and tumbled capitals"* in an open space in Rome.

During Wagner's time, architects had, for the most part, not yet found and documented antique architecture in Germany. The Romans never made it to Saxony, and Wagner never visited Trier, "Germany's Rome," the oldest city in Germany. The Roman amphitheater in Trier was only rediscovered and freed of debris and grape vines at the beginning of the 20th century. Based on Wagner's swooning for antiquity, it would be expected that he, like Goethe in his own day, could hardly wait to finally travel to Italy or even to (now liberated) Greece to admire the living evidence of antiquity. In 1850, Wagner indeed dreamt of *"fleeing the world"* and running off to Greece with the woman he was having an "affair" with, Jessie Laussot: *"For the time being, I've closed the door on the modern world. I hate it and want nothing to do with it nor with what people are calling 'art' these days."*

But Wagner only made it as far as Italy – the first time in 1852 (by foot across the Alps). He had planned to travel to Rome with his friend Semper in 1855/56. *"My servant, who had served the Pope in Rome, tells me a lot about it. It is his deepest desire that I travel there with him soon. He says it is very beautiful there,"* he writes to Otto Wesendonck in Rome.

According to the sources, Wagner didn't encounter antique architecture until 1876, when he traveled south following the first festival in Bayreuth. Along the way he visited the antique amphitheater in Verona, the Arena, but neither he nor Cosima commented on it: *"Up early with Richard and the children, Piazza dei Signori, Piazza d[elle] Erbe, the Arena, and finally breakfast à l'Italiana on the banks of the Etsch. Plenty of good cheer."* On March 16, 1878 Wagner recalls Verona, talking fondly of the *"Scaliger monuments"* in the narrow streets and corners. The incorrigible Wagner remembers not the antique theater, but rather the palaces of the Ghibellinic Scaligeri family from the Middle Ages.

In his "Art and Revolution" (1849), and later as well, Wagner theorized about the antique amphitheater, celebrating it as an "ideal" theater and a model for the present. *"The whole population gathered for per-*

besichtigt, doch weder von R. noch von C. kommentiert: „*Früh auf mit Richard und Kindern, Piazza dei Signori, Piazza d[elle] Erbe, die Arena, und schließlich ein Frühstück à l'Italiana am Ufer der Etsch. Viel Heiterkeit.*"[1] Am 16. März 1878 erinnert Wagner sich an Verona und schwärmt von den in enge Gassen und Ecken gestellten „*Monumenten der Scaliger*"[2]. Nicht das antike Theater, sondern wiederum die mittelalterlichen Paläste der ghibellinischen Scaliger sind dem Unverbesserlichen unvergesslich.

Schon in „Die Kunst und die Revolution" (1849) hatte er sich wie auch später theoretisch mit dem antiken Amphitheater beschäftigt und dieses als ein „ideales" Theater und Vorbild für die Gegenwart gefeiert: „*In den weiten Räumen des griechischen Amphitheaters wohnte das ganze Volk den Vorstellungen bei; in unseren vornehmen Theatern faulenzt nur der vermögende Teil desselben.*"[3] Doch solche Huldigungen waren rein theoretisch, die Originaltheater fanden erstaunlicherweise sein Interesse nicht.

Das versunkene Pompeji, die römische Stadt bei Neapel, die im Jahre 79 nach Christus durch den Vesuvausbruch verschüttet, 1748 offiziell wiederentdeckt und seit 1860 systematisch ausgegraben wurde, wurde von Wagners am 23. Oktober 1876 besichtigt. Doch Cosima, die immer gewissenhaft jede Regung und noch so launische Bemerkung des Meisters in ihr Tagebuch notierte, lässt jeden Kommentar zu diesem Ausflug vermissen. Pompeji, das wie keine andere archäologische Stätte ein lebendiges Bild antiken Lebens und einer späthellenistischen Kultur vermittelt und mit seinen Wandfresken und Mosaiken einen einzigartigen Blick auf die lange versunken geglaubte Malerei der Antike gewährte, war und ist Pflichtprogramm eines jeden Italienreisenden. Der sogenannte pompejanische Stil kam im 19. Jahrhundert in Mode, prägte einen „archäologischen Historismus" und zum Beispiel auch die

formances in the expansive space of the Greek amphitheater. Today, only the well-off portion of the population lazes around in our highbrow theaters.*" But such hymns of praise were only theoretical. Astonishingly, the original theaters were of little interest to him.

The Wagners visited the buried city of Pompeii on October 23, 1876. This Roman city near Naples was buried in ash when the Mt. Vesuvius volcano erupted in 79 AD, was officially rediscovered in 1784, and had been systematically dug out since 1860. Cosima, who otherwise painstakingly recorded the maestro's every move and observation, no matter how much the product of a bad mood, did not record a word about this excursion. Unlike any other architectural location, Pompeii offers a true-to-life view of antique life and late-Hellenistic culture. Its wall frescos and mosaics are a unique document of antique painting long believed to have sunk. It was and is a mandatory destination for every traveler to Italy. During the 19th century, the so-called Pompeii style came into fashion, influencing an "archeological historicism" and, for example, Bavarian King Ludwig I's buildings. Wagner's, however, were not influenced. He does not even mention the theater in Pompeii that was excavated during his lifetime. The family would return to Pompeii on June 3, 1880, but this time only the children would be sent in.

The Wagners are also left cold by Rome, every antiquity and architecture fan's dream destination. Richard's and Cosima's comments reiterate their fundamental aversion against Renaissance and Baroque architecture. But they do not praise the antique architecture there especially, either. True to form, they visit the Roman Forum and the Capitol, it being the site of one of the scenes in RIENZI, the antiques in the Vatican, Via Appia and the Caracalla Thermal Baths. They visit but make no comment of the largest and most famous antique theater, the Coliseum. "*Wagner despises Rome, he is not interested in ruins [...]*" In 1878, Cosima writes: "*This evening R. spoke very anti-apathetically about Rome, saying all of*

Bauten des bayerischen Königs Ludwig I. Wagners jedoch bleiben davon unberührt. Selbst das zur Zeit Wagners bereits ausgegrabene Theater in Pompeji wird nicht erwähnt. Ein zweites Mal findet sich die Familie am 3. Juni 1880 in Pompeji ein, doch schickt man nur die Kinder hin.

Auch Rom, das Traumziel eines jeden Antiken- und Architekturfreundes, lässt das Ehepaar Wagner eher kalt. R. und C. bestätigen sich zunächst in ihren Aversionen gegen die Architektur der Renaissance und des Barock. Aber auch die antike Architektur wird nicht sonderlich geschätzt. Pflichtgetreu werden das römische Forum und das Kapitol, immerhin ein Handlungsort im RIENZI, die Antiken im Vatikan, die Via Appia und die Caracalla-Thermen besichtigt. Das größte und berühmteste Theater der Antike, das Kolosseum, wird zwar besucht, doch nicht kommentiert! *„Rom ist Wagner zuwider, Ruinen interessieren ihn nicht."* 1878 erzählt Cosima: *„Abends sprach R. über Rom mit großer Antipathie; alle Denkmäler dort sprächen nur von schändlichen und geknechteten Menschen; von den römischen Kaisern an bis zu den Jesuiten-Kirchen oder den Palästen der Kardinäle."*[1]

1881 reist man erneut gen Süden mit Ziel Sizilien. Im März 1882 wird Taormina besucht, wo Wagner eigentlich vom antiken Theater schwärmen sollte, aber wieder mehr *„durch den Anblick der immer höher aufgenisteten Burgen der mittelalterlichen Landesherren"*[2] beeindruckt ist. Das griechisch-römische Theater in Taormina wird immerhin etwas genauer angeschaut, wie Cosima überliefert: *„In Taormina erfreuen die Säulen R. ganz besonders. Bei der Heimfahrt bespricht er es, wie traumhaft es ist, derlei zu sehen, wie es einen eigentlich gar nicht berühre."*[3] Das idealisierende Bild der Antike war also doch nur eine Träumerei, die sich an den traurigen Trümmern der Realität nicht mehr entzünden wollte.

Dass jene Säulen in Taormina korinthisch sind, wie die im Inneren seines damals schon erbauten Festspielhauses, sagt Wagner nicht. Und wieder wird eine Bildungslücke offenbar, seine Unkenntnis der antiken Stilbegriffe der Architektur, die spätestens seit der Wiederentdeckung des Vitruv im Zeitalter der Renaissance von gebildeten Menschen benutzt wurden. Gemeint sind die „toskanischen", „dorischen", „ionischen" und „korinthischen" Säulenordnungen, Begriffe, die bei Wagner allenfalls eine Landschaft, einen Staat oder eine Sprache benennen. Nur ein einziges Mal nennt Wagner in seinen Schriften eine antike Säulenordnung: ein *„Peristyl mit jonischer Säulenordnung"*[4] in der Beschreibung eines allegorischen Gemäldes von Delaroche.

Fazit

Wagner blieb – wie die Zitate aus allen Lebensphasen belegen – stets seinen letztlich kindlichen Prägungen treu, die ihn selbst in Italien und vor dem Angesicht antiker Architektur als einen ewigen Romantiker offenbaren, der die mittelalterliche Baukunst über alles schätzte, sodass sogar die Theater in Taormina und Pompeji, das Kolosseum in Rom und die Arena in Verona kaum beachtet wurden. Renaissance, Barock und Rokoko lehnte er grundsätzlich als falsche Rezeption der Antike ab. Als er ab 1876 selbst vor den Zeugnissen der griechischen und römischen Antike stand, blieb jede Begeisterung aus. Vielleicht kritisierte er diese Bauten generell als imperiale Architektur Roms. Doch wusste man damals, dass die Römer letztlich nur die Ideen der Griechen weiterentwickelt hatten, und Taormina war tatsächlich das Theater einer griechischen Kolonie. Wagners Verhältnis zur antiken Architektur und dem von ihm nicht wahrgenommenen Klassizismus überrascht, um nicht von Enttäuschung zu sprechen. Theoretisch jedoch verehrte er die Antike und ihre Architektur, wie seine ersten Visionen eines idealen „Theaters der Zukunft" zeigen werden.

the memorials are to immoral and downtrodden people; starting with the Roman Emperors and down to the Jesuit churches or the cardinals' palaces."

In 1881 Wagner returned south heading toward Sicily. In March of 1882 he visits Taormina, where one would, theoretically, expect him to rave about the antique theater. But again he is more impressed by *"the sight of the medieval fortresses of the rulers of the area nested one on top of the other."* As Cosima records, Wagner at least takes a closer look at the Greek-Roman theater in Taormina: *"The columns in Taormina are especially appealing to R. During the return ride he talks about how dreamlike it is to see things like that, how it actually doesn't matter at all."* It seems the idealized image of antiquity was nothing more than a passing dream that the sad broken blocks of reality couldn't bring back to life.

Wagner does not mention that these columns are Corinthian like those inside his Festspielhaus, which had been built by then. Another gap in his education is noticeable – his lack of familiarity with the terms for antique orders of architecture that educated people started using no later than the rediscovery of Vitruv's book on architecture during the Renaissance Age: "Tuscan," "Dorian," "Ionian," and "Corinthian" pillars. For Wagner, these terms refer at best to a landscape, a state or a language. Wagner only refers to an antique pillar order in his writings when describing an allegorical painting by Delaroche: a *"peristyle with Ionic order of pillars."*

Summary

As quotations from all periods of his life support, Wagner always remained true to his basically childlike preferences that reveal him to be a die-hard Romantic even in Italy and when confronted with antique architecture. He appreciates medieval architecture most, hardly even noticing the theaters in Taormina and Pompeii, the Coliseum in Rome and the Arena in Verona. He rejects Renaissance, Baroque and Rococo on principle as incorrect antique receptions. When he sees actual examples of Greek and Roman antiquity from 1876 on, he is not at all excited. Perhaps he was critical of these constructions in general as examples of imperial architecture. However, back then, people already understood that the Romans only further developed the Greeks' ideas, and Taormina had been a Greek colony's theater. Wagner's relationship to antique architecture and his tendency to ignore Classicism is surprising, if not disappointing. Theoretically, however, he admired antique society and architecture, as his early visions for an ideal "theater of the future" will demonstrate.

Taormina

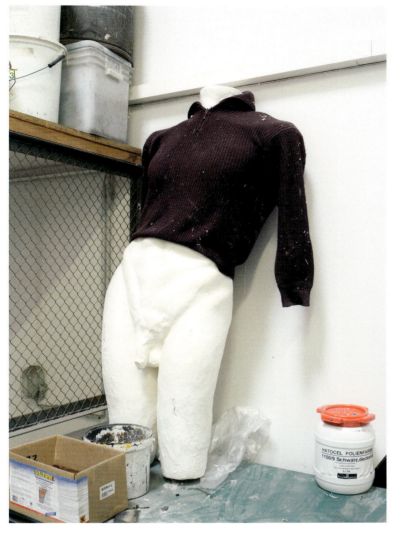

„Gipsgrieche" im kalten Norden – Malersaal
"Plaster Greek" in the cold north – paint shop

„Ich glaube nicht,
dass es einen für das klassische Altertum
begeisterteren Knaben und Jüngling
gegeben haben kann, als mich."

"I don't think there could have been any boy more
enthralled with classical antiquity as I was."

Richard Wagner

Visionen eines idealen Theaters

Wagners Theater der Zukunft
1849

In seiner Schrift „Das Kunstwerk der Zukunft"¹ beschäftigt sich Wagner zum ersten Mal (!) etwas ausführlicher theoretisch mit Architektur und schenkt ihr ein eigenes Kapitel, das einzige Kapitel in seinen sehr umfangreichen Schriften. Er skizziert sie als Teil einer Vision von einem Gesamtkunstwerk und beruft sich dabei auf die Anfänge der griechischen Theaterarchitektur. Er erzählt pathetisch vom „Ur-Hellenen", der seine Religion, seinen kultischen Tanz und die Musik in den „grünenden Baumsäulen des Götterhains" lebte, ehe er „unter dem schön gefügten Giebeldache und zwischen den sinnig gereihten Marmorsäulen des Göttertempels" ein festes Gebäude fand.

Aus diesem Göttertempel habe sich das hellenistische Theater entwickelt, wo die Tragödie ihren Platz gefunden habe, die er als die „vollendete griechische Kunst" schlechthin bezeichnet. Anstelle des Heiligtums sei nun die Bühne getreten, womit Wagner die „orchestra" des griechischen Theaters meint. Viel später in seinem Stück EINE KAPITULATION, einem „Lustspiel in antiker Manier", gibt Wagner diese Situation als Bühnenbild vor: „Das Proszenium, bis in der Mitte der Bühnentiefe [...] wird im Verlaufe des Stückes im Sinne der antiken ‚Orchestra' verwendet; in der Mitte steht, statt der ‚Thymele', ein Altar der Republik."

Diese hohe Wertschätzung des Theaters sei neu zu beleben, doch dürfe sie sich in einem Theater der Zukunft architektonisch nicht in übersteigerter Monumentalität und Prunkentfaltung äußern, sondern müsse die „erhabene Einfalt und die tiefsinnige Bedeutsamkeit griechischer Gebäude zur Zeit der Blüte der Tragödie" aufweisen. „Krause Schnörkel und Zierraten" lehnt Wagner als überflüssige Dekoration ab. Hiermit ist ein klares, jedoch etwas spätes Bekenntnis zum Klassizismus formuliert, zur „edlen Einfalt, stillen Größe", einem Diktum, das der 1768 gestorbene J. J. Winckelmann, dessen Schriften Wagner nachweisbar kannte, als gleichermaßen ethisches wie ästhetisches Ideal apostrophiert hatte. Dagegen führt Wagner kritisch die antiken Bauten des imperialen und luxuriösen Rom an, wie auch die Bauten des Historismus seiner Zeit.

Visions for an ideal theater

Wagner's theater of the future
1849

In his essay "The Artwork of the Future", Wagner theorizes in more detail about architecture for the first time (!), dedicating a chapter to it. This is the only chapter dedicated to architecture in his extensive writings. He outlines architecture as part of a vision of a complete artwork, referring to the beginnings of Greek theater architecture. He talks loftily about the *"Ur-Hellene,"* who lived his religion, his cult dance and his music in the *"lush tree pillars in the grove of the Gods"* until he established a solid building *"under the elegant gable roof and between the well-construed rows of marble pillars of the temple of the Gods."*

In his account, the Hellenistic theater developed from this temple of the Gods, providing a forum for the tragedies, which he calls the epitome of *"fully-mature Greek art."* The stage, which Wagner understands as the "orchestra" of the Greek theater, took the place of the sanctuary. In his much later work A CAPITULATION, a *"comedy in antique style,"* Wagner describes the set as follows: *"The proscenium up to the middle of the depth of the stage [...] is used throughout the play like the antique 'orchestra'; an altar to the Republic takes the place of the 'thymele' at the center."*

Wagner considers it important to rekindle high esteem for the theater, but does not think the theater of the future should express this through exaggerated monumentality or showiness, but should mirror the *"sublime simplicity and the deep meaningfulness of Greek buildings at the height of the tragedy."* Wagner rejects *"frilly embellishments and ornaments"* as superfluous decoration. This formulation is a clear though somewhat late avowal to Classicism, to *"noble simplicity and quiet grandeur,"* a dictum that J. J. Winckelmann, who had died in 1768 and whom Wagner read, had apostrophized as an ethical and aesthetic ideal. Wagner critically cites structures of imperial and luxurious Roman antiquity and the Historicist buildings of his time as opposing examples.

„Unter dem schön gefügten Giebeldache und zwischen den sinnig gereihten Marmorsäulen des Göttertempels."

"Under the elegant gable roof and between the well-construed rows of marble pillars of the temple of the Gods."

Richard Wagner

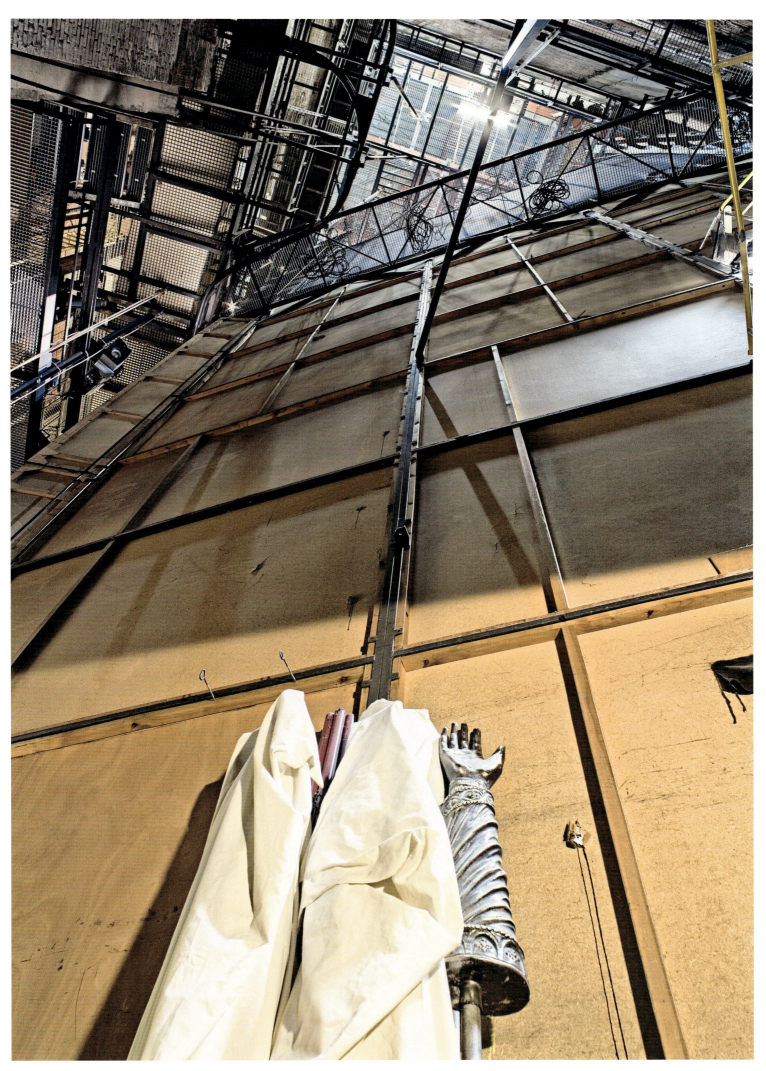

Blick von der Bühne in den Schnürboden
View of the flies from the stage

Auf der anderen Seite kritisiert Wagner nicht nur die Prunkbauten, sondern auch die allzu „einfältigen" Nutzbauten des imperialen Rom und seiner eigenen Zeit, in der die Barbarei des reinen „Nützlichkeitsmenschen" dem Schönheitssinn des „künstlerischen Menschen der Zukunft" gewichen sei. Wiederum lobt Wagner den „Ur-Hellenen", der in seinen privaten Wohnbauten nur den einfachsten und edelsten Bedürfnissen gefolgt sei. Diese Architektur sei zunächst „aus Holzstämmen gezimmert und – ähnlich dem Zelte des Achilleus – nach den einfachsten Gesetzen der Zweckmäßigkeit gefügt" und erst in der „Blütezeit hellenistischer Bildung mit glatten Steinwänden" gebaut worden. Wagner erkennt, „dass das wahrhaft Schöne insofern auch das Allernützlichste ist". Dies ist ein Bekenntnis zu einem bewusst einfachen, doch nicht einfältigen, sondern von hellenistischer Ursprünglichkeit beseelten Zweckbau (aus Holz), der sich – einem griechischen Göttertempel gleich – dem höchsten Ideal menschlichen Seins, der Kunst des Dramas verschrieben hat.

Auch für die innere Konzeption eines idealen Theaters fordert Wagner schon 1849 gleichermaßen eine Synthese aus Schönheit und Zweckmäßigkeit. Für den Zuschauerraum sucht er optimale optische wie akustische Bedingungen, die dem „Verlangen nach dem Kunstwerk" (dem Drama auf der Bühne) gerecht werden müssen, „zu dessen Erfassen er durch Alles, was sein Auge berührt, bestimmt werden muss". Nur so könne der Zuschauer mit dem Darsteller verschmelzen, wie auch der Darsteller mit dem Publikum eins werden solle, das schließlich aus dem Zuschauerraum verschwindet und nur noch in dem Kunstwerke selbst „lebt und atmet". „Solche Wunder entblühen dem Bauwerke des Architekten, solchen Zaubern mag er realen Grund und Boden geben."

Von der Bühne fordert Wagner ein „lebendiges Abbild der Natur", die dem Zuschauer ein möglichst veristisches „Bild des menschlichen Lebens vorführen soll", eine Forderung nach einer optimal erzeugten Illusion, die sich vor allem an die Kulissenmalerei richtet. Dieser größtmöglichen Unmittelbarkeit des Dramas dient auch die schon 1849 erdachte Versenkung des Orchesters aus dem Blickfeld des Betrachters, die wohl wichtigste Idee Wagners für ein Theater der Zukunft: „Das Orchester ist … der Boden unendlichen, allgemeinen Gefühles [...] es löst den starren, unbeweglichen Boden der wirklichen Szene gewissermaßen in eine flüssigweich nachgiebige, eindruckempfängliche, ätherische Fläche auf, deren ungemessener Grund das Meer des Gefühls selbst ist. [...] und deshalb als Lokalität sehr richtig auch außerhalb des szenischen Rahmens in den vertieften Vordergrund gestellt [wird]."

Fazit

Konkret betrachtet, werden also lediglich für den Außenbau das griechische Tempeldach und die griechischen Säulen, für den Innenraum eine unmittelbar vor den Betrachter gerückte Bühne und die Versenkung des Orchesters ausdrücklich genannt. Wagner fordert also für ein ideales Theater eine „edle Einfalt, stille Größe", eine radikale Schmucklosigkeit und Zweckmäßigkeit des Gebäudes (gerne aus Holz), das dem Wesentlichen, dem Drama, dienen solle, dem die Architektur die besten optischen und akustischen Bedingungen zu setzen habe. Auf der Bühne möge ein veristischer Illusionismus die Kunst der Darsteller mit dem Publikum verschmelzen lassen, wozu ein versenktes Orchester eine unsichtbare Musik erklingen lässt.

However, Wagner criticizes not only the pompous buildings, but also the "base" functional buildings of imperial Rome and his own time – a time in which he sees the barbarianism of the purely *"functional person"* giving way to the aestheticism of the *"artistic people of the future."* In turn, Wagner praises the *"ur-Hellene,"* who only fulfilled the simplest, most noble needs in creating his own private living spaces. He praises this architecture as *"constructed out of logs and – like Achilleus' tent – following the simplest rules of functionality"* and first built *"with smooth stone walls"* at the *"height of Hellenistic education."* Wagner recognizes *"that true beauty is therefore at once the most practical."* This is an avowal to a consciously simple, though not simplistic functional (wooden) architecture in the spirit of Hellenistic nativeness, an architecture like a Greek temple to the Gods, committed to the highest human ideal, the drama.

Similarly, in 1849, Wagner proposed an interior concept for the ideal theater synthesizing beauty and expediency. He sought optimal optical and acoustic conditions for the auditorium that were able to fulfill the *"desire for the artwork"* (the drama on the stage). *"Everything [the audience] sees must be dedicated to receiving [this artwork]."* Only in this manner can the viewer become one with the actor, just as the actor should become one with the audience that, in the end, disappears out of the auditorium and only *"lives and breaths"* through the artwork itself. *"Miracles like this are the product of the architect's buildings. He can give magic real solid substance."*

Wagner expects the stage to be a *"living image of nature"* that offers viewers a *"picture of human existence"* that is as true-to-life as possible. This call for an optically created illusion is directed principally at the painted scenery. The idea of lowering the orchestra out of view of the audience, which Wagner had already formulated in 1849, also served to achieve the highest possible immediacy of the drama. This was likely Wagner's most important idea for the theater of the future. *"The orchestra is [...] the basis of endless general feeling (...) to a degree, it transforms the rigid, immovable floor of the real scene into a fluidly soft, yielding, impulse-receptive, ethereal surface, whose unmapped depth is the sea of feeling itself [...] and which [will] therefore [be] quite correctly localized outside the scenic frame in the lowered foreground."*

Summary

In concrete terms, Wagner only specifically names the Greek temple roof and Greek columns for the exterior and a stage located directly in front of the audience and a sunken orchestra pit for the interior. Wagner requires that an ideal theater have "noble simplicity and quiet grandeur," and that it be radically free of ornament and fit for purpose (preferably made of wood). Its architecture should provide the best possible optical and acoustic conditions for it to serve the most important element, the drama. On the stage, a true-to-life illusionism should allow the performers' art to meld with the audience and a sunken orchestra should produce invisible music.

Eine Vision konkretisiert sich
1862

Als Kapellmeister oder Musikdirektor in Bad Lauchstädt, Magdeburg, Riga und Dresden hatte Wagner zahlreiche frustrierende Erfahrungen mit der Realität des deutschen Theaterbetriebs gemacht. Andererseits hatte er in seiner Pariser Zeit einen in vielen Belangen vorbildlichen Theaterbetrieb der Oper kennengelernt. Schon als Kapellmeister in Dresden wurde seine Kritik am Bestehenden immer lauter und gipfelte 1847 in einem tatkräftigen Plan für ein neues Konzertgebäude in der Nähe des Zwingers: *„Ich hatte mich hierzu mit Architekten und Bauunternehmern in das ausführlichste Vernehmen gesetzt; die Pläne waren vollständig ausgearbeitet"*, doch erhielt er auf seinen Vorschlag den summarischen Bescheid, *„dass man es für besser fände, wenn alles beim alten verbliebe."*[1] Das Aussehen und der Verbleib dieser Pläne sind leider unbekannt.

Später war Wagner vor allem über die Aufführungen seiner eigenen Stücke an diversen Bühnen in Deutschland frustriert, da er – selbst wenn er selbst die Regie übernehmen konnte – niemals optimale szenische und technische Bedingungen vorfand. Seinen RING jedoch, den er schon 1848 skizziert hatte und als sein Hauptwerk ansah, wollte er diesen Verhältnissen nicht aussetzen und plante parallel zur Dichtung und Komposition des RING eine Uraufführung in einem eigenen, von ihm erdachten, temporären Theater.

Als erste schriftliche Nennung dieser Idee, aus der schließlich die Festspiele entstanden, gilt ein Brief Wagners an Theodor Uhlig, 1850, worin er für Zürich *„auf einer schönen Wiese bei der Stadt von Brett und Balken ein rohes Theater nach meinem Plane herstellen und lediglich bloß mit der Ausstattung an Dekorationen und Maschinerie versehen lassen [wollte], die zu der Aufführung des SIEGFRIED nötig sind."*[2] Nach geglückten Vorstellungen wollte er die ganze Bretterbude wieder einreißen und die Partitur verbrennen. In einem Brief an Ernst Benedikt Kietz vom 14. September 1851 wiederholt sich der Festspielgedanke: *„Er brauche 10000 Taler, dann wolle er aus Brettern ein Theater errichten – und wieder abbrechen."*[3]

Ein hölzernes Theaterprovisorium erscheint auch in einem Bühnenwerk Wagners, in den MEISTERSINGERN, im ersten Aufzug: Wo Lehrbuben in der Mitte der Bühne ein größeres Gerüst mit Vorhängen aufschlagen, sowie *„ein geringeres Brettbodengerüste"*, auf dem der Meistersang stattfinden kann. Als solch hölzernes Provisorium stellte sich Wagner – sicherlich nicht zu Unrecht – ein mittelalterliches „Theater" vor, wie auch die Bühne des von ihm so verehrten Shakespeare, die dieser *„im Drange nach unmittelbarem Leben mit dem rohen Gerüste seiner Volksbühne"*[4] schuf.

Jenes ursprüngliche Shakespeare-Theater „The Globe", das im 19. Jahrhundert schon lange nicht mehr stand, wurde 1996 rekonstruiert und zeigt eine Bretterbühne, ist wie das Bayreuther Festspielhaus ein Fachwerkbau und mag als Musterbeispiel eines mittelalterlich-frühneuzeitlichen Theaters gelten.

A vision takes concrete form
1862

Wagner had had many frustrating experiences with the reality of the German theater scene as music director in Bad Lauchstädt, Magdeburg, Riga and Dresden. But during his time in Paris, he also became acquainted with an opera theater that was exemplary in many regards. As music director in Dresden his critique of existing conditions grew ever more vehement, culminating in a concrete plan for a new concert house near the Zwinger: *"In preparation, I had had detailed briefings with architects and construction companies. The plans were completely developed."* In response, he received a summary notice: *"That it would be preferable if everything stayed the way it is."* Unfortunately, the content and whereabouts of his plans are not known.

Wagner was later frustrated over how his own works were being performed on various stages in Germany because he was never provided with the right scenic and technical conditions, even when he himself was directing. He had no intention of subjecting his RING, which he had already sketched in 1848 and considered his primary work, to these conditions. Parallel to composing the lyrics and the music for the RING, he was planning to hold its premiere in a provisional theater he was conceiving for the very purpose.

The first written record of this idea, which would, in the end, become the Festival, is in a letter from Wagner to Theodor Uhlig in 1850, in which he describes his intention *"to have a raw theater made of boards and beams erected according to my plans on a beautiful field near the city [of Zurich], equipped only with the decorations and machinery necessary to produce SIEGFRIED."* After several successful performances, he wanted to tear down the whole wooden hut and burn the score. In a letter to Ernst Benedikt Kietz from September 14, 1851, he repeats his festival concept: *"He needs 10,000 thalers to build a wooden theater – and then tear it down again."*

There is also mention of such a provisional wooden theater in one of Wagner's stage works, in Act I of DIE MEISTERSINGER, where young apprentices unfold a large frame with curtains and *"a simple wooden framed floor"* on which the master singer competition can take place. Wagner imagined a medieval "theater" to have been such a provisional wooden structure, and surely not incorrectly. He also imagined his great idol Shakespeare to have had a similar stage, which Shakespeare created to meet *"the driving urge for direct theater using the raw frame of his people's theater."*

Shakespeare's original "Globe" Theater was long gone by the 19th century and was reconstructed in 1996 with a wooden stage. Like the Bayreuth Festspielhaus, it is a half-timbered construction, and may be regarded as an exemplary medieval-early modern theater.

Shakespeare-Bühne „The Globe" in London (Rekonstruktion 1996)
Shakespeare's "Globe" stage in London (1996 reconstruction)

1862 konkretisieren sich Wagners Ideen in seinem Vorwort zur Herausgabe der (bereits 1852 vollendeten) Dichtung des Bühnenfestspiels DER RING DES NIBELUNGEN[1]. Wichtig war Wagner die Lage seines Festspielhauses in einer *„der minder großen Städte Deutschlands"*, um die Berührung mit dem *„großstädtischen eigentlichen Theaterpublikum und seinen Gewohnheiten"* zu vermeiden, was indirekt eine Abkehr von den Prunkbauten der Gründerzeit bedeutet und sich gegen ein – in Wagners Augen – dekadentes und allein vergnügungssüchtiges Publikum richtet.

In Bayreuth fände der Besucher *„ein provisorisches Theater, so einfach wie möglich, vielleicht bloß aus Holz, und nur auf künstlerische Zweckmäßigkeit des Inneren berechnet"*. Kein äußerer Prunk solle von der eigentlichen Kunst, dem Drama auf der Bühne, ablenken. *„Einen Plan hierzu, mit amphitheatralischer Einrichtung für das Publikum, und dem großen Vorteile der Unsichtbarmachung des Orchesters, hatte ich mit einem erfahrenen, geistvollen Architekten in Besprechung gezogen."*

Dieser Architekt war bekanntlich sein Freund und Barrikadenbauer aus Dresdner Revolutionsjahren, Gottfried Semper. Wagner nennt erstmals den Begriff Amphitheater, den er jedoch grundsätzlich falsch verwendet. – Amphitheater sind römischen Ursprungs und besitzen eine ellipsoide Anordnung der aufsteigenden Sitzreihen um eine mittlere Arena (für Gladiatorenkämpfe und Tierhatzen), während sich beim (echten) griechischen Theater die aufsteigenden Sitzreihen halbrund um die „orchestra" gruppieren. – Doch der an sich falsche Begriff hat sich bei Theaterbauten der Moderne allgemein eingebürgert und bezeichnet auch halbrunde Theater.

All diese Bedingungen sollten eine optimale Vorstellung des RING ermöglichen. *„Zur Vollendung des Eindruckes einer solchermaßen vorbereiteten Aufführung"* gehöre nicht nur die Unsichtbarkeit des Orchesters, sondern auch eine *„architektonische Täuschung"*, die erst durch die amphitheatralische Einrichtung des Zuhörersaals möglich ist. Ohne dass Wagner es klar ausdrücken würde, meint er damit einen Verzicht auf die Seitenlogen, die in der Tat in jedem anderen Theater schräge Einblicke hinter Kulissen oder gar in den Schnürboden erlauben. Wagner aber ist eine Unsichtbarmachung der Bühnentechnik, der *„mechanischen Hilfsbewegungen beim Vortrage der Musiker"*, und der *„Fäden, Schnüre, Leisten und Bretter der Theaterdekorationen, welche, aus den Kulissen betrachtet, einen bekanntlich alle Täuschung störenden Eindruck machen"*, sehr wichtig – und das von allen Plätzen aus! Wagners Vorstellung von aufsteigenden Sitzreihen ist also durch optische Gründe motiviert und erstaunlicherweise nicht als Reminiszenz an die alten Griechen gedacht! Das antike Theater spielt in dem Vorwort von 1862 ohnehin keine Rolle mehr!

Die allerwichtigste Forderung Wagners an sein ideales Theater aber ist der versenkte Orchestergraben, der das Bühnengeschehen unmittelbar vor das Publikum rückt und darüber hinaus – des Musikers wichtigstes Anliegen – eine akustische Wirkung evoziert.

Fazit

Wagner wollte schon 1850/51 ein (hölzernes) Provisorium. 1862 bedenkt er auch die Lage eines Festspielhauses und wünscht sich eine kleine Provinzstadt, wo er ein „unverdorbenes" Publikum erwartet, das sich ganz seiner Kunst in einem hierfür im Innern ganz zweckmäßig eingerichteten Theater hingeben möge. In einen aufsteigenden „griechischen" Hörsaal gebannt, soll es einem ganz unmittelbaren Bühnengeschehen folgen. Dies müsse durch eine architektonische Unsichtbarmachung der Bühnentechnik besorgt werden und durch einen versenkten Orchestergraben, der die Sänger näher und verständlicher an das Publikum vorrücken ließe und darüber hinaus einen verklärenden Klang der Musik besorge.

Wagner's ideas take more concrete form in the 1862 foreword to the edition of the lyrical text he wrote for the stage festival DER RING DES NIBELUNGEN (completed in 1852). It was important to Wagner that his Festspielhaus be situated in one of the *"smaller cities in Germany"* in order to avoid contact with the *"actual theater-going audience from the large cities and their habits."* Indirectly, this represents a retreat from the pompous buildings in Wilhelminian style. Wagner's comment targets what he considers a decadent audience addicted solely to entertainment.

In Bayreuth, the visitor would encounter a *"provisional theater, as simple as possible, perhaps built only out of wood, and only designed to serve the artistic needs of the interior."* No additional pomp should divert one's attention from the actual art at hand, the drama on the stage. *"I have initiated discussions about a plan for such a theater with an experienced, brilliant architect, including an amphitheater-like seating area for the audience and the huge advantage of putting the orchestra out of sight."*

Naturally, this architect was his friend and cobarricade comrade from Wagner's revolutionary years in Dresden, Gottfried Semper. This is Wagner's first mention of the term amphitheater, which he uses basically incorrectly. – Amphitheaters are of Roman origin and have rows of tiered seating arranged in elliptical form around a center arena (for gladiator combat and animal slaughter). This contrasts with the (true) Greek theater, in which the rows of tiered seating are grouped in a semicircle around the "orchestra." – However, the actually incorrect term gained general acceptance in modern theater construction and now also refers to semicircular theaters.

All of these conditions should make an optimal performance of the RING possible. *"Perfecting the impact of a performance thus prepared"* involves not only removing the orchestra from sight, but also achieving the *"architectonic illusion"* made possible only by arranging the auditorium in the form of an amphitheater. Although Wagner never expressed it clearly, what he means by this is to eliminate the side loges that actually permit angled views behind the scenery or even of the rigging loft. Needless to say, it is important to Wagner to make the theater technology, the *"mechanical movements needed to play the music,"* and the *"ropes, rigging, rails and boards belonging to the theater decoration that clearly disrupt the illusionary effect of the scenery"* invisible – from every seat, no less! Thus, Wagner's idea of tiered seating is optically motivated and, amazingly, is not meant to recall the ancient Greeks. In fact, there is no further mention of the antique theater in the 1862 foreword.

Wagner's most important demand on his ideal theater, however, is the sunken orchestra pit, which serves to bring the events on the stage directly to the audience, and which creates an acoustical effect Wagner valued above all as a musician.

Summary

As early as 1850/51 Wagner wanted a (wooden) provisional theater. In 1862 he considers where his Festspielhaus should be located, favoring a small provincial city where he expects an "unspoiled" audience willing to direct all of its attention to his art in a theater with a totally functional interior. Seated in a "Greek" auditorium with tiered seating, the audience should follow the events on the stage quite directly, without obstacle. This is achieved by using architectonic methods to make the stage technology invisible and by sinking the orchestra pit bringing the singers nearer to the audience, making them more easily understood and creating a pure musical sound.

Bayreuther „Bretterbude" mit Amphitheater
Bayreuth "wood board hut" with amphitheater

Gescheiterte Visionen für München
1865

1864 lernte Wagner den jungen König Ludwig II. von Bayern kennen, der sich fortan leidenschaftlich für die Person und das Werk Richard Wagners engagieren sollte und sich aufgefordert fühlte, Wagner dieses von ihm ersehnte ideale Festspielhaus zu realisieren. Die Geschichte und das Scheitern des für München gedachten und von Gottfried Semper entworfenen Projekts ist bei Heinrich Habel[1] ausführlich geschildert und soll hier nur kurz interessieren. Ludwig und Gottfried wollten natürlich keine provisorische Bretterbude, sondern ein monumentales und repräsentatives, einer Residenzstadt des Königs würdiges Theater. München hätte aber genau jene Kollision mit einem von Wagner so verachteten Repertoiretheater und einem großstädtischen Publikum bedeutet. Das konnte dem in seinem Leben stets kompromisslosen Wagner nicht behagen.

Immerhin ließ sich Semper auf die Wünsche Wagners ein und realisierte jenen aufsteigenden, „amphitheatralischen" Zuschauerraum ohne Seitenlogen, rückte die Bühne nahe ans Publikum und versenkte den Orchestergraben. Er gab dem Zuschauerraum eine konvexe Fassade, die das antike Halbrund auch außen sichtbar machte, und setzte dem Bühnenturm ein griechisches Tempeldach mit Akroterien auf. Alles andere aber widersprach den Visionen Wagners. Semper wählte – wie auch bei der Oper in Dresden oder dem Burgtheater in Wien – als stilistisches Gestaltungsmittel die dem Komponisten so verhasste Neorenaissance, schmückte die Fassade mit Bögen und Kolonnaden, so wie sie Wagner in Venedig als „langweilig, phantasie- und erfindungslos" empfunden hatte. Ein zweiter Entwurf sah vor, ein provisorisches Festspielhaus im Münchner Glaspalast zu errichten, doch auch diese Idee wurde verworfen.

Zwar äußert sich Wagner in Briefen an den König höflich und respektvoll über Sempers ersten Entwurf: „Das prächtige an Sempers Bau ist die Einheit, die Harmonie, der feierliche ernste Stil."[2] Doch war Wagner letztlich gegen das Projekt, wie diese Tagebuchnotiz vom 9. September 1865 sehr deutlich macht: „Mir geht's nicht gut. Meine armen Nerven! – Ein Schreck: Semper ist da! [...] Soweit bin ich, dass mir Sempers Besuch widerwärtig ist. Gott, was geht mich ein provisorisches, oder ein definitives Festtheater, was geht mich alle Baukunst der Welt an! [...] Wie hasse ich dieses projektierte Theater, ja – wie kindisch kommt mir der König vor, dass er so leidenschaftlich auf diesem Projekte besteht: nun habe ich Semper, soll mit ihm verkehren, über das unsinnige Project sprechen! Ich kenne gar keine größere Pein, als diese mir bevorstehende."[3]

Failed visions for Munich
1865

In 1864 Wagner met the young King Ludwig II of Bavaria, who would untiringly and passionately support Richard Wagner and his works from then on. Ludwig felt called to make Wagner's ideal Festspielhaus a reality. The history and the failure of the project planned for Munich with designs by Gottfried Semper is described in detail in Heinrich Habel's book and is only of limited interest for our purposes. Naturally, both Ludwig and Gottfried did not want a provisional wooden board hut, but rather a monumental, representative theater worthy of the King's city of residency. Yet building in Munich would have meant colliding with a repertory theater Wagner so disdained and the large-city audience he meant to avoid. Wagner found no pleasure in that idea.

At least Semper was receptive to Wagner's wishes and designed an "amphitheatrical" auditorium with stepped rows of seating, left out the side loges, drew the stage close to the audience, and sank the orchestra pit. He also gave the auditorium a convex facade to make the antique semi-circle visible from the outside, and he topped the stage tower with a Greek temple roof with acroteria. But everything else contradicted Wagner's visions. As was the case with the Dresden Opera and the Vienna Burgtheater, he selected neo-Renaissance stylistic elements that the composer so loathed, decorated the facade with arches and colonnades, creating a look Wagner had found *"boring, unimaginative and uncreative"* in Venice. A second design proposed constructing a provisional Festspielhaus inside the Munich Glass Palace, but this idea was rejected as well.

Granted, Wagner's letters to the King adopt a polite and respectful tone regarding Semper's first design: *"What makes Semper's building splendid is its uniformity, its harmony, its solemn serious style."* But, as this remark in his journal from September 9, 1865 clearly demonstrates, in the end, Wagner was against the project: *"I'm not feeling well. My poor nerves! – A horror: Semper is here! [...] Alas, I have reached the stage of finding Semper's visit repulsive. God, what do I care about a provisional or a definitive Festspielhaus, what do I care about all the architecture in the world! [...] How I hate this projected theater. The King seems so childish to me for insisting on this project so passionately: now Semper is here, I should keep company with him and talk to him about the absurd project! I know no greater torment than the one facing me."*

Sempers Entwurf für ein monumentales Festspielhaus in München 1865
Semper's 1865 design for a monumental Festspielhaus in Munich

Gottfried Semper
Gottfried Semper

König Ludwig II. von Bayern
King Ludwig II of Bavaria

Decision to build in Bayreuth
1871

After the Munich Festspielhaus projects failed and because of the scandals caused by his associations with still-married Cosima von Bülow, Wagner had to leave Munich. King Ludwig II owned the rights to the RING and wanted to have each of the works performed in Munich as soon as they were complete, but Wagner always wished to direct a complete performance of all four works together. This fact may have driven obstinate Wagner to look for his own theater. In a discussion with Cosima on March 5, 1870 in his new exile, Tribschen near Luzern, Switzerland, he coincidentally mentions the city of Bayreuth. In this often discussed "moment of conception of the Bayreuth idea," Wagner looks up the city in an encyclopedia and reads about a large opera house there. By the following March, the Bayreuth idea had matured. On March 1, 1871 he writes a letter to the King's secretary informing the King that he had found a town in Bavaria where *"it wouldn't be necessary to build a theater [...] not even a provisional one."*

This was a strategically wise choice of location: a provincial city in the King's domain, but far from Munich and therefore not too close to the King himself. Wagner also had his eye on Berlin and was hoping to arouse national interest in his project. Further advantages of Bayreuth included its central location in Germany, its geographical proximity to Prussia, and its Prussian tradition between 1791 and 1810, during which time the Prussian King Frederick the Great's sister Wilhelmine had developed Bayreuth as a residency.

On April 17, 1871, the Wagners traveled to Bayreuth and looked at the opera house there on April 19. *"The only thing that we didn't like there was the theater; so build, all the better."* That would pinpoint April 19, 1871 as the day Wagner decided to build his own Festspielhaus. A decision had been reached on that memorable Wednesday, and right away the Wagners wanted to *"find a house, so we rode all around the city with the castle caretaker but nothing suited us perfectly, so we'll build for ourselves, too."*

All at once, everything happened very quickly. Between April 25 and the beginning of May, Wagner was staying in Berlin, practically obsessively eager to build, where he initiated negotiations with the Berlin architect Wilhelm Neumann. This now completely forgotten but then very active architect was charged with revising Semper's plans. Neumann's new plans were too "grandiose," so he was asked to tone them down. Apparently Neumann was not interested in building a provisional theater that would do little for his status as an architect. On April 24, 1872 Wagner and Neumann parted ways. Only a vague sketch of his designs remains.

The county manor in Tribschen where Wagner lived from 1866 to 1872

Bayreuth, entrance to royal garden, historical postcard

DAS BAYREUTHER FESTSPIELHAUS

Die Baugeschichte

Bezaubernd ist dieser Punkt

Am 8. Mai 1871 hatte Wagner seinen (sehr) entfernten Verwandten, den Bayreuther Bankier Friedrich Feustel, kennengelernt, der zu einem der wichtigsten Wegbereiter des Projekts vor Ort wurde. Ihn bat Wagner, sich nach einem geeigneten Terrain von mindestens zweihundert (preußischen) Quadratfuß umzuschauen, und hoffte auf ein Geschenk der Stadt, die von solchen Festspielen nur profitieren könne. Ursprünglich hatte Wagner an ein Grundstück im Hofgarten gedacht. In einem Brief vom 3. November 1871 äußerte Feustel Bedenken wegen der Erdarbeiten für die Unterbühne, die bis in eine Tiefe von dreißig bis vierzig (bayerische) Fuß führen würden, befürchtete Probleme mit dem Grundwasser und empfahl (als Erster) eine (später so pathetisch gedeutete, doch sehr pragmatisch motivierte) Hügellage. Außerdem machte er auf die hiesigen, sehr ergiebigen Sandsteinbrüche aufmerksam, die Wagner jedoch kaum in Anspruch nehmen sollte. *„Der Bau kann in Sandstein und Backstein ausgeführt werden"*[1], schreibt Feustel, womit erstmals das Wort „Backstein" fällt.

Am 7. November 1871 beschloss der Bayreuther Stadtrat, das Projekt großzügig zu unterstützen und ihm ein geeignetes Grundstück zur Verfügung zu stellen. Das war klug, denn auch andere Städte machten dem mittlerweile berühmten Komponisten Angebote, wie Baden-Baden, Darmstadt, später Reichenhall, Berlin, London, ja sogar das 1871 abgebrannte Chicago!

„Am 14. Dezember bin ich in Bayreuth", schreibt Wagner in einem Brief sehr „großherzig", *„um das Terrain in Empfang zu nehmen."*[2] Am 15. Dezember 1871 werden die in Frage kommenden Bauplätze besichtigt, und man entscheidet sich für den in der Vorstadt St. Georgen gelegenen Stuckberg. Der Besitzer, der Zuckerfabrikant Rose, will aber nicht verkaufen, sodass der Bürgermeister Muncker Wagner die heutige Stelle an der Bürgerreuth anbietet und sogar bereit ist, privates Land dazuzukaufen. Wagner aber ist davon zunächst nicht begeistert, droht, Bayreuth ganz fallen zu lassen und fordert beleidigt: Die *„gesamte Einwohnerschaft muss mir gewogen sein!"*[3] Cosima vermittelt erfolgreich, und schließlich ändert Wagner seine Meinung: *„Entzückend – bezaubernd ist dieser Punkt."*[4] Der Grund bleibt freilich Eigentum der Stadt und wird erst 1891 den Erben Wagners geschenkt.

THE BAYREUTH FESTSPIELHAUS

Construction history

Enchanting – this spot is magical

On May 8, 1871 Wagner met a distant relative, Bayreuth banker Friedrich Feustel, who would become important in paving the way locally for the project. Wagner asked him to look around for a suitable terrain with at least two hundred (Prussian) square feet, and was hoping the city would offer it up as a present, seeing as they would only profit from such a festival. Wagner originally considered a parcel in the Hofgarten. In a November 3, 1871 letter, Feustel expressed his concerns about removing enough earth to create a thirty to fourty (Bavarian) foot deep sub-theater and about problems with the water table. It was he who (first) recommended building on a hill (which would later be described in such lofty terms, but which was really quite pragmatically motivated). He also drew Wagner's attention to the productive local sandstone quarries, which Wagner would later hardly make use of. Feustel is also the first to mention using brick: *"The building can be finished in sandstone and brick."*

On November 7, 1871, the City Council of Bayreuth decided to support the project generously and to offer Wagner a suitable plot of land. This was a smart move, seeing as other cities were making the now famous composer offers, including Baden-Baden, Darmstadt and later Reichenhall, Berlin, London and even Chicago following the Great Fire of 1871!

Wagner responds in a „generous" letter, *"I will be in Bayreuth on December 14 to receive the terrain."* On December 15, 1871 an inspection of the potential building sites is held and a plot in Stuckberg in St. Georgen on the outskirts of the city is chosen. The owner, however, the sugar manufacturer Rose, does not want to sell the plot, so the mayor, Muncker, offers Wagner the current location in An der Bürgerreuth and is even prepared to buy additional private land. At first Wagner is not excited about the spot and threatens to drop Bayreuth altogether, demanding offended: *"The entire population has to be in favor of me!"* Cosima successfully negotiates, and, in the end, Wagner changes his opinion: "Enchanting – this spot is magical." Naturally, the property remains in city hands until it is turned over to Wagner's heirs in 1891.

Tu Geld in deinen Beutel!

Für die Finanzierung seines Bayreuth-Gedankens hoffte Wagner weiterhin auf die Gunst des Königs, ohne sehen zu wollen, dass dieser dadurch seine Exklusivrechte verlor und von Bayreuth nicht begeistert sein konnte. So zeigen sich der König und sein Sekretär Düfflipp sehr distanziert. Ludwig finanzierte zunächst lediglich die Kosten für Grundstück und Bau von Wagners Villa Wahnfried mit 75000 Talern, weil er den Meister natürlich in Bayern halten wollte. Beim Festspielhaus blieb der König jedoch außergewöhnlich charakterstark und verweigerte jedwede Zuwendung, sodass der beleidigte Wagner in seinem verletzten Stolz sogar auf das Wohnhausgeschenk verzichten wollte und drohte, Bayern ganz zu verlassen. Erst zum Jahreswechsel 1873/74, als die Bauarbeiten aus Geldnot eingestellt werden mussten und man bereits die Fassade vernagelte, damit „*sich keine Eulen einnisten*"[1], erkannte Ludwig seine Verantwortung und schrieb Wagner am 25. Januar 1874. „*Nein, nein und wieder nein! so soll es nicht enden! Es muss da geholfen werden!*"[2] Ludwig gewährte einen Kredit von 100000 Talern, den die Familie Wagner bis 1906 zurückgezahlt hat.

Wagner hatte mit Freunden ein privates Finanzierungsmodell entwickelt und eine Patronatsgesellschaft gegründet. Die Kosten wurden auf je 100000 Taler für den Bau, für Technik und Dekorationen (Bühnenbilder, Kostüme) und für die Künstlergagen kalkuliert. Durch den Verkauf von mindestens 1000 Patronatsscheinen, einer Art Aktie in Höhe von 300 Talern, erhoffte man die Summe von 300000 Talern aufzubringen. Die ersten Scheine wurden im Mai 1871 ausgegeben, verkauften sich jedoch nicht wie gehofft. Der Mannheimer Emil Heckel veranlasste die Gründung der ersten Wagner-Vereine. Wagner dankte ihm mit einem seiner gefürchteten Gedichte: „*Hat jeder Topf seinen Deckel, / jeder Wagner seinen Heckel, / dann lebt sich's ohne Sorgen, / die Welt ist dann geborgen!*"[3]

Die Festspiele organisierten sich durch die Bildung eines Verwaltungsrats, dem der Bürgermeister Muncker, der Bankier Feustel und der Advokat Käfferlein angehörten, eine sehr sinnvolle Trias aus Politik, Finanz- und Rechtswesen. Die Finanzierung jedoch blieb bis zuletzt schwierig, und Wagner nannte das Festspielhaus später einmal sein „*Qualhall*"[4]. Er träumte in dieser Zeit schwer: „*R. sagt, er erkläre sich seine häufig wiederkehrenden Träume eines Geldbetruges durch den Alp, den ihm der Anblick des Theaters hinterlässt, gleichsam, ob er nicht ein Schwindler sei?*"[5]

Besonders enttäuscht war Wagner vom deutschen Adel, der nicht wie gehofft Interesse zeigte. Immerhin kam am 13. September 1873 der preußische Kronprinz Friedrich Wilhelm nach Bayreuth. Man bereitete ihm einen großen Empfang. „*'Jetzt nicht mehr gefackelt, sondern geflaggt', scherzt R. zur Haushälterin.*"[6] Doch der Prinz mied den Hügel. Das Festspielhaus wird eigens illuminiert: „*Wie eine Geistererscheinung, wie Wotans Bau ragt es zweimal in rotem Lichte empor. [...] Sehr ergriffen von dem Anblick des Theaters umarmen wir uns, und R. spricht: Es ist mit unserem Blute gerötet!*"[7]

Wagner gibt Konzerte (in Wien und Pest) und stiftet die Erlöse; man versucht die Baukosten zu drücken, wo es nur geht. Die geplanten Honorare für die Künstler werden in „Entschädigungen" umbenannt: „*Wer nicht aus Ehre und Enthusiasmus zu mir kommt, den lasse ich wo er ist.*"[8] Selbst nach der Uraufführung des RING 1876 sollte ein Defizit von 160000 Mark bleiben, das durch Wagners Privatvermögen, Cosimas Erbe, durch Verkauf der Tantiemen an die Münchner Hofoper und den Verkauf der RING-Dekorationen an den Theaterunternehmer Angelo Neumann aufgefangen wurde. Das Festspielhaus blieb bis 1882 geschlossen.

All das klingt nach einem finanziellen Fiasko, doch mit heutigen Augen betrachtet, waren die ersten Festspiele keineswegs so desaströs: Die Endabrechnung ergab, dass für den Bau tatsächlich

Put money in your pocket!

Wagner continued to hope that the King would finance his Bayreuth idea without wanting to admit that the King would therefore lose his exclusive rights and be anything other than excited about Bayreuth. For their part, the King and his secretary Düfflipp held their distance. At first, Ludwig only offered 75,000 to finance property and building costs for Wagner's villa, "Wahnfried." Naturally, he wanted to keep the maestro in Bavaria. When it came to the Festspielhaus, however, the King showed unusual strength of character and denied all funding. This offended Wagner's pride so much that he even thought of refusing the King's present of a residency and threatened to leave Bayreuth altogether. It wasn't until around the new year of 1874 when construction had been halted due to lack of funds and the facade was being boarded up to keep *"owls from nesting"* that Ludwig saw it as his responsibility to step in. On January 25, 1874 he writes to Wagner: *"No, no, thrice no! This isn't how it should end! Help must be given!"* Ludwig approved a credit of 100,000 thalers, which the Wagner family finished paying off in 1906.

Wagner had developed a private financing model with friends and founded a patron's society. The cost of building, technology and decoration (sets, costumes) and for artist fees were calculated at 100,000 thalers. He hoped to raise 300,000 thalers by selling at least 1,000 patron notes, akin to stock shares, valuing 300 thalers each. The first notes were sold in May of 1871, but sales were not as high as had been hoped. Then Emil Heckel took steps to found the first Wagner Society in Mannheim. Wagner thanked him with one of his dreaded poems: *"If every pot has its lid, and every Wagner has his Heckel, then life has no worries, and all the world is safe!"*

The advisory board established to organize the festival included the major, Muncker, the banker, Feustel, and a lawyer, Käfferlein – a sensible triad covering politics, finances and law. But financing the project remained difficult right up to the end, causing Wagner to later call the Festspielhaus his *"Qualhall,"* or hall of torture. He was plagued by bad dreams during this time: *"R. says the horror he feels when he sees the theater is the reason for his frequently returning nightmare involving fraud, quasi, whether he is a fraud?"*

Wagner was especially disappointed that the German nobility did not show interest like he had hoped. At least Prussian Crown Prince Friedrich Wilhelm visited Bayreuth on September 13, 1873. He was received with great ceremony: *"R. joked with the housekeeper, 'don't light the torches, bring out the flags.'"* The Festspielhaus was lit up especially for the occasion: *"It rose up in the double red lights like a ghost, like Wotan's building. [...] We hugged each other at the sight of the theater and R said: 'It is red with our blood.'"*

Wagner conducted concerts (in Vienna and Pest) and donates the proceedings. Construction costs were cut wherever possible. The intended fee for the artists was renamed a compensation: *"Anyone who doesn't come to me out of honor and enthusiasm will be left where he is."* The deficit of 160,000 marks remaining even after the premiere of the RING, 1876 was covered by Wagner's private estate, Cosima's inheritance, by selling royalties to the Royal Munich Opera, and by selling the RING decorations to theater producer Angelo Neumann. The Festspielhaus remained closed until 1882.

That may all reek of financial fiasco, but from a modern-day perspective, the festival was not disastrous at all. In the final account, the construction only cost one third of the original estimate. Private funding covered fifty-six per cent of all costs (including new construction), and "public" funds (the King's credit) accounted for only twenty-four per cent. The Wagner family covered twenty per cent of the cost personally. The proportion paid by the public hand (public subventions) today average forty per cent, making the Bayreuth Festival one of the most economically successful festivals in the world.

nur ein Drittel der ursprünglich veranschlagten Gesamtsumme verbraucht wurde. Alle Kosten (inklusive Neubau) wurden zu zirka sechsundfünfzig Prozent durch privates Geld und nur zu zirka vierundzwanzig Prozent durch „öffentliches" Geld (den Krediten des Königs) finanziert. Das Eigenkapital der Wagners deckte zwanzig Prozent der Kosten. Heute liegt die „Staatsquote" (der öffentlichen Zuschüsse) bei vierzig Prozent, womit die Bayreuther Festspiele zu den wirtschaftlich erfolgreichsten weltweit gehören.

Wie heißt eigentlich der Architekt?

Wagner, der ein höchst unpraktischer Mensch war und nachweislich keinen Nagel gerade in die Wand brachte, hatte bis dahin höchstens Bauwerke aus dem ihm vertrauten Material errichtet, wie eine Anekdote aus seiner ersten Pariser Zeit überliefert, als er mit „60 Klavierauszügen ein sonderbar konstruiertes Bauwerk"[1] um seinen Arbeitstisch aufbaute.

Für sein eigenes, parallel zum Festspielhaus errichtetes Wahnhaus in Bayreuth hatte Wagner schon 1856 eigene Entwürfe für einen Bauplan angefertigt, „welchen ich zuletzt mit allem Material eines Architektur-Zeichners ganz korrekt auszuarbeiten versuchte"[2]. 1872 folgten weitere Skizzen für Wahnfried, die zeigen, dass Wagners Ziehvater Geyer einst irrte, als er versuchte Richard für die Malerei zu begeistern: „Sobald es aber von dieser naiven Kleckserei zu ernsteren Zeichnungsstudien übergehen sollte, hielt ich, vielleicht schon durch die pedantische Manier meines Lehrers (eines langweiligen Vetters) abgeschreckt, nicht aus."[3]

Für das Festspielhaus sind solche Skizzen erster Hand leider nicht vorhanden. Nicht einmal ein Bierdeckel. Auch die Pläne der wechselnden Architekten sind nicht vollständig überliefert oder exakt zuzuweisen. Geradezu tragisch ist der Verlust fast aller Pläne zum Festspielhaus in einer geplanten permanenten Richard-Wagner-Ausstellung im Stadtgeschichtlichen Museum Leipzig im Zweiten Weltkrieg. Die schriftlichen Quellen zur Baugeschichte sind nicht lückenlos. Vieles wurde wohl nur mündlich verhandelt. Während Wagner Wahnfried bis ins Detail mit Architekten und Bauleuten diskutierte, ist dies beim Festspielhaus anscheinend nicht geschehen. Ästhetische oder stilistische Diskussionen um die Architektur sind nicht überliefert und wohl nicht geführt worden.

Wagner war primär an der Bühnentechnik zur Umsetzung seiner Kunst interessiert, sodass ihm der Bühnenmeister Carl Brandt (aus Darmstadt) als Homo technicus wichtigster Vertrauter wurde. Der Architekt hatte eine eher zweitrangige Stellung. Nachdem man sich von Neumann getrennt und der Kreisbaurat Franck abgewinkt hatte, brachte Brandt den Herzoglich Sachsen-Altenburgischen Hofbaumeister Otto Brückwald ins Spiel, den er vom Neubau des Altenburger Theaters kannte.

What was the architect's name, anyway?

Wagner was anything but practical and reportedly couldn't drive a nail straight into the wall. As an anecdote from his time in Paris confirms, before constructing the Festspielhaus, he had, at best, only undertaken construction projects using materials he was familiar with. It seems he constructed *"a peculiarly built structure out of 60 piano scores"* around his desk.

In 1856 he drew his own architectural designs for his home in Bayreuth being built parallel to the Festspielhaus: *"I attempted to draw them in detail using all the materials available to an architectural draftsman."* Later sketches for "Wahnfried" from 1872 demonstrate that Wagner's foster father Geyer had erred when he tried to interest Richard in painting: *"But as soon as we were supposed to advance from naive dabbling with paints to the more serious study of drawing, I was lost, perhaps because my teacher (a boring cousin) had such a pedantic manner."*

Unfortunately, there are no sketches by Wagner of the Festspielhaus. Not even on a beer coaster. The various architects' plans are also incomplete and not precisely attributable. It is nothing less than tragic that almost all plans for the Festspielhaus in a planned permanent Richard Wagner exhibit in the Museum of City History in Leipzig were lost during World War II. The written sources about the construction history are not free of gaps, either. It would seem that quite a bit was negotiated orally. Whereas Wagner discussed every detail of "Wahnfried" with architects and builders, this was apparently not the case for the Festspielhaus. There are no records of aesthetic or stylistic discussions about the architecture, and there were likely none.

Wagner was principally interested in what stage technology would enable him to produce his art. Accordingly, the homo technicus stage master Carl Brandt (from Darmstadt) became Wagner's most important confidant. The architect was of lesser importance. Once Neumann was out of the picture and the district building officer, Franck, had been waved off, Brandt called in the ducal court architect from Saxony-Altenburg, Otto Brückwald, whom he knew from the Altenburg Theater, a new construction project.

Little thought has been given to who the actual architect of the Festspielhaus was. Wagner himself is considered the spiritus rector of the project and saw himself as its ideational architect. At this point, Semper was litigating because of Munich, and Wagner only wanted to see his plans used to the degree that *"they are his intellectual property."* This positions Semper's successors, Neumann and Brückwald, as third-class figures. Some have even wondered whether the stage master, Brandt, was the architect, or even the developer Carl Wölfel, who had built "Wahnfried." The construction manager Carl Runckwitz and the district building officer, Franck, also developed plans for Bayreuth, and even Cosima provided important impulses. As a result, the question of authorship can not be answered without doubt (even by Habel). Nonetheless, Otto Brückwald is the official architect of the Festspielhaus. His biography depicts him as an interesting designer with building experience even before Bayreuth.

Bühnenbauer (Carl Brandt), Bauunternehmer (Carl Wölfel), Baumeister (Otto Brückwald), Bauleiter (Carl Runckwitz) in Bayreuth
Stage builder (Carl Brandt), building contractor (Carl Wölfel), master builder (Otto Brückwald), construction foreman (Carl Runckwitz) in Bayreuth

Wagners berühmtes Selbstporträt
Wagner's famous self portrait

Bisher wurde kaum über den eigentlichen Architekten des Festspielhauses nachgedacht. Wagner selbst gilt als Spiritus rector des Ganzen und verstand sich auch als idealler Architekt: Die Pläne des wegen München mittlerweile prozessierenden Semper wollte Wagner nur soweit benutzt sehen, *„als sie sein geistiges Eigentum sind"*[1]. Die Nachfolger Sempers, Neumann und Brückwald, erscheinen so lediglich als drittklassige Figuren. Es wurde sogar überlegt, ob nicht der Bühnenmeister Brandt der Architekt sei oder gar der Bauunternehmer Carl Wölfel, der Wahnfried gebaut hatte. Der Bauleiter Carl Runckwitz und ein Kreisbaurat Franck haben ebenfalls Pläne für Bayreuth gezeichnet, ja sogar Cosima hat entscheidende Anregungen gegeben, sodass die Autorenfrage (selbst von Habel) nicht zweifelsfrei zu klären ist. Otto Brückwald jedoch ist der offizielle Architekt des Festspielhauses, und seine Biografie offenbart einen interessanten Baukünstler, der schon vor Bayreuth Theater gebaut hatte.

Paul Otto Brückwald (1841 – 1917) stammte wie Wagner aus Leipzig, sodass es keine Verständigungsschwierigkeiten gab. Er galt als liebenswürdig, obwohl das Verhältnis zu dem stets ungeduldigen Wagner immer gespannt war und niemals ein freundschaftliches wurde. Brückwald, wie Wagner aus eher bescheidenen Verhältnissen, hatte zunächst Maurer gelernt und dann bis 1863 an der Königlichen Akademie in Dresden studiert, in der Klasse Georg Hermann Nicolais, einem Schüler des (Münchner) Klassizisten Leo von Klenze. Für seinen ersten Auftrag zeichnete er Pläne für den Neubau des Leipziger Stadttheaters unter der Leitung des Schinkel-Schülers Carl Ferdinand Langhans, dem Sohn des Erbauers des klassizistischen Brandenburger Tors in Berlin. Langhans jr. hatte schon die Theater in Breslau, Liegnitz und Dessau errichtet. Brückwald wohnte damals in Berlin und studierte die dortige Architektur. 1866 bis 1868 wurde er verantwortlicher Bauleiter am Leipziger Neuen Stadttheater und eröffnete danach ein eigenes Büro in Leipzig. Sein prominentester Auftrag war der Neubau des (heute noch stehenden) Herzoglichen Hoftheaters im sächsischen Altenburg, das er nach seinen Plänen schuf und 1871 vollendete.[2]

Am 24. April 1872, knapp einen Monat vor der Grundsteinlegung (!), erreicht ihn, den 31-Jährigen, das Telegramm aus Bayreuth *„Haben Sie Lust und Zeit, Wagnertheater Bayreuth zu bauen?"*[3] Am 24. Mai wird der Vertrag unterzeichnet. Obwohl Brückwald etwas überfallen wurde und in seiner Arbeit nicht ganz frei war, wäre es doch verwunderlich, wenn sich dieser erfahrene und wohlstudierte Mann, Kenner der Schinkelschen Backsteinarchitektur und des deutschen Klassizismus, nicht auch ästhetisch in Bayreuth eingebracht hätte. Sein Lieblingsstil war sicherlich die Neorenaissance und Habel rückt ihn in die Nähe von Semper (den Brückwald freilich erst beim *„Einweihungsschmause"* 1876 in Bayreuth trifft).[4]

Das Altenburger Theater ist zwar ohne jeden Backstein im Stil der italienischen Neorenaissance errichtet, doch zeigt es eine offensichtliche Verwandtschaft zum Bayreuther Festspielhaus, das ja auch Renaissanceelemente im hellen Haustein aufweist. Ähnlich sind die Unvermitteltheit der Baukörper, der isolierte hohe Bühnenturm, eine Art Lüftungslaterne über dem relativ niedrigen Zuschauerraum, typische Doppelfenster und die segmentbogenrunde Fassade des Zuschauerraums mit einem Portikus wie dem „Königsbau". Innen jedoch findet sich ein klassisches Logentheater ohne amphitheatralisches Halbrund. Hätte Brückwald – so ließe sich spekulieren – mehr Geld zur Verfügung gehabt, um ein formal ansprechendes und anständiges Theater zu bauen, sähe sein Theater in Bayreuth – zumindest außen – heute vielleicht wie das in Altenburg aus.

Like Wagner, Paul Otto Brückwald (1841 – 1917) was from Leipzig, so there were no communication difficulties. He was considered quite likeable, even though his relationship with ever-impatient Wagner was always strained and never developed into a friendship. Also like Wagner, Brückwald came from a relatively humble background. He was trained as a mason and later studied architecture at the Königliche Akademie in Dresden under Georg Hermann Nicolai, himself a student of the (Munich) Classicist Leo von Klenze. Brückwald's architectural debut was to draw up plans for the new construction of the Leipzig Stadttheater under the direction of Schinkel's student Carl Ferdinand Langhans, Jr. Langhans was the son of the designer of the classicistic Brandenburg Gate in Berlin. He had already built theaters in Breslau, Liegnitz and Dessau. At the time, Brückwald was living in and studying the architecture of Berlin. From 1866 to 1868 he was the construction supervisor for the Neues Stadttheater in Leipzig, and after that he opened his own office in Leipzig. His most prominent commission was the new construction of the (still standing) Herzogliches Hoftheater in Saxon Altenburg, which he built according to his own plans and completed in 1871.

On April 24, 1872, just under a month before the cornerstone would be laid (!), the then 31-year-old Brückwald received a telegram from Bayreuth *"Do you want to and do you have time to build the Wagner Theater in Bayreuth?"* The contract was signed on May 24. Even though Brückwald was taken a bit by surprise and was never totally free in his work, it would be quite surprising if this experienced man with such strong academic qualifications, who was familiar with Schinkel's brick architecture and German Classicism, had not brought his own aesthetic to the job in Bayreuth. His favorite style was surely the neo-Renaissance and Habel places him in the Semper camp (though the two would first meet at the consecration party in Bayreuth in 1876).

Although the Altenburg theater was built in the brickless style of the Italian neo-Renaissance, it nonetheless shows similarities to the Bayreuth Festspielhaus, which also has Renaissance elements in light-colored hewn stone. Similar elements include the directness of the building, the isolated tall stage tower, a type of ventilation lantern above a relatively low auditorium, and a portico resembling the "Königsbau." The interior, however, is a classical theater with loges lacking the amphitheater semi-circular seating. It could be speculated that if Brückwald had had more money at his disposal to build a formally attractive, respectable theater, the exterior of the theater in Bayreuth would perhaps resemble the theater in Altenburg.

Theater Altenburg von Otto Brückwald (von 1871)
Otto Brückwald's Altenburg theater (of 1871)

Bayreuth blieb Brückwalds letztes Theater. Er erhielt dafür zwar noch einen bayerischen Orden, baute aber nichts Großes mehr und fiel am Ende seines Lebens sogar verarmt in Vergessenheit, galt 1906 bereits als verstorben. 1916 besuchen ihn Herren des Leipziger Wagner-Vereins im Johannisstift für mittellose Künstler: *„Sie finden ihn über das Reißbrett gebeugt, dessen Zeichnung den Plan des Festspielhauses aufwies!"*[1]

Bayreuth would be Brückwald's last theater. Even though he received a medal from Bavaria for it, he never built anything else big and even fell, forgotten, into poverty. He was thought to have died in 1906, but in 1916 members of the Leipzig Wagner Society visited him in the Johannes home for poor artists: *"They find him bent over his designs for the Festspielhaus on the drawing board!"*

Der Grundstein wird gelegt
1872

The cornerstone gets laid
1872

Am 22. Mai 1872, also zwei Tage vor (!) dem Vertragsabschluss mit Brückwald, kam es nun tatsächlich zur Grundsteinlegung eines Gebäudes, das der Architekt noch zu zeichnen hatte und das erst während des Baus (am 13. Juni 1872) behördlich genehmigt wurde. Brückwald berichtet, dass er bis zum Vertragsabschluss nur die defekten Pläne eines Kreisbaurats Franck vor Augen hatte und die Pläne Sempers nie gesehen habe. Brückwalds später maßgeblichen Pläne lagen bei der Grundsteinlegung also noch nicht vor und wurden erst am 30. August 1872 vorgelegt. Trotzdem hatte man schon am 29. April den ersten Spatenstich getan. Verständlich, dass kaum jemand an den Erfolg dieses Projekts glaubte, wie etwa ein Bayreuther Architekt, der ausrief: *„Wenn dieser Hochstapler* [Richard Wagner] *imstande ist, den Bau des Theaters über die Grundmauern hinauszuführen, dann laufe ich barfuss nach Jerusalem und wieder zurück."*[2] Es ist nicht überliefert, ob jener Ungläubige sein Versprechen 1876 eingelöst hat.

On May 22, 1872, two days before (!) Brückwald singed the contract, the cornerstone gets laid for a building that the architect still had to draw and that the authorities would first approve during construction (on June 13, 1872). Brückwald reports that until he signed his contract he had only seen the defective plans by the district building officer, Franck, and that he never saw Semper's plans. At the time the cornerstone was laid, Brückwald's later definitive plans had not yet been drawn. These would be submitted on August 30, 1872. But the first shovel of dirt was removed on April 29 nonetheless. It is understandable that hardly a soul believed the project would be a success. For example, a Bayreuth architect proclaims: *"If this conman* [Wagner] *is able to raise his theater above the foundation, then I'll run barefoot to Jerusalem and back."* There is no record whether the disbeliever followed through on his promise in 1876.

Die Grundsteinlegung erfolgte also am 59. Geburtstag des Meisters trotz der *„Ungunst des Wetters, welche die Vornahme des Aktes der Grundsteinlegung belästigte, die heiter erregte Laune nicht einzuschüchtern vermochte."*[3] In den Grundstein, den Richard Wagner selbst unter Tränen mit dem Hammer versenkte, wurde eine Blechkapsel eingeschlossen, darin ein telegrafischer Weihegruß von König Ludwig II., die Statuten des ersten Wagner-Vereins (in Mannheim), weitere Glückwunschtelegramme, diverse Münzen und ein Vers des Dichterkomponisten: *„Hier schliess ich ein Geheimnis ein, da ruh' es viele hundert Jahr': so lange es verwahrt der Stein, macht es der Welt sich offenbar."*[4]

The cornerstone was laid on the maestro's 59th birthday, despite the *"unfavorable weather that made it more difficult to lay the cornerstone, but that did not disrupt the positive atmosphere."* Richard Wagner tearfully laid the cornerstone himself, inserting a metal capsule containing a dedication greeting from King Ludwig II sent by telegraph, the statutes of the first Wagner Society (in Mannheim), additional congratulatory telegrams, various coins, and a verse by the poet composer: *"A secret I do bury here for centuries, may it be: doth the stone yet persevere, its truth the world shall see."*

Unter der Gedenktafel im Foyer soll sich der Legende nach der Grundstein liegen, doch dem ist nicht so. Er befindet sich vermutlich einen Schritt südlicher. Wolfgang Wagner allein kennt wohl den genauen Ort, doch *„er wahrt den neidlichsten Schatz"*.

Legend has it that the cornerstone is located beneath the plaque, yet that is not the case. It is presumably located a step further south. Wolfgang Wagner' alone probably knows the exact spot, but *"he is preserving the jealously guarded treasure."*

Im Markgräflichen Opernhaus hielt Wagner eine (sicherlich mehr als einstündige) Rede vor einem sitzenden Publikum, die *„die ernstesten Männer"*[5] zu Tränen gerührt haben muss, wie Cosima notiert. Um fünf Uhr dirigierte Wagner dann den Kaisermarsch und seine Lieblingssymphonie, Beethovens Neunte.

Wagner held a speech (certainly lasting over an hour) in front of a seated audience in the Margravial Opera House that Cosima writes brought even *"the most serious of men"* to tears. At five o'clock Wagner directed the Kaiser March and his favorite symphony, Beethoven's 9th.

Wagner dirigiert zur Grundsteinlegung Beethovens IX. Symphonie im Markgräflichen Opernhaus, einem klassischen Logentheater, das Wagner ablehnte, nicht zuletzt wegen eines nicht immer auf die Bühne konzentrierten Publikumsverhaltens.
Wagner directing Beethoven's 9th Symphony at the cornerstone-laying ceremony in the Margravial Opera House, a classical loge theater. One reason Wagner would not accept this platform for his festival was because it encouraged the audience to not focus their attention toward the stage at all times.

Otto Brückwalds Aufgabenstellung

Die Rede zur Grundsteinlegung 1872[1] ist eine der authentischsten und ausführlichsten Quellen, um die Intentionen Wagners für Bayreuth kennenzulernen, obgleich sie vieles aus dem Vorwort zur Nibelungen-Dichtung von 1862 wiederholt, während die Visionen von 1849 in den Hintergrund geraten sind. Wagner hat ihren Text im folgenden Frühjahr 1873, zusammen mit sechs Holzschnitten der Pläne Brückwalds, publiziert.

Wagner betont erneut den provisorischen Charakter des projektierten Gebäudes und spricht von einer im *„dürftigsten Materiale ausgeführten äußeren Umschalung"*, die *„im glücklichsten Falle"* an die *„flüchtig gezimmerten Festhallen"* und an die für einen baldigen Abbruch gebauten Sängerhallen erinnere. In einem späteren Brief von 1872 schreibt er: *„Mir wäre es recht, wenn es ganz nur aus Holz wäre, wie Turner- und Sängerfesthallen; keine andere Solidität, als die welche es vor Einsturz sichert."*[2] In einem Brief Wagners am 17. April 1872 heißt es: *„Ich gestatte einen vollständigen Holzbau, so sehr dies auch meine Bayreuther verdrießen sollte, welche gern schon jetzt ein stattliches Gebäude von Außen sehen möchten. [...] Und: Ich akzeptiere selbst ein Balkengesperre."*[3]

Überraschenderweise ist dieses „Balkengesperre", das schöne Fachwerk samt Backsteinen, auf den Plänen Brückwalds am Zuschauerhaus und an der Südfront des Bühnenturms nicht zu sehen! Sie zeigen stattdessen scheinbar verputzte oder zumindest getünchte weiße Außenwände. Daraus ist zu folgern, dass die Fachwerkarchitektur hier nicht vorgesehen war, sondern erst im Verlauf der Bauzeit zwischen 1872 und 1876 – vermutlich aus Kostengründen – als unverkleideter Rohbau „übrig blieb".

Brückwald musste außerdem auf seinen hübschen Girlandenschmuck verzichten (doch vielleicht war der nur als temporärer Festschmuck gedacht?). Wagner hatte Brückwald für die Edition jener sechs Holzschnitte um Zusendung der noch nicht fertigen Pläne angefragt und gebeten *„alle Embleme und Ornamente fortzulassen"*. In Klammern fügte er an: *„Es versteht sich ganz von selbst, dass Sie bei der Ausführung dann die Freiheit zurück erhalten, gefällige Verziehrungen anzubringen."* (2. April 1873).[4] Der Plan mit Wagners eigenhändigem Kommentar *„Die Ornamente fort"* ist erhalten, Wagners Versprechen wurde aber nie eingelöst.

Die Fachwerkarchitektur, wie sie schließlich am Zuschauerhaus realisiert wurde, war also nicht geplant und gehört damit keinem ästhetischen Grundkonzept an! Sie erscheint in den Plänen lediglich am funktionalsten Teil des Gebäudes, dem Bühnenturm, und da nur an den Seiten. In Wagners Rede ist keine Rede von einem romantischen oder gar neugotischen Fachwerkbau. Wagners lebenslange Burgenbegeisterung spielt für Bayreuth keine Rolle mehr, sodass dem heutigen Betrachter nur die durchaus legitime Anmutung einer romantischen Aura bleibt, die diese Architektur umfängt.

Otto Brückwald's job definition

Wagner's speech at the cornerstone laying ceremony in 1872 is one of the most authentic and detailed sources for understanding Wagner's intentions for Bayreuth. It repeats quite a bit from the 1862 foreword of the Nibelungen poem, shifting his 1849 visions somewhat into the background. Wagner published his speech and six woodcuts of Brückwald's plans in the spring of 1873.

In his speech, Wagner re-emphasizes the provisional character of the projected building, referring to an *"exterior shell constructed out of simple materials"* that *"in the best case scenario"* should recall the *"hastily built banquet halls"* and the master singers' halls built to be torn down soon thereafter. In a later letter of 1872, Wagner writes: *"It would be fine with me if it were built completely out of wood, like gymnasiums or master singers festival halls, lacking any more solidity than is needed to keep it from collapsing."* In a letter on April 17, 1872, he adds: *"I approve of an entirely wooden construction, even though the citizens of Bayreuth will be annoyed. They would prefer to see a building with a stately exterior right away. [...] I'm even willing to accept timber binders and joists."*

Surprisingly, the "timber binders and joists," the beautiful timber framing with bricks on the auditorium and the south face of the stage tower, is not included in Brückwald's plans. Instead, his plans show stucco or at least whitewashed exterior walls. Presumably the timber framing we see was not intended, but was left unfinished during construction during 1872 and 1876, probably for cost reasons.

Brückwald also had to forfeit his pretty garland decorations (or perhaps that was only planned as temporary festival ornamentation?). Wagner had asked Brückwald to send him his incomplete plans for the edition of the six woodcuts, asking him to *"remove all emblems and ornaments."* He added parenthetically: *"It goes without saying that you will be free to add agreeable decorations when it comes time to build."* (April 2, 1873). The plan containing Wagner's comment *"Remove the ornaments"* survives, but he never fulfilled his promise.

So, the timber framing found on the auditorium was not planned and was not part of a basic aesthetic concept. The only place it appears in the plans is on the most functional part of the building, the stage tower, and even there only on the sides. In his speech, Wagner does not mention a Romantic, let alone neo-Gothic half-timbered building. Wagner's lifelong fascination for fortresses is no longer relevant for Bayreuth. The observer is left only with a quite legitimate impression of a Romantic aura surrounding this architecture.

Ein wirklich gotisches Theater ist das Stadttheater Zwickau, das, wie auch andere Häuser, in Leipzig zum Beispiel, ein ehemaliges Gewandhaus darstellt, das 1823 und 1855 in ein Theater umgewandelt wurde.
The Zwickau Stadttheater is truly Gothic. Like other theaters, such as in Leipzig, it was an old storage depot and was converted into a theater in 1823 and in 1855.

Neugotische Sängerhalle in Nürnberg 1861
Neo-Gothic Master Singer Hall in Nurnberg, 1861

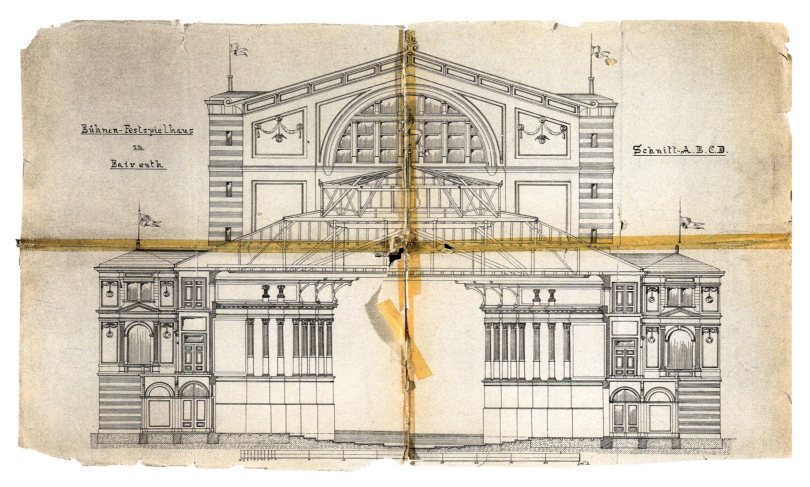

Einziger erhaltener Originaleingabeplan Brückwalds von 1872 im Stadtarchiv Bayreuth
The only remaining original structured drawing by Brückwald from 1872 in the Bayreuth City Archives

Brückwalds Aufriss der Südfassade 1872
mit Wagners Kommentar „*Die Ornamente fort!*"
Otto Brückwald's 1872 draft of the south facade
with Wagner's comment *"Remove the ornaments!"*

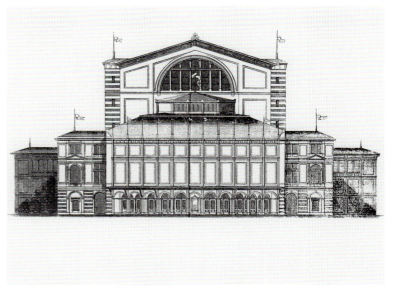

Von Wagner 1873 edierter Holzschnitt: Aufriss der Südfassade (noch ohne
Königsbau) mit noch offenen Arkaden im Erdgeschoss unter dem Zuschauerraum.
1873 woodcut revised by Wagner: draft of the south facade (still lacking Königsbau)
with open arcade on the ground floor beneath the auditorium.

Über *„die äußere Gestalt des ganzen Theaterbaues"* sagt Wagner in seiner Rede völlig unromantisch, wie ein einst von ihm selbst kritisierter Nützlichkeitsmensch, dass diese *„nicht in das Gebiet der uns zur Aufgabe gestellten Erfindung zu rechnen war"* und verweist mehrmals auf die fehlenden Finanzen, die zur *„Errichtung eines monumentalen Ziergebäudes"* nötig gewesen wären. In einem Brief an Brandt (16. Februar 1873) bezeichnet er das Äußere gar als *„uninteressant"*[1]. Auch Otto Brückwald schämte sich wohl ein wenig und nennt das Festspielhaus in seinem Rückblick von 1894 ein *„neues eigentümliches Gebäude"*, *„bei welchem von Anwendung edler Architekturformen oder schöner Verhältnisse der Gebäudeteile zueinander abzusehen war"*[2].

Wagner begreift das Äußere also als reines Provisorium, das später einmal, vielleicht erst nach ihm, vollendet werden sollte. Wichtig ist ihm allein das Innere: *„Was von diesem Gebäude jedoch auf einen dauernden Bestand berechnet ist, soll Ihnen dagegen immer deutlicher werden, sobald Sie in sein Inneres eintreten."* Erst am Ende seiner Rede geht er noch einmal auf den Außenbau ein, der allein dadurch interessant sei, dass man an ihm die Idee zu diesem Theater ablesen könne, das *„den inneren Geist auch nach außen kundgeben"* wolle.

Wichtigster Gebäudeteil ist die Bühne, die quasi den Maßstab für den restlichen Bau liefert. Wagner will für sein Theater die Möglichkeit, Kulissen sowohl nach oben als auch nach unten vollständig verschwinden lassen zu können, was nicht neu aber im Vergleich zum Barocktheater mit seiner Kulissen-Soffittenbühne immer noch modern war. Der Bühnenturm müsse deshalb das dreifache Volumen des Bühnenraums besitzen, wovon ein Drittel im Boden, die anderen zwei Drittel als Turm aus dem Gebäude aufragen sollten. Das Zuschauerhaus solle die Bühne an Höhe nicht überragen: *„Über dem eigentlichen Parterre bedarf die Bühne daher ihrer doppelten Höhe, während für den Zuschauerraum nur die einmalige Höhe nötig ist."*

Diese Proportionen sind im Querschnitt von Runckwitz und in der Seitenansicht zu sehen. Wagner greift hier eine Anregung Cosimas auf, die diese am 25. Mai 1872 geäußert hatte: *„Der Architekt [...] Brückwald kommt am Morgen, [...] ich rate für den Theaterbau kühn das Bühnenhaus hervortreten zu lassen, als Hauptsache, nicht es zu verdecken, sondern den Zuschauerraum möglichst niedrig zu halten wie eine Art niedrige Vorhalle zur Bühne."*[3]

Wagner kritisiert in seiner Rede andere Theaterbauten, die diese Verhältnisse zu kaschieren versuchen, indem sie einen Übergang gestalten, um *„den Zuschauerraum bedeutend aufsteigen zu lassen, außerdem aber auf diesem noch leere Räume zu konstruieren"*. Das ist in Bayreuth außer einer Lüftungslaterne in der Tat nicht geschehen. Viele Theater hätten, so Wagner, aus solchen Gründen den Zuschauerraum mit Logenrängen in *„oft unmäßiger Höhe"* gestreckt, sogar über die Höhe der Bühne hinaus, wo man die dortigen Plätze *„nur den ärmeren Klassen der Bevölkerung anbot, welchen die Beschwerde der dunstigen Vogelperspektive [...] zugemutet wurde. Allein diese Ränge fallen in unserem Theater hinweg"*. Wagner wollte jedoch solche extreme Sichtverhältnisse vermeiden und jedem Besucher eine möglichst horizontale Sichtperspektive gewährleisten.

Dieses additive Verfahren, einzelne funktional getrennte Gebäudeteile auch äußerlich zu trennen, war nicht neu und findet sich als genuin romanische Bauweise in der Architekturgeschichte, wie es Wagner zum Beispiel am Wormser Dom hätte studieren können. In der Theaterarchitektur war es Gottfried Semper, der dieses (sehr moderne) „form follows function"-Prinzip etabliert hatte, wie schön am Burgtheater in Wien oder an der zweiten Semper-Oper in Dresden zu sehen ist. Zu diesem Konzept gehörte auch die äußere Sichtbarmachung des antikisierenden Zuschauerraums, des halbrunden „Amphitheaters", das Semper ebenfalls als Erster in die moderne Architektur eingebracht hatte und als

Sounding just as completely unromantic as the people defined by functionality he had formerly criticized, Wagner comments in his speech on *"the exterior appearance of the whole theater"* that *"it is not within the bounds of the creative task we are undertaking"* and refers on several occasions to the lack of financial means that would be needed to *"erect a monumentally decorated building."* In a letter to Brandt (February 16, 1873) he goes as far as to call the exterior *"uninteresting."* In his 1894 retrospect, Otto Brückwald appears to have been somewhat ashamed as well, calling the Festspielhaus a *"peculiar new building"* for which he *"refrained from using noble architectural forms or from creating a beautiful relationship between the parts of the building."*

Wagner therefore understood the exterior to be purely provisional, postponing its completion to a later time, perhaps even a later generation. The only thing important to him is the interior. *"It will be more and more clear to you what aspect of this building was designed to last once you step inside."* At the end of his speech, Wagner again refers to the exterior, which he says is only of interest because it mirrors the idea behind the theater that wants to *"proclaim its inner spirit externally as well."*

The most important part of the theater is the stage, which in a way sets the standard for the rest of the building. Wagner wants it to be possible to make the scenery in his theater *completely* disappear up out the top and down into the floor as well. This is not new, but still very modern compared with the Baroque theater's backdrops and soffitts. To achieve this, the stage tower had to had three times the volume of the stage area, one third would extend below the floor and two thirds would extend upward in a tower outside the main building. The auditorium should not be much higher than the stage: *"The stage therefore needs twice its height above the actual first floor, whereas the auditorium only needs the single height."*

Runckwitz's cross section shows these proportions well. Wagner seizes on a suggestion Cosima makes on May 25, 1872: *"The architect, [...] Brückwald, came by this morning [...] and I boldly suggested that he let the stage building of the theater stand out, as its main feature. Instead of covering up the stage tower, he should keep the auditorium as low as possible, like a vestibule to the stage."*

In his speech, Wagner criticizes other theaters for trying to disguise this relationship by creating an add-on *"to make the auditorium significantly higher and also to create empty spaces on top of it."* With the exception of a ventilation lantern, that is not the case at all. Wagner says that many theaters stretch the auditorium to *"frequently extreme heights"* with loge balconies for this reason, even ranging above the height of the theater. The seats there *"are offered only to the poorer segments of the population, [..] expecting them to put up with the ill effects of a hazy bird's-eye perspective. In our theater, however, there are no such balconies."* Wagner wanted to avoid such extreme viewing conditions and ensure that the perspective is as horizontal as possible for every visitor.

This additive method of externally splitting up functionally divided parts of buildings was not new. There are genuinely Roman examples of this architecture in history, as Wagner could have studied at the Worms Cathedral. Gottfried Semper is attributed with establishing this form-follows-function principle in theater architecture. His Burgtheater in Vienna and the second Semper Opera in Dresden are ready examples. Another aspect of this concept is to make the classical auditorium, the semi-circular "amphitheater," visible from the outside. Semper was also the first person in modern architecture to view this as a revival of a tradition from Roman antiquity. In Historicism after Semper, the resulting visible curve in the facade even became the standard way of clearly identifying buildings as concert or theater halls. Wagner does not discuss this curvature in his speech. Wilhelm Neumann's "defective" drawing still disguises the amphitheater, placing it in a square architecture, resulting in a straight finish.

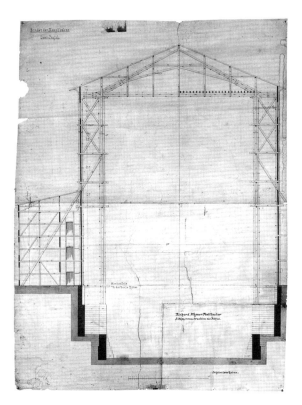

Querschnitt durch den Bühnenturm von Runckwitz
Cross-section of the stage tower by Runckwitz

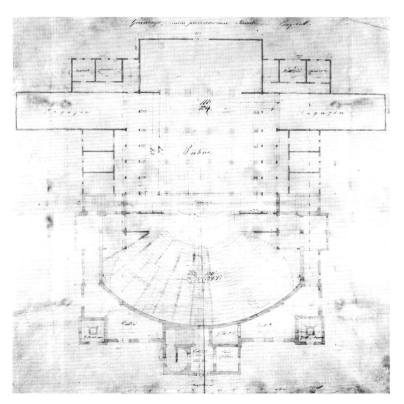

Einziger Wilhelm Neumann zugeschriebener Plan mit geradem Fassadenabschluss
The only plan attributed to Wilhelm Neumann, calling for a straight facade finish

Otto Brückwalds Aufriss der östlichen Seitenfassade (Holzschnitt 1873)
Otto Brückwald's sketch of the east facade (1873 woodcut)

Aufnahme von 1875 (ohne Königsbau) mit offenem Foyer
Photograph from 1875 (without Königsbau) with open foyer

Wiederbelebung der römischen Antike verstand. Das bedeutete eine auch äußerlich sichtbare Rundung der Fassade, die im Historismus nach Semper sogar zum Standard gereichte, und Bauten deutlich als Konzert- oder Theatergebäude auswiesen. Wagner geht in seiner Rede auf die Rundung seiner Bayreuther Fassade nicht ein. Jene „defekte" Zeichnung von Wilhelm Neumann zeigt noch eine Kaschierung des Amphitheaters, das in eine rechtwinklige Architektur gestellt wird und so einen geraden Abschluss erhält.

Auf „Flügelanbaue, etwa für Bälle, Konzerte u. dgl.", wie sie noch der Entwurf Sempers für das Münchner Projekt vorsah, verzichtet Wagner ebenso, damit niemand vom Hauptzwecke seines Besuchs abgelenkt werde und es nicht „wieder so hergehe, wie es eben im Operntheater der ‚Jetztzeit' der Fall ist". Darüber hinaus verschont er sein Theater vor der Kunst der Bildhauer, denen nur „immer wieder die Motive der Renaissance mit uns nichts sagenden, unverständlichen Figuren und Zierraten einzig einfallen". Das Bayreuther Festspielhaus zeigt in der Tat keinen Skulpturenschmuck, wie jedes andere Theater des 18. und 19. Jahrhunderts.

Wagner spricht in seiner Rede zur Architektur seines Theaters nur noch über die Fassade, die er grundsätzlich ablehnt, wie er auch im März 1873 Cosima mitteilt: „R. bemerkte, dass außer der gotischen Kirche alle Gebäude eigentlich für die Fassaden gebaut seien und wir keine eigentlichen freistehenden schönen Monumente haben."[1] In seiner Rede kritisiert Wagner, dass alle anderen Opernhäuser „einzig eine Fassade für den, dem Eingange zugewendeten, schmalen Teil des Gebäudes" besäßen.

Sein Festspielhaus dagegen zeige sich selbstbewusst auf einem „hochgelegenen freien Raum", womit es eine Art Allansichtigkeit erhält, die jeder Bayreuth-Besucher kennt, der Rundgang ums Haus ist Ritual. Sein Theater aber verzichte auf eine „ewig unerlässlich dünkende Hauptfassade." [...] „Ein Zugang zu diesem Gebäude enthält dagegen einen, gleichsam nur übermauerten Vorhof". Gemeint ist die offene Loggia unter dem Zuschauerraum, die auf alten Fotos (siehe Seite 67) noch sichtbar ist und erst 1933 mit Glastüren geschlossen wurde.

Fazit

Wagner wünschte sich für den Außenbau seines in den Plänen noch nicht ausgereiften, aber schon begonnenen Theaters eine Art provisorischer Sängerhalle, zur Not mit einem radikalen Balkengesperre errichtet (obgleich diese Holzarchitektur in den Plänen Brückwalds nur an den Seiten erscheint). Der äußerlich nicht ornamentierte und von jedem Skulpturenschmuck befreite Bau soll von innen nach außen – wie eine gotische Kirche – errichtet werden und so – den Konzepten Sempers folgend – die Funktionalität seiner Teile sichtbar machen: einen Zuschauerraum ohne Logen, der nicht höher als die Bühne ist und eine horizontale Sicht erlaubt, darüber keine weiteren Bauten. Der Bühnenturm rage mit dem gleichen Volumen wie die Bühne ohne Kaschierung aus dem Baukörper hervor. Das Theater habe keine Hauptfassade, sondern eine Allansichtigkeit und lediglich offene Foyers unter dem Zuschauerraum. Flügelbauten für weitere Nutzungen sind nicht erwünscht. Alles Äußere soll erst nachträglich in einer monumentalen Bauweise vollendet werden, während das Innere – wovon noch ausführlich die Rede sein wird – bereits für den Bestand errichtet werde. So lautete die Aufgabenstellung für den Architekten Otto Brückwald.

Wagner also rejected *"wings for balls, concerts, etc.,"* which Semper's proposal for the Munich project had included. Wagner didn't want anyone to get distracted from the main reason for their visit and wanted to prevent things from *"getting to be like in 'modern day' opera theaters."* He also spared his theater sculptors' artistry, who *"have no other ideas than to incessantly repeat Renaissance motifs, carving figures and decorations that mean nothing to us and that we don't understand."* The resulting Bayreuth Festspielhaus lacks the sculptured decoration common to every other theater from the 18th and 19th centuries.

Wagner then directs his speech about the architecture of his theater to the facade, which he fundamentally disapproves of. For example, in March 1873, Cosima writes: *"R. remarked that all buildings except Gothic churches are actually built for their facade and that there aren't really any beautiful freestanding monuments."* In his speech, Wagner criticizes that *"all other opera houses only have a facade for the narrow part of the building facing the entrance."*

In contrast, his Festspielhaus stands self-assuredly in a *"free, elevated location,"* making it pleasing to look at from all sides. Every Bayreuth visitor knows this, and taking a walk around the theater has become ritual. His theater, however, he adds, will not have one *"main facade considered absolutely essential."* [...] *"Access to this building, in contrast, will be through a simple covered vestibule."* He is referring to the open loggia below the auditorium still visible in old photographs (see page 67). Glass doors were added to close in the loggia in 1933.

Summary

Construction began on Wagner's theater even before its plans were fully developed. Wagner wanted the exterior to resemble a provisional master singers' hall, if necessary with timber binders and joists. (Brückwald's plans only called for this wooden architecture on the sides.) The building should be erected from the inside out like a Gothic church and its exterior should be free of sculptured ornament. Following Semper's concepts, the functionality of the building's parts should be visible. For example, to achieve a horizontal perspective, the auditorium should not be higher than the stage and there should be no balconies. Therefore, there should be no additional structures on top of the auditorium. Rather, the stage tower should extend above the auditorium building with the same volume as the stage itself, without effort to disguise this. The theater should not have a main facade, but rather should be pleasing to look at from all sides. It should have simple open foyers below the auditorium but no wings for other purposes. The exterior should be finished later in monumental style, whereas the interior, which will be discussed below, should be built to last. That's how the architect Otto Brückwald's job was defined.

Heidelberger Stadthalle im Stil der „Deutschen Renaissance" von 1903 mit signifikanter Fassadenwölbung, schmückenden Lyren und interessanten Scheitelsteinen

The 1903 Stadthalle in Heidelberg in "German Renaissance" style with significant curved facade, decorative lyres and interesting apex blocks

Vision von einer deutschen Architektur

Wagner beschreibt in seiner grundsteinlegenden Rede[1] jene additive und funktionelle Bauweise als eine genuin deutsche Bauart: *„Dies aber ist das Wesen des deutschen Geistes, dass er von Innen baut"* – im vermeintlichen Gegensatz zur *„welschen"* Architektur, die mehr an Fassaden, Äußerlichkeiten und Dekorationen interessiert sei. (Aus diesen Gründen habe er auch *„eine andere Stätte, als die des italienisch-französischen Opernsaales"* des Markgräflichen Opernhauses als Ort der Festspiele finden müssen.) Wagners Rede hat einen sehr patriotischen Ton, der in heutigen Ohren oft unerträglich chauvinistisch klingt. Zwar weist er Absichten, in Bayreuth ein deutsches Nationaltheater bauen zu wollen, von sich, doch schürt er den Patriotismus und benutzt ihn sogar, die Unvollkommenheit seines Festspielhauses zu entschuldigen: *„Alle äußere Form des deutschen Wesens"* sei seit Jahrhunderten *„eine provisorische"*.

Hieraus sprechen die Identitätssuche einer erst vor kurzem geeinten Nation, wie auch Wagners alte Ressentiments gegen die kulturelle Vormachtstellung des 1871 besiegten Feindes Frankreich. Und wieder werden die großen Vertreter des *„deutschen Geistes […] Winkelmann, Lessing, Goethe und endlich Schiller"* (den Bayreuther Jean Paul alias Friedrich Richter nicht vergessend) beschworen, die großen Klassiker, die Klassizisten. An dieser Stelle wünscht man sich einen Satz wie diesen: „Deshalb, verehrte Gemeinde, habe ich einen klassizistischen Bau im Geiste Winckelmanns und all der anderen Kenner und Verehrer der griechischen Antike errichten lassen, im Geiste der größten deutschen klassizistischen Architekten Gilly, Schinkel und Klenze, denn das ist deutsch, das Erbe der Antike in seiner tiefsten Wahrhaftigkeit zu erkennen und dem rein Äußerlichen des Franzosen oder Italieners entgegenzustellen." Doch die 1849 noch so verehrte Antike ist 1872/73 vergessen, die klassizistische Architektur kein Begriff.

Stattdessen nimmt seine Rede eine überraschende, eine höchst kühne Wendung. Neben den fehlenden Finanzen sieht Wagner nämlich auch eine ästhetische Not: *„Wäre uns selbst ein edleres Material […] zur Verfügung gestellt gewesen, so würden wir […] zurückgeschrocken sein, und hätten uns nach einer Hilfe umsehen müssen, die wir mit Sicherheit so schnell kaum […] irgendwo angetroffen haben würden. Es stellte sich hier uns nämlich die neueste, eigentümlichste und deshalb, weil sie noch nie versucht werden konnte, schwierigste Aufgabe für den Architekten der Gegenwart (oder der Zukunft?) dar."* Diese Sätze bedeuten schlicht und einfach, dass er gar nicht gewusst hätte, wie ein solcher Monumentalbau auszusehen habe. Jedenfalls wollte Wagner *„keine der überkommenen Ornamente zu verwenden wissen, sodass wir unser Gebäude für jetzt in der naivsten Einfachheit eines Notbaues erscheinen lassen müssen"*. Nun wird verständlich, warum sich das Festspielhaus stilistisch so schwer einordnen lässt, denn es hat – obigem Zitat zufolge – gar keinen Stil!

„In welchem Style sollen wir bauen?" heißt eine berühmte, 1828 erschienene Schrift des Architekten Heinrich Hübsch (1795–1863), die als grundlegende Studie zur Architektur des Historismus im 19. Jahrhundert gilt und bereits im Titel eine gewisse Ratlosigkeit ausdrückt. Die Architektur war im 19. Jahrhundert ästhetisch in der Krise und sollte erst durch die Moderne im 20. Jahrhundert eine neue Sprache finden. Wagner selbst hatte den Historismus in seinem Eklektizismus kritisiert. Für sein revolutionäres Festspielhaus aber wünschte er sich einen neuen Stil im deutschen Geiste, der noch gar nicht gefunden war.

Wagner schließt sogar seine Rede mit der kühnen Hoffnung, dass sein Festspielhaus *„zur Auffindung eines deutschen Baustiles hingeleitet"* habe. *„Bis zur Ausbildung einer monumentalen architektonischen Ornamentik, welche etwa mit der*

Vision of a German architecture

In his speech at the cornerstone-laying ceremony, Wagner describes building additively and functionally as a genuinely German architecture: *"But it is at the core of the German spirit to build from the inside"* – intending to contrast this style with a *"Welsh"* architecture more interested in facades, superficialities and decoration. (These were the reasons he had to find *"a site other than the Italian-French opera house,"* the Margravial Opera House, for the festival.) Wagner's speech has a very patriotic tone that sounds unbearably chauvinistic for modern ears. Although he denies his desire to build a German national theater in Bayreuth, he still stokes patriotism and even uses it to excuse the imperfection of his Festspielhaus: *"All external forms of the German character"* have been *"provisional"* for centuries.

This verbalizes the search for identity by a nation that had only united a short while before, as well as Wagner's old resentment against France's cultural supremacy, the enemy defeated in 1871. Once again, the biggest proponents of the *"German spirit […] Winkelmann, Lessing, Goethe and, finally, Schiller"* are evoked (not to forget Jean Paul, aka Friedrich Richter), the great classics, the Classicists. At this point, you hope for a statement like, "And for that reason, dear friends, I have chosen to build in Classicist style in the spirit of Winckelmann and all other people who know and admire Greek antiquity, in the spirit of greatest German classicistic architects: Gilly, Schinkel and Klenze because that is German. It is German to recognize the inheritance of antiquity in its deepest truth and it is German to stand up against the pure superficiality of the French or the Italians." But the antiquity so admired in 1849 has been forgotten by 1872/73, classicist architecture means nothing.

Instead, Wagner's speech takes a surprising, wildly bold turn. In addition to financial difficulties, Wagner also sees an aesthetic crisis: *"Even if we had had […] more noble materials at our disposal, we would […] have shied away and looked to others for help, which we surely would hardly have found […] anywhere. For we were facing a brand new, highly specific and, because it could never be attempted before, most difficult task for the architect of the present (or of the future?)."* Put simply, these sentences mean that he wouldn't have known what such a monumental building would have looked like. Wagner was only sure that he didn't want *"to see any outdated ornaments used, so for now we will let our building resemble the most naive simplicity of a temporary shelter."* Now it is understandable why the Festspielhaus is so difficult to categorize stylistically. According to the quotation above, it doesn't have any style at all!

In a study of the architecture of 19th century Historicism published in 1828, architect Heinrich Hübsch (1795 – 1863) asks, "What style should we build in?" Even the title of this foundational study expresses a degree of perplexity. In the 19th century, architecture was in crisis and would only find a new language in the Modernity of the 20th century. Wagner himself criticized the eclecticism of Historicism. He desired a new style in German spirit for his revolutionary Festspielhaus, but that style had not yet been found.

Wagner closes his speech with the bold hope that his Festspielhaus would *"lead the way to the discovery of a German architecture."* *"There is plenty of time to develop a monumental architectural ornamental language that can rival the Renaissance or the Rococo in its richness and diversity […] until the 'Reich' decides to participate in our work. So let our provisional construction, one only gradually reaching monumentality, be a warning to the German world."*

From this perspective, then, the brick walls of the Festspielhaus are only the walls of an unfinished shell that future generations should finish in "German style." This is a truly spontaneous idea that was in no way prepared in anything Wagner wrote. Is it all just rhetoric? Did Wagner just want to capture the interest of the Reich, particularly Bismarck, to drive the financing and ensure the security of his Festspielhaus? Was he stoking a sense of aesthetic pride while really only thinking about

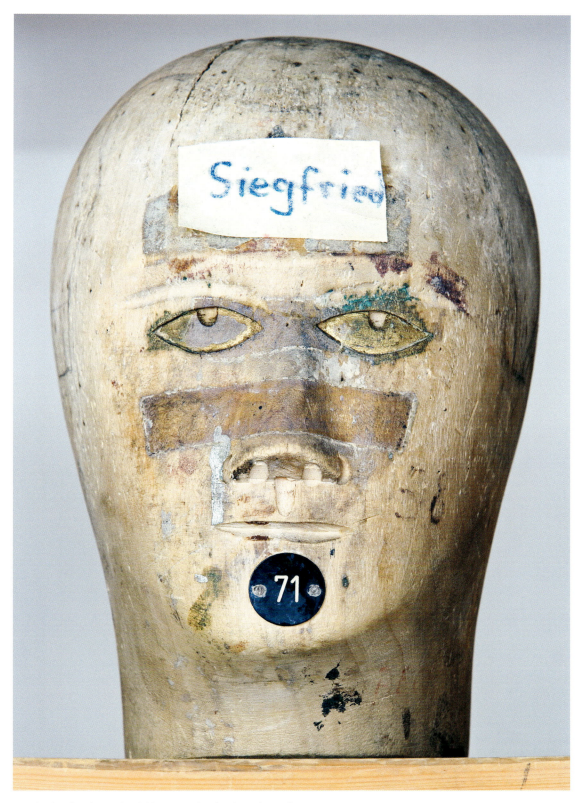

Perückenkopf in der Maskenbildnerei Wig head in the make-up shop

„… wehe dann die Fahne des deutschen edlen Geistes über Deutschland,
an welcher ich webe,
und welche mein herrlicher Siegfried dann hoch über die Länder schwinge."[1]

"… may the flag of the noble German spirit wave above Germany,
the flag which I am weaving
and which my wonderful Siegfried will bear high across the states."

Richard Wagner

Renaissance oder des Rokoko in Reichtum und Mannigfaltigkeit wetteifern sollte, hat es hierbei gemächlich Zeit [...] bis das ‚Reich' sich zur Teilnahme an unserem Werk entschließt. Somit rage unser provisorischer, wohl nur sehr allmählich sich monumentalisierender Bau, für jetzt als ein Mahnzeichen in die deutsche Welt hinein."

In diesem Sinne sind die Backsteinmauern des Festspielhauses also nur Mauern eines unfertigen Rohbaus, den künftige Generationen mit einem „*deutschen Stil*" verkleiden sollen. Eine wahrlich plötzliche Idee, die sich in keiner Weise in den Schriften Wagners vorbereitet hätte – ist das alles nur Rhetorik? Wollte Wagner einfach nur das Interesse des Reichs, namentlich Bismarcks, wecken, um die weitere Finanzierung und Sicherung seines Festspielhauses zu erzwingen, indem er einen ästhetischen Ehrgeiz schürte, doch eigentlich nur das Geld im Sinne hatte? Wagner macht die Not zur Tugend und behauptet frech, dass die „Hässlichkeit" Konzept sei. Wollte er damit provozieren, wusste er doch, dass eine solche Architektur niemandem gefallen konnte, sodass jedem sichtbar würde, dass man diesen Bau weiter fördern und vollenden müsse? Das wäre raffiniert gedacht.

Doch so radikal stellt sich das Bayreuther Festspielhaus nicht dar. Es ist kein seelenloser Betonklotz unserer Zeit und auch keine krude Fabrikhalle mit rohen Mauern. Wenn es als ein absolut reiner Nutzbau errichtet worden wäre, hätte Wagner Architekturgeschichte geschrieben und müsste als Pionier des „International Style" der 20er und 30er des 20. Jahrhunderts gefeiert werden. Aber was ist mit den Schmuckelementen außen wie innen, mit dem antiken Tempeldach und den Akroterien, Voluten, was mit den Renaissanceelementen in schmuckem Haustein, dem dekorativ gezeichneten Fachwerk, mit den korinthischen Säulen im Zuschauersaal und so weiter und so weiter und so weiter? Hatte Wagner selbst nicht richtig hingeschaut? Zumindest hat er während der Bauzeit und nach der Eröffnung des Festspielhauses nie wieder über dessen Architektur geschrieben. Er schaute kaum hin, weil sie in seinen Augen nicht fertig war. Gustav Adolph Kietz[1] überliefert in seinen Erinnerungen, dass Wagner sich die monumentale Vollendung tatsächlich mehr als alles gewünscht hat, doch dies ist freilich nie geschehen.

Architektonische Zukunftsmusik

Der von Wagner so patriotisch geforderte deutsche Baustil blieb auch nach seinem Tode eine unerfüllbare Hoffnung. Auch der mit dem Regierungsantritt von Kaiser Wilhelm II. 1888 zum deutschen Reichsstil erhobene Neobarock wäre für Wagner nicht in Frage gekommen. Noch 1895 plante Cosima Wagner gar eine Verlegung der Festspiele nach Mainz (-Kastell), den „*monumentalen Ausbaues unseres Theaters an dem Punkte, welchen sein Erbauer dafür gedacht hat (nämlich da, wo der Main in den Rhein sich ergießt), mit der Bestimmung, dass, sollten wir noch leben, wir die Festspiele dort veranstalten!"*[2]

Ab 1906 war das Unternehmen Bayreuth entschuldet, die Familie blickte auf ein millionenschweres Vermögen und ein von Wagner gewünschter Ausbau war in den Bereich des Möglichen gerückt. Cosima und Siegfried Wagner jedoch hatten dies offensichtlich zu keiner Zeit betrieben. Siegfried Wagner, selbst studierter Architekt, hätte hier (ab 1908) viel einbringen können: Der Jugendstil hätte dem Bayreuther Festspielhaus eine neue ästhetische Gestalt gegeben, wenn man zum Beispiel einen Ernst Bernhard Sehring (Theater in Cottbus und Bielefeld, Theater des Westens, Berlin) gerufen hätte, um das Festspielhaus in der deutschen, geometrischen Spielart des Jugendstils umzugestalten. Aber auch der Jugendstil war kein genuin deutscher Stil, sondern einer von vielen internationalen Versuchen, sich vom abendländischen Erbe zu befreien und die Architektur zu erneuern.

money? Wagner made a virtue of necessity, brazenly claiming that the "*ugliness*" was concept. Was he being provocative? He knew that no one would like that type of architecture, making it clear to everyone that the building had to be given further support and be completed. That would have been ingenious.

But the Bayreuth Festspielhaus isn't really all that radical. It isn't like the spiritless concrete monstrosities of our time, nor is it a crude manufacturing facility with raw walls. If it had been built as an absolutely pure functional building, Wagner would have written architectural history and would have to be celebrated as the pioneer of the "International Style" of the 1920s and 1930s. But what about the interior and exterior decorative elements, the antique temple roof, the acroteria and volutes? What about the Renaissance elements in ornamental hewn stone, the decoratively positioned timber framing, the Corinthian pillars in the auditorium, etc., etc., etc.? Didn't Wagner himself look closely? At least he never wrote anything further about the architecture of the Festspielhaus during its construction or after it was opened. He barely looked because the architecture was not yet finished. In his memoirs, Gustav Adolph Kietz claims that Wagner really wished more than anything that his theater would be finished in monumental style, but of course this never happened.

Architectural dreams of the future

The German architectural style Wagner so patriotically called for remained an unfulfillable desire even after his death. Even the neo-Baroque, declared the style of the German Reich when Kaiser Wilhelm II took power in 1888, would not have been an option for Wagner. As late as 1895, Cosima Wagner planned to move the festival to Mainz (Kastell), initiating a "*monumental expansion of our theater on the spot which its builder had originally intended (that is, where the Main flows into the Rhine), with the purpose, if we should still be alive, of holding the festivals there!*"

By 1906 the festival organization had paid off its debts and the company possessed an asset worth millions. The expansion Wagner had desired had entered the realm of possibility. However, Cosima and Siegfried Wagner apparently never followed through on this. Siegfried Wagner, a trained architect, could have achieved a lot at this point (from 1908 on). Art Nouveau could have given the Bayreuth Festspielhaus a new aesthetic appearance if, for example, Ernst Bernhard Sehring (theaters in Cottbus and Bielefeld, Theater des Westens in Berlin) had been engaged to redesign the Festspielhaus in the German geometrical variety of Art Nouveau. But Art Nouveau wasn't a genuinely German style, either, but rather one born of numerous international attempts to break free of the western legacy and rejuvenate architecture.

Anbauten aus der Ära Siegfried Wagner (Hinterbühnenmagazin, 1924/25)
Buildings added during Siegfried Wagner's era (back stage repository, 1924/25)

Der Expressionismus von Peter Behrens oder Erich Mendelsohn hingegen war ein typisch deutscher (und niederländischer) Sonderweg, der bekanntlich den roten Backstein sehr schätzte. Doch Siegfried Wagners An- und Umbauten von 1924/25 als Hinterbühnenmagazin für die plastischen Dekorationen des neuen RING (Architekt Franz Rank) zeigen zwar Backsteine (ohne Fachwerk), verraten aber einen konservativen, neoklassizistischen Stil, wie die Fassade des Hinterbühnenhauses von 1924 verrät, mit klassischer Gliederung durch Lisenen und Attikazone und einem neoklassizistischen Tympanon auf toskanischen Säulen. Ein Stil, den auch seine Witwe Winifred in den 1930er Jahren (Baugeschäft Häffner und Keil, Architekt Hans C. Reissinger) weiter pflegte.

Das „Bauhaus", das in Deutschland zu Hause war, so doch einer übernationalen Bewegung, dem „International Style", zuzurechnen ist, findet in dem funktionalistischen Provisorium Brückwalds schon fünfzig Jahre früher durchaus verwandte Ideen. Man kann in diesem „form follows function" und einer ideellen wie intellektuellen Konzeption von Architektur eine typische Mentalität in der deutschen Architekturgeschichte erkennen (B. Neumann, Gilly, Schinkel, Semper und andere), die schließlich im „Bauhaus" gipfelte. Diese Avantgarde war den Nazis in den 1930er Jahre suspekt, nicht zuletzt wegen der vielen jüdischen Architekten, sodass ein eigener nationalsozialistischer Stil kreiert wurde, der freilich sehr undeutsch war und die Architektur des imperialen Roms zum Vorbild nahm. Doch wurde allein in der Nazizeit wirklich über eine Vollendung des Festspielhauses nachgedacht. Emil Rudolf Mewes plante 1940 einen gigantischen Neubau im neoklassizistischen Stil eines Albert Speer. *„Aber glücklicherweise sind Pläne dazu da, dass sie nicht ausgeführt werden"* (Wolfgang Wagner).

The form of Expressionism coined by Peter Behrens or Erich Mendelsohn, however, was a uniquely and typically German (and Dutch) style, which, as is widely known, favored the use of red bricks. But although Siegfried Wagner's additions and modifications for the back stage storehouse for carved decorations for the new RING (architect Franz Rank) from 1924/25 use brick (without timber framing), his constructions adhere to a conservative, neo-Classicist style. The 1924 facade of the back-stage building reveals this style, which his widow Winifred continues to use in the 1930s (construction company Häffner und Keil, architect Hans C. Reissinger).

The "Bauhaus" style at home in Germany was part of a larger, international movement known as the "International Style." Some of its ideas are related to Brückwald's functionalist provisional construct from fifty years earlier. One may recognize an architecture based on "form-follows-function" and a concept based on ideas and intellect as a typical mentality in German architectural history (B. Neumann, Gilly, Schinkel, Semper and others), which reaches a pinnacle in "Bauhaus." The Nazis were suspicious of these avant-gardes in the 1930s for reasons including the large number of Jewish architects. In response, they created their own "National Socialist Style," which was naturally quite un-German, following the architectural models of imperial Rome. Yet the only real thought was given to completing the Festspielhaus during the Nazi period. In 1940, Emil Rudolf Mewes planned a gigantic new building in the neo-Classicist style of an Albert Speer. *"But thankfully plans are there to be not implemented."* (Wolfgang Wagner).

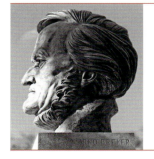

Emil Rudolf Mewes, Modell für einen Neubau 1940
Emil Rudolf Mewes, model for new building, 1940

Wagnerkopf von Arno Breker Wagner bust by Arno Breker

Plakette an der Parkmauer Commemorative plaque at the wall in the park:
„Zum Gedenken an die in der nationalsozialistischen Gewaltherrschaft ermordeten Sängerinnen der Bayreuther Festspiele: Ottilie Metzger, •15.6.1878 Frankfurt/Main, in Bayreuth 1901 – 1911 •1943 Konzentrationslager Auschwitz; Henriette Gottlieb: •1.6.1884 Berlin, in Bayreuth 1927 – 1930 •1943 in unbekanntem Konzentrationslager"

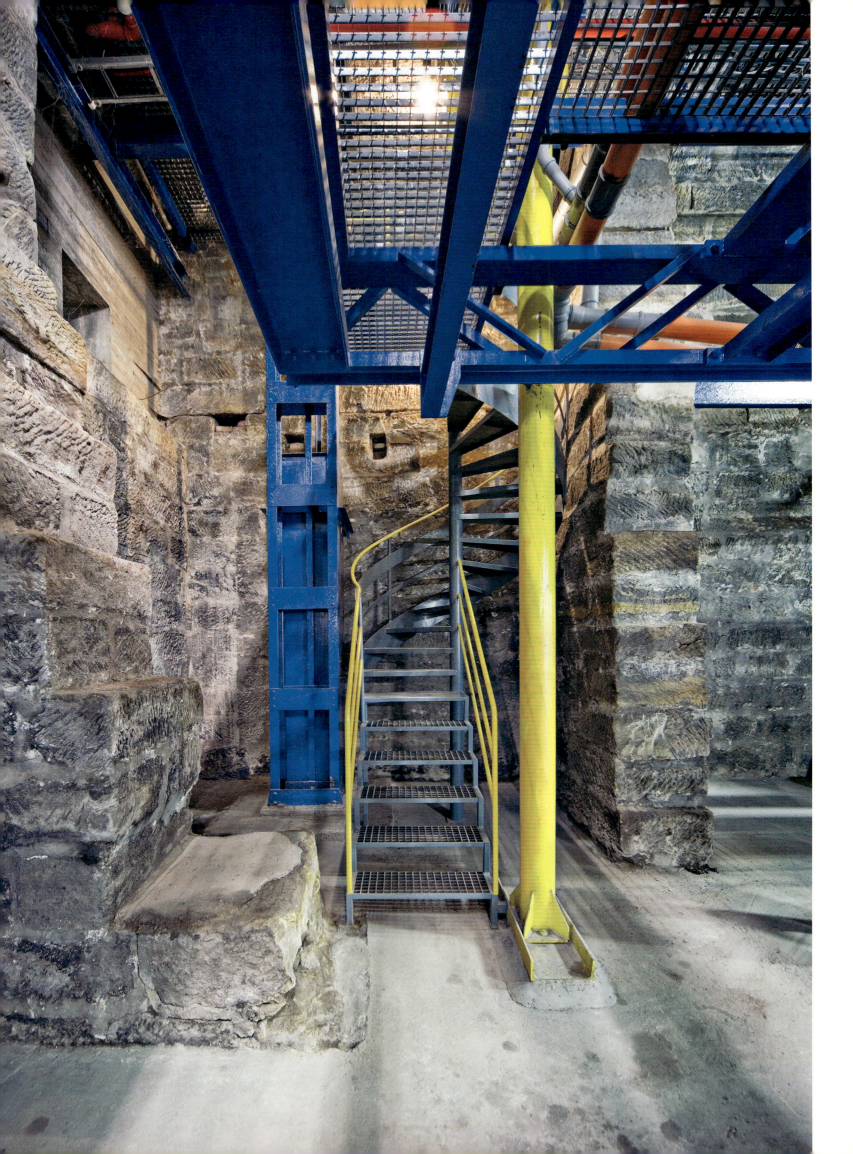

Die Fundamente

Zurück auf die Baustelle und das Jahr 1872. Im April wurde der erste Spatenstich getan und eine riesige Grube ausgehoben. Erdarbeiten kannte Wagner in seinem bisherigen Leben allenfalls von den Beerdigungen seiner so geliebten Hunde. Schon in seiner Pariser Zeit hatte sich Wagner um die letzte Ruhestätte seines Hundes große Sorgen gemacht und versucht, *„die Leiche dem gewöhnlichen Lose gestorbener Hunde in Paris, nämlich auf die Straße geworfen und des Morgens vom Unrathabräumer mit aufgelesen zu werden, zu entziehen"*[1]. Eine eigenhändige Hundebeerdigung ist auch aus seiner Biebricher Zeit überliefert. In Bayreuth kurz vor Baubeginn wurde *„Fitzo von dem Eisenbahnzug gerädert"*[2] und anschließend feierlich begraben, wie Cosima dem großen Philosophen Nietzsche ausführlich berichtet.

Für sich selbst und seine Frau ließ sich Wagner im Garten seiner Villa eine Gruft ausheben. Eines Tages fand man darin Mäuse und anderes Getier, sodass Wagner scherzte: *„Wer sich eine Grube gräbt, dem fallen die andren hinein!"* Sehr zornig allerdings wurde Wagner, als ein Hausangestellter ein Junges seiner Hündin Molli, die dem neuen Bernhardiner mit Namen Fafner verfallen war und ihren alten Wurf verstieß, in jener Grube entsorgen wollte: *„Er rief den Gärtnergehilfen, und dieser zog es vorsichtig mit dem Rechen heraus, wobei es sich denn als unbeschädigt erwies. Wenn er die spielenden Hündchen übereinander liegen sah, verglich er sie dem Amorettenhaufen in der Venusbergszene."*[3]

Bei all den heiteren Anekdoten darf nicht vergessen werden, dass diese Erdarbeiten die endgültigen Fundamente des Gebäudes legten, steinerne Mauern, die heute noch in der Unterbühne des Festspielhauses wie ein archäologischer Befund zu bestaunen sind. Cosima notiert am 19. Juli Juli 1872: *„Furchtbare Grabungsarbeiten; R. sagt mir, die Leute müssen denken, ob der wahnsinnig ist, uns so tief unten hier arbeiten zu lassen, damit er da oben sein Stück aufführt."*[4] Wagner wusste also um seine Verrücktheit: *„Ich baue da in Bayreuth darauf los und weiß nicht, ob wir nicht am Ende stecken bleiben."*[5] Die Bevölkerung Bayreuths jedenfalls war von der Baustelle des Festspielhauses fasziniert, wie ein Zeitgenosse schildert, *„dass ganz Bayreuth wieder heute sich um den ‚Schlund' versammelt hatte und beständig von nichts anderem spräche als von dem Theaterbau"*[6].

Hier im tiefsten Keller des Festspielhauses ereignete sich das allererste musikalische Konzert im Jahr 1873 noch vor Vollendung des Baus. Der Bildhauer Gustav Adolf Kietz (aus Leipzig), in den 1860er Jahren bekannt geworden durch seine Tätigkeit am Luther-Denkmal in Worms, der nun Richard und Cosima modellierte (übrigens ein Bruder des berühmten *„Pinselauswaschers"* Ernst Benedikt, eines Leidensgenossen Wagners in Paris), berichtet 1875 von einem Besuch der Baustelle. Der Bühnenmeister Carl Brandt hatte ihn aufgefordert, sich umzusehen: *„Da bin ich überall herumgekrochen, es war ja alles von höchstem Interesse für mich, auf der Bühne und unter der Bühne, wo ich mit Wagner noch vor zwei Jahren dem ersten Konzert im angefangenen Hause lauschte, nämlich dem der Frösche, die den nassen Untergrund sehr zahlreich bevölkerten, was den Meister höchlichst ergötzte."*[7]

Das alte Fundament der Unterbühne

The foundations

We return to the construction site and the year 1872. In April, the first shovel of dirt is removed and soon a huge hole is dug out. Up until then, Wagner's only experience with dirt had been burying his much-loved dogs. Even when he was living in Paris, he was very concerned about finding an appropriate final resting place for his dog and tried *"to spare the cadaver from the traditional Parisian fate of being tossed into the street and swept up in the morning by the street cleaners."* There is also record of him digging a grave for a dog while he was living in Biebrich. Shortly before construction was begun in Bayreuth, *"Fitzo was run over by the train"* and then formally buried, as Cosima describes in detail to the great philosopher Nietzsche.

Wagner had a grave dug for himself and his wife in the garden of their villa. One day mice and other small animals were discovered inside, leading Wagner to joke *"If you dig yourself a trap, others will fall in!"* Wagner did get really angry when one of the domestic servants used the grave to dispose of one of the puppies of Wagner's dog Molli, who had a case of puppy love for a new St. Bernhard named Fafner and had rejected her litter. *"He called the gardener, who carefully pulled it out and found it unharmed. When he saw the dogs playfully draped all over each other, he compared them with the 'Amorettenhaufen' in the Mt. Venus scene."*

Despite all of these happy-go-lucky anecdotes, it is important to bear in mind that all this digging prepared the foundation for the building, stone walls that can still be awed in the bowels of the Festspielhaus like an archeological dig. On July 19, 1872, Cosima notes: *"Horrible excavation work; R. told me that the people must wonder whether he'd gone crazy digging down so deeply just to be able to perform his works up top."* Wagner apparently knew he was crazy: *"I've simply started to build in Bayreuth without knowing if we'll get stuck in the end."* At least the population of Bayreuth was fascinated by the Festspielhaus building site. One contemporary reports *"that all of Bayreuth has gathered around the 'abyss' again today and talks about nothing but the theater construction the whole day."*

It was here, in the deepest basement of the Festspielhaus, that the very first musical concert took place in 1873, even before the building was complete. Sculptor Adolf Kietz (of Leipzig), who became known in the 1860s for his work on the Luther monument in Worms (and whose brother, incidentally, was the famous *"paintbrush-washer"* Ernst Benedikt, one of Wagner's companions in misfortune in Paris), writes in 1875 about visiting the construction site. The stage master, Carl Brandt invited him to take a look around: *"I crawled around everywhere and found it all incredibly interesting – on the stage and under the stage, where I had heard the very first concert with Wagner shortly after work on the theater had been started – a concert of the multitude of frogs living in the moist cavern. The maestro was absolutely tickled."*

The original foundation of the stage

„Wer sich eine Grube gräbt, dem fallen die andren hinein!"

"If you dig yourself a trap, others will fall in"!

Richard Wagner

Im September 1873 kam ein weiterer Besucher nach Bayreuth. Kietz erzählt: „*Als ich gestern Nachmittag bei meiner Arbeit noch allein war, brachte der Diener Wagners ein Fässchen Bier herein. Ich frug: ‚Was soll das?' und er antwortete: ‚Es kommt Besuch.' Nicht lange darauf kamen Wagner, seine Frau und ein kleiner Herr, den mir Wagner als Herrn Anton Bruckner, Komponisten aus Wien vorstellte.*" Es wurde viel getrunken. Habel erzählt, dass während dieses Besuchs auch die Baustelle besichtigt wurde: „*Bruckner unterhielt sich in seiner volkstümlichen Art mit Erdarbeitern und Maurern; bei seiner sehr gründlichen Besichtigung der Baustelle stürzte er rücklings in einen leeren Mörteltrog.*"[1]

Für das Zuschauerhaus wurde das Fundament dagegen nicht so solide ausgeführt, sondern, nach einer Aussage Wolfgang Wagners, teilweise mit ungebrannten Ziegeln unterlegt, was dazu führte, dass ein Teil des Zuschauerraums im Laufe der Zeit absank und heute noch einen deutlichen Knick aufweist.

Ähnliche Verschiebungen sind im Foyer – an den Pfeilerstützen neben dem Gedenkstein – zu erkennen. In den nicht unterkellerten Foyers ruhten die Stützbalken auf der blanken Erde, der rechte Balken neben dem Gedenkstein ist um einige Zentimeter abgesunken. Viele Pfeiler des Foyers waren am Fuß verfault und mussten noch vor den Sanierungen der 1990er Jahre solide mit Kunststoff ausgegossen werden.

Bereits am 30. November 1873 hatten Zeitungen darüber berichtet, „*das Theater habe sich gesenkt*"[2], was von den Wagners als Lüge und Verleumdung aufgefasst wurde. „*Mich*", so Wolfgang Wagner in einem Gespräch, „*hätte man damals nicht so bescheißen können.*" Doch Richard Wagner war kein guter Bauherr, wie er einmal selbst am 12. April 1872 in einem Brief zugab: „*Anders ist es, wenn man mit Bauleuten, Zimmerleuten, Holz, Leinwand, Blech, Pinseln und Maschinen zu tun hat: da habe ich keine Macht, sondern muss nur anordnen und befehlen können.*"[3] Brückwald war nicht immer vor Ort und hatte den unerfahrenen 23-jährigen Carl Runckwitz aus Altenburg als Bauleiter bestellt (womit mit Brandt und Brückwald die Altenburger Skatrunde komplett war).

Langsam nahm der Bau Gestalt an. Wagner erschrak selbst darüber, dass seine Vision nun Wirklichkeit wurde: „*R. geht zum Theaterplatz, kommt sehr ergriffen davon heim, erhaben nehme sich die Anlage aus, nun sei er verpflichtet, nun sei er nicht mehr frei, gebunden sei er, seine Phantasie und der Glaube einzelner habe dies hervorgebracht, er könne nun nicht mehr zurück. Er ist sehr ernst. Um 5 1/2 Uhr zünden wir den Baum an.*"[4] Am 15. Dezember 1872 war die Unterbühne ausgemauert und die Fundamente der Bühnentürme standen bis auf halbe Höhe. Ähnlich empfindet Cosima am 5. Juli 1873: „*Ein Gefühl von Angst, das ich nicht beschreiben kann, überfällt mich, wie ich das riesige Gerüst sehe und den breiten Zuschauerraum! So lange die Idealität bloß in uns lag, erschrak mich ihr Abstand von der Realität nicht, nun aber, da sie geformt vor uns ist, erschreckt mich die Kühnheit, mir erscheint dann alles wie ein Grab (Pyramiden!).*"[5]

In September of 1873, someone else visited Bayreuth. Kietz writes: "*When I was alone at work yesterday afternoon, Wagner's servant brought in a bottle of beer. I asked 'What's this about?' and he answered: 'Company is coming.' Shortly thereafter, Wagner, his wife and a short man Wagner introduced as Mr. Anton Bruckner, a composer from Vienna, came in.*" The alcohol flowed freely. According to Habel, the visit also included a tour of the construction site, during which "*Bruckner was conversing in his down-to-earth manner with excavation workers and masons when he tumbled backwards into an empty mortar trough.*"

The foundation below the auditorium was built less solidly. According to Wolfgang Wagner, even unbaked bricks were used. As a result, part of the auditorium sank over time so that a clear "dip" is noticeable today.

There is other evidence of settling in the foyer – on the pillar blocks adjacent to the commemoration stone. In the foyer, which does not have a cellar, the supporting beams were resting on bare earth, such that beam on the right, next to the memorial stone, had sunk several centimeters. Many of the pillars of the foyer had decayed at the base and had to be solidly cast in synthetics before restoration in the 1990s.

There were reports about this in the newspaper as early as 30 November 1873: "*The theater is reported to have sunk down,*" which the Wagners interpreted as lies and slander. In an interview with Wolfgang Wagner, he said, "*You couldn't have pulled that on me back then.*" But Richard Wagner was not a good builder, as he admitted in a letter on April 12, 1872: "*Dealing with builders, carpenters, wood, canvas, tin, brushes and machines is different – in that world I have no power, but rather only have to be capable of requesting and ordering.*" Brückwald was not always on site and had engaged the 23-year-old rookie Carl Runckwitz from Altenburg as construction manager (completing the Altenburger Skat group including Brandt and Brückwald).

The building was slowly taking shape. It shook Wagner up to witness his vision becoming reality: "*R. walked over to the theater site, returning home very moved. The theater gives a lofty impression. He says now he's committed, he's no longer free, he's tied down, his fantasy and individuals' belief have created this, there's no turning back now. He was very serious. We lit the tree at 5:30.*" On December 15, 1872 the sub-stage walls were finished and the stage tower foundation was halfway up. On July 5, 1873, Cosima expresses similar sentiments: "*A feeling of fear that I can't describe takes hold of me whenever I see the huge frame and the expansive auditorium! As long as the ideal was only inside us, I was not overwhelmed by its distance from reality. But now that it is taking form in front of us, I am taken aback at the audaciousness, and everything appears like a grave (pyramids!) to me.*"

Mörteltrog 1965
Mortar trough, 1965

Der hauseigene Brunnen in der Unterbühne (Foto von 1999)
The theater's own well below the stage (1999 photograph)

Knick im Gemäuer aufgrund schlechter Fundamente des Zuschauerhauses
Dip in the wall due to poor foundation under auditorium

Rechts neben dem Gedenkstein im Foyer die abgesenkte Stütze
The sunken pillar block to the right of the commemoration stone

Das Richtfest
1873

Am 2. August 1873 erfolgte das Richtfest, die Vollendung der von den Zimmerleuten errichteten Holzkonstruktion. Wagner wollte nicht als Bauherr gefeiert werden und dichtete deshalb noch schnell ein Gedicht auf den „deutschen Geist", ehe man sich am Nachmittag zur Baustelle begab. „*Zum ersten Mal wird ein Theater für eine Idee und für ein Werk aufgeführt, sagt der Vater*"[1], zitiert Cosima ihren Vater Franz Liszt und hebt hervor, dass dabei „*wirkliche Arbeitersleute sich einfinden und schlicht grüßen und dazu die letzten Hammerstöße erschallen*". Wagner hatte ein gutes Verhältnis zu seinen Arbeitern, den Handwerkern im Allgemeinen, und wird auf dem Fest wie Hans Sachs im dritten Aufzug der MEISTERSINGER zum „Spruchsprecher"[2]:

Nun setzen wir auf's Haus das Dach;
bewahr es Gott vor Sturz und Krach!
Laß' ich jetzt den Bauherrn leben,
welchen Namen soll ich ihm geben?
Ob Wagner, oder seine Patrone,
oder gar der im Lande trägt die Krone?
Der sich als besten Bauherrn erweis't,
es lebe, so ruf' ich, der deutsche Geist! Hoch!

Zum Hebefest, das hoch oben im Dachstuhl stattfand, schrieb Wagner das folgende, ausführliche Gedicht, ganz im Stile des Meistersangs gereimt, ein eher unbekanntes Werk des Meisters, worin er das Chaos während der Bauzeit parodiert und sogar enthüllt, wer letztlich die Pläne zu seinem Theater gezeichnet hat[3].

„Sollt' ich euch nach rechtem Gewichte danken,
ich glaub', unter der Wucht müßte der Dachstuhl schwanken:
damit wir aber Alle unversehrt bleiben,
sag' ich nur ohne jed' Übertreiben,
dass ich wohl Bescheid davon weiß,
was ich verdank' eurem redlichen Fleiß.
Jetzt haben wir Alle zwar gut Lachen,
da hoch in der Luft wir uns lustig können machen:
als wir aber noch tief im Erdboden staken,
da hatte das Ding manch' schlimmen Haken;
da hieß es: was graben denn die dort unten?
Wird dort der Stein der Weisen gefunden?
Den ließen wir liegen; doch Mauersteine
stemmten wir auf zum festen Gebeine,
darauf in die Luft wir hoch
uns schwangen aus dem tiefen Loch.
Die Zimmerer mit ihren langen Stöcken
die mussten das Gerüst in die Höhe recken,
darauf wir nun stehen und weithin schauen,
uns zu bedenken, was noch zu bauen.
Verstehn's noch nicht Alle, doch Ein's ist gewiß:
das Ding geht nach einem sich'ren Plan und Riß.
Ihr ließ't sie leben, die beide erdacht;
doch wissen's sie selber kaum, wer sie gemacht.
Ganz richtig zwar that jeder das Seine,

The topping-out ceremony
1873

The topping-out ceremony took place on August 2, 1873, marking the completion of the carpentry work on the wood frame construction. Wagner did not wish to be celebrated as builder, and so quickly wrote a poem to the *"German spirit"* before they walked over to the construction site. Cosima quotes her father Franz Liszt: *"Father called this the first time a theater is built for an idea and a work,"* emphasizing that the *"real workers gather and greet each other politely while the last nails are pounded."* Wagner had a good relationship with his workers and with the handicraftsmen in general, and took his position as "spokesman" like Hans Sachs in Act 3 of DIE MEISTERSINGER:

Now we are putting a roof on the house;
may God shield it from storms and collapse!
I raise a toast to the builder,
what name shall I give him?
Perhaps Wagner or his benefactor,
or even he who wears the crown in this land?
The one who proves the best builder,
I toast to the German spirit! Here, here!

Wagner wrote the following long poem for the topping-out ceremony that took place high up in the truss. Like the poem quoted above, this poem also rhymes in the style of the Mastersingers. It is one of the maestro's little-known works in which he parodies the chaos of the construction period and even reveals who drew up the final plans to his theater.

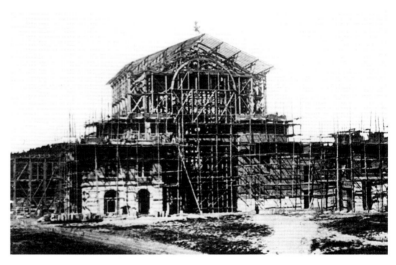

Aufnahme vom 2. August 1873
Photograph from August 2, 1873

Sanierung des Dachstuhls des Bühnenhauses und Austausch der Holz- durch eine Stahlkonstruktion 1964/65.
Renovation of the roof truss of the stage building and replacing the wooden frame with iron, 1964/65.

und daß ihr gleich seht, wie die Sach' ich meine, –
ohne den Brückwald, seinen Riß und Plan,
kamen wir sicher nicht auf dieß Gerüst heran.
Betrachtet's genau: das war eine Kunst,
solch' Werk wächst nicht aus Nebel und Dunst!
Ich glaub', daß keine deutsche Stadt
solch' kühnen Zimmerbau aufzuweisen hat.
Der kam vom Papier nun auf das tiefe Loch,
meint man, er wär' draus herausgewachsen doch!
Wie kamen wir heraus aus Lehmen und Koth?
's half Einer dem Andern, und Allen die Noth:
und war's nicht ein Helfer, so war es ein Hölfel,
dem Zimmermeister Weiß half der Maurermeister Wölfel.
Das alles ist klar, und Jedermann weiß es; doch bedarf's
noch immer eines Beweises, wie das Alles mit rechten
Dingen zuging,
daß man hier solchen Baues sich unterfing.
Die Sache hat einen dunklen Grund,
gleich dem, auf dem dieß Gerüst entstund:
nun ihr aus dem Grund es heraufgebracht,
so sag' ich euch auch, wer den Plan gemacht.
Mag wer will Teufelswerk drin erschauen,
ich sag's: den Plan entwarf – das Vertrauen!
Ein tief unergründlich deutsches Verlangen
sollt' wieder einmal zum Vertrauen gelangen:
es vertraute Einer auf deutsches Wesen;
nun hört, ob er damit unglücklich gewesen!
In langen Jahren schuf er sein Werk:
ihm gab das Vertrauen Kraft und Stärk':
und daß er sein Werk getrost vollende,
reicht' ein König ihm selbst die Hände.
Im Bayerischen Frankenland
bot ihm der Bürger nun auch die Hand;
und hatt' er auf sich selbst vertraut,
Vertrauen nun auch das Haus ihm baut,
darin sein Werk aus seinem Plan
nun deutlich auch tret' an die Welt heran. –
Drum sag' ich, der Grund, auf dem wir bauten,
ist, daß mir Bayreuths Bürger vertrauten.
Und das ist nicht nur so bildlich gesprochen:
der Grund, in den wir dieß Loch gebrochen,
das ist Bayreuther Grund und Boden;
den sollten wir dießmal nicht ausroden,
sondern mit solchen Kunstbäumen bepflanzen,
die wir umzäunen zu einem festen Ganzen,
darin der Welt sich bald solle zeigen,
was deutsches Vertrauen sich schaffe zum Eigen.
Und will ich euch allen Helfern nun danken,
so faß' ich Alles in einen Gedanken,
der Alles, was ich jetzt sagte,
und kühn anzudeuten wagte,
wie ein edles Bild im festen Rahmen,
einschließt in einen Namen:
ich denke, keiner von euch es bereut,
ruft er mit mir: – es lebe Bayreuth!"

Abstract

The burden of expressing the thanks you all deserve for your hard work would cause this truss to sway, so I must trim it down. We are all in good spirits because we're high up in the air, but there were tough moments when we were digging out the earth. They wondered whether we were digging to find the Stone of Wisdom, but instead we were putting in a stone foundation so we could cast ourselves out of that hole. The carpenters wielded their poles to stretch the frame up high. From this vantage point, you can still see how much there is to be built. But no worries, we are progressing according to a concrete plan. It was you who brought the plans to life barely knowing who designed them. While it is true that everyone, even I, did their part, if it hadn't been for Brückwald, we would not be standing up here. It's a great achievement. A building doesn't just spring up out of the fog. No other German city has such a bold construction. How did we make it leap from the paper and grow out of the hole? One person helped the other, and necessity helped us all. The masons helped the carpenter, that's clear, but how did it even come to be that we are building this? Its reason is as dark as the earth on which it was built, and since you raised the building, I'll tell you who drew up its plans. Some may say the Devil was involved, but I say it was trust! A deep unexplainable German desire should evolve into trust. One person trusted in the German character, creating his work over years. Trust gave him strength to complete his work, and even a king offered his hand. The citizens of Bavarian Franconia offered him their hands, too. And Trust built him a theater where he can share his plan with the world. And so I tell you, the rock on which this building stands is the trust that Bayreuth's citizens have shown me. And I do not mean this figuratively, this is Bayreuth's land. This time, let's not dig it out, but rather plant it with trees of art and make it a whole to show the whole world what German trust is capable of. In thanks to all of you helpers, I'll summarize it in one thought, a thought that frames all I have said in one name: I doubt any of you will regret cheering with me, Long Live Bayreuth!

Modell des Festspielhauses und seiner originalen Nebengebäude von Georg Steingräber (1888)
Model of Festspielhaus and the other buildings in the original complex by Georg Steingräber (1888)

Bewahr es Gott vor Sturz und Krach!

Am 29. September 1873 musste der erste schwere Unfall auf der Baustelle beklagt werden, Cosima berichtet, *„dass ein Arbeiter vom hohen Gerüst des Theaters herab gefallen und tot gefunden worden sei. Sehr trauriger Eindruck – […] nun ist es da und wird schweigsam [als] Zeichen empfangen."*[1] Wenige Tage später: *„R. besucht das Theater, kehrt schweigsam heim, die Leute werden mit dem Rohbau nicht fertig! Der herabgestürzte Arbeiter ist nicht gestorben, aber sehr verstümmelt."*[2] Am Vormittag noch hatte Wagner einen Traum erzählt, *„dass er in seinem Theater wäre und von der Fürstengalerie den ganzen schönen fertigen Raum überblickte. ‚Wie uns wohl zumute sein wird, wenn es zur Aufführung kommt?' fragt er."*[3] Solche Unfälle machten die Realität deutlich und schürten natürlich auch die Ängste und den Pessimismus, der die Wagners während der ganzen Bauzeit begleitete. Am 25. Dezember 1875 sollte ein Maurer tatsächlich zu Tode stürzen.

Vollendet das ewige Werk

Der Außenbau näherte sich Ende des Jahres 1873 seiner Vollendung. Cosima beschreibt am 24. September die von ihr als schön empfundene Fachwerkarchitektur: *„Herrliche Ausschmückung angegeben durch die Balkenkragungen, welche einfach übermalt werden, eine förmlich primitive Kunst ist damit gewonnen; keine willkürliche Ornamentik, die Ziegelsteine geben das Rot an. Die Balken die Linien, welche gelb angestrichen wie Gold in der Sonne glänzen."* Und fügt in einer romantischen Ergriffenheit hinzu: *„Wie ein Märchen steht das Ding da in der plumpen Wirklichkeit."*[4]

Friedrich Nietzsche erzählt von einem Besuch einer Delegation der Wagnervereine am 1. November 1873: *„Der Bau sieht viel schöner und proportionierter aus, als wir nach den Plänen vermuten."*[5] Einer der Delegierten, Dr. Adolf Stern, bestätigt, dass alles *„im Rohbau vollendet"*[6] sei. Ein offizieller Abschluss der Bauarbeiten am Äußeren findet sich in den Quellen nicht, doch Otto Brückwald schreibt am 18. Dezember 1874: *„Zur Zeit ist der Bau im Äußeren ganz, im Inneren nahezu ganz vollendet und man ist gegenwärtig hauptsächlich mit der Einrichtung der Bühne beschäftigt."*[7] Das ewige Werk wird erst zur Eröffnung der Festspiele 1876 vollendet.

May God shield it from storms and collapse!

On September 29, 1873, the first serious injury was reported. Cosima writes *"that a worker is said to have fallen from a high platform in the theater and had been found dead. Very saddening […] now it has happened and is being silently taken [to be a] sign."* A few days later *"R. visited the theater and returned deep in thought, the workers aren't managing to finish the frame! The fallen worker did not die, but was seriously maimed."* In the late morning Wagner had told her about a dream *"that he was in his theater looking out over the whole complete hall from the Prince's gallery. He asked, 'What will it be like when there is actually a performance?'"* Accidents like these bring reality into focus and fuel the fears and the pessimism that accompanied the Wagners throughout the entire construction period. On December 25, 1875 a mason would actually fall to his death.

The eternal work is complete

By the end of 1873, the exterior was nearly finished. On September 24, Cosima describes the timber framing she finds so beautiful: *"The beam collars provide wonderful decoration and can be simply painted over, creating a simple primitive art; no arbitrary ornaments, the bricks determine the red, the beams the lines that are painted yellow and shine like gold in the sun."* She adds with romantic emotionality: *"It stands there in raw reality like a fairy tale."*

Friedrich Nietzsche tells of a visit from a delegation from the Wagner Societies on November 1, 1873: *"The building looks much more beautiful and better proportioned than we would guess from the plans."* A member of the delegation, Dr. Adolf Stern, confirms that everything *"in the frame is complete."* There is no official conclusion to the exterior construction work in the sources, but Otto Brückwald writes on December 18, 1874: *"The building's exterior is finished and its interior is nearly complete. The main focus at the moment is on building the stage."* The eternal work would be finally completed in time for the opening of the festival in 1876.

Blick in den Dachstuhl des Zuschauerhauses mit Balken und Brettern der ursprünglichen Zimmermannsarbeit von 1876
View into the truss of the auditorium with beams and planks from the original carpentry work of 1876

Der liebliche Hügel

Auch wenn vielen Festspielgästen heute oder anno dazumal die Architektur des „Wagner-Theaters" nicht gefällt, von der Lage war und ist fast jeder angetan. G. A. Kietz zum Beispiel schwärmt: *„Schon die Lage dieser neuen Kunststätte macht sicher auf jeden einen weltentrückenden, weihevollen Eindruck."*[1] Cosima, in ihrem Urteil freilich etwas voreingenommen, spazierte zwischen 1872 und 1876 unzählige Male mit der Familie oder mit Gästen auf den Hügel und erfreute sich an der schönen Lage: *„Spaziergang mit R. und den Kindern durch die Wiesen, das Theater in voller Pracht erblickt."*[2] Oder: *„Bei schönem Sonnenschein erblicken wir das Theater, das sich mächtig erhebt, in der Ferne. Schöner großer Eindruck."*[3] Und: *„Mit den Kindern nach dem Theater und der Bürgerreuth, freundlicher Blick, das Land gefällt uns immer mehr, möchte es eine freundliche Heimat für die Kinder werden! Mir ist es, als ob ich nicht mehr recht lebte und nur noch träumte, so wunschlos fühle ich mich für mich."*[4]

Andererseits wird der Hügel auch als Leidensberg empfunden: *„Ich wandere am Nachmittag zum Theater, es mit Ernst, ja Kummer zu betrachten!"*[5] Am Karfreitag des Jahres 1874 *„besteigen wir den Hügel, der auch ein Leidensberg für uns ist"*[6]. Diese fast religiöse Assoziation wiederholt sich in einem Ausspruch der sehr katholisch erzogenen, inzwischen zum Protestantismus konvertierten Cosima, der die „ärmliche" Holzarchitektur aufgreift: *„Das Theater begrüßt! Dem andren Theater in der Welt Marmor und kostbaren Schmuck, dir, dem Erhabenen gewidmet, Holz und Ziegel, ich gedenke der Krippe unseres Heilandes!"*[7]

Die exponierte Lage auf einem Hügel hat in der Kulturgeschichte natürlich eine große Tradition und lässt an die Bergheiligtümer früherer Kulturen denken oder an die alten Griechen, die ihre Tempel auf ihre Akropolis bauten. Kirchen sind außer Wallfahrts- und Wehrkirchen eher selten auf Bergen oder Hügeln zu finden. Auch hätte sich Wagner gegen einen Vergleich seines Theaters mit einer christlichen Weihestätte gewehrt. Seine bösen Kritiker griffen diesen Vergleich jedoch gerne auf, um ihr eigenes Leiden an einer von ihnen unverstandenen Musik auszudrücken: *„All diese Sachen in Wagnerscher Manier singen hören zu müssen, breitspurig, in endloser Melodie, die keine Melodie ist, unterbrochen und begleitet von unzähligen Motiven, Tonmalereien und Orchestersätzchen, jede Möglichkeit ausgeschlossen, einen Satz verstehen zu können, ist das Grausamste, was einem Menschen zugemutet werden kann. In solchen Stunden kommen über den Hörer alle Leiden der Märtyrer auf einmal und man begreift, wie man den Wagnerhügel mit einem Golgatha und Calvarienberg vergleichen konnte."*[8]

The pleasant hill

Even if many festival guests don't like the architecture of the "Wagner Theater" these days or at any time, almost everyone loves its location. For example, G. A. Kietz praises it, saying, *"The location of this new artistic center alone makes it seem far removed from the world and consecrated."* Although her opinion is understandably somewhat partial, Cosima took frequent walks to the hill with her family or with guests between 1872 and 1876 and always enjoyed the beautiful location: *"Took a walk with R. and the children across the fields, saw the theater in all its glory."* Or: *"We saw the theater on this sunny day rising up powerfully in the distance. Wonderful grand impression."* And: *"Walked to the theater and the Bürgerreuth with the children, pleasant view, we like the area more and more. May it become a friendly home for the children! It feels as though I am no longer really living and am only dreaming – that's how few desires I have for myself."*

Sometime, however, the hill is experienced as a mountain of suffering: *"I walked over to the theater in the afternoon, looking at it full of seriousness, even sorrow!"* On Good Friday in 1874 *"we climbed up the hill, our mountain of suffering."* Cosima, who was raised a strict catholic and had by this time converted to Protestantism, brings up this almost religious association in reference to the *"humble"* wooden architecture: *"Hail, o theater! Other theaters in the world boast marble and valuable decoration while you, dedicated to the sublime, wood and brick – Our Savior's manger comes to mind!"*

Naturally, the exposed location on a hilltop has a long tradition in the history of cultures. Consider early cultures' sanctuaries on top of the mountain, or the ancient Greeks, who built their temples on the Acropolis. With the exception of those built for pilgrimage or defense, churches are seldom built on the top of mountains or hills. Certainly Wagner would have objected to having his theater compared with a consecrated Christian site. His ill-intending critics frequently made such comparisons to express their suffering at hearing music they didn't understand: *"Having to hear such things sung in Wagnerian style – dense, in an endless melody that isn't a melody at all, interrupted and accompanied by countless motifs, tonal paintings and orchestral interludes, without the faintest hope of understanding a sentence – that is that most horrible thing you can expect a person to endure. At times like that, the listener can't help but think about the martyrs and suddenly the comparison between Wagner's hill and Golgatha and Mount Calvary is completely comprehensible."*

> *„Und draußen auf einem Hügel vor der Stadt haben sie ein eigenes Gebäude errichtet, um dort die Orgien der musikalischen Neuromantik zu feiern."*[8]
>
> *"They've constructed a building on a hill on the outskirts of the town to hold their musical neo-Romantic orgies."*
>
> Albert Lavignac, 1897

Auffahrt zum Hügel in den 1920er und 1930er Jahren mit geänderter Verkehrsführung
Approach to the hill in the 1920s and 1930s with revised traffic management

DER AUSSENBAU

Theoretisch gut präpariert und mit der Baugeschichte vertraut, lässt sich nun der Außenbau mit neuem Interesse anschauen, wobei eine grobe Gliederung für Klarheit sorgen soll: die Betrachtung einer eher nördlich anmutenden Architektur, die sich durch Fachwerk und Backsteine artikuliert, und einer mehr südlich wirkenden Bauweise, die sich durch Zitate aus Antike und Renaissance präsentiert.

Bei diesen Betrachtungen sollte man sich vom Meister selbst nicht irritieren lassen. Denn dieser hat sein Provisorium, die Baracke, die Bretterbude selbst kaum richtig angeschaut. Das musste den armen Otto Brückwald und all die qualifizierten Handwerker, die dieses *„Qualhall"* errichtet hatten, im Nachhinein sehr kränken. Diese Bauleute und vor allem Brückwald verdienen jedoch eine stärkere Würdigung, wie auch die aufwendigen Sanierungs- und Restaurierungsmaßnahmen der letzten fünfzig Jahre, die sich im Großen wie in vielen Details um die Wiederherstellung eines Originalzustands bemüht haben.

Die Pausen in Bayreuth sind lang, wie auch die oft nur schwer zu füllende (vor allem kartenlose) Zeit im *„kleinen, abgelegenen, unbeachteten Bayreuth"*. Eine ausführliche Baubeschreibung und Analyse des keineswegs so kunst- und zierlosen Gebäudes können durchaus neue Anregungen geben und den (in anderem Zusammenhang geäußerten) Satz Wagners widerlegen: *„Oh, wie schrecklich! ich mag nicht hinsehen!"*[1]

Der Fachwerkbau

Theater-Scheune auf dem Hügel

Das Wort „Scheune" ist sicherlich das häufigste „Kompliment", das der Architektur des Festspielhauses zuteil geworden ist. Wagners Hofbiograf Carl Friedrich Glasenapp spricht noch sehr höflich von einem Gebäude, das *„trotz des einfachen Materials, roter Ziegel mit Fachwerk, mit imponierender Majestät dem Hinaufwandelnden entgegenschaut"*[2], während sein weit kritischerer Nachfolger Martin Gregor-Dellin von einer *„roten Theater-Scheune auf dem Hügel"*[3] spricht. Scheunenviertel wurden wegen Brandgefahr übrigens überall vor den Toren einer Stadt errichtet.

Bereits die Zeitgenossen urteilten ähnlich, wie ein anonymer Franzose 1875: *„Es ist groß, einförmig, kalt und hässlich wie eine ungeheure Scheune oder eine mächtige Feldbaracke."*[4] Ein anderer erkennt ebenfalls einen landwirtschaftlichen Nutzbau, ein *„Fourragemagazin"*[5]. Wagner selbst spricht am 8. November 1878 gar von einer *„Baracke"*[6].

Wagner hatte schon einmal Theater in einer echten bäuerlichen Scheune erlebt, als Gymnasiast auf einer Wanderung durch Sachsen: *„[...] wo wir [...] in einer großen Scheune übernachteten, trafen wir ein großes Puppentheater mit Marionetten von fast menschlicher Größe an."*[7] Seine Freunde amüsierten sich laut, zum Unmut des „naiven Publikums", und Wagner nahm Partei für die Bauern. Eine weitere Begegnung mit einer echten Bäuerin erlebte Wagner einmal auf dem Festspielhügel selbst: *„R. [...] geht zum Theater hinaus und begegnet dort einer Bauernfrau, mit welcher er sich heiter unterhält, er spricht ihr von dem schlechten langen Weg, den sie zurückzulegen hat bis zu ihrem Dorf, ‚ach! lieber Herr, wenn man den 30 Jahre lang jeden Tag zu machen hat, denkt man nicht mehr, ob er schlecht oder gut ist'."*[8]

THE EXTERIOR

Theoretically well prepared and with an understanding of the construction history, we can now focus on the exterior with new attention. For the sake of clarity, our discussion will be roughly structured between aspects of the architecture with a northern feel articulated by timber framing and brick, and those aspects with a more southern aura presented in quotations from antiquity and the Renaissance.

During this examination, we should not let ourselves get pulled off track by the maestro himself, who barely took a good look at his provisional building, his barrack, his wood plank hut. That must have angered poor Otto Brückwald and all of the other qualified craftsmen once they finished erecting this *"Qualhall"* (Hall of torment). Yet these builders, and especially Brückwald, deserve far more recognition. The extensive renovation and restoration efforts during the last fifty years have attempted to restore the building to its original condition, both on a large scale and in detail.

The intermissions in Bayreuth are long, and it is not always easy to fill the time in *"small, far off, unnoticed Bayreuth"* (especially if you don't have tickets). A detailed description of the building and an analysis of this in no way artless or plain building could possibly provide new impulses and contradict a statement Wagner made (in a different context): *"Oh, how awful! I don't want to look!"*

The half-timbered building

The theater barn on the hill

The word "barn" is surely the most frequent "compliment" given to the architecture of the Festspielhaus. Wagner's personal biographer, Carl Friedrich Glasenapp, describes it relatively politely as a building that *"greets those approaching with impressive majesty despite simple materials, red bricks and timber framing,"* while his far more critical successor, Martin Gregor-Dellin, calls it the *"red theater barn on the hill."* Incidentally, barn districts were built outside the city gates all over the world because they were fire hazards.

Even contemporaries had a similar opinion. An anonymous Frenchman writes in 1875: *"It is big, monotonous, cold and ugly – like a huge barn or a vast field barrack."* Another also sees in it an agricultural functional building, a *"fourragemagazin."* Wagner himself even used the term *"barrack"* on November 8, 1878.

Wagner once experienced theater in an actual farmer's barn when he was an upper level pupil on a hike through Saxony: *"[...] where we [...] spent the night in a big barn and happened on a big puppet theater with practically life-sized marionettes."* Wagner's friends were boisterously amused, to the consternation of the "naive audience," while Wagner himself stood up for the farmers. Wagner had another contact with an actual farmer's wife on the festival hill itself: *"R. [...] walked over to the theater and ran into a farmer's wife. They conversed and he mentioned the long, bad path she took to walk to her village. 'Oh, dear sir, if you have to walk along that path every day for 30 years, you don't think much about whether it's bad or good.'"*

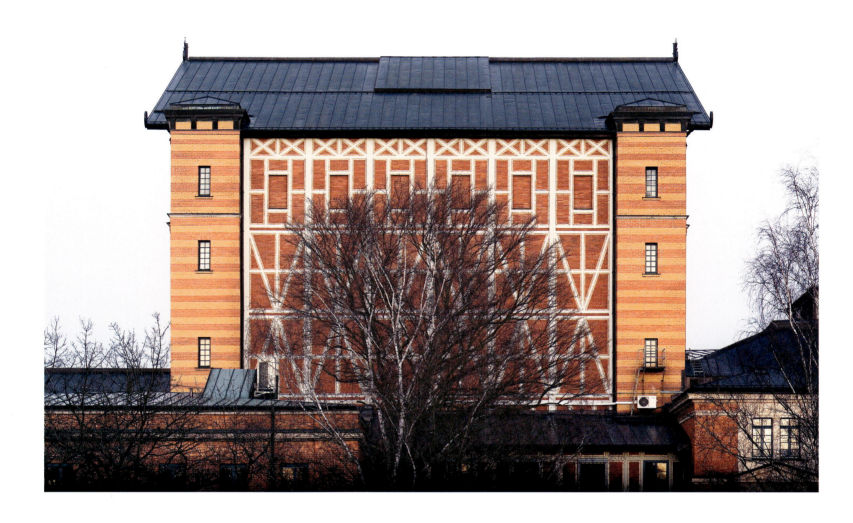

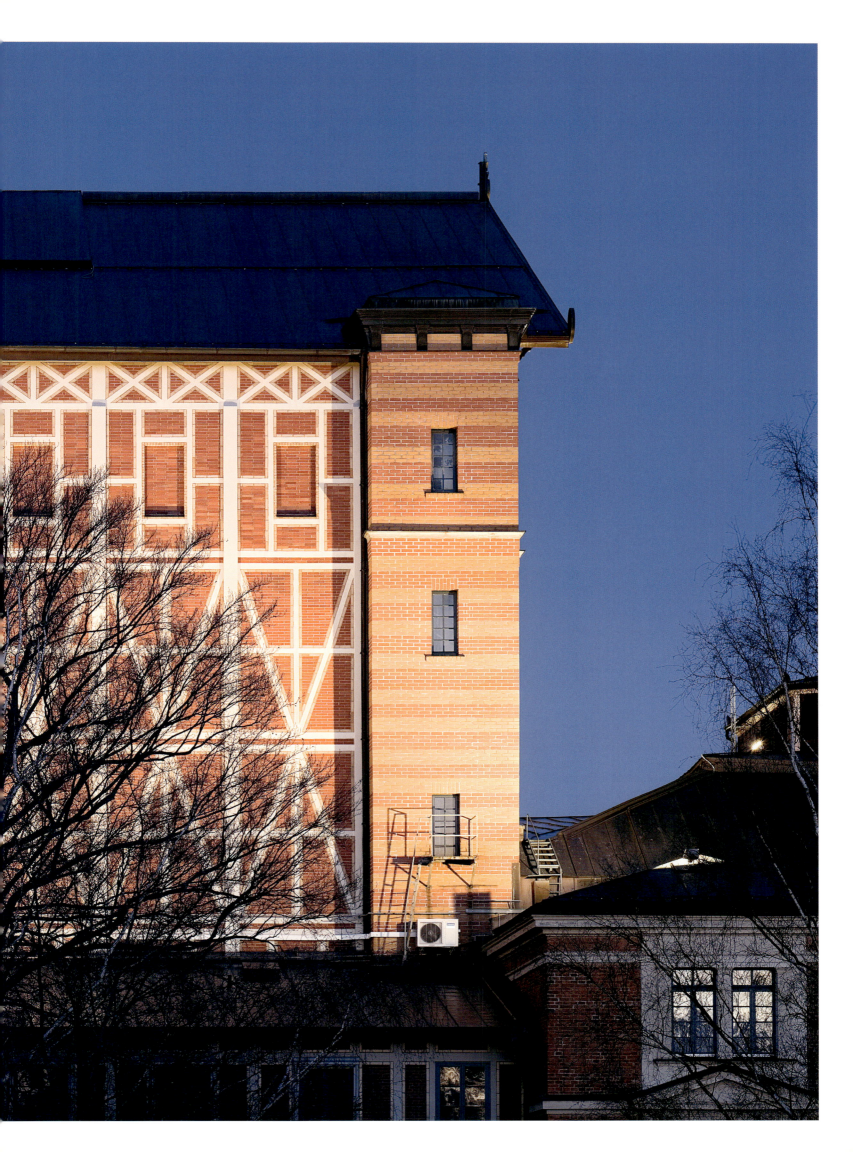

Nordisches Fachwerk in Oberfranken

Fachwerkarchitektur findet sich traditionell in Europa überall, wo es Eichenbäume gibt oder einmal gab. Man vermutet ihren Ursprung in den Nordprovinzen des Römischen Reichs, wo sich die im mediterranen Altertum bereits bekannte Bauweise mit den Traditionen der nordischen Völker mischte. Wagner hätte in diesem Fachwerkstil eine germanische und sehr deutsche Bauweise erkennen können, was jedoch nicht geschah, obwohl er in seiner Rede zur Grundsteinlegung über Römer und Germanen spricht und patriotisch hervorhebt, dass die Römer nie in den *„ungeheuren hercynischen Wald"*, den Frankenwald, vorgedrungen seien.

Das am Bayreuther Festspielhaus zu sehende Fachwerk ist mit Backsteinen ausgefacht, was besonders typisch für das Siedlungsgebiet der alten Germanen ist, für Skandinavien, England, Norddeutschland. Im Süden Deutschlands (wie auch in Franken) dagegen herrscht ein mit Lehm gefülltes Fachwerk vor. Das Wagner-Theater ist also in weiten Teilen seiner Architektur in einem norddeutschen Stil erbaut, ohne dass Wagner diese Tatsache bewusst gewesen wäre!

Der Bayreuther Fachwerkstil ist zudem ein typisch preußischer. Das mag man nicht überbewerten, doch lässt dies das Festspielhaus im oberfränkischen Bayreuth als einen Fremdkörper erscheinen. Hierin ein politisches Kalkül Wagners zu vermuten, die Preußen in der Reichshauptstadt Berlin mit einer ihnen vertrauten Architektursprache anzusprechen, führt sicherlich zu weit, obgleich ein Zitat Wagners zumindest die entsprechende Metapher aufgreift: *„,Nicht einen Balken', sagt R., ,den der nationale Gedanke mir eingebracht.'"*[1]

Der Begriff Fachwerk oder Riegelwerk ist in den Schriften Wagners übrigens nicht zu finden. Auch Brückwald hat darüber in seinen Äußerungen über Bayreuth nicht reflektiert. Semper dagegen verfasste darüber sogar einen theoretischen Aufsatz. Die Tatsache, dass das Fachwerk im endgültigen Bau nicht überputzt oder -tüncht wurde, mag Wagner aber durchaus gefallen haben – man denke nur an sein geliebtes „Asyl" in Zürich. Seine Liebe zum Mittelalter und seine Burgenromantik mag hier indirekt und unversehens doch noch zum Zuge gekommen sein.

Eine altertümliche Skelettbauweise

Die Fachwerkarchitektur des Festspielhauses mag einen gewissen romantischen Charme besitzen, doch stellt sie auch die damals billigste Konstruktionsbauweise dar. Um 1870 waren aber bereits die moderneren Skelettbauweisen der Eisenarchitektur üblich geworden. Semper hatte für sein Münchner Festspielhaus eine Eisenkonstruktion vorgesehen. Schon 1786 war der Dachstuhl des Théatre Français aus Eisen errichtet worden. Eisen hatte schon ab 1860 die Wolkenkratzer Amerikas in den Himmel aufragen lassen und sollte 1889 den Eiffelturm in Paris zum Mahnmal eines neuen Industriezeitalters aufrichten. Die Architektur des späten 19. Jahr-

Nordic timber framing in Upper Franconia

Timber framing architecture is traditional everywhere in Europe where there are or were at one time oak trees. Its origin is usually considered the northern provinces of the Roman Empire where the familiar architecture of Mediterranean antiquity mixed with Nordic traditions. Wagner could have recognized the timber framing as a Germanic and very German architectural style, but he didn't, even though he talks about the Roman and the Germanic peoples in his speech at the cornerstone laying ceremony, patriotically stressing that the Romans never pushed their way into the *"ominous Hercynian Forest,"* the Franconian Forest.

The timber framing visible on the Bayreuth Festspielhaus was infilled with bricks. This is especially typical in the areas settled by the old Germanic tribes in Scandinavia, England and Northern Germany. In southern Germany (and in Franconia), however, half-timber constructions are predominantly infilled with clay. Given this fact, the Wagner theater was, to a large degree, built in a north German style without Wagner having been aware of it!

In fact, the Bayreuth timber framing is typically Prussian. That needn't be overemphasized, but it does contribute to the Festspielhaus looking out of place in Upper Franconian Bayreuth. Chalking this up to political calculation on Wagner's part, an attempt to appeal to the Prussians in the Reich capital, Berlin, by speaking an architectural language familiar to them, surely goes too far. Still, one quotation from Wagner uses the appropriate metaphor at least: *"Wagner said 'nation building didn't contribute even one single beam.'"*

There is incidentally no mention of the term timber framing or half-timbered in Wagner's writings, nor does Brückwald reflect on it in anything he wrote about Bayreuth. Semper, on the other hand, wrote a theoretical essay on the topic. It may well have pleased Wagner that the timber framing was not covered in stucco or whitewashed – consider his beloved "asylum" in Zurich. His love for the Medieval period and his romantic affection for fortresses may have indirectly and unintentionally found a voice after all.

A traditional skeletal architecture

The timber framing of the Festspielhaus may have a certain amount of romantic charm, but it is also the most economical construction method. By 1870, the more modern skeletal architecture using iron was already common. Semper had proposed an iron frame for his Munich Festspielhaus. The roof truss of the Théatre Français had been built in iron back in 1786. Iron was making skyscrapers in the US possible by 1860, and would be the material of choice for the memorial to a new industrial age in Paris, the Eiffel Tower. The architecture of the late 19th century was being built ever more frequently by engineers, often leaving only the facade for the architects to design. If Wagner had accepted the offer from Chicago, the Festspielhaus would most certainly have been constructed of steel. But in Bayreuth, the old carpentry and masonry guilds still reigned strong!

Fränkisches Fachwerk in Bayreuth
Franconian timber framing in Bayreuth

Sanierung der Ostfassade 1966 und heutiger Zustand
Restoration of the east facade, 1966 and current condition

hunderts wurde zunehmend von Ingenieuren gebaut, während den Architekten oft nur noch die Fassadengestaltung übrig blieb. Hätte Wagner das Angebot aus Chicago angenommen, wäre das Festspielhaus sicherlich als Stahlkonstruktion errichtet worden. In Bayreuth jedoch regierten damals noch die alten Zünfte der Zimmermänner und Maurer!

Die Festspielidee sollte in München mit einer solch modernen Stahlkonstruktion in Verbindung kommen. Nachdem das Projekt für ein monumentales Festspielhaus nicht vorankam und Wagner stets auf ein provisorisches gedrängt hatte, entwarf Semper 1864 bis 1868 – nie ausgeführte – Pläne, die ein kleineres Theater in den Münchner Glaspalast eingestellt hätten. Dieser Palast, nach dem Vorbild des (ebenfalls provisorischen) Kristallpalasts der Londoner Weltausstellung 1851, stand in München von 1854 bis 1931. Sempers Entwürfe zeigen ein antikes „Amphitheater" nach dem Vorbild des in Pompeji ausgegrabenen Theaters, mit einem versenkten Orchester und einem nach oben offenen Zuschauerraum, der von dem Dach des Glaspalasts geschützt, dem antiken Theater in freier Natur sehr nahegekommen wäre (siehe Abbildung Seite 116).

The festival concept would cross paths with the modern steel construction style in Munich. Seeing that his project to build a monumental Festspielhaus was not making headway, and since Wagner had always pushed for a provisional theater, Semper drew up plans between 1864 and 1868 – which were never realized – for building a small theater inside the Munich Glass Palace. Modeled after the (likewise provisional) Crystal Palace of the London World's Fair in 1851, this palace stood in Munich between 1854 and 1931. Semper's plans show an antique "amphitheater" modeled after the theater uncovered in Pompeii, with a sunken orchestra and an auditorium protected by the roof of the glass palace, but with an otherwise very similar feel to an open-air theater from antiquity (see page 116).

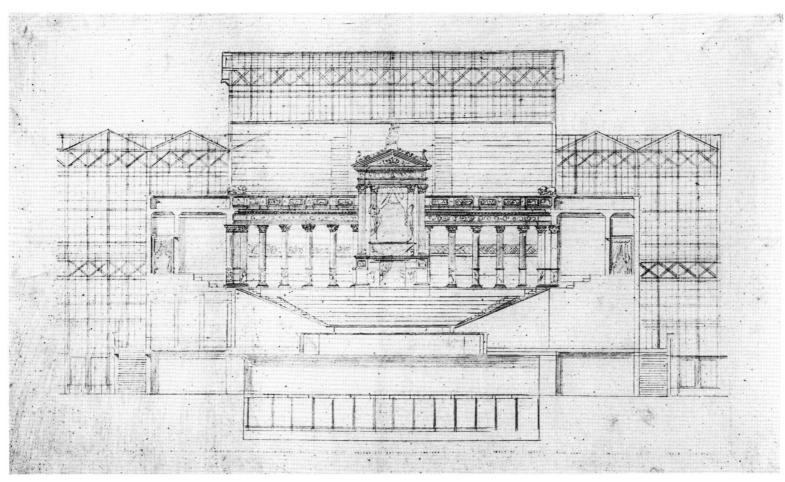

Sempers Modellzeichnung für ein provisorisches Festspieltheater im Münchner Glaspalast (1864 bis 1868)
Semper's design for a provisional festival theater in the Munich Glass Palace (1864 to 1868)

Moderne Skelettbauweise des Münchner Glaspalastes (1854 – 1931) aus Eisen und Glas; archaische Holzkonstruktion der Foyers des Bayreuther Festspielhauses
Modern skeletal architecture of the Munich Glass Palace (1854 – 1931) made of iron and glass; archaic wooden construction of the foyer of the Bayreuth Festspielhaus

Andreaskreuze und Wilde Männer

Brückwalds Fachwerkkonstruktion war also eher eine Reverenz an die Zeit der Meistersinger als ein revolutionäres Gebäude, wenn man es lediglich technisch betrachtet. Ästhetisch angeschaut, hat Brückwald, oder haben die Zimmermänner Vogel und Weiß, ein durchaus ansprechendes „Design" geschaffen, denn ein rein technisch motiviertes Fachwerk hätte man auch einfacher und noch billiger ausführen können. Das Bayreuther Fachwerk besitzt durchaus ornamentalen Charakter, und man könnte beinahe von einer fantasievollen Geometrie sprechen, die mit Rauten, Andreaskreuzen und „Stehenden" beziehungsweise „Wilden Männern" (drei gekreuzte Balken) traditionelle Motive verwendet, die recht schmuckvoll erscheinen.

Von der zitierten Wahrnehmung Cosimas gelb-golden gestrichener Balken ist nichts mehr zu sehen. Die ursprünglichen Pläne Brückwalds und alte Fotos zeigen dunkle Balken, die von weißen Linien (Fugen) umrandet wurden. Beim heutigen Bau erscheint das Fachwerk hell, fast weiß, mit abschattierender Umrandung, die keine Fugung mehr ist. Dieser Farbkontrast, wie er sich heute zeigt, ist in der Geschichte des Fachwerks sehr selten, da nicht der Balken, sondern das Gefach in der Regel weiß ist. In diesem Sinne könnte man von einem negativen oder inversiven Fachwerk sprechen. Das gleiche Phänomen findet sich am Bühnenturm, dessen Fachwerk heute ebenfalls jene Balkenköpfe vermissen lässt. Dieses Detail legt die berechtigte Vermutung nahe, dass jene Balken und damit die ganze Holzkonstruktion des Inneren heute nicht mehr existieren.

Die Fenster innerhalb des Fachwerks wurden in Bayreuth ganz traditionell zwischen Schwelle, Brust- und Sturzriegel eingestellt, dass hier die Balkenköpfe der tragenden Deckenbalken sind heute verschwunden.

St. Andrew's cross and wild men

From a purely technical perspective, Brückwald's half-timbered construction was a stronger reference to the time of the master singers than a revolutionary building. Aesthetically, Brückwald, or the carpenters Vogel and Weiß, created a very pleasing design. If the motivation behind using timber framing had been purely technical, they could have built it simpler and less expensive. The Bayreuth timber framing is clearly ornamental as well. One could almost speak of a fantasy-filled geometry, using traditional lozenges, St. Andrew's crosses and "wild men" (three crossed beams) motifs in very decorative manner.

There is nothing more to be seen of the yellow-golden painted beams Cosima is quoted as enjoyed. Brückwald's original plans and old photographs show dark beams framed by white lines (joints). The timber framing of today's theater is a very light, almost white, color framed by hues of white. The color contrast seen today is very rare in the history of timber framing, since typically the infill is white, not the beams. One could call it negative or inverse timber framing. The same phenomenon can be seen on the stage tower, this timber framing is also missing the beam ends. This detail leads to the justified suspicion that these beams, and thus the entire interior timber construction, no longer exist today.

In Bayreuth, the windows within the framing were placed between the abutment, breast rail and the cross timber, as was the tradition. The beam ends of the bearing floor beams have disappeared.

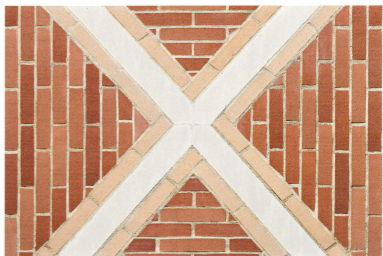

Alte Andreaskreuze aus Holz vor der Sanierung
Old wooden St. Andrew's crosses prior to the restoration

Raute, Andreaskreuz, „Wilde Männer" (Aufnahme 1962)
Lozenge, St. Andrew's cross, "Wild men" (photo from 1962)

Fachwerk à la Mondrian
Timber framing à la Mondrian

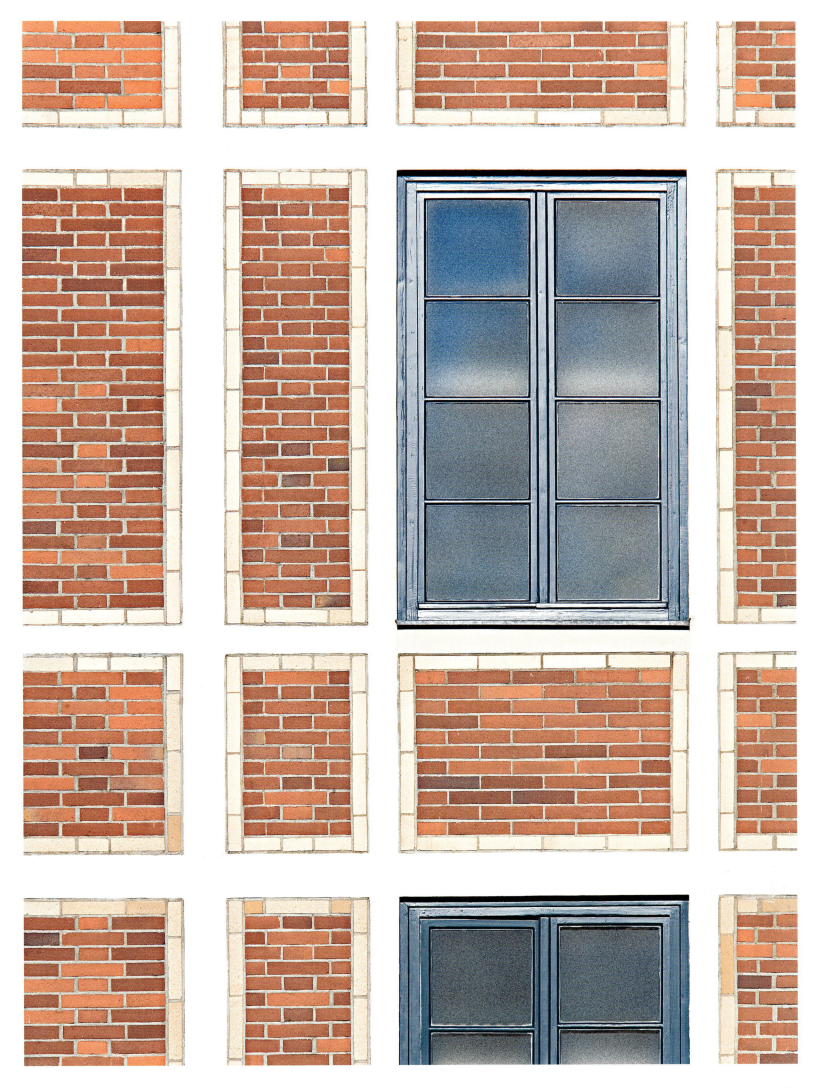

Potemkinsches Theater

Das Fachwerk, das der heutige Besucher der Bayreuther Festspiele sieht, ist also nicht original, weder im Sinne der Brückwaldschen Pläne, noch in der Ausführung von 1876, doch besteht große Ähnlichkeit. 1958 bis 1968 wurde das gesamte Fachwerk des Festspielhauses abschnittsweise erneuert. 1958/59 begann man mit der Sanierung der Südfassade des Zuschauerhauses, nachdem ein Teil der Vorderwand während der Generalproben 1958 herausgefallen war, wobei das Fachwerk völlig verschwand und einer einfachen Ziegelmauer weichen musste.

Erst 1995/96 kehrten die Rauten und Andreaskreuze als vorgeblendete Fassade auf der gebogenen Südfassade zurück, ein Verdienst des Bauherrn Wolfgang Wagner, dem es freilich immer um eine möglichst zweckmäßige und preiswerte Sanierung ging. Darüber hinaus ist dem von 1961 bis heute mit dem Bau betrauten Architekten Helmut Jahn aus Bayreuth sowie anderen, am Denkmalschutz interessierten Männern, wie Hans Heid, Ministerialrat der Obersten Baubehörde in München, die Rekonstruktion des Festspielhauses in der „original Optik" zu danken.

Damit war ein weiterer Schritt in dem Bemühen getan, das Provisorium Wagners und Brückwalds in seiner charakteristischen Erscheinung zu erhalten und das Gedankengebäude Wagners zu dokumentieren. Die wahrgenommenen Veränderungen, wie das inversive Fachwerk und die geometrische Vereinfachung desselben, sind nicht unbedingt als unhistorisch zu werten, sondern als eine behutsame Adaption, die keine Holzkonstruktion vortäuschen, sondern historische Ursprünglichkeit andeuten will.

1962/63 (immer in der festspielfreien Zeit) wurden der Garderobentrakt und das Zuschauerhaus im Osten saniert und mit einem Neubau für eine Probebühne und die Schneiderei ergänzt, wobei alles Fachwerk durch Betonpfeiler ersetzt wurde. Brückwald und seine Zimmermänner hatten meist Weichholz und keine Eichenbalken verwendet, sodass die Konstruktion knapp hundert Jahre später zum Teil gefährlich morsch geworden war. Viele Holzpfeiler steckten direkt in der blanken Erde und waren zum Teil von unten her verfault. Hinzu kamen neue brandschutztechnische Argumente, die einen Austausch durch Beton rechtfertigten. Die Optik wurde freilich gewahrt, das „Betonfachwerk" in Sichtbauweise gezeigt und hell gestrichen.

Nur im Dachstuhl des Zuschauerhauses, unter der Zuschauertribüne (den Besuchern unsichtbar) und in den Foyers (sichtbar) sind heute noch echte und originale Fachwerkkonstruktionen zu sehen. Hier wurden bereits von Brückwald Eichenpfeiler verwendet, die heute noch erhalten sind, während die Binder meist von der hauseigenen Schreinerei (als eine Art Bühnenbild) gezimmert wurden. Alle anderen scheinbar hölzernen Fachwerkelemente des Bayreuther Festspielhauses sind potemkinsche Dörfer.

Smokescreen theater

We can thus determine that the timber framing that festival visitors see nowadays was neither part of Brückwald's original plans, nor the same as, though similar to, the way it was in 1876. Between 1958 and 1968 the entire timber framing on the Festspielhaus was restored section by section. In 1958/59 restoration work on the south facade of the auditorium was started after part of the front wall fell off during the dress rehearsal in 1958. In this case, the timber framing had to be completely removed and replaced by a simple brick wall.

The lozenges and the St. Andrew's crosses were only added back on as a superimposed facade on the curved south facade in 1995/96. This is attributable to the builder Wolfgang Wagner, who naturally favored the most practical and inexpensive restoration possible. Other individuals dedicated to reconstructing the Festspielhaus in its "original appearance" include Helmut Jahn, the architect entrusted with building renovations since 1961, and other men interested in monument preservation, such as Hans Heid, ministerial advisor to the highest building authority in Munich.

This was a further step in the effort to preserve the characteristic appearance of Wagner's and Brückwald's provisional building and to document Wagner's thought construction. The changes made, such as reversing the timber framing color scheme and simplifying its geometry, should not necessarily be written off as unhistorical, but instead interpreted as careful adaptation intended to reference historic originality rather than to feign timber-framed construction.

In 1962/63 (always during the off-season), the coat room and the east side of the auditorium were renovated and a new building was built for a rehearsal stage and tailoring. During this time, the entire timber framing was replaced by concrete posts. Brückwald and his carpenters had used mainly soft wood rather than oak beams, so that the construction had grown dangerously unsound in the almost hundred years since. Many wooden posts had been driven directly into the earth and some of them were rotting from the bottom up. New fire prevention arguments also legitimized replacing the wood by concrete. The appearance was preserved by making the "concrete timber framing" visible and painting it a light color.

The only places genuine and original timber framing can be found today are in the roof truss of the auditorium, under the auditorium tribune (not visible to visitors) and in the foyers (visible). The oak beams Brückwald used in these locations are still sound, and the braces were cut in the theater woodshop (as a sort of set). All other seemingly wooden timber framing in the Bayreuth Festspielhaus is smokescreen.

Das Fachwerk der gebogenen Hauptfassade seit 1996
The timber framing of the curved facade of the main building since 1996

Neue Andreaskreuze und Füllen des „Betonfachwerks" (1963)
New St. Andrew's crosses and filler for the "concrete timber framing" (1963)

Von der hauseigenen Schreinerei 1973 rekonstruierte Andreaskreuze für das Foyer
St. Andrew's crosses for the foyer reconstructed in the theater workshop in 1973

Asketische Architektur

1963 bis 1967 wurde auch das Bühnenhaus saniert, wobei die Seitenmauern zwischen den Stütztürmen jeweils um 3,10 Meter nach außen rückten (1963/64) und so den Bühnenraum vergrößerten, um Platz für eine neue Obermaschinerie zu schaffen. Das Fachwerk ersetzte man – insbesondere im Dachstuhl – durch Stahlträger. An der Nordseite verschwand das Fachwerk unter dem großen Bogenfenster mit seinen „Wilden Männern" (1965/66) und wurde auch in den 1990er Jahren nicht wieder rekonstruiert. 1963/64 sanierte man den Westteil des Zuschauertrakts analog zum Ostteil.

Die Entscheidungen der 1960er und der 1990er Jahre, den Fachwerkcharakter des Festspielhauses zu wahren beziehungsweise zu rekonstruieren, offenbaren eine denkmalpflegerische Gesinnung, die freilich nur an der Optik haftet. Der funktionale Charakter dieser altertümlichen Skelettbauweise betont das Asketische dieser Architektur bis in unsere Zeit, sodass Wagners Wunsch, dass nichts von seinen Werken auf der Bühne ablenken möge, noch einhundertdreißig Jahre später gilt. Der Werkstatt-Charakter der Festspiele wird so betont, wie auch der Verzicht auf alle eitlen Äußerlichkeiten der Opernwelt, die schon Wagner kritisiert hatte und heute kaum weniger selten sind. Dies mag ein Blick auf und in den östlichen Garderobentrakt und das spartanische Gemach hinter schlichtem Gefach deutlich machen.

Ascetic architecture

The stage building was also renovated between 1963 and 1967 and the side walls between the support towers were all moved out by 3.10 meters (in 1963/64) to enlarge the stage area and make room for new equipment in the fly gallery. The timber framing was largely replaced by steel girders, especially in the roof truss. The timber framing with its "wild men" below the large semi-circular window on the north side was removed altogether (1965/66) and was not reconstructed in the 1990s. In 1963/64, the west side of the auditorium was restored analogue to the east side.

The decisions in the 1960s and 1990s to preserve or re-construe the timber framing character of the Festspielhaus are evidence of a conservational approach limited solely to appearance. To this day, the functional character of this classical skeletal construction reinforces the ascetic nature of this architecture. In this light, Wagner's wish to avoid anything that would divert attention away from his works on the stage is still honored even one hundred and thirty years later. This emphasizes the festival's workshop character and the conscious abnegation of the vain superficialities of the opera world that Wagner had criticized in his day, and that are not less frequent today. A look at and inside the east dressing rooms with their Spartan furnishings behind simple beams bring this into focus.

Solistengarderobe für die Weltstars, so spartanisch wie die Chorgarderoben
Soloist dressing rooms for international stars, as Spartan as the chorus dressing rooms

Neuer Anbau von 1968 bis 1872 mit Probebühne I., Kostümwerkstätten und Garderoben
New addition from 1968 to1972 with Rehearsal Stage I, costume shop and dressing rooms

„Jetzt hab' ich die Garderoben einzurichten.
Muss ich das alles selbst tun?"[1]

"Now I have to set up the dressing rooms.
Do I have to do everything myself?"

Richard Wagner (an Richard Fricke am 10. April 1876)

Der Backsteinbau

Zur Not auch Backstein

Wagner hat in all seinen Äußerungen über sein provisorisches Theater immer nur von Holz als möglichem Material gesprochen, über Back- oder Ziegelsteine nie – bis auf eine einzige Ausnahme, in einem Brief an Semper vom 13. Dezember 1864, worin er mitteilt, dass ihm eine monumentale Ausführung des Münchner Festspielprojekts in Stein nicht behagt, und dass es ihm „*vorsichtiger und außerdem zweckmäßiger erscheint, für das erste, aber sofort die Konstruktion eines provisorischen Theaters in Holz und etwa Backstein in Angriff zu nehmen.*"[1] Hierin spiegelt sich die Furcht Wagners vor einem festen Haus, da er seine Ideen, wie die des versenkten Orchestergrabens, gerne erst (akustisch) ausprobiert hätte. Das obige Zitat ist die einzige Fundstelle des Wortes Backstein in einem konkreten architektonischen Zusammenhang im nicht gerade lakonischen Gesamtwerk Wagners. In einigen Stellen erscheinen Back- beziehungsweise Ziegelsteine lediglich metaphorisch und werden „*Marmorblöcken*" oder „*Granitblöcken*"[2] entgegengestellt, was die Wertschätzung Wagners für den Backstein als minderes Material klar belegt.

Der gelernte Maurer Otto Brückwald jedoch machte reichlich Gebrauch davon, getreu dem Motto „*Hat er nur Steine zu hauen gelernt, so haue er Steine, vermag er aber schöne Gebäude aufzurichten, so überlasse er das Steinhauen anderen.*"[3] Die Maurerarbeiten nahmen mit fünfunddreißig Prozent sogar den größten Posten in den Gesamtkosten des Baus ein, noch vor den Zimmerarbeiten. Brückwald beziffert die Gesamtkosten des Theatergebäudes bei einer bebauten Grundfläche von 3319 Quadratmetern auf 428.384,09 Mark oder 129,07 Mark pro Quadratmeter.[4]

Backsteine sind so alt wie die menschliche Zivilisation. Bereits die Sumerer, Babylonier und Assyrer bauten mit gebrannten Ziegeln, so auch den Turm zu Babel (mit blau glasierten Ziegeln). Cosima empfängt am 25. Dezember 1873 einen „*grandiosen Eindruck, wie ein assyrischer Bau erhebt sich das Ganze*"[5].

Im Mittelalter finden sich Backsteinbauten in werksteinarmen Gebieten, im Flachland also, wiederum im Gebiet der alten Germanen, von den Niederlanden bis ins Baltikum, in Skandinavien und den Britischen Inseln. „Backsteininseln" sind darüber hinaus die Lombardei und die Südwestecke Frankreichs (um Toulouse). Eine ästhetische Qualität des Backsteins in Sichtbauweise entwickelte sich vor allem in der Backsteingotik des Nordens. In der Renaissance sind Mischformen aus Back- und Haustein häufig, im Barock waren Backsteinbauten meist verputzt.

Brückwald hätte, wie seine Pläne zeigen, alle Backsteinwände gerne weiß verputzt, die Sparsamkeit ließ sie jedoch roh, sodass unversehens eine ästhetische Verwandtschaft zu anderen Backsteinstilen der Architekturgeschichte entstand. Zum Beispiel die Weserrenaissance in Norddeutschland kennt die Verbindung von absichtlich unverputzten Backsteinwänden mit Zierelementen aus Haussteinen (Bremer Rathaus) genauso wie die Renaissance und der Barock in den Niederlanden oder in Skandinavien. Besonders treffend ist der Vergleich mit dem Georgian-Style in England und seinen Überseekolonien zwischen 1714 und 1820, der genau diese Kombination aufweist: schlichte Backsteinwand mit Zierelementen an Fenstern und Türen im Stil der Renaissance des Palladio. In England gab es sogar Theater in diesem Stil, wie das City of London Theatre.

Brick building

If need be, even brick

Whenever Wagner makes reference to a provisional theater, he always only mentions wood as a possible material. With only a single exception, in a letter to Semper on December 13, 1864, he never mentions clinkers or bricks. In this letter, Wagner expresses his disapproval of Semper's monumental designs for the Munich Festspielhaus, thinking it *"more careful and also more practical, at least initially, to start building a provisional theater straight off out of wood and perhaps brick."* This statement is an expression of Wagner's fear of building a permanent structure without first (acoustically) trying out his ideas, such as the sunken orchestra pit. The above quotation is the only reference to the term brick specifically related to architecture in his not exactly laconic oeuvre. On several occasions he uses the term clinker or brick metaphorically in contrast to *"marble slabs"* or *"granite blocks."* This clearly evidences Wagner's high opinion of bricks as a cheaper material.

Otto Brückwald, a trained mason, used bricks widely, in keeping with the motto *"[...] if he only learned how to hammer stones, so he shall hammer stones, but if he can build beautiful buildings, he'll leave the stone hammering to others."* Masonry costs accounted for thirty-five per cent of total construction costs, the largest item even above carpentry. Brückwald reports the total costs of building the theater at 428,384.09 marks with a construction footprint of 3,319 square meters, or 129.07 marks per square meter.

Bricks are as old as human civilization. The Sumerians, the Babylonians and the Assyrians built with burned bricks. For example, the Tower of Babel was built using blue glazed bricks. On December 25, 1873, Cosima describes a *"grand impression, rising up like an Assyrian building."*

Bricks were commonly used in the Middle Ages in areas lacking building stone, that is, in the flatlands, the area inhabited by Germanic tribes from the Netherlands into the Baltic, in Scandinavia and on the British Isles. There are also "islands of brick" in Lombardy and in the southwest corner of France (around Toulouse). Brick takes on an external aesthetic quality in the brick Gothic of the north. It was common in the Renaissance to mix bricks and hewn stones, and most brick buildings were coated with stucco in the Baroque.

As his plans show, Brückwald wanted to apply stucco to all of the brick walls. Thrift, however, left them red, creating an unintended aesthetic resemblance to other brick styles in architectural history. For example the Weser Renaissance in northern Germany combined intentionally plain brick walls with decorative elements made of hewn stone (Bremen city hall), as did the Renaissance and the Baroque in the Netherlands and in Scandinavia. A comparison with the Georgian style in England and its oversea colonies between 1714 and 1820 is especially fruitful, as this exact combination is frequently used: plain brick walls with decorative elements on the windows and doors in the Renaissance style of Palladio. There were even theaters built in this style in England, such as the City of London Theater.

City of London Theatre im Georgian-Style
Georgian-Style: City of London Theatre

Neubau eines Verwaltungstrakts an der Westseite aus der Ära Winifred Wagner von 1930/31 (heute Kartenbüro, Festspielleitung, und Verwaltung)
New administrative tract built on the west side in 1930/31 during Winifried Wagner's era (today ticket office, festival management and administration)

Marienburg, Manchester und der Maurerstil

Erst das 19. Jahrhundert sollte den so lange verachteten Backstein wieder hinter Putz und Farbe hervorholen. Der klassizistische Architekt Friedrich Gilly gilt als Erster, der 1794 im Angesicht der ostpreußischen Marienburg einen nackten Backsteinbau als schön empfunden hat und als preußisch-vaterländisches Monument pries. Sein Schüler Karl Friedrich Schinkel schuf 1817 bis 1840 zahlreiche, zum Teil neogotische Backsteinbauten in Preußen, die das „Preußische", aber auch die Industriearchitektur Englands (Manchester) zum Vorbild hatten. Der Backstein erfuhr dadurch eine gewisse Ästhetisierung, da nun ein präzises Mauerwerk gefordert wurde, das das Handwerk des Maurers nobilitierte. Schinkel folgten diverse jüngere Architekten wie Persius, Stüler und Martin Gropius, die mit ihrem sachlichen, sogenannten Berliner Maurerstil bis ins Kaiserreich stilbildend waren.

Otto Brückwald kannte diese kurz geraffte Geschichte der modernen Backsteinarchitektur gewiss, Richard Wagner sicherlich nicht, sonst hätte er hier erneut einen tudesken Stil erkennen können. Dieser behauptete sich ganz bewusst gegen die von der Pariser École des Beaux Arts offiziell in Frankreich protegierte und von hier aus auch in Deutschland beliebte Neorenaissance, als dem Repräsentationsstil des gehobenen Bürgertums und des Adels. Wagner spottet darüber in seiner Rede zur Grundsteinlegung: *„Einer Pariser Dirne fällt es ein, ihrem Hute eine gewisse extravagante Form zu geben, so genügt dies, um alle deutschen Frauen unter denselben Hut zu bringen; oder ein glücklicher Börsenspekulant gewinnt über Nacht eine Million, und sofort lässt er sich eine Villa im St. Germain-Style bauen, zu welcher der Architekt die gehörige Fassade in Bereitschaft hält."*[1]

Marienburg, Manchester and masonry style

The long-distained brick was not freed of its stucco and paint cover until the 19th century. The classicist architect Friedrich Gilly is considered the first to have considered a naked brick building, the East Prussian Marienburg, beautiful and proclaim it a monument to the Prussian fatherland. His student Karl Friedrich Schinkel created many brick structures in Prussia between 1817 and 1840, many in neo-Gothic style, modeled after "Prussianness," but also the industrial architecture of England (Manchester). This gave the brick an aesthetic boost, requiring precision masonry and raising the status of the masons' craft. Various younger architects following Schinkel, such as Persius, Stüler and Martin Gropius, created the dry, so-called Berlin masonry style and had an influence on style right up to the Kaiser Reich.

Whereas Otto Brückwald was certainly familiar with this compact history of modern brick architecture, Richard Wagner surely wasn't. Otherwise he again would have recognized a "tudesque" style quite consciously opposing the neo-Renaissance style officially sponsored by the Parisian École des Beaux Arts in France and spreading in popularity to Germany as the representational style of the haut bourgeoisie and the nobility. Wagner made fun of this style in his speech at the cornerstone laying ceremony: *"The moment some girl in Paris decides to give her hat a certain extravagant shape, it's enough to convince all German women to buy a hat like that. If a lucky stock market speculator wins a million over night, he immediately has a villa built in St. Germain style and the architect has the appropriate facade ready and waiting."*

Interessante Nahtstelle zwischen alten und neuen Mauern (am südöstlichen Eckpavillon)
Interesting juncture between an old and a new wall (on the southeast corner pavilion)

Blockverband, Läuferverband, „Wagnerverband". Die Zuganker sind rein dekorativ und ohne Funktion, 1993 erneuert.
English bond, stretcher bond, "Wagner bond." The tie rods, refurbished in 1993, are purely decorative and do not have a function.

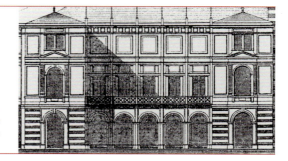

So blieben für die Architekten der Schinkel-Schule meist nur Schulen, Kasernen, Fabrikbauten, Bahnhöfe, Friedhofskapellen oder Festspielhäuser übrig. Brückwald wählte den Backstein primär als billigstes Baumaterial, doch wusste er sicherlich, dass man selbst dem billigsten und funktionalsten Bau einen gewissen Stil geben konnte, wenn man ihn der Ästhetik der Schinkel-Schule anzunähern verstand. Hier sind seine Pläne besonders aufschlussreich.

Der Plan beweist, dass Brückwald für das Zuschauerhaus keinen Backsteinstil vorgesehen hatte, sondern nur für die nicht repräsentativen Teile des Theaters. Er näherte sich – wie die eleganten Rundbögen im Erdgeschoss zeigen – auch in den Seitenfassaden eher der Neorenaissance der Hauptfassade. Küfners Bauaufnahmen von 1916 bestätigen, dass das letztlich im Backsteinstil errichtete Zuschauerhaus so nicht geplant war, sodass eine Affinität zur Ästhetik der Schinkel-Schule nicht gewollt war und nachträglich nicht hineinprojiziert werden sollte. Die Pläne beweisen außerdem, dass die Entscheidung für den rohen Backsteinbau während der Bauzeit getroffen worden ist, und wohl tatsächlich aus Kostengründen fiel, um den Verputz zu sparen und um das von Wagner so gewünschte Provisorium deutlich zu demonstrieren.

Darüber hinaus wird deutlich, dass die Baumaßnahmen der 60er und 90er Jahre des 20. Jahrhunderts keinen Versuch unternahmen, den ursprünglichen Entwurf Brückwalds auszuführen, sondern den 1876 tatsächlich ausgeführten Bau nachempfunden haben. Die Eckpavillons zeigen übrigens kaum Änderungen (außer einem Umbau der Erdgeschossfenster in Türen), denn sie waren nicht provisorisch gedacht, sondern schon „monumental" ausgeführt, wie Brückwald schreibt, als massive „Stützpunkte"[1] der Holzkonstruktion, wie auch die vier Türme des Bühnenturms.

Das alte Mauerwerk wurde bis in die 1930er Jahre im Blockverband des ursprünglichen Baus gemauert, was dem geübten Maurerauge eine gewisse Stärke der Mauer offenbart. Die neuen Mauern ab den 1960er Jahren sind im (dünnen) Läuferverband gemauert, da sie nur flache Verklinkerungen darstellen. Alt und Neu lassen sich am Verband oder an der Steinfarbe und Verwitterung erkennen.

Daneben findet sich an ganz neuen Bauten eine wilde Mischung aus Kreuzverband und gotischem Verband, nennen wir ihn einfach „Wagnerverband".

As a result, the buildings left for architects from the Schinkel school are mainly schools, military bases, factories, train stations, cemetery chapels and a Festspielhaus. Otto Brückwald chooses brick primarily because it is the least expensive building material, but he also knew that it is possible to give even the least expensive and most functional building a certain amount of style by applying the aesthetic of the Schinkel school. In this case, the plans are especially revealing.

The plan proves that Brückwald did not intend to use brick for the auditorium, but rather only for non-representative parts of the theater. As the elegant arches on the ground floor show, he leans toward the neo-Renaissance of the main facade for the side facades as well. Küfner's building plans from 1916 confirm that the auditorium built in brick style after all was not planned, implying that an affinity to the aesthetic of the Schinkel school was unintentional and should not be projected onto it. The plans also prove that the decision for the plain brick must have come during the construction phase, and was likely reached to save stucco costs and to clearly demonstrate Wagner's concept of a provisional theater.

It is also clear that no attempts were made during the renovation and construction efforts during the 1960s and the 1990s to realize Brückner's original design. Instead, the building as it was built in 1876 served as the model. Incidentally, the corner pavilions have hardly changed (except that the windows on the ground floor were converted into doors), as they were never considered provisional. Instead, as Brückwald writes, they were designed *"monumentally"* as massive *"anchors"* of the wooden construction, just like the four corner tower of the stage tower.

Until the 1930s, the old bricks were laid in English bond, giving the wall a strong appearance to the trained bricklayer's eye. The new walls from the 1960s are in (thin) stretcher bond, since the bricks are all laid flat. Old and new can be differentiated based on the bond, the color of the stone and the weathering.

Brand new buildings contain a mixture of cross bond and Flemish bond, which we'll call "Wagner bond."

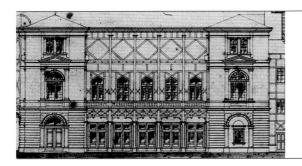
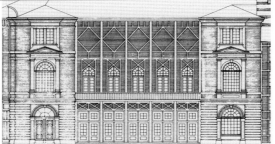

Brückwalds Plan 1873
Brückwald's plan, 1873

Zustand vor den Umbauten 1916
Condition before the renovations, 1916

Zustand nach allen Umbauten 1962 bis 1966
Condition after all renovations, 1962 to 1966

Bunte Backsteine

Einige architektonische Gestaltungsmotive des Bayreuther Festspielhauses lassen sich jedoch eindeutig der Schinkel-Schule zuordnen. Das sind zum einen die großen Rundbogenfenster am Bühnenturm (siehe Seite 112) und die bunten Backsteinbänder am Bühnenturm: der Wechsel von gelben und roten Backsteinen, wie an der Heilandskirche in Sacrow von Persius 1844. Das Motiv ist in den Plänen Brückwalds zu erkennen, wurde tatsächlich realisiert, bei der Übertünchung mit Ölfarben vor dem Ersten Weltkrieg berücksichtigt und ist bei den Sanierungen des 20. Jahrhunderts nicht verschwunden.

Dieses Streifenmotiv war nicht neu und findet sich ähnlich schon in romanischen Bauten (wie den Domen in Trier und Aachen). Wagner selbst bestaunte in seinem Lieblingsdom von Siena die „Säulen aus hell-dunkel geschichtetem Marmor und bewunderte, was dann Sarah Kirsch in einem Gedicht ‚dieses sechzehnbeinige Zebra mit den Skalpen der Päpste' genannt hat."[1] Das Thema Polychromie in der Architektur war den Wagners sogar bekannt: „Spaziergang nach der Stadt; wobei Besprechung der Polychromie Sempers, weil ich jetzt dessen Broschüre über diesen Gegenstand lese."[2]

Archäologische Befunde hatten vermuten und dann auch beweisen lassen, dass die antike Architektur (und Plastik) keineswegs so rein weiß war, wie noch Herr Winckelmann glaubte. Der Marmor, der in seiner abstrakten Weißheit als Ausdruck von Idealität verstanden wurde, war im Gegenteil ganz volkstümlich bunt gefasst. Auch das Festspielhaus besitzt ein wenig von der leidenschaftlich diskutierten Polychromie, wie Cosima am 23. Juli 1878 notiert: „Wir freuen uns, dass das Haus da steht, wie ein ewiger Sonnenuntergang sieht es unter den Bäumen aus; seine schlichte Polychromie machte uns Freude."[3]

Die Sanierungen seit den 1960er Jahren haben nicht viele alte Backsteine des Originalbaus übrig gelassen. Schuld an dem schlechten Zustand vieler Steine war die Bemalung mit Ölfarbe. Schon Brückwald hatte für seinen Bau keine verschieden gebrannten oder glasierten Steine genommen, sondern diese lediglich farbig anstreichen lassen. In der Ära Siegfried Wagners sollen sogar alle Backsteinwände des Festspielhauses gestrichen worden sein (um 1910). Ölanstriche aber ruinieren Backsteine auf Dauer, sodass hier spätestens in den 1960er Jahren höchster Handlungsbedarf gefordert war. An den Türmen des Bühnenturms zum Beispiel wurden sie nicht völlig entfernt, aber großzügig abgeschlagen und anschließend mit Klinkersteinen neu eingemauert. Süd- und Nordfassade wurden ebenfalls großzügig abgerissen, wobei beim Wiederaufbau alte Steine zum Teil wiederverwendet wurden, die freilich ein anderes Maß als die neuen hatten, weshalb sogar Ziegel in den Originalmaßen nachgebrannt wurden.

Colorful bricks

Several architectural design motifs of the Bayreuth Festspielhaus are, however, clearly from the Schinkel school. For example, the large round arched window on the stage tower (which will be discussed below) and the colorful brick bands on the stage tower alternating between yellow and red bricks like on the Heilandskirche in Sacrow built by Persius in 1844. This motif is part of Brückwald's plans, was actually constructed that way, was maintained when the walls were painted with oil paints before the First World War, and did not disappear during the restoration efforts in the 20th century.

This strip motif was not new. A similar form can be seen in Romanesque buildings (such as the cathedrals in Trier and Aachen). In his favorite cathedral, in Siena, Wagner himself wondered at the *"pillars of alternating light and dark layers of marble and admired what Sarah Kirsch called 'the 16-legged zebra with the Popes' scalps' in a poem."* The Wagners were familiar with the topic of polychromy in architecture: *"Took a walk into the city and discussed Semper's polychromy, as I am now reading his brochure about this topic."*

Archeological finds confirmed the speculation that antique architecture (and sculptures) were not as purely white as Winckelmann still believed. The marble's abstract whiteness was interpreted as an expression of ideality, whereas in reality it was as colorful as everyday life itself. As Cosima noted on July 23, 1878, the Festspielhaus also has a little of the polychromy the Wagners so passionately discussed: *"We are happy to see the theater standing there, looking like an eternal sunset under the trees. Its simple polychromy pleased us."*

Restoration efforts since the 1960s have not left many of the bricks from the original building in place. The oil paints used to paint the bricks are the reason why so many are in poor condition. Even Brückwald didn't use any differently burned or glazed bricks for his building, but rather simply had them painted. During Siegfried Wagner's era, in fact, all of the brick walls of the Festspielhaus are said to have been painted (around 1910). But over time, oil paint ruins bricks, so that by the 1960s, reparations were critically necessary. For example, the bricks from the corner towers of the stage tower were not completely removed, but they were knocked out generously and then bricked over with clinker bricks. The south and north facades were also torn down in great swaths and many of the old bricks were re-used. Since these bricks were a different size than new bricks, bricks of the original dimensions were burned for the purpose.

1984 wurden die originalen Backsteine an den Bühnentürmen grob abgeschlagen und durch Klinker ersetzt. An der Bühnenhaussüdwand sind alte Backsteine eingeflickt.
In 1984 the original bricks of the stage tower were knocked out generously and replaced by clinker bricks. On the south wall of the stage building old bricks were laid back in.

Heilandskirche von Persius, 1844 in Sacrow
1844 Heilandskirche by Persius in Sacrow

Ein Theater als Fabrik

Die Backsteinarchitektur des Bayreuther Festspielhauses ist und war für ein Theater eigentlich eine bodenlose Provokation, eine Kühnheit, die jede im 19. Jahrhundert geltende Modenorm ignorierte und sich in seiner Hässlichkeit auf einem gut von überall sichtbaren Hügel postierte. Schon ein Zeitgenosse erkannte dies, Romain Rolland: „*Das Theater sieht einem Industriebau ähnlicher als einer Kunststätte.*"[1]

Andererseits empfand Wagner Fabriken als hässlich, wie Glasenapp erzählt: „*Auf dem Rückweg erblickte er [Wagner] den Rauch einer der ersten Bayreuther Fabriken [...] und bemerkte: er stiege gerade so senkrecht auf, wie die Lerche, nur mit einem Unterschiede: ‚die eine singt, der andere stinkt'. Was würde er erst heute sagen, wo die pietätvollste Pflege seines damals noch in den Anfängen begriffenen großen Werkes [...] , sich durch immer neu sich erhebende Fabrikschlote mehr das Äußere eines der Industrie als der Kunst gewidmeten Ortes zu verleihen, und seine poesievollsten Ausblicke durch ungefüge rote Ziegelsteinmassen und daraus hervorragende rauchende Schornsteine zu entstellen!*"[2] Glasenapp will nicht sehen, dass das aus „*rohen Ziegelsteinmassen*" gefügte Festspielhaus selbst einer profanen Fabrik gleicht. Zwar hat Wagner seine „Fabrik" immer mit dem Hinweis auf fehlendes Geld und dergleichen entschuldigt, doch war dies vielleicht ebenfalls nur Rhetorik. Wollte er in Wahrheit die von ihm stets verachtete bürgerliche und adlige Opernwelt mit seinem proletarischen Bauwerk schockieren? Vielleicht wollte er so sichtbar machen, dass er sich ein anderes, ein neues Publikum erhoffte.

Sollte in Bayreuth sogar der alte Revolutionär, Sozialist und Anarchist Wagner wieder lebendig geworden sein, so wie er sich 1848 in seiner Schrift „Deutschland und seine Fürsten" über das Elend des Proletariats geäußert hat: „*Ein emsig Summen, Stampfen und Sausen schallt euch entgegen aus jenem Hause; es ist eine Fabrik. Tretet hinein und ihr seht hundert fleißige Hände, künstlich gebaute Maschinen in fruchtbarer Tätigkeit. [...] Nun blickt hin auf die Menschen! Seht die bleichen, abgehärmten Gesichter, die matten, glanzlosen Augen, die ausgehungerten, nackten, frierenden Körper, seht auch hier das wahre Bild des Jammers und des Elends mitten im Überflusse! Und wieder frage ich: Muss das so sein?*"[3]

Fazit

Die Backsteinarchitektur des Bayreuther Festspielhauses war primär aus Kostengründen motiviert, selbst beim Äußeren des repräsentativen Zuschauerhauses, das Brückwald so nicht geplant hatte. Darin einen ästhetischen Willen zu vermuten, ist ein interessanter Versuch, der am Ende jedoch nicht vollständig zu beweisen ist. Eine Verwandtschaft zur Backsteinarchitektur der Schinkel-Schule ist nur indirekt als eine (zufällige) Affinität zu erkennen und lediglich bei den Zebramustern der Bühnentürme und dem großen Segmentfenster statthaft. Letzteres kann stilistisch aber auch der Renaissance und dem Klassizismus zugerechnet werden.

Offensichtlicher als jede so schwierige Stilzuweisung ist eine für das 19. Jahrhundert höchst seltene „Stillosigkeit", die das Theater und alle seine (auch neueren) Nutzbauten bis heute prägt und damit den Werkstatt-Charakter Bayreuths in einer betonten Sachlichkeit und ästhetischen Ökonomie präsentiert. In der Fabrikarchitektur des Festspielhauses einen politischen Hintergedanken zu erkennen und den Revolutionär Wagner wieder aufleben zu lassen ist legitim, gerade im Hinblick auf die vielen „demokratischen" Theaterneubauten in Deutschland nach 1945. Im 19. Jahrhundert war dies jedoch sehr gewagt und bildete einen provokanten Kontrast zur modischen Opernwelt des Adels und der Bourgeoisie.

A theater as a factory

For a theater the brick architecture of the Bayreuth Festspielhaus is and was brazenly provocative, an audacity ignoring every fashion norm of the 19th century. It stood in all its ugliness on a hill, plainly visible from all around. Even Romain Rolland, a contemporary, recognized this: "*The theater looks more like an industrial building than a site of art.*"

But as Glasenapp notes, Wagner thought factories were ugly: "*On the way back, [Wagner] saw the smoke of one of the first factories in Bayreuth [...] and commented: it climbs straight up like the lark, but with only one difference: 'one sings and the other stinks.' What would he say today seeing the reverential treatment for his work then only just in its conception [...] , in a place filled with more and more factory smokestacks looking more like an industrial center than of a place dedicated to art, and his most poetic views marred by raw red brick masses with smoking chimneys jutting up between!*" Glasenapp does not want to see that the Festspielhaus is also made of "*raw brick mass*" and itself resembles a profane factory. Wagner always excused his "factory" by pointing to the lack of funds and other such reasons, but that may have all been rhetoric. Did he actually want his proletariat building to shock the bourgeoisie and noble opera world he so looked down on? Maybe he wanted to make it visible to express his hope for a different, new audience.

Is, in fact, the old revolutionary, socialist and anarchist Wagner rising up again in Bayreuth, the Wagner who described the misery of the proletariat in his essay "Germany and its Princes" in 1848? "*A busy humming, stamping and whirling come at you out of every house; it's a factory. Go inside and you will see a hundred hardworking hands, artificially made machines productively at work. [...] Now look at the people! Notice the pale faces worn with worry, the dull eyes lacking all shine, the underfed, naked, freezing bodies. Look again at the true face of lament and squalor amid such overabundance! And again I ask: must it be like this?*"

Summary

The brick architecture of the Bayreuth Festspielhaus was motivated mainly by cost, even for the exterior of the representative auditorium, and was not planned that way by Brückwald. It is interesting to attempt to interpret a willful aesthetic in this architecture, but in the end, it is not completely provable. Its relationship with the brick architecture of the Schinkel school reveals only an indirect (coincidental) affinity: the only elements that stand close scrutiny are the zebra stripes on the stage tower and the large segmental window, whereby the latter could be traced to the Renaissance or to Classicism as well.

The most obvious trait of the theater and all of the functional buildings added onto it (even the newer ones) it a "lack of style". This is highly uncommon for the 19th century and makes it difficult to position the theater within an existing style. The high level of practicality and aesthetic economy emphasizes Bayreuth's workshop character. Especially given the many "democratic" theaters built in Germany after 1945, it is legitimate to read a political subtext into the factory architecture of the Festspielhaus, rekindling Wagner's revolutionary background. But this was quite daring in the 19th century and can be interpreted as a provocative contrast to the opera world of the nobility and the bourgeoisie.

*Mit einem ihm gegenüber wohnenden Schmied oder Schlosser,
so berichtet Frau Wesendonck,
hatte er eigens einen Vertrag geschlossen,
wonach dieser am Vormittage nicht hämmern durfte,
weil er „Siegfrieds Schmiedelied" komponiere.[1]*

*According to Ms. Wesendonck,
he signed contract with a blacksmith or locksmith
who lived across from him forbidding him to hammer in the mornings
because he was composing "Siegfried's Blacksmith Song."*

Schlosserei Metal shop

Schreinerei Woodworking shop

*„Summ' und brumm', du gutes Rädchen,
munter, munter dreh' dich um!
mein gutes Rädchen, braus' und saus'!"*

Mädchen in DER FLIEGENDE HOLLÄNDER
2. Aufzug Act 2

Werkstätten für Malerei, Dekoration, Kostüme und Schuhe – auch für Hunde und Riesen (Kothurne für Fafner und Fasolt)
Shops for painting, decoration, costumes and shoes – even for dogs and giants (cothurns for Fafner and Fasolt)

„Doch seit mein Schuster ein großer Poet,
gar übel es um mein Schuhwerk steht."

Beckmesser in DIE MEISTERSINGER VON NÜRNBERG
1. Aufzug Act 1

Fundus für Schuhe, Beleuchtung, Kostüme und Bühnenmaterial
Storage for shoes, lighting, costumes and stage material

Antikensehnsucht

Römische Schwitzbadfenster

Ein zweites Motiv des Bayreuther Festspielhauses, das sich der Schinkel-Schule als Stilmerkmal zuordnen lässt, ist das große Segmentbogenfenster am Bühnenturm, das freilich auch ein eindeutig antikes Motiv ist. Heute nur an der südlichen Hauptfassade, befand sich an der Nordseite ursprünglich ein Pendant, das 1966 beim Wiederaufbau des Bühnenturms nicht mehr realisiert wurde.

Solche großen Bogenfenster werden in der Architekturgeschichte Thermenfenster genannt oder diokletianische Fenster, da sie erstmals in der römischen Antike unter Kaiser Diokletian erscheinen und ursprünglich für große Thermen und Schwitzbäder verwendet wurden, was in manchem Bayreuther Sommer durchaus Sinn macht. Die Familie Wagner hat auf ihrer Italienreise 1876 sogar ein antikes Original gesehen, am 15. November: *„Nachmittags Thermen des Caracalla, Via Appia!!"*[1] Doch niemand fühlte sich dabei an Bayreuth erinnert. Klassische Thermenfenster haben zwei markante Vertikalstreben, doch werden oft alle Segmentbogenfenster dieses Ausmaßes Thermenfenster genannt. Das Motiv wurde durch den Renaissancearchitekten Palladio neu belebt, findet sich auch in Kirchenbauten des Barock. In der Revolutionsarchitektur und im Klassizismus erscheint es sehr häufig und schmückt sogar viele Bühnentürme klassizistischer Theater, dort wo – in einer noch nicht elektrifizierten Zeit – viel natürliches Licht verlangt wurde.

Longing for the antique

Roman sweat bath windows

A second motif of the Bayreuth Festspielhaus that can be placed firmly in the style of the Schinkel school and that is also a distinctly antique motif is the large segmented semi-circular window on the stage tower. Originally there was a pendant on the north side such as that found on the south main facade, but it was not rebuilt in 1966 when the stage tower was reconstructed.

In architectural history, large semi-circular windows such as this are called thermal or Diocletian windows because they were first used in Roman antiquity during the reign of Emperor Diocletian in large thermal and sweat baths. This seems perfectly appropriate during some Bayreuth summers. During their 1876 trip to Italy, the Wagner family actually saw an antique original on November 15: *"Afternoon, Caracalla thermal baths, Via Appia!"* But no one was reminded of Bayreuth. Classical thermal windows have two prominent vertical mullions, but all large segmented semi-circular windows are often referred to as thermal windows. The Renaissance architect Palladio began to use this motif again, and it is also found in Baroque churches. It is very common in revolutionary architecture and in Classicism, even decorating many stage towers of Classicist theaters, providing natural light where a lot of light was needed and before there was electric lighting.

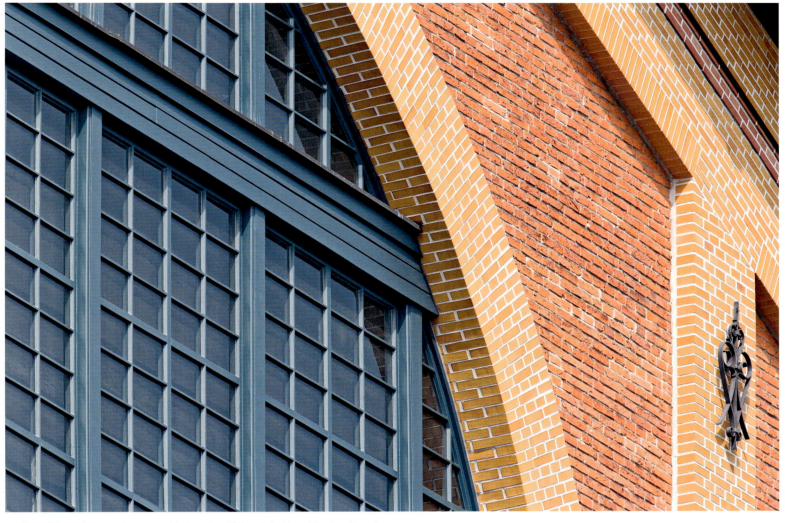

Nachträglich geschwärzte Fenster verhindern den Blick auf die hinterblendete Brandmauer
Window panes darkened later prevent the firewall behind the window from being seen

Das Festspielhaus von Preußen kommend aus betrachtet
The Festspielhaus seen when approaching from Prussia

Das Wagner wohlbekannte, klassizistische Zürcher Theater mit Thermenfenster
The Classicist Zurich Theater with thermal windows that Wagner certainly knew

Das Bühnendach wurde 1964 abgerissen, das Nordfenster 1966 zugemauert
The stage roof was torn down in 1964 and the north window was walled closed in 1966

Blaue Fenster, blaue Türen

Die Farbe Blau ziert alle Fenster und Türen beim Altbau wie auch bei den neueren Neben- und Anbauten, dort sogar alle Gatter und Tore, wodurch ein koloristisch reizvoller Komplementärkontrast zu den (orange-)roten Backsteinen und eine harmonische Gesamterscheinung entstehen. Blaue Fenster sind aus dem Süden Europas bekannt, wo sie Fliegen vertreiben sollen. Die Farbe Blau besitzt aber auch eine apotrophäische Funktion im Aberglauben vieler Völker, böse Blicke abzuhalten. In Bayreuth sind damit vielleicht die kritischen Gedanken der blauen „Tintenmänner" gemeint.

Wagner hatte einen durchaus sensiblen Farbensinn. Ob er diesen auch synästhetisch in seine Musik eingebracht hat, so wie Nietzsche dem LOHENGRIN einmal viel „*blaue Musik*" attestiert hat, führt etwas weit. Wagner bevorzugte in seinen Wohnungen rote Vorhänge, aber auch grüne und blaue Tapeten. Er kleidete sich oft sehr farbenfroh, berühmt ist sein rosafarbener Schlafrock. Rosa muss als seine Lieblingsfarbe gelten, was heute sicherlich viele überrascht: „*In der Frühe spricht er heiter von dem Vergnügen an Farben, und dass mit Rosa eigentlich das Leben begänne. Gelb, Blau etc., alles Übrige sei Haltung und Freundlichkeit und was man wolle, Rosa aber sei Leben.*"[1] Zur Farbe Blau ist kein signifikantes Verhältnis zu erkennen, allenfalls ein meteorologisches, denn Wagner liebte den blauen Himmel, insbesondere den italienischen Äther, weshalb er im winterlichen Bayreuth oft litt: „*Heitrer Himmel, R. augenblicklich wohler, er braucht das Blau durchaus.*"[2]

Blue windows, blue doors

All of the windows and doors of the old and new buildings, annexes and additional buildings and even the gates and entranceways of the latter are painted blue. This provides a striking complementary color contrast to the (orange) red bricks and creates a harmonious overall appearance. Blue windows are common in southern Europe, where they are supposed to drive away flies. In the superstitions of many cultures, the color blue also has the apotrophaic function of warding off the evil eye. Perhaps the blue "ink men's" critical thoughts are meant in Bayreuth.

Wagner had a sophisticated sense of color. It goes too far to wonder whether he applied this synaesthetically to his music, though Nietzsche did once claim that LOHENGRIN has a lot of *"blue music."* In his apartments, Wagner preferred red curtains, but also green and blue wallpapers. He often dressed in many colors, and his pink bathrobe is famous. His favorite color must be pink, which must surprise many people today: *"This morning he spoke happily about the joy he finds in colors, and that life actually began with the color pink. Yellow, blue, etc., everything else may well be poise and friendliness and whatever you want, but pink is life."* He does not have a recognizably significant relationship with blue, except perhaps a meteorological one, since Wagner loved the blue sky, especially the Italian ether, causing him to suffer frequently during the winters in Bayreuth: *"Clear sky, R. feeling better immediately, he truly needs the blue."*

Wagner kannte die romantischen Dimensionen der Farbe Blau und auch ihre seit der Ritterzeit volkstümlich gewordene Symbolbedeutung als Farbe der Treue: *„Die blaue Blume der Romantik, wie sie auf den Inseln der Seligen blüht, ist mir nie in den Sinn gekommen, aber (…) Männerwert und Tapferkeit! Treue bis in den Tod für Vaterland und Frauenliebe! In diesem Sinne blühten die Träume der Romantik auf in mir."*[1]

Häufiger jedoch erscheint die Bedeutung der Farbe Blau als Symbol des Glaubens, wie ein Zitat aus einem Brief König Ludwigs beweist, sodass die überreiche Verwendung der Farbe Blau am Bayreuther Festspielhaus wohl in diesem Sinne verstanden werden kann: *„Die blaue Farbe des Saphirs (Farbe des Glaubens) möge Ihnen ein Symbol des festen Glaubens und unerschütterlichen Vertrauens sein, welche mich beseelen und mir den Muth verleihen, Alles was an mir liegt zu tun, um das große, das EWIGE Werk erbauen zu helfen."*[2]

Der blaue Anstrich ist aber leider nicht historisch und wurde von Wieland Wagner eingeführt. Alle Hölzer waren bis dahin grundsätzlich braun gestrichen. Als in den 1950er Jahren einmal eine neue Farbe zur Diskussion stand, entschied man sich – wie Wolfgang Wagner erzählt – für Blau, *„denn Braun hat man schließlich genug gehabt"*[3].

Wagner was familiar with the Romantic dimensions of the color blue and the color's commonly known symbolic meaning since the days of the knights as the color of fidelity: *"The blue blossom of the Romantic that blossoms on the islands of the blessed never entered my mind, but [...] manly values and bravery! Fidelity to the death for fatherland and a woman's love! In this regard the dreams of the Romantic blossom within me."*

The color blue is more commonly used as a symbol of faith, as a quotation from a letter from King Ludwig illustrates, providing a possible explanation for the heavy use of blue for the Bayreuth Festspielhaus: *"May the blue color of the sapphire (the color of faith) be a symbol of a strong faith and an unshakable trust that fill me and give me the courage to do everything in my power to help build the ETERNAL work."*

Unfortunately, the blue paint is not historic and was added by Wieland Wagner. Up until then, all the wood was painted brown. As Wolfgang Wagner explains, when a new color was discussed in the 1950s, blue was chosen *"because people had had enough of brown."*

Griechischer Tempel im Industriezeitalter

Die Bayreuther Hügelscheune, die rote Ziegelfabrik hat – wenn man genau schaut – ein etwas merkwürdiges Dach mit einer Firstblume und Schnörkeln am Giebel, wie sie schon in den Plänen Brückwalds erscheinen. Diese Verzierungen sind 1939 Opfer eines Unwetters geworden, das große Teile des Dachs zerstörte. Beim Neubau des Bühnenturms 1964/65 und Austausch des hölzernen Dachstuhls durch eine Stahlkonstruktion wurden sie nicht wieder ergänzt, sondern erst 1994 rekonstruiert, womit sich erneut ein Bekenntnis zum Originalbau offenbart.

Jene so lange verschwundenen Zierelemente mögen viele überrascht haben, weil sie nicht zum preußischen Theaternutzbau passen, sondern Motive einer antikisierenden Architektur darstellen. Das Satteldach mit einer dreieckigen Giebelform entspricht zwar einer durchaus normalen Dachform eines Fachwerkbaus, doch die Voluten verleihen ihm eine antike Anmutung, die seit der Renaissance auftaucht. In den Entwürfen Sempers für die beiden Münchner Projekte erscheinen sie nicht, sind also eine Zugabe Brückwalds.

Semper hatte in seinen Münchner Plänen einen klassischen Dreiecksgiebel, ein Tympanon mit Figurenschmuck, vorgesehen, wie es beim antiken Tempelbau üblich war und den Theaterbau als Musentempel pointiert. Auch der nördliche Anbau des Festspielhauses von 1924 zeigt ein echtes Tympanon. Brückwald jedoch nimmt solche Tempel-Assoziationen zurück, indem er die Katheten seines Giebeldreiecks nicht durch eine Hypotenuse schließt, sondern mit dem Radius des Thermenfensters durchkreuzt.

Trotzdem wurde das Bayreuther Festspielhaus immer wieder gerne mit einem Tempel verglichen, ja sogar von Wagner selbst, der – wie eingangs zitiert – die Anfänge der Theaterarchitektur im griechischen Tempel sah: „Wonnige Ruhe und edles Entzücken fasst uns dagegen beim heiteren Anblicke der hellenistischen Göttertempel"[1] schreibt er in „Das Kunstwerk der Zukunft". Auch im übertragenen Sinne blieb dem Theaterreformer Wagner der griechische Tempel als Vorbild für sein ideales Theater gültig, wie Cosima berichtet: „Das Theater seines Gedankens ist ein Tempel, und das jetzige Theater eine Jahrmarktsbude, er redet die Sprache des Priesters, und Krämer sollen ihn verstehen!"[2]

A Greek temple in the industrial age

If you look closely, the Bayreuth barn on a hill, the red brick factory has a somewhat strange roof with a finial and scrolls on the gable that were even on Brückwald's plans. These decorations were damaged during a storm in 1939 that destroyed large segments of the roof. When the new stage tower was built in 1964/65 and the wooden truss was replaced by a steel construction, the decorative elements were not added, but were reconstructed in 1994, another display of commitment to the original building.

After having disappeared for so long, these decorative elements may have surprised many visitors because they do not match the Prussian functional theater, but are rather motifs from classical architecture. The saddleback roof with a triangular gable is completely in line with the normal roof shape of a timber-framed building, but the volutes give it an antique feel only in use since the Renaissance. They are not found in Semper's designs for either Munich project, so Brückwald must have added it on.

Semper's Munich plans called for a classical triangular gable and a tympanum decorated with figures. Such elements were typical for antique temples and would have flagged the theater as a temple of the Muses. The north addition from 1924 also has a true tympanum. Brückwald de-emphasized such temple associations by not spanning a hypotenuse between the legs of the gable triangle, but instead by crossing through the radius of the thermal window.

Nonetheless, people frequently compare the Bayreuth Festspielhaus to a temple, even Wagner himself who, as quoted earlier, identifies the beginnings of theater architecture in the Greek temple. In "The Artwork of the Future" he writes, *"We were awash in a feeling of pleasant calmness and noble delight at the lovely sight of the Hellenistic temples to the Gods."* As Cosima writes, the Greek temple remained a model for Wagner in the figurative sense as well, in his efforts to reform the theater: *"The theater of his thoughts is a temple, and the current theater is a carnival stall. He speaks the priest's language and grocers are supposed to understand him!"*

„Wonnige Ruhe und edles Entzücken
fasst uns dagegen beim heiteren Anblicke
der hellenistischen Göttertempel."

"We were awash in a feeling of pleasant calmness and
noble delight at the lovely sight
of the Hellenistic temples to the Gods."

Richard Wagner

Modell von 1865 des von Semper als griechischer Tempel mit unbedachtem Zuschauersaal geplanten Theaters für den Münchner Glaspalast
1865 model of the theater Semper planned in the form of a Greek temple without a roof for the Munich Glass Palace

Außen Antike – innen High-tech
Antique exterior, high-tech interior

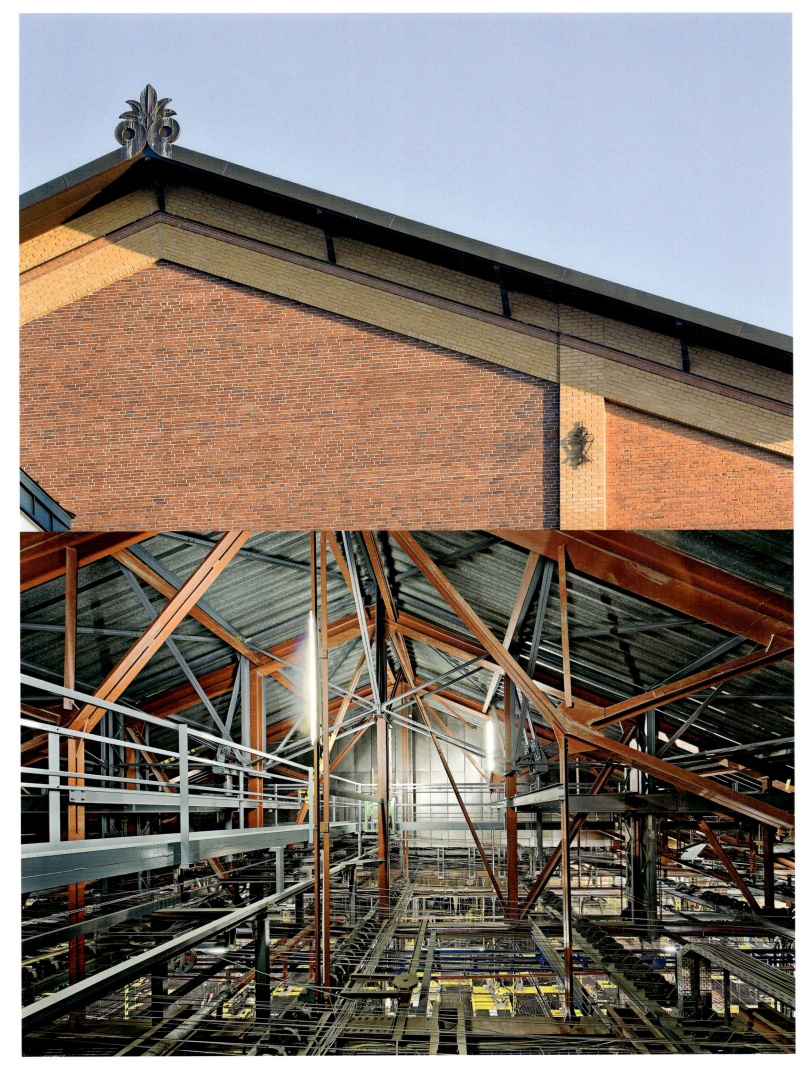

Voluten, Palmetten, Akroterien

Die Voluten am Nord- wie am Südgiebel des Bühnenturms mögen so manche Assoziation wecken. Volute ist lateinisch und bedeutet ganz abstrakt „das Gerollte", sodass ein musikalisch gebildeter Mensch an die Schnecke einer Violine denken mag. Wagnerianer und andere Germanisten können auch an den gerollten Bug eines Wikingerschiffs denken oder an die Spiralornamente germanischer Goldschmiedearbeiten. Architekten wie Otto Brückwald jedoch verbanden die Volute mit der antiken Architektur, wo sie vor allem im ionischen und korinthischen Kapitell erscheint. Schon die Ägypter vor über 3500 Jahren kannten die Volute als Abstraktion einer sich einrollenden Lotosblume oder Palmette. Giebelvoluten wie die in Bayreuth kennt die antike Architektur allerdings nicht; sie sind erst seit der Renaissance in Gebrauch, insbesondere in der deutschen Renaissance am sogenannten Volutengiebel überaus reich. Hier mag auch Brückwald sein Vorbild gefunden haben.

Erscheinen die vier Bayreuther Giebelvoluten als Motive einer Neorenaissance, so ist die Firstblume, eine klassische Palmette, eher ein Motiv des Klassizismus um 1800. Sie hat eindeutig antike Vorbilder, wie etwa auf dem Parthenon in Athen, und wurde in einem archäologischen Historismus als echtes Motiv gerne verwendet. Die Palmette (französisch Palmbäumchen) ist die symmetrische Abstraktion eines Palmenwipfels und findet sich als Ornament in den frühesten Kulturen, häufig – wie in Bayreuth – in Verbindung mit ebenfalls vegetabil verstandenen Voluten. Der Ursprung solcher Motive liegt in dem magischen Glauben, Gebäude durch solche Akroterien (griechisch akrotérion – der äußerste vorragende Teil) vor bösen Geistern und Kritikern schützen zu wollen.

Die Palmette ist das klassische Siegeszeichen, das in Bezug zum Festspielhaus viele Motivationen haben kann: die Realisierung des Festspielhauses darf als ein großer persönlicher Sieg Wagners gewertet werden, als Sieg über das scheinbar Unmögliche, als Sieg der Kunst über die Ignoranz und den Geiz dieser Welt. Zumindest hätte ein Mensch des 19. Jahrhunderts solche pathetischen Gedanken empfinden können. An keiner Stelle der vielen gesichteten Schriften zum Festspielhaus wird dieses besondere i-Tüpfelchen wahrgenommen und auch heute kaum beachtet.

Dabei verleiht die exponierte Lage eines solchen Akroterions jedem Gebäude einen besonderen Akzent, der oft die Funktion eines Baus erkennbar macht. Sempers Oper in Dresden und sein Entwurf für das Münchner Festspieltheater zeigen eine antike Lyra, das Attribut des Musenvaters Apoll, das Sinnbild der Musik. Darüber hinaus waren Theatermasken beliebt oder eine Pallas Athene, eine Quadriga oder die Siegesgöttin Nike.

Neben dem figurativen Palmen-Akroterion am First zeigt das Bayreuther Festspielhaus weitere abstrakt-geometrische Akroterien: je eine geachtelte Kugel am Übergang zwischen gebogener Südfassade des Zuschauerhauses und den Eckpavillons, sowie acht sphärische Dreiecke auf den acht Ecken der Lüftungslaterne auf dem Dach des Zuschauerhauses. Solche geometrischen Akroterien sind seit dem Klassizismus und der Revolutionsarchitektur bekannt. Sie sind schon auf den Plänen Brückwalds zu finden, wurden 1876 gebaut, haben das 20. Jahrhundert mit seinen Unwettern und Sanierungen überstanden und gehören zu den wenigen Originalteilen der Festspielarchitektur.

Volutes, palmettes, acroteria

The volutes on the north and south gables of the stage tower awaken certain associations. Volute has Latin roots and means, abstractly, "rolled" reminding a musically educated person of the scroll of a violin. Wagnerians and other Germanists may also recall the spiral at the head of the prow of a Viking ship or on the spiral ornaments common in Germanic goldsmith work. Architects like Otto Brückwald, however, associate volutes with antique architecture, where they are especially common in Ionic and Corinthian capitals. Even the Egyptians used volutes 3,500 years ago as an abstraction of a rolled-up lotus flower or palmette. Gable volutes like those in Bayreuth, however, were not found in antique architecture, but were introduced during the Renaissance, and were especially common in so-called volute gables in the German Renaissance. This may have been Brückwald's model.

Whereas the four Bayreuth gable volutes are motifs of the neo-Renaissance, the finial, a classical palmette, is more of a motif from Classicism around 1800. It has unambiguous antique models, such as on the Parthenon in Athens, and was used as a genuine motif in archeological historicism. The palmette (diminutive of French palme) is the symmetrical abstraction of the crown of a palm tree and was frequently used as an ornament in the earliest cultures – as in Bayreuth as well – in connection with plant-like volutes. Such motifs have origins in the magical belief that such acroteria (Greek akrotério = the part extending out the farthest) protect the building from evil spirits and harsh critics.

The palmette is the classical sign of victory that could have been motivated in many ways with regard to the Festspielhaus: the realization of the Festspielhaus can be considered a personal victory for Wagner, as victory over the seemingly impossible, as victory of art over ignorance and greed in the world. At least people could have had such lofty thoughts in the 19th century. This special detail is not mentioned anywhere in the many documents about the Festspielhaus we studied, and is hardly noticed today either.

The exposed location of such acroteria, however, gives any building a special accent, often revealing the building's function. Semper's opera in Dresden and his design for the Munich Festspieltheater called for an antique lyre, the attribute of Apollo, the leader of the Muses, and the symbol of music. Theater masks, Pallas Athena, a quadriga or Nike, the goddess of victory, were also common.

In addition to the figurative palmette acroteria on the ridge, the Bayreuth Festspielhaus also has further abstract geometrical acroteria: an eighth of a sphere on each transition between the curved south facade of the auditorium and the corner pavilions and eight spherical triangles on the eight corners of the ventilation lantern on the roof of the auditorium. Geometrical acroteria of this type have been common since Classicism and revolutionary architecture. They were part of Brückwald's plans, were built in 1876, survived the storms and remodeling of the 20th century and are some of the few remaining original parts of the Festspielhaus architecture.

Akroterien: Palmetten am Giebeldach, geachtelte Kugeln am Zuschauerhaus und sphärische Dreiecke auf der Lüftungslaterne
Acroteria: palmettes along the gable roof, an eighth of a sphere on the auditorium and spherical triangles on top of the ventilation lantern.

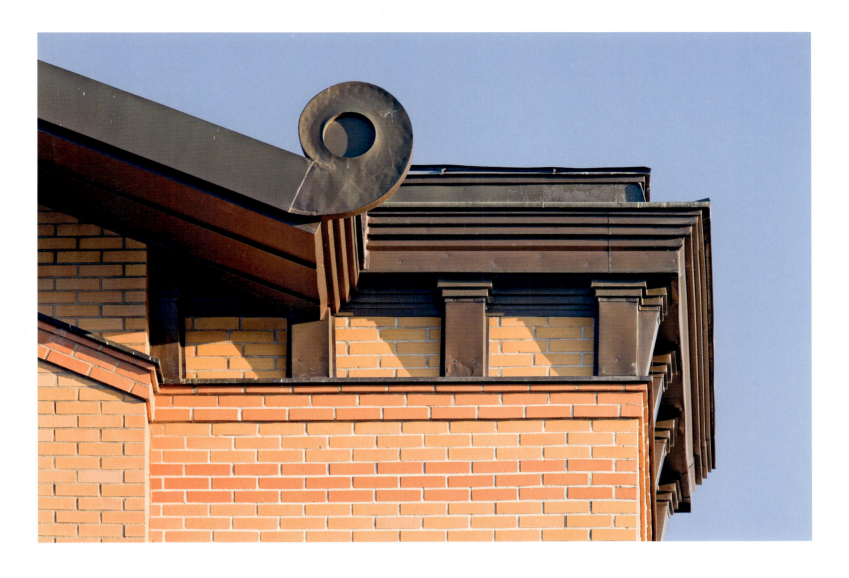

Fazit

Diese Details sind – schon rein quantitativ – nicht von überragender Bedeutung, doch sind diese wenigen Zierelemente eines ansonsten kunstlosen Gebäudes nicht unwichtig und ganz sicher nicht unbedacht. Voluten, Palmetten und Akroterien markieren Akzente, nobilitieren die rote Theater-Scheune und rücken sie in die Tradition des Klassizismus, wo sie vor allem die griechische Antike als architektonische Allusion wachrufen. Sie sind quasi der minimalisierte sichtbare Rest einer einst so pathetisch zelebrierten Antikenbegeisterung Richard Wagners. Im Historismus des 19. Jahrhunderts wird bisweilen der Begriff des „romantischen Hellenismus" benutzt, um Bauten der Schinkel-Schule zu beschreiben, die nordische Backsteine mit griechischen Elementen kombinieren, eine Stilzuweisung, die auch für große Teile des Bayreuther Festspielhauses sinnvoll ist.

Summary

From a purely quantitative perspective, these details do not have great meaning, but these few decorative elements on an otherwise artless building are not unimportant and were surely not added thoughtlessly. Volutes, palmettes and acroteria provide accents, making the red theater barn more noble and bringing it closer to the Classicist tradition as architectonic allusions to Greek antiquity. They are quasi the minimized visible remains of Wagner's once so loftily celebrated fascination with antiquity. The term "romantic Hellenism" is sometimes used in the historicism of the 19th century to describe buildings from the Schinkel school that combine Nordic brick with Greek elements. This term could be used to categorize many aspects of the Bayreuth Festspielhaus as well.

1994 wurden die 1939 bei einem Unwetter verloren gegangenen Voluten und Palmetten aus Kupferblech rekonstruiert; das Satteldach wurde wieder vorgekragt
In 1994, the volutes destroyed in a storm in 1939 were reconstructed out of copper sheet and the saddleback roof was also cantilevered again

Die Eckpavillons

Neorenaissance mit Natursteinen

Teure Hausteine aus gelbem Sandstein prägten bei der Eröffnung des Hauses 1876 allein die Eckpavillons des Zuschauerhauses (der Königsbau wurde erst 1882 gebaut). Sie schmücken bis heute die Rustika und die Umrandungen von Türen und Fenstern im Erdgeschoss. Letztere wurden im ersten und zweiten Obergeschoss nur mit Putzmauerwerk eingefasst, erscheinen aus der Distanz aber wie echte Hausteine. Diese massive Bauweise war für die Treppentürme seitens der Feuerschutzgesetze gefordert. Ein anderer Grund für die teure Bauweise mag darin motiviert gewesen sein, dass im nordwestlichen Eckpavillon im ersten Obergeschoss ein Speisesaal und im nordöstlichen ein Fürstensalon für hohe Gäste eingerichtet war, wovon heute nichts mehr erhalten ist. Darüber hinaus offenbart die hier erfolgte Verringerung billiger Backsteine eine Entscheidung für edlere und dauerhaftere Materialien an jenen Gebäudeteilen, die nicht als Provisorium gedacht waren.

Wie die Pläne zeigen, sind die Pavillons von Brückwald fast so gebaut worden, wie sie entworfen wurden: Nur die Fenster im Parterre rückten in die symmetrische Mitte und der Girlandenschmuck sowie die weißen Putzwände „durften" so nicht ausgeführt werden. Die Eckpavillons sind heute noch original erhalten, wurden bei keiner Sanierung abgerissen und zeugen so von der originalen Bausubstanz, auf der „das Auge des Meisters geruht" hat.

Wagner geht in seiner Rede zur Grundsteinlegung allerdings mit keinem Wort auf diese massiv ausgeführten Eckpavillons ein, nennt das ganze Festspielhaus ein Provisorium, was genau betrachtet eine rhetorische Finte ist. Sie sind nicht zier- und schmucklos, sondern stilistisch gestaltet, und zwar ganz eindeutig im Stil der italienischen Neorenaissance. Damit erinnern sie an die Pläne Sempers für München, und man kann darüber nachdenken, ob Brückwald, der diese Bauteile 1875 lediglich als „Stützpunkte"[1] bezeichnet, nicht doch von Semper beeinflusst war.

Wagner selbst erinnert in seiner Rede von 1872 an Semper (allerdings nur beim Innenraum), „welchem zuerst die Aufgabe zuerteilt war, das Theater im Sinne einer monumentalen Ausführung zu entwerfen" und sich dabei „der architektonischen Ornamentik im edelsten Renaissance-Stil" bediente. Doch „da wir für das provisorische Festtheater in Bayreuth jedem Gedanken an ähnlichen Schmuck, wie er nur durch ein kostbares edles Material Bedeutung erhält, entsagen mussten"[2], wurde einfacher gebaut.

Die letztlich doch im Stil der Renaissance in „edlen Materialien" errichteten Eckpavillons markieren also den Beginn der monumentalen Vollendung des ganzen Theaters! Das verwundert, schätzte Wagner die Renaissance bekanntlich so gar nicht. Schon die Entwürfe Sempers für München (1864/65) werden von Wagner

The corner pavilions

Neo-Renaissance with natural stone

When the theater opened in 1876, only the corner pavilions of the auditorium boasted expensive hewn stone of yellow sandstone (the Königsbau wasn't built until 1882). To this day, this stone decorates the rustica and the door and window frames on the ground floor. On the second and third floors, the door and window frames were only framed with plaster, although from a distance it looks like real hewn stone. Fire code dictated this massive construction for the stairwell. Another motivation for this expensive construction may have been that there was a dining room on the second floor of the northwest corner pavilion and a Prince's Salon in the northeast pavilion for important guests. Neither of these still exist today. In addition, the less frequent use of inexpensive bricks is an indication of the decision to use sturdier construction materials on the parts of the building not conceived as provisional.

As the plans show, the pavilions were built almost exactly as Brückwald had designed them. Only the windows on the ground floor were shifted into the symmetrical center and the festoon decoration and the white plaster walls "weren't allowed" to be built that way. The corner pavilions are still original and were never torn down during restoration. They display the original building substance that "the maestro's eye rested on."

In his speech at the cornerstone laying ceremony, Wagner makes no mention of these massively constructed corner pavilions, calling the Festspielhaus a provisional building. On closer look, this was a rhetorical maneuver. They do not lack detail and decoration, but rather are stylishly decorated, definitely in the style of the Italian neo-Renaissance. In this regard, they recall Semper's plans for Munich. It is worth considering whether Brückwald wasn't influenced by Semper after all, even though he only calls these building sections "support points" in 1875.

Wagner himself mentions Semper in his 1872 speech (but only regarding the interior), *"who was first given responsibility for creating a monumental design for the theater,"* using *"the most noble architectonic ornaments in Renaissance style"* to do so. But *"since we had to abandon every thought about such decoration for the provisional festival theater in Bayreuth because it would only be realizable using expensive, noble materials,"* the building was built simpler.

The corner pavilions built in the style of the Renaissance using "noble materials" thus mark the beginning of the monumental completion of the whole theater! That is surprising, given Wagner's low opinion of the Renaissance. Wagner even criticizes Semper's designs for Munich (1864/65) on January 6, 1872: *"R. looked at Semper's drawings and was not satisfied with the exterior solution. In the end it was a good thing that theater wasn't built!"* Many years later, on October 24, 1882, Cosima writes: *"Yesterday we spoke about Semper's buildings and agreed that his motifs were mostly borrowed from Italy and that he did not use decoration very successfully, 'a person like him only sees straight lines and nothing more.'"* And on November 7, 1882, Cosima notes:

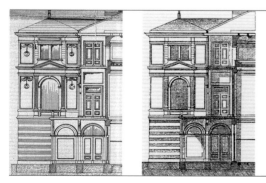

Eingabeplan 1872 Plan submitted, 1872

Holzschnitt 1873 woodcuts, 1873

Heutiger Zustand Current condition

noch am 6. Januar 1872 kritisiert: „*Die Zeichnung Sempers betrachtend, und nicht befriedigt mit der Lösung nach außen, sagt R., am Ende sei es ein Glück gewesen, dass es nicht zur Ausführung kam!*"[1] Viele Jahre später, am 24. Oktober 1882, schreibt Cosima: „*Gestern sprachen wir von den Semper'schen Bauten, kamen überein, dass die Motive meist von Italien übernommen seien und dass er in der Dekorierung nicht sehr glücklich gewesen sei, ‚so einer sieht nur gerade Linien und weiter nichts'.*"[2] Und am 7. November 1882 notiert Cosima: „*Beim Kaffee sprachen wir von der Renaissance; ob es überhaupt unbedingt ein Glück war, dass die Antike ausgegraben wurde?*"[3] Trotz dieser vernichtenden Urteile ließ Wagner sein Wahnfried und jene Eckpavillons im Stil der italienischen Renaissance bauen – einer von vielen Widersprüchen im Werk und Leben Richard Wagners.

"*We talked about the Renaissance over coffee, whether it was necessarily a good thing that the Antique was dug out?*" Yet despite these scathing judgments, Wagner had his "Wahnfried" and these corner pavilions built in the style of the Italian Renaissance – one of the many contradictions in the life and work of Richard Wagner.

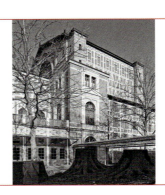

Eckpavillons mit Hausteinelementen im Stil der italienischen Renaissance
Corner pavilions with hewn stone elements in the style of the Italian neo-Renaissance

Theatermotiv mit Tympanon

Wagner liebte sein Italien, doch was macht diese Eckpavillons nun so italienisch? Es sind zwei Elemente: die Sockelzone und die Fenster beziehungsweise Türen. Die Fenster der ersten Etage der Eckpavillons werden von einer Ädikula lateinisch Häuschen, Tempelchen) gerahmt, einer dekorativen Scheinarchitektur – so als habe die Wand einen kleinen Tempel verschluckt. Sie ist seit der griechisch-römischen Antike bekannt und wurde von der Renaissance Italiens wiederbelebt. Sie umfasst die Fenster mit einer rechteckigen Kolonnade, bestehend aus einem flachen Wandpfeiler (Pilaster) mit kaum differenziertem toskanischen Kapitell und einem ebenso schmucklosen Balken, der einen Dreiecksgiebel, ein Tympanon, stützt. Zu dieser Ädikula tritt ein weiteres Motiv: In die Kolonnade ist eine Archivolte (Rundbogen) eingestellt. Diese Kombination aus Kolonnade und Archivolte erscheint am Kolosseum in Rom (das von Wagner allerdings erst am 1. Dezember 1876 besichtigt wurde) und wird deshalb Theatermotiv (oder Tabularium-Motiv) genannt! In allen Theatern von Semper ist dieses für ein Theater überaus sinniges Motiv das häufigste Element der Fassadengliederung, wie auch bei vielen anderen Theatern des 19. Jahrhunderts. Eine besonders elegante Dekoration findet sich in einer geschwungenen Spange (Agraffe), die den Scheitelstein der Archivolte mit dem Gebälk der Kolonnade verklammert und damit das sogenannte Theatermotiv schließt und pointiert.

Das zweite so italienische Element der Eckpavillons ist die Sockelzone, mit einem Wechselspiel von glatten und rauen Steinen. Es handelt sich um eine bandierte Rustika, ein seit der Antike bekanntes „bäuerliches", sprich primitives Gemäuer mit grob behauenen Steinen (Bossen), die noch deutlich die Spuren des Steinmetzen tragen. Die Renaissance entdeckte darin eine ästhetische Qualität und führte die Rustika bei Palästen in Rom oder Florenz wieder ein. Dabei ziert eine Rustika meist die Sockelzone und grenzt die prächtige Beletage von den einfachen, womöglich bäuerlichen Zeitgenossen der Straße ab. Eine Rustika suggeriert also Distanz und ist damit ein eher „undemokratisches" Bauelement.

Auch im Erdgeschoss finden sich Archivolten um die Türen, deren Steine radial geschnitten sind und den Bogen sichtbar wölben. Die Rundbögen sind in ein vorspringendes Wandfeld eingestellt, das oben mit einem vorkragenden Gebälk schließt, doch ohne Dreiecksgiebel. Da diesem Gebälk eigene Säulen fehlen, kann man hier nicht von einem Theatermotiv sprechen.

Theater motif with tympanum

Wagner loved Italy, but what is it that makes these corner pavilions so Italian? Two elements are critical: the base zone and the windows and/or doors. The windows on the 2nd floor of the corner pavilions are framed by aedicules (Latin: small house or temple), a decorative mock architectural treatment looking as though the wall had swallowed a small temple. Aedicules have been common since classical antiquity and were brought back into fashion in the Italian Renaissance. In this style, a square colonnade comprising a flat wall column (pilaster) with a barely differentiated Tuscan capital and a likewise undecorated beam supporting a triangular gable, a tympanum, frames a window. Another motif accompanying the aedicule is an archivolt (round arch) set into the colonnade. This combination of colonnade and archivolt was used on the Coliseum in Rome (which Wagner first visited on December 1, 1876) and is for that reason known as the theater (or tabularium) motif! This motif, which is perfecting appropriate for a theater, is the most frequent element structuring the facade of all of Semper's theaters as well as of many other theaters built in the 19th century. The curved hook (agraffe) that clamps the keystone of the archivolt with the beam of the colonnade is an especially elegant decoration. It helps close and emphasize the "theater motif."

The second especially Italian element of the corner pavilion is the base zone with alternating smooth and raw stone. This so-called banded rustica, considered a "rural" or primitive wall style since antiquity, features roughly hewn stones (bosses) still showing clear marks from the stonecutters. The Renaissance saw an aesthetic quality in banded rustica and used it for palaces in Rome and Florence. Rustica typically decorates the base zone, dividing the piano nobile from the simple, possibly peasant, streetwalkers with their dogs. Rustica thus suggests distance and is therefore an "undemocratic" building element.

There are also archivolts around the doors on the ground floor with radial cut stones that visibly vault the arch. The round arches are set in a projected wall segment topped with a cantilevered beam, but without a triangular gable. Since this beam does not have its own columns, this would not be considered a theater motif.

There is a special detail on the southeast corner pavilion: a hook to the right of the sales window on the rustica. Anyone fond of a man's best friend, which Wagner also loved so much, will comprehend its function immediately. *"After dinner R. spoke of man's best achievement: the dog. This fact dates back long before history, and now he gets tied up, creating a wild animal out of him again."*

Eine Gouache mit Firnis von unbekannter Hand vom Winter 1882/83 zeigt Richard und Cosima Wagner vor dem Palazzo Vendramin (Landseite) in Venedig, vielleicht in die Betrachtung eines klassischen Theatermotivs mit Tympanon versunken.
A gouache with varnish by unknown artist from winter 1882/83 of Richard and Cosima Wagner in front of the Palazzo Vendramin (street side) in Venice, possibly deeply engaged in observing a classical theater motif with tympanum.

Agraffe, Hundehaken und Türbeschlag mit Löwen- und Narrenkopf.
Agraffe, dog leash hooks and door fittings with lion's head and fool's head.

Rustika im Stil der Palazzi des Cinquecento Rustica in the style of the palaces of the cinquecento

Ein besonderes Detail lässt sich am südöstlichen Eckpavillon entdecken, ein Haken rechts neben dem Verkaufsfenster an der Rustika, dessen Funktion jeder sofort erfasst, der jene Menschenfreunde mag, die auch Wagner so sehr liebte. *„Nach Tisch spricht R. von der schönsten Errungenschaft des Menschen: dem Hund; diese Tat sei vor aller Geschichte vor sich gegangen, und nun binde man ihn an, mache ihn gleichsam wieder zum wilden Tier."*[1]

Wilde Tiere lassen sich an einem weiteren Detail entdecken, an den Türbeschlägen, die im dekorativen Stil einer deutschen (!) Neorenaissance gegossen sind: mit typischem „Beschlagwerk". Alle Beschläge sind einem letzten Original nachgegossen worden, das sich am Königsbau bis in die 1990er Jahre erhalten hatte. Trotz Wagners ausdrücklichen „Verbots" von figurativen Zierelementen erkennt man einen Löwenkopf, der an die wilden Bestien des römischen Amphitheaters erinnern mag. Darunter einen Narrenkopf, der an Wagners Satz vom 7. Mai 1874 denken lässt: *„Komme ich mir nicht selber vor wie ein Narr, mit meinem Theater da draußen."*[2]

Fazit

Die vier Treppentürme beziehungsweise Eckpavillons des Bayreuther Festspielhauses präsentieren sich in einer heute noch originalen, massiven Bauweise, die den Beginn der monumentalen Vollendung des Theaters markiert. So also hätte das ganze Festspielhaus aussehen können, wenn man mehr Geld besessen hätte. Als neues Gestaltungselement wird hier der Haustein ins Spiel gebracht, der in seiner Verbindung mit dem ungewollt unverputzten Backstein unversehens an lombardische und nordeuropäische Vorbilder, insbesondere an den englischen Georgian-Style, denken lässt. Es handelt sich um einen gelben Sandstein, der an Feustels Brief vom 3. November 1871 erinnert, worin Sandsteinbrüche der Stadt Bayreuth genannt werden. Diese Haussteine schmücken die Sockelzone als Distanz suggerierende Rustika und die Umrandungen von Fenstern und Türen, die in der Beletage das sinnige Theatermotiv plus Tympanon aufweisen. Beide Elemente sind typisch für italienische Paläste des Cinquecento und kennzeichnen einen Stil, der eindeutig als italienische Neorenaissance zu bezeichnen ist. Damit folgt Brückwald dem Einfluss Sempers und wählt den um 1870 beliebtesten Stil des Historismus, obwohl sich Wagner immer gegen den Historismus und gegen die Renaissance ausgesprochen hatte einschließlich der Neorenaissancebauten Sempers für München. Damit wird seine Forderung nach einem „deutschen" Stil letztlich ad absurdum geführt.

There are wild animals to be found in another detail – on the door fittings – cast in decorative German (!) neo-Renaissance style with typical fittings. All fittings were cast from a mold of the last original that survived on the Königsbau until the 1990s. Although Wagner explicitly "forbade" figurative decorative elements, you can see a lion's head possibly reminiscent of the wild beasts of the Roman amphitheater. Underneath there is a fool's head bringing to mind a statement Wagner made on May 7, 1874: *"Don't I feel like a fool myself with my theater out there."*

Summary

The four staircase towers/corner pavilions of the Bayreuth Festspielhaus have retained their original massive architecture that marks the start of the monumental completion of the theater. The whole Festspielhaus could have looked like this if there had been enough money. Hewn stone is introduced as a new design material. Combined with the unintentionally bare bricks lacking stucco, they unintentionally bear resemblance to models from Lombardy and northern Europe, especially the English Georgian style. Yellow sandstone was used, like Feustel mentions in his letter of November 3, 1871, when he names the sandstone quarries near the city of Bayreuth. These hewn stones decorate the base zone, creating a rustica suggesting distance, and are arranged in appropriate theater motifs with tympana framing windows and doors in the piano nobile. Both elements are typical of Italian palaces of the cinquecento and are unmistakably typical of the Italian neo-Renaissance style. This shows that Brückwald was following Semper's influence by choosing the most popular style of Historicism around 1870, even though Wagner often spoke out against Historicism and against the Renaissance, including Semper's neo-Renaissance buildings in Munich. This essentially reduces Wagner's demand for a "German" style ad absurdum.

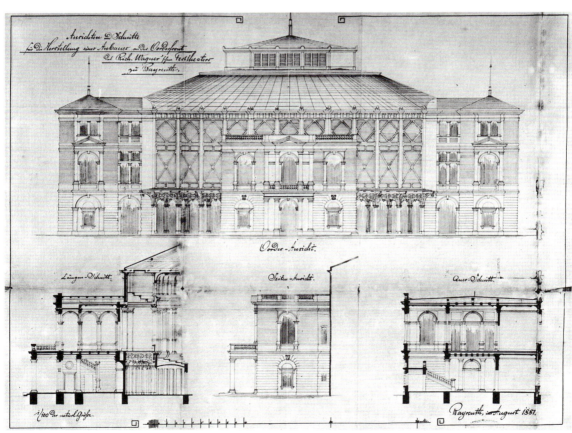

Originaler Eingabeplan Otto Brückwalds für den Königsbau, 1881
Original plan submitted by Otto Brückwald for the Königsbau in 1881

Der Königsbau

Königsbau ohne König

Schon 1876 wurde der Gedanke gefasst, einen zentralen Anbau speziell für den König zu errichten. Nachdem Wagner seine Pläne vom Mai 1877, alles abreißen zu lassen und nach Amerika auszuwandern, aufgegeben hatte und beschloss, seinen PARSIFAL in Bayreuth uraufzuführen, wurde der Königsbau erneut in Planung genommen. Am 15. Mai 1881 hatte Otto Brückwald einen Plan dafür vollendet. Einen Tag später schreibt Wagner an König Ludwig über sein Theater: *„Dieses sonderbare Gebäude ist doch ein unleugbarer Erwerb, eine Wirklichkeit, gegen die sich nichts sagen lässt. Nun wird aber dafür gesorgt, dass auch unser großer, lieber, herrlicher Protektor in diesem ungemütlichen Bauwerke Sich ein wenig behaglicher fühlen soll: der Baumeister Brückwald, [...] arbeitet jetzt den Plan zu dem Vorbau aus, welcher die besondere Anfahrt, dann ein möglichst anständiges Gelass (Salon genannt) mit unmittelbarem Eingang in eine geräumige, gänzlich abgeschlossene Loge in der so genannten Fürsten-Galerie unserem erhabenen Protektor zur Verfügung stellen soll."*[1]

So wie das Wiesbadener Theater eine „Kaiserfahrt" erhielt, um dem durch Attentatsversuche gefährdeten Kaiser einen unauffälligen Zugang zu ermöglichen, wollte Wagner, der nach wie vor der Gunst des Königs bedurfte, seinem menschen- und lichtscheuen Freund eine exklusive Behandlung zukommen lassen. Dadurch erhielt das Festspielhaus nachträglich eine Art Mittelrisalit, der ursprünglich jedoch nicht – wie heute – als ein Haupteingang für alle gedacht war. Noch 1931 war im Parterre der Durchgang zum allgemeinen Foyer durch eine Nische verschlossen und wurde erst später geöffnet.

Der Vergleich von Plan und Wirklichkeit zeigt, dass Brückwald endlich so bauen durfte, wie er es geplant hatte und den Sandstein nicht nur im Parterre (wie bei den Eckpavillons), sondern am gesamten Bau verwenden konnte. Daneben sind (erstmals) Backsteinwände im ersten Obergeschoss eingezeichnet, die also nicht verputzt werden sollten! Brückwald plante diesen Anbau sehr geschmackvoll im Renaissancestil der Eckpavillons unter Verwendung gleicher Materialien und Motive. Selbst Wagner war diese Harmonie wichtig, wie er in jenem Brief an Ludwig schreibt: *„Es ist dafür zu sorgen, dass dieser Vorbau sich in gute Verhältnisse zu dem Ganzen setzt, damit einmal, wann ich endlich doch gestorben bin und die ‚deutsche Nation' sich einheitlich hinter mir zu rühren beginnt, der Beibehaltung des Grundbaues – der ja ganz solid ist – nichts entgegensteht, sobald das Ganze nun mit massiver Architektur umgeben und mit monumentaler Ornamentik ausgestattet werden soll."*[2] Diese Zeilen sind sehr bedeutsam, weil sie verraten, dass der Königsbau wie die Eckpavillons der Anfang eines monumentalen Ausbaus darstellen und der hier verwendete Renaissancestil für den Gesamtbau maßgeblich gewesen wäre!

Die renaissanceistische Rustikazone ist geometrisch sehr schön gestaltet, indem die grob behauenen Bossenbänder zum Rundbogen der Fensterzone abknicken, so einen radialen Strahlenkranz bilden und die tektonischen Zugkräfte eines Bogens abstrahieren, ein Motiv, das ebenfalls von italienischen Palästen des 16. Jahrhunderts bekannt ist.

Mittelpunkt des Königsbaus ist ein von vier Stützen getragener Altan mit einer Balustrade aus Sandstein (heute Beton). Er wird durch toskanische Säulen und Pfeiler aus schön marmoriertem Sandstein getragen mit sehr schlichten Kapitellen und undekoriertem Gebälk. In der Beletage wird ein Risalit im Risalit hervorgehoben: Die leicht vortretende Ädikula mit Theatermotiv wird links und rechts um je einen Pilaster samt Wandfeld aus Sandstein erweitert. Hinter dem Tympanon bildet eine massive Attikazone den Abschluss.

The Königsbau

Königsbau without a king

The idea was already in place in 1876 to build a central addition especially for the King. After Wagner abandoned his plans in May of 1877 to tear down everything and immigrate to America and decided to hold the premiere of PARSIFAL in Bayreuth, his plans to build a Königsbau were taken up again. Otto Brückwald had finished drafting a plan for it by March 15, 1881. The next day, Wagner wrote to King Ludwig about his theater: *"This special building is an undeniable acquisition, a reality that can't be denied. We are now taking measures to ensure that our great, dear, wonderful Protector will feel a little more at ease in this uncomfortable building. The architect Brückwald [...] is currently completing his plans for a frontal building designed to accommodate special transportation and provide a receiving area (called the salon) with direct access to a spacious, fully enclosed loge in the so-called Prince Gallery for the use of our honorable Protector."*

Just as the Wiesbaden Theater was given a so-called Kaiserfahrt to give the Emperor safe and inconspicuous access to the theater in a time when he was being threatened with assassination attempts, Wagner wanted to give his friend, who preferred to avoid people and light and whose graces Wagner still needed, exclusive treatment. This gave the Festspielhaus a sort of central risalit after the fact that was originally not intended as a main entrance for everyone, as is the case today. The access to the public foyer was still blocked by a niche in 1931 and was only opened later.

A comparison between the plan and reality shows that Brückwald was finally allowed to build as he had planned, using sandstone not only on the ground floor (like on the corner pavilions), but on the entire structure. Adjacent to the stone, brick walls not meant to receive stucco are drawn (for the first time) for the second floor! Brückwald planned this extension very tastefully in the same Renaissance style as the corner pavilions using the same materials and motifs. As Wagner writes in a letter to Ludwig, this harmony was important even to him: *"Care should be taken to match this extension with the style of the whole so that when I have finally passed away and the 'German nation' starts to join ranks unanimously behind me, it will not be a problem to keep the basic – quite solid – structure, expand it with massive architecture and adorn it with monumental ornamentation."* These words are critically important because they reveal that the Königsbau, like the corner pavilions, was meant to be the beginning of a monumental expansion and that the entire building would have been modeled on the Renaissance style used on these sections!

The Renaissance style rustica zone is beautifully geometrically designed. The roughly hewn boss bands bend toward the round arch of the window zone, creating a radial ray-like crown as an abstraction of the tectonic forces of an arch. This motif is also common on Italian palaces built in the 16th century.

The center of the Königsbau is a balcony carried by four supports with a balustrade of sandstone (today concrete). It is carried by Tuscan columns and pillars of marbled sandstone with very simple capitals and an undecorated beam. The piano nobile features a risalit within a risalit. The slightly protruding aedicule with theater motif is expanded by a pilaster and a wall section of sandstone on both sides. A massive attic zone behind the tympanum provides closure.

Die seitlichen Fenster im ersten Obergeschoss sind ohne Kolonnaden (wie bei den Eckpavillons im Erdgeschoss) als einfache Rundbogenfenster mit Agraffen ausgeführt. Sie finden sich an der Südfassade und an den Flanken. Sie entsprechen in Form und Proportion der Eingangstür, die allerdings wieder in eine Ädikula eingestellt ist und ein Theatermotiv bildet. Die blau gestrichene Holztür ist original und zeigt Diamantbossen im unteren Drittel.

Die Attika verkleidet das flache Dach im Sinne eines „toit caché". Attikazonen lassen immer an südliche Gefilde denken, oft werden sie von Statuen antiker Götter bewohnt. In Bayreuth findet sich links und rechts des Mittelrisalits eine Balustrade aus Sandstein mit Balustern, die in ihrer vasenförmigen Bauchung etwas barock anmuten, so doch in der Renaissance seit Michelangelo bekannt sind.

Alles in allem wurde beim Königsbau eine recht ansehnliche Fassade gestaltet, die an einen kleinen italienischen Adelspalast des Cinquecento erinnert. Habel spricht sogar von einem *„harmonischen Kabinettstück"*[1] und vom künstlerisch wertvollsten Teil des Außenbaus. So also hätte das ganze Festspielhaus aussehen können, wenn da nicht wieder das Rot der Backsteine frech herausschauen würde. Da an diesem Königsbau keineswegs so geizig wie bisher gespart wurde, hätten die wenigen Quadratmeter rohen Mauerwerks für ein paar hundert Mark auch noch verputzt werden können. Doch Brückwald hat sie (nicht wie bei allen Plänen vorher) nicht verputzen wollen. Warum das? Hatte man sich inzwischen mit dem Backstein angefreundet und die ästhetische Nähe zur Schinkel-Schule oder zum Georgian-Style verstanden? Oder wollte man das Understatement eines Provisoriums aus taktischen Gründen wahren und Mitleid bei den Gönnern wecken? Noch heute lässt Wolfgang Wagner nur ungern renovieren: *„Man könnte ja glauben, dass wir reich seien."*[2]

Portikus plus preußische Kappen

Bei der Fassade des Königsbaus handelt es sich um einen von Säulen getragenen Portikus. Wagner selbst mochte einen Portikus ganz besonders, den am Dogenpalast in Venedig, *„R.'s Lieblingsplatz"*[3], wie Cosima ihn nennt (30. September 1882). Einen Tag zuvor schreibt sie: *„Vor allem erfreut ihn das Sitzen unter dem Portikus zwischen den Säulen, so möchte er gemalt sein."* Das wundert ein wenig, hatte er von hier aus doch jene langweiligen Renaissancebauten vor Augen. Am 16. Oktober 1882 schreibt Cosima nach einem Spaziergang durch die Stadt: *„Er setzt sich aber bald mit mir unter den Bogen des Dogen-Palastes; die Ziegelsteine [Venedigs], […] gewähren ihm keinen erfreulichen Anblick!"*[4]

Neben den „unerfreulichen" Ziegelsteinen zeigt der Königsbau als einziger Bauteil am Außenbau solide, schön marmorierte Säulen und Pfeiler aus Sandstein im Stil der toskanischen Säulenordnung. Diese wiederholen sich auch in der Beletage, wo nach klassischer Tradition eigentlich eine „ranghöhere" ionische Säule hingehört. Damit mag erneut Schlichtheit und Sparsamkeit ausgedrückt werden, doch diese einfachste aller antiken Säulenordnungen hätte sich für einen Königsbau eigentlich verbieten sollen. Zudem ist sie römischen Ursprungs und passt nicht recht zum Hellenismus Wagners und den korinthischen Säulen im Inneren. Doch mag der archaische Charakter dieser Säulen gereizt haben, die ursprünglich ein hölzernes Gebälk trugen und somit gut zum Bayreuther Fachwerk passen. Alberti, der große Architekturtheoretiker der Renaissance, schreibt in seinen „I quattro libri dell' architectura", dass sie sehr zweckmäßig seien bei *„Villen, um Wagen und andere bäuerliche Geräte unterzustellen, und auch wegen der geringen Kosten"*[5]. Als Kutschenauffahrt also legitim, doch für einen König nicht standesgemäß.

The windows on the side on the second floor lack a colonnade (like on the corner pavilions on the ground floor), and are simple round arched windows with agraffes. They can be found on the south facade and on the sides. Their form and proportions match the entranceway, which is embedded in an aedicule with a theater motif. The wooden door now painted blue is original and has diamond bosses on the lower third.

The attic decorates the flat roof as a sort of "toit caché." Attic zones always recall southern regions and often include statues of Gods from antiquity. To the left and right of the center risalit in Bayreuth there is a sandstone balustrade including balusters with a vase-like bulge looking somewhat Baroque, though they were already common in the Renaissance since Michelangelo.

All said and done, the facade of the Königsbau is pleasing to the eye and looks like something from a small palace of a member of the Italian nobility from the cinquecento. Habel even refers to it as a *"harmonious showpiece,"* calling it the most valuable part of the exterior. To think that the entire exterior of the Festspielhaus could have looked like that if the red bricks wouldn't shine through again so prominently! Since costs weren't cut nearly as miserly for the Königsbau as for the rest, a few hundred marks could have been spent to give the few square meters of raw brick a layer of stucco. However, Brückwald didn't want to cover them with stucco (unlike in all previous plans). Why not? Had people grown to like the brick and to understand the aesthetic similarity to the Schinkel school or the Georgian style? Or was the understated look of a provisional building kept for tactical reasons to win the sympathy of supporters? To this day, Wolfgang Wagner is hesitant to undertake restoration work: *"Someone might think we are rich."*

Portico with Prussian barrel vaults

The facade of the Königsbau features a portico supported by columns. Wager was especially fond of the portico on the Doge's Palace in Venice, which Cosima calls *"R.'s favorite spot"* (September 30, 1882). A day earlier she writes: *"He especially likes to sit under the portico between the columns – he'd like to be painted there."* That comes as a bit of a surprise, since from that vantage point he would be facing what he considered boring Renaissance buildings. On October 16, 1882, after a walk through the city, Cosima writes: *"But soon thereafter he sat down with me under the arch of the Doge's Palace; he does not particularly enjoy the sight of […] the bricks [of Venice]."*

Aside from the "not enjoyable" bricks, the Königsbau is the only part of the exterior building with solid, beautifully marbled sandstone columns and piers in the style of Tuscan column order. These are repeated in the piano nobile, where in the classical tradition "higher ranking" Ionic columns belong. This may be another expression of simplicity and thrift, but this simplest of all antique column orders should actually not have been used at all for the Königsbau. In addition, it is a Roman style and does not fit in well with Wagner's Hellenism and the Corinthian columns on the interior. Perhaps the archaic character of these columns was attractive, as they originally supported a wooden beam and therefore match the Bayreuth timber framing. The great Renaissance architectural theoretician Alberti writes in his "I quattro libri dell' architectura" that they served very practical purposes in *"villas to house wagons and other farming equipment, also because they were inexpensive."* So they may be legitimate for a carriage drive, but not suitable to the ranks of a king.

Eine weitere „Unanständigkeit" lässt sich entdecken, wenn man dem Altan „unter den Rock schaut" und hier flache Gewölbe entdeckt, die den Namen Segmentbogenkappen, preußische Kappen oder Berliner Gewölbe tragen, und als Erfindung von Karl Friedrich Schinkel gelten, der diese erstmals in seiner Berliner Bauakademie einbaute. Häufig verwendet wurde dieses Industriebaumotiv ab 1870, vorwiegend für Keller- und Stalldecken. Die Neorenaissance hätte an dieser Stelle eine antikisierende Kassettendecke vorgesehen. Doch siegte erneut die Sparsamkeit und bescherte dem bayerischen König eine preußische Stalldecke, die Ludwig (zum Glück) nie gesehen hat. Er kam 1882 nicht zur Premiere des PARSIFAL und hat den ihm gewidmeten Bau nie betreten.

Laternen mit Lindwürmern

Der gesamte Platz vor dem Königsbau und um das Festspielhaus herum wurde 1991 bis 1996 phasenweise neu gestaltet, wobei man den Boden mit einem die Hitze abweisenden Granit gepflastert hat. Alte Aufnahmen zeigen noch den etwas ländlichen Zustand des Platzes als eine Wiese. Im Zuge dieser Maßnahmen wurden die Brüstungsgitter zur Stadt nach Vorbild des Balkongitters der Villa Wahnfried nachgegossen, die alten Glaskugellaternen der 1960er Jahre entfernt und durch historisierende Laternen ersetzt, die man alten Fotoaufnahmen nachempfunden hat. Sie sind also nicht original, passen aber stilistisch recht gut, besitzen sogar kleine Palmetten-Akroterien, womit sie die Firstblume auf dem Bühnenturm en miniature aufgreifen. Ganz scharfe Augen können im Rankenwerk des Gusseisens sogar ein kleines Fabeltier erkennen, das man – dem Genius loci entsprechend – durchaus einen Lindwurm nennen könnte.

Fazit

Der schon 1876 geplante und 1882 nach den (unveränderten) Plänen Otto Brückwalds errichtete Königsbau sollte einem licht- und menschenscheuen König einen exklusiven und separaten Zugang zum Festspielhaus gewähren, ein Luxus, den Ludwig II. nie wahrgenommen hat. Heute ist der Königsbau mit Zugang zum Foyer für alle Gäste offen und präsentiert sich als eine Art Haupteingang. Architektonisch bildet er den künstlerisch wertvollsten Teil des gesamten Außenbaus und stellt einen Portikus mit Altan dar, der harmonisch im Stil der älteren Eckpavillons ausgeführt wurde. Dabei wurde die italienische Neorenaissance noch schmuckvoller ausgebaut mit einer geometrisch reizvollen Rustika im Erdgeschoss, einem Risalit in der Beletage mit Theatermotiv sowie Balustraden am Balkon und auf der italienisch anmutenden Attika.

Das alles hinderte jedoch nicht, die Wandflächen wiederum mit roten Backsteinen zu mauern, als habe man sich mit dieser Ästhetik letztlich versöhnt. Brückwald wollte sie nicht verputzen lassen und zeichnete sie in seine Pläne. Andere Sparmaßnahmen, wie die schlichten preußischen Kappen, finden sich als schlichte Decke unter dem Altan und geziemen einem König eigentlich nicht, wie auch die sehr einfachen toskanischen Säulen. Wagner selbst bezeichnet den Königsbau als Beginn einer monumentalen Vollendung seines Theaters, womit erneut ein widersprüchliches Bekenntnis zur Renaissance ausgesprochen wird und der „deutsche" Stil endgültig als rhetorischer Unsinn entlarvt ist.

If you look "under the skirts" of the balcony, you will discover another "indecency." The flat structures there are called segment arch caps, Prussian barrel vaults or Berlin vault, and are considered an invention of Karl Friedrich Schinkel, who first used them in his Berliner Bauakademie. This was a common industrial building motif starting around 1870, especially for basement and stable ceilings. The neo-Renaissance would have called for an antique coffered ceiling on this spot, but thrift triumphed yet again, giving the Bavarian King a Prussian stable ceiling, which Ludwig (luckily) never saw. He did not go for the 1882 premiere of PARSIFAL and never entered the annex dedicated to him.

Lanterns with lindworms

The entire square in front of the Königsbau and surrounding the Festspielhaus was redesigned in phases between 1991 and 1996. The ground was covered with heat-reflective granite. Early photographs show that the original square was more rural, a field. During this phase, the parapet lattice toward the city was modeled after the balcony lattice of the "Wahnfried" Villa, the old glass globe lanterns from the 1960s were removed and replaced with antique looking lanterns based on old photographs. Although they are not original, the style matches well. They even have small palmette acroteria, complimenting the finial on top of the stage tower en miniature. Very sharp eyes will even recognize a mythical animal in the arabesques of the cast iron that, in the genius loci, could well be a lindworm

Summary

The Königsbau was built in 1882 based on unaltered plans drawn up by Otto Brückwald in 1876. Its purpose was to give the King, who avoided people and light, exclusive and separate access to the Festspielhaus. Ludwig II never availed himself of this luxury. Today, all visitors have access to the foyer through the Königsbau, which acts as something of a main entrance. From an architectural standpoint, it is the artistically most valuable part of the entire exterior. It represents a portico with a balcony that matches the style of the older corner pavilions. It displays a more ornate version of the Italian neo-Renaissance with a geometrically attractive rustica on the ground floor, a risalit with theater motif in the piano nobile and balustrades on the balcony and on the Italian-looking attic.

None of this prevented the wall surfaces from being built of red brick again, as if this aesthetic had gained acceptance after all. Brückwald did not want to cover the brick with stucco and drew the brick into his plans. Other cost-cutting measures, such as the simple Prussian barrel vaults comprising the simple roof under the balcony, and the very simple Tuscan columns are not fitting of a king. Wagner describes the Königsbau as the start of a monumental completion of his theater, another contradictory commitment to the Renaissance revealing the desire for a "German" style as rhetorical nonsense.

Preußische Kappen für den bayerischen König Prussian barrel vaults for the Bavarian king

„Vor allem erfreut ihn das Sitzen unter dem Portikus zwischen den Säulen, so möchte er gemalt sein."
"He especially likes to sit under the portico between the columns – he'd like to be painted there."

Cosima Wagner, Venedig, 16. Oktober 1882

Rustikale Männer vor der Rustika verlegen das neue, hitzeabweisende Granitpflaster, Mitte 1990er Jahre
Rustic men in front of the rustica laying the new heat-reflective granite in the mid 1990s
Das Festspielhaus auf der grünen Wiese, um 1900
The Festspielhaus in a green meadow around 1900

Historisierende Lampen mit Lindwürmern
Antique looking lanterns with lindworms
Drachen müssen draußen bleiben!
No dragons allowed!

Architektur für ein neues Publikum

Garantiert und gratis

Ein ideales Theater im Sinne Richard Wagners verlangte auch nach einem neuen Publikum. In seiner ersten Vision eines Festspielhauses (für Zürich), dem Brief an Theodor Uhlig 1850, wollte er seine Mustervorstellungen des RING für alle *„Freunde des musikalischen Dramas"* einrichten, die er durch Zeitungsannoncen zum Besuch des *„dramatischen Musikfestes"* auffordern mochte: *„Wer sich anmeldet und zu diesem Zwecke nach Zürich reist, bekömmt gesichertes Entree, natürlich wie alle Entree: gratis! Des Weiteren lade ich die hiesige Jugend, Universität, Gesangvereine u.s.w. zur Anhörung ein."*[1]

Wie haben sich die Zeiten gewandelt. Die relativ niedrigen Kartenpreise in Bayreuth sind im Vergleich zu anderen Festspielen immer noch demokratisch, doch die Karten sind alles andere als garantiert. Die heutige durchschnittliche Wartezeit auf eine Karte beträgt mindestens zehn Jahre. Ein emeritierter Heidelberger Jura-Professor zum Beispiel fragte nach vierzehn Jahren erfolgloser Bestellung beim Kartenbüro an, ob er sich zu seinen Lebzeiten noch Hoffnung machen könne oder ob er seine Jahre der Anwartschaft gegebenenfalls vererben könne und ob dafür ein notarieller Akt nötig sei. Junge Wagnerianer haben immerhin die Möglichkeit, ein Stipendium des Wagnerverbands wahrzunehmen und so – ganz im Sinne Wagners – Karten zu bekommen. Wagner wollte wahrlich kein elitäres Festival.

Polarisiertes Publikum

Wagners Verhältnis zum damaligen Publikum war ambivalent. Jeder Künstler wünscht sich Anerkennung beim Publikum, doch diese wurde dem damals avantgardistischen Komponisten erst sehr spät zuteil. Seine „Zukunftsmusik" polarisierte ein Publikum, das von französischen und italienischen Opern geprägt war, insbesondere in den Hauptstädten Paris, Wien oder Berlin. In Paris wurde der TANNHÄUSER noch 1861 gar gnadenlos mit Trillerpfeifen ausgepfiffen. Wagner hasste das großstädtische Opernpublikum geradezu und wählte nicht zuletzt deshalb Bayreuth als Standort für seine Festspiele.

Zahllos sind Wagners bittere Äußerungen über ein „verdorbenes" Publikum, das er als geistesträge oder nur oberflächlich angeregt kritisierte, als allein schau- und sensationslustig, als dekadent und eitel, nicht an der Kunst interessiert, sondern allein an der eigenen Zurschaustellung. In dieser Kritik zeigt sich der verletzte Künstler, aber auch der politische Ideologe, denn die Oper war zu seiner Zeit nach wie vor eine Domäne des Adels und des erfolgreichen Bürgertums, eine Repräsentationskunst einer Ständegesellschaft, die der 1848er-Revolutionär Wagner stets abgelehnt hat. 1876 hatte Wagner längst den Durchbruch beim Publikum geschafft und die Premieren in Bayreuth gereichten zu umjubelten Triumphen seiner so lange verkannten Kunst.

Architecture for a new audience

Guaranteed and free

Richard Wagner's concept of an ideal theater also requires a new audience. In his first vision for a Festspielhaus (for Zurich) outlined in an 1850 letter to Theodor Uhlig, he expresses his desire to hold model performances of RING for all *"friends of the musical drama"* that he would invite to a *"dramatic music celebration"* via newspaper ads: *"Whoever signs up and travels to Zurich for this purpose will be guaranteed entry, as with every entry, free! I also invite the local youth, university, choirs, etc. to come listen."*

How times have changed. The relatively inexpensive tickets at Bayreuth are still democratic compared with other tickets to other festivals, but tickets are anything but guaranteed. The average time spent waiting for a ticket is at least ten years. For example, after fourteen years of trying unsuccessfully to order tickets, an emeritus professor of law in Heidelberg asked at the ticket office whether he could still have hope during this lifetime, whether he might bequeath the time he spent waiting, and whether such an action would need to be notarized. At least young Wagnerians have the opportunity to apply for a scholarship from the Wagner Society and in this manner to receive a ticket, as Wagner foresaw. Wagner wanted anything but an elite festival.

Polarized audience

Wagner had an ambivalent relationship to the audience of his day. Every artist wants to be recognized by the public, but the then avant-garde composer didn't receive such recognition until very late in life. His "music of the future" polarized an audience shaped by French and Italian operas, especially in the capital cities of Paris, Vienna and Berlin. Even in 1861, the Parisian audience pulled out their whistles to boo TANNHÄUSER mercilessly. Wagner downright hated the big city opera audience, which was one reason he chose Bayreuth for his festival.

Wagner made countless bitter statements about the "rotten" public, criticizing it as slow of wit or simply superficially interested, as eager only for visual or sensationalist pleasure, as decadent and conceited, as not interested in art, but rather only in being seen themselves. These are the words of a bruised artist, but also of a political ideologue. In his day, opera was still the domain of the nobility and of the successful bourgeoisie, the representational art of a society based on estate that Wagner, an activist in the 1848 revolution, had always spurned. By 1876, Wagner had long had a breakthrough with his public, and the premieres in Bayreuth were no less than applauded triumphs for his long-misunderstood art.

Doch es waren nicht die „Freunde des musikalischen Dramas", die Intellektuellen und jungen Enthusiasten, die das Bild der ersten Bayreuther Festspiele beherrschten. Es war die Prominenz jener Gesellschaft, die Wagner für seine Erfolge letztlich brauchte, doch insgeheim als „Klassenfeind" verachtete – nicht nur als junger Revolutionär, sondern selbst noch im reifen Alter. So äußert er sich am 6. September 1878 über die deutschen Fürsten: „Sie schaden durch das, was sie nicht nützen, denn nützen könnten sie noch unendlich, und ihre Unnützigkeit ist der Schaden."[1] In Beziehung auf die vielen adligen Gäste in Bayreuth resümiert Cosima am 9. Oktober 1876 enttäuscht: „Nicht eine von den Fürstlichkeiten, nachdem sie Orden an alle Ausübende verteilt, hat R. gefragt, was für ihn zu tun sei, wie ihn zu unterstützen oder [ihm] beizustehen!"[2] Dabei hatte es Wagner einmal selbst in der Hand, den höchsten aller deutschen Fürsten zu stürzen, wie Cosima vom 14. August 1876 nach der Premiere des RHEINGOLD berichtet: Der Kaiser „nimmt Abschied, geht einen Schritt zurück, merkt die Schwelle nicht, strauchelt so arg, dass R. nur mit dem größten Kraftaufwand ihn zurückhalten kann und überzeugt ist, dass dieser Fall rücklings der Tod des kaiserlichen Herrn gewesen wäre!"[3]

„Welcher Fürst hat denn Ehrgefühl außer dem König von Bayern"[4], äußerte Wagner am 5. März 1874. Ludwig war der einzige Fürst, der ihn unterstützte und den er deshalb gelten ließ, doch kam dieser menschenscheue Freund nicht zur Premiere, sondern nur zur Generalprobe und zum dritten Zyklus. In der so genannten Fürstenloge vertraten ihn der Deutsche Kaiser und König von Preußen Wilhelm I. und weitere regierende Staatsoberhäupter wie der Kaiser Dom Pedro von Brasilien und der Großherzog Friedrich von Baden nebst seiner Gemahlin, der Großherzogin Luise, der Großherzog von Schwerin mit Gemahlin und Tochter [...] Großfürstin Wladimir), der Großherzog Karl Alexander von Sachsen-Weimar, Prinz Wilhelm von Hessen, die Herzöge von Anhalt, Dessau, Schwarzburg-Sondershausen und so weiter. „Bayreuth is Germany", soll ein Engländer damals ausgesprochen haben.

Die Intellektuellen dagegen waren nicht so prominent vertreten, obwohl Wagner damit gerechnet hatte, dass „viele Künstler selbst, der übrigen deutschen Theater, schon aus bloßer Neugierde"[5] kommen würden. Der Komponistenkollege Tschaikowsky zählt 1876 „eine ganze Menge bekannter Repräsentanten der Tonkunst", doch „die musikalischen Berühmtheiten ersten Ranges glänzten durch Abwesenheit: Verdi, Gounod, Ambroise Thomas, Brahms, Anton Rubinstein, Raff, Joachim, Hans von Bülow waren nicht nach Bayreuth gekommen."[6] Einer Anekdote zufolge soll der wiederverheiratete Bülow nach dem Grund seines Fernbleibens gefragt worden sein, worauf er geantwortet habe, „ich hatte Angst, dass Wagner mir auch meine zweite Frau nehmen und vor allem mir die alte wieder zurückgeben würde". Zugegen waren lediglich „Franz Liszt, dessen Anwesenheit bei den nahen verwandtschaftlichen Beziehungen und seiner langjährigen Freundschaft zu Wagner ja selbstverständlich ist"[7]. Dazu kamen Anton Bruckner, der längst wieder aus dem Mörteltrog herausgefunden hatte, Saint-Saëns, der mit den Wagners eng verbundene Nietzsche und Gottfried Semper, mit dem sich Wagner kurz zuvor in Wien wieder versöhnt hatte.

Soweit die Wirklichkeit. Das ideale Publikum, das sich Wagner vorstellte und wünschte, sah etwas anders aus. Hier interessierte ihn weder Stand noch intellektueller Rang, sondern der Mensch an sich, den er – zumindest theoretisch – optimal für seine Kunst empfänglich machen wollte. Damit nähern wir uns einer psychologischen und soziologischen Dimension von Architektur, denn Wagners Theater wurde nicht für das klassische, adlige und bourgeoise, sondern für ein neues Publikum errichtet, wie es die schlichte Architektur in ihrer Sprache deutlich formuliert.

The first Bayreuth Festivals were not, however, dominated by *"friends of the musical drama,"* intellectuals and young enthusiasts, but rather prominent members of the societal estate that Wagner needed for his success, but secretly scorned as "class enemies" – not only as young revolutionary, but in later years as well. For example, on September 6, 1878 he writes about the German princes: *"They cause harm even by doing nothing, because they could achieve so much, and their uselessness is the damage."* On October 9, 1876, Cosima sums up her disappointment in the numerous guests of noble blood in Bayreuth: *"After giving out medals to all the performers, not one of the princes asked R. what he needed, how they could support him or be of service to him!"* All the while, it was once within Wagner's grasp to permit the fall of the highest of the German Princes, as Cosima reports after the premiere of RHEINGOLD on August 14, 1876: the Emperor *"took his leave and took a step back without noticing the threshold. He stumbled so badly that it took R. all of his might to hold him back. R. is convinced that this fall surely would have led to the Emperor's death!"*

On March 5, 1874, Wagner asks *"what ruler other than the King of Bavaria has a sense of honor?"* Ludwig was the only ruler who supported Wagner and with whom Wagner was therefore satisfied. But his shy friend did not attend the premiere, but rather only the dress rehearsal and the third cycle. Instead, he was represented by the German Emperor and King of Prussia Wilhelm I and other governing heads of state, such as Emperor Dom Pedro of Brazil and Grand Duke Friedrich of Baden, and his wife, the Grand Duchess Luise, the Grand Duke of Schwerin with his wife and daughter (Grand Princess Wladimir), Grand Duke Karl Alexander of Sachsen-Weimar, Prince Wilhelm of Hessen, the Dukes of Anhalt, Dessau, Schwarzburg-Sondershausen, etc. A Brit is reported to have said: *"Bayreuth is Germany."*

Intellectuals, however, were not as prominently represented, even though Wagner had counted on *"many artists from other German theaters [coming] out of pure curiosity."* In 1876, his fellow composer Tchaikovsky counts *"a great number of people from the music world,"* but *"the famous musicians of the top tier were conspicuous by their absence: Verdi, Gounod, Ambroise Thomas, Brahms, Anton Rubinstein, Raff, Joachim, Hans von Bülow did not come to Bayreuth."* According to one anecdote, when the remarried Bülow was asked why he did not attend, he is said to have responded: *"I was afraid Wagner would steal my second wife as well, and worse, that he would give me back my old one."* In attendance were only *"Franz Liszt, whose presence was a matter of course given the close family tie and his old friendship with Wagner."* Then there was Anton Bruckner, who had long since found his way out of the mortar trough, Saint-Saëns, the Wagners' close friend Nietzsche, and Gottfried Semper, with whom Wagner had recently made amends in Vienna.

So much for reality. Wagner's imagined and desired ideal audience looked somewhat different. He was less interested in their estate or their intellectual rank, but rather in the person, whom he – at least theoretically – wanted to make receptive for his art. That brings us to a psychological and sociological dimension of architecture. Wagner's theater was not built for the classical nobility and haut bourgeoisie, but rather for a new public as spoken by its simple architectural language.

„Was er am Vormittag komponierte", so erinnerte sich Mathilde Wesendonck, „das pflegte er am Nachmittag auf meinem Flügel vorzutragen und zu prüfen. Es war die Stunde zwischen 5 und 6 Uhr; er selbst nannte sich der Dämmermann!"

Mathilde Wesendonck recalls, "in the afternoon he would come here and use my piano to play and test out the music he had composed in the morning. It was the hour between 5:00 and 6:00. He even called himself the Dämmermann [twilight man]!"

Besinnlichkeit der blauen Stunde

Schon 1862 in jenem Vorwort zur Edition der Nibelungendichtung schreibt Wagner: „*Ebenso wichtig, wie für die Aufführung selbst, müsste (…) der Erfolg einer solchen Aufführung hinsichtlich ihres Eindruckes auf das Publikum sein.*" Sein Publikum sollte „*nach dem gastlichen Ort der Aufführung reisen und hier zusammenkommen, eben um den Eindruck unserer Aufführung zu empfangen.*" In sehr philanthropischen Gedanken fühlt sich Wagner in die ganz menschlichen Bedürfnisse seines Publikums ein: „*Im vollen Sommer wäre für Jeden dieser Besuch zugleich mit einem erfrischenden Ausfluge verbunden, auf welchem er (…) sich von den Sorgen seiner Alltagsgeschäfte zu zerstreuen suchen soll. Statt dass er, wie sonst, nach mühsam am Comptoir, am Büro, im Arbeitskabinett oder in sonst welcher Berufstätigkeit, hin gequältem Tage, des Abends die einseitig angespannten Geisteskräfte wie aus ihrem Krampfe loszulassen, nämlich sich zu zerstreuen sucht, und deshalb, je nach Geschmack, eben oberflächliche Unterhaltung ihm wohltätig dünken muss, wird er diesmal sich am Tage zerstreuen, um nun, bei eintretender Dämmerung, sich zu sammeln: und das Zeichen zum Beginn der Festaufführung wird ihn hierzu einladen.*"[1]

Der Romantiker Wagner beschwört die Dämmerung, die auch in einigen seiner Stücke als symbolträchtige und subtile Stunde wirksam eingesetzt wird. In der blauen Stunde ist der Mensch besonders empfänglich: So wird „*der erste mystische Klang des unsichtbaren Orchesters zu der Andacht stimmen, ohne die kein wirklicher Kunsteindruck möglich ist. In seinem eigenen Begehren erfasst, wird er* [der Besucher] *willig folgen, und schnell wird ihm ein Verständnis aufgehen, welches ihm bisher fremd bleiben, ja unmöglich sein musste. Da, wo er sonst mit ermüdetem Hirn, zerstreuungssüchtig angelangt, neue Anspannung, und somit schmerzliche Überspannung finden musste, wo er deshalb bald über Länge, bald über zu großen Ernst, und endlich völlige Unverständlichkeit zu klagen hatte, wird er jetzt zu dem wohltätigen Gefühle der leichten Tätigkeit eines bisher ungekannten Auffassungsvermögens gelangen, welches ihn mit neuer Wärme erfüllt, und ihm das Licht entzündet, in welchem er deutlich Dinge gewahrt, von denen er zuvor keine Ahnung hatte.*"[2]

Erholung und Entspannung

Wagners Festspielhügel sollte also ein Ort der Besinnung sein. Dazu gehört ganz wesentlich die Erholung zwischen den einzelnen Aufzügen, den zeitlich sehr reich bemessenen Pausen. Diese hatte er nachweislich schon am 1. Oktober 1874 festgelegt, wie auch die Anfangszeiten am Nachmittag. Zum Erholungsraum wurde die Außenanlage als ein naturnahes Ambiente gestaltet. Schon nach dem ersten Spatenstich „*ward die ausgegrabene Erde sofort an den Fuß des Berges hinabgeschafft, um daselbst zur Planierung des gesamten Bodenkomplexes und zur Herstellung von Gartenanlagen zu dienen*"[3].

The sensuality of twilight

Wagner writes in the foreword to the 1862 edition of the Nibelungen poem: *"The success of such a performance based on the impression it makes on the audience […] should be equally as important as the performance itself."* His audience should *"travel to the hospitable performance location and gather here specifically to experience our performance."* Wagner empathizes with the very human needs of his public in highly philanthropic thoughts: *"At the height of summer, the visit would be appropriately combined with a refreshing excursion which guests would […] primarily use to distract themselves from their everyday concerns. After a tedious day at the sales counter, in the office, in the study or in whatever job, instead of spending the evening trying to tear the spirit free of its one-sided mental efforts by seeking diversion as usual, that is, by having to find relief in superficial entertainment of one's choice, this time the person will divert himself during the day and collect his thoughts as dusk falls: and the signal that the festival performance is about to begin will invite him inside."*

Wagner the romantic swears by twilight and uses it as a highly symbolic and subtle hour in several of his works. People are especially receptive during twilight: *"The first mystical sounds of the invisible orchestra will set the devotional mood without which no true artistic impression is possible. Caught up in an initial desire, he* [the visitor] *willingly follows. Soon an understanding takes form that had been foreign, even impossible up until then. At the point where he typically arrives, mentally exhausted and addicted to distraction, and finds instead new tension and therefore painful hypertension, where he therefore complains about the length, about over-seriousness and about endless complete incomprehensibility, now he will achieve the pleasant and brand new feeling of easy perceptivity which fills him with a new warmth and ignites the light for him that makes things clear to him that he had had no idea about before."*

Rest and relaxation

Wagner's festival hill should be a place of reflection. A critical part of that includes resting between the acts during the generous intermissions. These intermissions and the afternoon starting time had been set by Wagner by October 1, 1874. The theater grounds have been designed as a natural place of rest. As soon as the first shovel of earth was removed *"the dug out earth was immediately transported down to the foot of the hill to flatten out the grounds and to use in designing the gardens."*

„Doch um der Rasten willen weil' ich gerne,
für sie lass' dieser Welt Lauf ich besteh'n;
sie grüne, blüh', sie dämm're in die Ferne,
getrost mag ich an ihr vorüber geh'n."[1]

"But for the sake of rest I gladly stay,
for its sake I leave the world behind;
it sprout green, blossoms, lights up the sky at dusk,
comforted, I can move on."

Richard Wagner (25. August 1881)

Bier und Bratwurst

Auch für das leibliche Wohl wollte Wagner sorgen, obwohl die Prioritäten eindeutig sein mussten. *„Da wir hier zu einem Feste versammelt sind, und dieses heute ein Bühnenfest, nicht ein Eß- oder Trink-Fest ist, so könnte [...] in den [...] Zwischenakten jede mögliche Erfrischung, wie ich annehme – in sommerlich freier Abendluft, füglich mit zur Ökonomie der Geistestätigkeits-Entwickelung verwendet werden."*[1]

Es wurden sogar eigene Restaurationen auf dem Hügel gebaut. Am 22. Mai 1876 fand die Einweihung der kleinen Restauration (1976 abgerissen) statt und am 1. August die große für eintausend Gäste, dort wo auch heute das neue Restaurant steht, das außerhalb der Festspiele als Orchesterprobenraum benutzt wird. Applaus für die Sänger war bis 1951 während und nach den Aufzügen und am Ende der Vorstellung unerwünscht, und es wurde den Künstlern erst in der großen Restauration bei Sekt und Bier zugejubelt. Der Applaus im Festspielhaus sollte allein dem Werke Wagners gelten.

Ja selbst die fränkischen Grillbratwürste sind von höchster Stelle initiiert. Cosima berichtet am 11. Juli 1872 an den Mannheimer Heckel: *„Die Erlaubnis, die der Magistrat neulich gab – und zwar feierlich – Wurst auf dem Platz zu verkaufen, hat uns viel Vergnügen gemacht."*[2]

Die Versorgung der vielen Festspielgäste war in der Tat ein großes logistisches Problem. Peter Iljitsch Tschaikowsky berichtet in seinen „Erinnerungen an Bayreuth" (1876) darüber: *„Neben dem Wagnertheater sind große Zeltrestaurants aufgeschlagen, [...] aber es gehört wahrer Heroismus dazu, sich durch das Gewühl der Hungrigen hindurchzuarbeiten. Während der ganzen ersten Serie der Vorstellungen der Tetralogie bildete das Essen das allgemeine Gesprächsthema und schwächte ganz bedeutend das Interesse für die Kunst ab. Man hörte mehr von Beefsteaks, Schnitzeln und Bratkartoffeln als von Wagners Leitmotiven."*[3]

Beer and bratwurst

Wagner also wanted to see to it that visitors were well fed, but were to keep clear priorities in mind: *"Since we are gathered here today to celebrate, and this is a stage celebration and not a food and drink celebration, there could be [...] all types of refreshments [...] in the intermissions, as I assume – in the outdoor summer evening air, which will be suitable to serving the economy of the development of mental activity."*

Several restaurants were even built on the hill. The small restaurant was christened on May 22, 1876 (torn down in 1976), and the larger one for one thousand guests was opened on August 1, 1876. This is where the current new restaurant is located that is used as orchestra rehearsal space in the off-season. Up until 1951, there was no applause for the singers after the acts or at the end of the performance, but they were instead cheered in the large restaurant over sparkling wine and beer. Applause in the Festspielhaus was reserved for Wagner's works.

Even the Franconian grilled bratwursts were initiated from top levels. Cosima writes on July 11, 1872 to Heckel in Mannheim: *"We were quite pleased that the magistrate gave us permission – quite ceremoniously – to sell sausage on the square."*

Meeting the needs of so many festival guests was indeed a sizeable logistical problem. Peter Iljitsch Tchaikovsky comments on this in his "Memories of Bayreuth" (1876): *"There are big tent restaurants set up next to the Wagner Theater [...] but is an act of true heroism to make your ways through the hungry masses. Food was the main topic of conversation during the entire first series of performances of the tetralogy, significantly weakening the interest in the art. There was more talk of beefsteaks, schnitzels and fried potatoes than of Wagner's leitmotifs."*

Die kleine Restauration, Zeichnung von Ludwig Bechstein, 1876
The minor restoration, 1876 drawing by Ludwig Bechstein

> *„In den Pausen kokettieren die Franzosen,*
> *die Deutschen trinken Bier*
> *und die Engländer lesen den Operntext."*[4]
>
> *"During the intermissions, the French flirt,*
> *the Germans drink beer*
> *and the Brits read the libretto."*
>
> Romain Rolland (1891)

SB-Restaurant außerhalb der Saison
Restaurant in the off-season

Lüftungslaterne und leichte Kleidung

Wagner sorgte in seinem neuen Theater sogar für eine gute Luft, die bekanntlich wach hält und der Aufmerksamkeit für die Kunst sehr förderlich sein kann. Der Zeitgenosse Albert Lavignac berichtet 1897, *„dass, wohl infolge eines sinnreichen Lüftungssystems, im Saale nie jene verpestete Luft herrscht, wie in den meisten uns bekannten Theatern. Auch beim Eintritt befällt einen keine Empfindung des Erstickens, was anderswo oft recht unangenehm ist."*[1] Das war auch nötig. Schon die Proben und die Uraufführung 1876 litten unter einem sehr heißen Sommer, doch regierte *„trotz der draußen herrschenden tropischen Glut, ein überaus buntes und reges Leben, eine solche Frische und Lebendigkeit"*[2]. Die Hitze hielt bis zum dritten Zyklus an, doch *„das ganze Personal hielt sich wacker, trotz einer fortdauernd tropischen Temperatur, die von den Probentagen und -wochen in gleichmäßiger Heiterkeit angehalten hatte."*[3]

Bei den zweiten Festspielen 1882 wurde die Hitze zu einem ernsten, auch künstlerischen Problem. Wagner hatte im PARSIFAL den Damenchor der mittleren Höhe aus akustischen Gründen in den durch die Gasbeleuchtung zusätzlich aufgeheizten Schnürboden platziert. Die Damen jedoch beschwerten sich über die dort herrschende Hitze und drohten zu streiken. *„Der Meister stieg trotz seiner Erkältung selbst auf den Schnürboden, um die Höhe der Temperatur zu erproben; er fand, dass die Beschwerde wohlbegründet und die dort herrschende Glut eine mehr als tropische war: es bliebe demnach nur das Auskunftsmittel einer sehr leichten Kleidung übrig."*[4]

Über das Lüftungssystem des Festspielhauses, namentlich des Zuschauerhauses, ist in den Schriften und Äußerungen Wagners nichts zu finden. Doch Brückwald schreibt 1875, dass *„dafür Sorge getragen worden [ist], dass an geeigneten Stellen und namentlich unter den Sitzen reine und abgekühlte atmosphärische Luft zugeführt wird."*[5] Schon Semper hatte in seinen Entwürfen einen durchfensterten Aufsatz auf dem Dach des Zuschauerhauses vorgesehen, den Brückwald in Bayreuth als achteckige Lüftungslaterne ausführte.

Wie die Lüftung einst funktionierte, weiß heute niemand mehr so genau. Vermutlich zog die Luft über dem Orchestergraben in das damals noch nach oben offene Proszenium direkt in den Dachstuhl, wie auch umgekehrt. Hier oben sind noch alte Lüftungsklappen direkt über dem Proszenium erhalten. 1990 wurde das Lüftungssystem völlig erneuert. Die Frischluft kommt nun über einen Lüftungskanal aus Beton, der zweihundertfünfzig Meter vor dem Haus sechsunddreißig Kubikmeter frische Luft pro Stunde mittels Schaufelrädern ansaugt, in den Pausen sogar das Doppelte.

Unter dem Orchestergraben, zwischen diesem und der ersten Reihe existiert ein Gang aus Beton mit Rohren, die die Luft auch in den Hohlraum unter dem Parkett blasen, sodass jene von Brückwald genannten Schlitze unter den Sitzen funktionieren –

Ventilation lantern and light clothing

Wagner also provided fresh air in his new theater to keep the audience awake and help them dedicate their attention more fully to the art. Contemporary Albert Lavignac writes in 1897: *"Probably due to an intelligently designed ventilation system, the hall was never plagued by bad air, as is the case in most theaters we know. There is no sense of suffocation upon entering, either, which can be quite unpleasant elsewhere."* This was a necessity. Even the rehearsals for the premiere in 1876 suffered in the blazing summer heat. Nonetheless, *"despite the tropical weather outside, the atmosphere inside was colorful and active, fresh and lively."* Although the heat didn't let up through the third cycle, *"the whole team kept a stiff upper lip despite the unrelenting tropical temperature and nothing but clear skies carrying over from the days and weeks of rehearsals."*

During the second festival in 1882, the heat became a serious and artistic problem. For acoustic reasons, Wagner hat positioned the mezzo sopranos in the women's chorus for PARSIFAL in the fly gallery that was heated even more by the gas lights. But the women complained about the high temperature there and threatened to strike. *"Despite having a cold, the maestro climbed up into the fly gallery himself to test the temperature and found the complaint to be justified, as the heat up there was more than tropical: as a result, the only solution was for them to wear very light clothing."*

There is no mention of the ventilation system of the Festspielhaus, that is, the auditorium, in Wagner's writings. Brückwald, however, writes in 1875 that *"care has [been] taken that clean and cool atmospheric air is fed in at the appropriate spots, namely under the seats."* Even Semper's plans called for a structure with windows on the roof of the auditorium, which Brückwald designed as an octagonal ventilation lantern in Bayreuth.

No one knows exactly how the ventilation used to work. Presumably air flowed over the orchestra pit into the proscenium, which was still open at the time, and directly into the roof truss, and the other way around. There are still old ventilation flaps directly above the proscenium. In 1990, a new ventilation system was installed. Fresh air now enters through a concrete ventilation canal that draws thirty-six cubic meters of fresh air per hour using paddlewheels located two hundred and fifty meters away from the theater. In the intermissions the draw is doubled.

There is a concrete passageway between the orchestra pit and the front row of seats containing pipes that also blow air into the cavity below the parquet so that what Brückwald called slits under the seats work – this all takes place so quietly that the music is not disturbed. Together with all the expensive perfume odors and the sweet sweaty smells of a worn out audience, the exhaust flows outside through large pipes exiting in the northern part of the grounds.

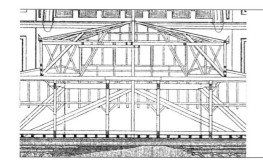

Lüftungslaterne unter Lebensgefahr vom Dach des Zuschauerhauses fotografiert
Photograph of ventilation lantern taken at risk of life and limb from the roof of the auditorium

Hölzerne Konstruktion der Lüftungslaterne, Detail aus dem Holzschnitt Brückwalds, 1872
Wooden ventilation lantern construction, detail from Brückwald's 1872 woodcut

Alte Lüftungsklappen über dem Proszenium/Orchestergraben Old ventilation flaps above the proscenium/orchestra pit

das alles so leise, dass die Musik nicht gestört wird. Die Abluft geht zusammen mit allen teuren Parfumdüften und den süßen Schweißgerüchen eines strapazierten Publikums über große Rohre nach draußen und findet im nördlichen Bereich des Geländes ihren Ausgang.

Fazit

Wagners Festspiele waren ursprünglich als Fest für die „Freunde des musikalischen Dramas" mit garantiertem und freiem Eintritt gedacht. Dieser Idealismus war letztlich durch seine Erfahrungen mit einem in seinen Augen dekadenten und vergnügungssüchtigen Großstadtpublikum entstanden, sodass er seine „alternativen" Festspiele bewusst in einer Provinzstadt ansiedelte. Hier wollte er die Menschen als Menschen verstehen und sie durch eine angenehme Atmosphäre und durch Erholungsräume im Grünen von ihrem Alltag befreien und auf ein besonderes Kunsterlebnis vorbereiten. Von der blauen Stunde erhoffte er sich psychologisch einfühlsam die rechte Besinnlichkeit und Aufnahmebereitschaft, die allein der Kunst zugedacht sein sollte. In diesem Sinne war die ganze Architektur in ihrer edlen Einfachheit ohne jede architektonische Eitelkeit der adäquate Rahmen. Fast väterlich sorgte Wagner auch für die leiblichen Bedürfnisse und eine gute Belüftung seines Theaters, was besonders bei den in Bayreuth häufig heißen Sommern sehr human war. Die Premieren zeigten jedoch, dass das von ihm erhoffte neue Publikum nur ein fernes Ideal blieb. Bayreuth entwickelte sich nicht zum Treffpunkt der Jugend und der Intellektuellen, sondern zu einem Schauspiel des Hochadels und jener Kreise, von denen Wagner kein rechtes Kunstverständnis erwartete. Ein elitäres Festival hat Wagner nie gewollt.

Summary

Wagner's festivals were originally conceptualized as a celebration for *"friends of the musical drama"* with guaranteed free entry. This idealism was born of Wagner's experiences with a large city audience he considered decadent and addicted to pleasure. This is why he consciously decided to hold his "alternative" festivals in a provincial city. In the small city, he wanted to understand people as people, freeing them from their everyday toils and preparing them for a special art experience by creating a pleasant atmosphere in a restful natural environment. Showing psychological empathy, he wanted to avail himself of twilight to awaken sensuality and receptiveness dedicated only to art. In this regard, the architecture in all its noble simplicity, free of architectural vanity, provides a suitable setting. Wagner also attended to the audience's need for food and a well-ventilated theater, a humanitarian, almost fatherly gesture considering the oft stifling summers in Bayreuth. But the premiere showed that the new public he had hoped for would remain a distant ideal. Bayreuth did not become a meeting place for the young generation and for intellectuals, but rather a showplace for the upper nobility and people of higher circles whom Wagner did not expect.

Keine Wagnertuben, sondern Gebläserohre in einem Lüftungsgang unter dem Orchestergraben, die Frischluft in den Zuschauerraum blasen
Not Wagner tubas, but rather pipes in a ventilation passageway below the orchestra pit that blow fresh air into the auditorium

THE INTERIOR

Leading up to the auditorium

Sunny illusionistic architecture

We currently live in a democratic society which since 1918 has allowed everyone to ignore arrogant zones of rustication and to enter the palaces of the kings – and that is also the case at Bayreuth, where the Königsbau has long since been opened up for public use. The architecture of the external facade is carried over, greeting visitors with two Tuscan pillars in beautifully marbled sandstone. Only malevolent voices would complain that this marbling has been manipulated by a painter's brush. After all, both the ancient world and, later, the Baroque age were familiar with such thoroughly artificial marbling.

The eye first notices the walls, painted in "giallo antico," a yellow ochre tone that Semper had also recommended. The walls appear to have been built of powerful ashlars and only at a second glance does it emerge that they are actually only imitation. Here, too, the models of antiquity were followed, in particular those of Pompeii, where the illusion of stone walls is created by means of the so-called incrustation style. In the early "first style" of this approach, the illusionistic joints were etched into the plasterwork and lightly shaded with paint in order to achieve a particularly sculptural effect. In Bayreuth the late stonework style was chosen (albeit unknowingly) in which only paint is used (200 to 80 BC).

A famous example of this is the Pompeianum of Ludwig's grandfather, King Ludwig I of Bavaria, in Aschaffenburg, which follows this pattern in its entire external structure. In Pompeii, which Wagner himself is known to have visited on October 23, 1876 and which he also had his children visit on June 3, 1880, one can see especially beautiful incrustations in the rooms of the Casa di Sallustio and the Casa del Fauno.

The whole interior of the Königsbau was renovated in 1998/99, with the colorful design faithfully adhering to the original conservational findings. All the colors and the marbling are therefore original. Unfortunately none of the original plans of the interior, the Königsbau, the foyer or the auditorium have survived. The lamps in the Königsbau are new (1998/99). The ceiling, however, is original. In its simple rafter construction, it too has an ancient or antique feel. Made of wood, it displays brown-painted, coffered crossbeams.

More interesting than the simple ceiling is the floor. This genuine mosaic floor cannot have been so inexpensive and is the most elegant flooring in the whole Festspielhaus. Helmut Jahn surmises that remnants from a nearby new church were used to build it. However, it is more than it seems and it too was based on models from antiquity. It is a classical Greek black-and-white mosaic, which in Pompeii was made of black lava and white marble and was called "lavapesta." An elaborate geometry suggests 3D effects and even what we would today call op-art effects. The eye focuses on various places, at one time falling more on the white triangles and squares, then more on the black ones, each time seeing a different pattern. The Tempio della Vittoria in Fossombrone in Italy is a suitable ancient model for the Bayreuth pattern.

King Ludwig I of Bavaria's Pompeianum in Aschaffenburg with yellow faux masonry and Pompeian red rustica

Zentraler Eingang Königsbau mit marmorierten Säulen und antikisierendem Schwarz-Weiß-Mosaik
Central entrance to the Königsbau with marbled columns and antique looking black-and-white mosaic

Salons und Studios

Links neben der Treppe findet sich eine kleine geheimnisvolle Tür, dahinter verbirgt sich ein winziges Appartement mit Toilette, das sich einst Winifred Wagner als Privatraum einrichten ließ. Heute dürfen sich hier gelegentlich hohe Gäste aufhalten, ausruhen oder umziehen. Die Treppenstufen sind – wie von der Feuerwehr gefordert – aus Granit ausgeführt. Das Geländer mit den Balustern folgt den Entwürfen Brückwalds, wie die Pläne zeigen, und wurde nach Auskunft von Helmut Jahn von Winifreds Hausarchitekt Reissinger in den 1930er Jahren erneuert. Es greift mit seinen Balustern (Docken) die Gestaltung des Balkons und der Attika auf und gibt dem Königsbau eine königliche Note.

Fenster und Türen sind durch Archivolten akzentuiert, ein verkröpfter Sockel markiert die Geschossgrenzen. Die Bemalung mit rot umrandeten Wandfeldern ist eine freie Gestaltung, die der Denkmalpfleger Hans Heid von der obersten bayerischen Baubehörde in München 1998/99 angeregt hat und die den pompejanischen Stil stark stilisiert. Erneut wurden Originalpläne der Inneneinrichtung schmerzlich vermisst.

In der ersten Etage findet sich jenes kleine *„möglichst anständige Gelass (Salon genannt)"* für den unsichtbaren König. Die Wandfarbe in Wagners Lieblingsfarbe Rosa ist frei gewählt. Zwei Aquarelle des Münchner Kunstprofessors Eduard Ille hängen an den Wänden, die König Ludwig Wagner 1865 schenkte. Dem TANNHÄUSER-Gemälde vis à vis steht die Bank, auf der die Fanfarenbläser jeweils auf ihren Aufruf warten. Die Decke wurde 1934 wegen des Einbaus eines Rundfunkstudios im darüberliegenden Balkongeschoss tiefergelegt.

Salons and studios

To the left beside the staircase is a mysterious little door concealing a tiny apartment complete with a toilet, which Winifred Wagner once furnished as her own private room. Today, high-ranking guests are occasionally allowed to use this room to rest or to change. The steps of the staircase are – as required by fire code – made of granite. The plans show that the balustrade and balusters follow Brückwald's designs and, according to information supplied by Helmut Jahn, were renovated by Winifred's personal architect, Reissinger, in the 1930s. With its balusters, it continues the design of the balcony and attica, giving the Königsbau a royal note.

The windows and doors are accentuated by archivolts, an offset plinth marking the limits of the stories. Hans Heid, responsible for the preservation of historical monuments at the highest Bavarian building authorities in Munich, encouraged the freely designed red border framing the wall sections in 1998/99, a strong stylization of the Pompeian manner. Once again the original plans for the interior furnishings were painfully lacking.

A small *"chamber (known as the Salon), made as respectable as possible"* for the invisible king is located on the second floor. The paint on the wall was chosen freely in Wagner's favorite color, pink. There are two watercolors on the walls by the Munich art professor Eduard Ille, which King Ludwig gave to Wagner as a present in 1865. Opposite the TANNHÄUSER painting is the bench where the fanfare players wait for their cue. In 1934 the ceiling was lowered to make room for a radio studio in the balcony level above.

Freie Farbgestaltung des Treppenhauses und des Salons im ersten Obergeschoss des Königsbaus (1998f), zum Teil in der Lieblingsfarbe des Meisters
Freely chosen paint colors in the stairwell and the salon in the 2nd floor of the Königsbaus (1998 et seq.), some in the maestro's favorite color

Gedenkstein gleich Grabstein

Tritt man die Treppe wieder hinunter, findet sich in der Symmetrieachse des Hauses die Gedenktafel, die am 2. August 1876 zur Erinnerung an die Mitwirkenden der Uraufführung errichtet und von den Maurer- und Zimmermannsmeistern gestiftet wurde. Sie zeigt einen Stein gewordenen Theaterzettel in schwarzem (echten) Marmor, der freilich während der ersten Festspiele verhängt blieb, da man die nicht genannten Orchestermusiker und Choristen nicht zu früh beleidigen wollte. Auch andere schienen über den Stein verärgert wie Albert Niemann, der Sänger des „Siegmund": *„Wenn ich einmal in der richtigen Laune bin, schmeiße ich den Leichenstein um."*[1]

Der Stein erinnert in der Tat an einen Grabstein, zu dem er längst geworden ist, oder an den Eingang in ein Mausoleum. Er zeigt eine klassische Ädikula mit Tempeldach und Pfeilern, in die Kanneluren eingemeißelt sind, sodass sie als dorische Pfeiler anzusprechen wären. Darunter sind Diamantbossen zu erkennen. Letztere besitzt auch die Eingangstür zum Königsbau, ein Motiv, das ebenfalls aus der italienischen Renaissance bekannt ist (Palazzo dei Diamanti in Ferrara) und vor allem ein Kennzeichen der „Deutschen Renaissance" ist und wie die Türbeschläge einen winzigkleinen Stilbruch darstellt.

Memorial stone and gravestone in one

If one descends the stairs again one finds in the symmetrical axis of the building the plaque which was set up on August 2, 1876 to commemorate the work of those involved in the premiere and donated by the master masons and carpenters. It shows a theater program in (genuine) black marble, which naturally was left draped during the first festival, since no one wanted to offend the members of the orchestra and choristers too early who had not been mentioned. Others, too, seem to have been annoyed by the stone, such as Albert Niemann, who sang the part of "Siegmund": *"When I am in the right mood, I'll knock the corpse stone down."*

The stone does actually remind one of a gravestone, which it has long since become, or of the entrance to a mausoleum. It shows a classical aedicule with a temple roof and columns, in which fluting has been engraved, giving them the look of Dorian pillars. Beneath them are diamond bosses like those also found on the entrance door to the Königsbau. This is also a familiar motif from the Italian Renaissance (Palazzo dei Diamanti in Ferrara) and is above all a distinguishing mark of the "German Renaissance." Like the door fittings, it represents a tiny breach of style.

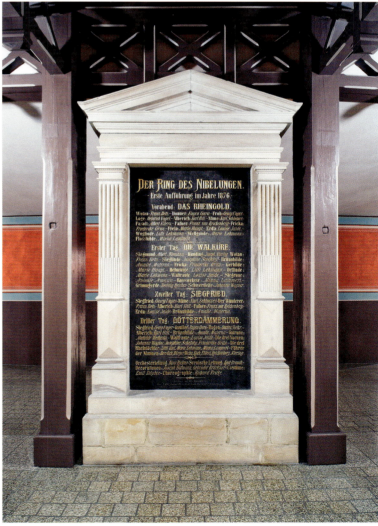

Pompejanische Polychromie

Ab 1994 wurde das Foyer des Festspielhauses aufwendig restauriert. Bis dahin herrschte der sachliche Stil der Umbauten durch Reissinger in den 1930er Jahren. Hinter den hell gestrichenen Wänden fanden die Restauratoren jedoch schon 1992 Reste einer überraschend bunten Originalbemalung, die im Folgenden wiederhergestellt wurde.

Es handelt sich um einen Akkord aus einem dunklen Rot, einem Gelb und einem helleren Blau – Farben, wie sie in Pompeji in diesem Dreiklang häufig waren, da sie die intensivsten und haltbarsten Pigmente der Antike repräsentieren: Eisenoxidgelb (Ocker), Ägyptisch- oder Pompejanischblau und Rot aus Zinnober oder Mennige, das später sogar den Namen Pompejanischrot erhielt und im Klassizismus sehr geschätzt war, wie zum Beispiel im Pompejanum in Aschaffenburg oder in Schinkels Altem Museum in Berlin. In Bayreuth kamen noch neutrale Weiß- und Schwarztöne sowie ein sehr gedecktes Purpurviolett hinzu.

Hier mag der Einfluss Sempers gewirkt haben, wie Wagner schreibt: *„Semper klärte uns, als er vor siebzehn Jahren aus Griechenland zurückkehrte, in seiner berühmten Schrift ‚Bemerkungen über vielfarbige Architektur und Skulptur bei den Alten' (Altona 1834) über die wesentlichen Gründe jener Erscheinungen auf."*[1] Wagner gestaltete die Räume seiner Villa Wahnfried ebenfalls bunt. Die Hallenwände sind in einem braunen Pompejanischrot zu sehen. *„Dagegen waren die umlaufenden Wände der oberen Galerie himmelblau gehalten, auf Malwidas Empfehlung, welche diese dem Auge wohltuende Farbenzusammenstellung auf ihren Reisen in Griechenland beobachtet hatte."*[2] Der Familie Wagner wurden übrigens am 1. September 1870 *„einige Photographien nach Wandgemälden aus Pompeji!"* geschenkt.[3]

Doch nirgendwo verliert Wagner selbst ein Wort über die Farbgestaltung seines Festspielhauses, wie auch Brückwald nicht. Schön, dass ihre Nachfolger diesen Farbensinn zurückgewonnen haben und das Foyer wieder in alter Pracht zu sehen ist.

Pompeian polychromy

From 1994 onwards the foyer of the Festspielhaus was restored with great care. Up until then, Reissinger's matter-of-fact style of the 1930s had predominated. However, in 1992 the restorers found the remains of a surprisingly colorful original painting behind the brightly painted walls, which was also subsequently restored.

It displays a chord of dark red, yellow and lighter blue – colors frequently used in this triad in Pompeii, since they represent the most intensive and lasting pigments of antiquity: iron oxide yellow (ochre), Egyptian or Pompeian blue and red made from vermilion or minimum, which later was even given the name Pompeian red and was highly prized in classicism, as e.g. in the Pompeianum in Aschaffenburg or in Schinkel's Altes Museum in Berlin. In Bayreuth, neutral white and black tones, as well as a very muted purple-violet were also added.

This could signal Semper's influence, as Wagner writes: *"Semper explained to us about the essential reasons for those manifestations upon his return from Greece seventeen years ago, in his famous essay 'Observations on the Polychromatic Architecture and Sculpture of the Ancients' (Altona 1834)."* Wagner had also designed the rooms of his villa "Wahnfried" in a colorful manner. The walls of the hall are a brown Pompeian red. *"In contrast, the surrounding walls of the upper gallery were sky blue, upon the recommendation of Malwida, who had found this color combination so pleasant to the eye on her travels in Greece."* Incidentally, on September 1, 1870, the Wagner family was given *"several photographs based on the wall paintings of Pompeii!"*

Wagner himself does not even mention the color design of his Festspielhaus, nor in fact does Brückwald. It is good that their successors have regained this sense of color and that the foyer has been restored to its entire former splendor.

Pompejanische Wandbemalungen in allen Foyers, 1994 bis 1997 nach wenigen Originalbefunden rekonstruiert
Pompeian wall painting in all of the foyers reconstructed between 1994 and 1997 according to the original findings

Das ansteigende Amphitheater des Zuschauerraums „sitzt" schräg auf den Säulen des Foyers The graded auditorium amphitheater "sits" at an angle on top of the foyer pillars

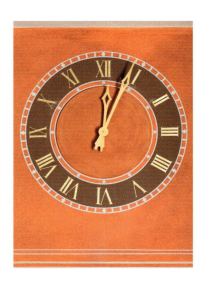

Wanduhr im Foyer mit römischen Ziffern. Die Vorstellungen beginnen pünktlich. Zu spät Kommende haben keine Chance, denn die Uhr ist mit der Atomuhr in Braunschweig gekoppelt und hat immer Recht.
Clock on the foyer wall with Roman numerals. Performances always start on time. Late arrivers don't have a chance because the clock is linked to the atomic clock in Braunschweig and is always right.

Auch bei den Garderoben wurde die antike Bemalung erneuert. Sie befinden sich übrigens direkt unter dem ansteigenden Amphitheater, deshalb die schräge Decke. Die Spiegel wurden Mitte der 1990er Jahre erneuert.

Der Verzicht auf jede äußere Prunk- und Prachtentfaltung mag die dunkle Farbgestaltung der Treppenaufgänge zum Zuschauerraum erklären. Es handelt sich um ein sehr gedecktes Violett, im Abendland die klassische Symbolfarbe der Trauer, der Demut und des Büßertums. Sie ziert in der Karwoche die katholischen Kirchen und passt recht gut zu jeder PARSIFAL-Aufführung. Doch darf hier nicht überinterpretiert werden: Das Braun-Violett steht einfach im Kontrast zum herrschenden Lichterglanz und Gold herkömmlicher Theaterfoyers.

1933 wurden die Zugänge zum Zuschauerraum nach außen verlegt sowie das ganze Foyer entsprechend verbreitert. Die ebenfalls dunklen Türen sind nicht original. In ihrer Kassettierung erinnern sie an die Antike, doch Brückwald hatte eine andere Gliederung vorgesehen und auch realisiert (eine einzige Tür, die zum Orchester, ist noch original erhalten). Man wollte bei der Sanierung also noch pompejanischer sein als ursprünglich. Alle Türen sind übrigens nach neuen Sicherheitsbestimmungen sogenannte Paniktüren, die immer von innen zu öffnen sind, so streng die blauen Mädchen auch schauen mögen, sodass sich das peinliche Erlebnis des Theodor Fontane (siehe Seite 168) heute so nicht mehr ereignen kann.

Fazit

Der Eintritt in den Königsbau ist überraschend: Während die Außenfassade im Stil der Renaissance erscheint und eine ebensolche Innengestaltung erwarten lässt, findet sich hier ein vollkommen anderer Stil, der als neopompejanisch bezeichnet wird. Zwar sind beide Stile der Antike verpflichtet, doch offenbart sich hier – insbesondere im Inneren des Königsbaus – ein eklatanter Stilbruch. Im Historismus sind solche Brüche nicht ungewöhnlich, doch sprechen sie nicht gerade für eine konsequente Konzeption. Es wäre ein Leichtes gewesen, auch den Außenbau wie das Pompejanum in Aschaffenburg zu gestalten, womit eine klare ästhetische und programmatische Aussage getroffen worden wäre. So aber wird die um 1870 moderne Neorenaissance mit einer seit dem Biedermeier längst nostalgisch gewordenen Mode konfrontiert, die einem König Ludwig I. zwei Generationen zuvor gefallen hätte. Eine Ausschmückung im Stile der Neorenaissance mit viel Stuck wäre vermutlich zu teuer gewesen. Wesentlich billiger war es, die Wände in einem antikisierenden Stil nur anzumalen, das Mauerwerk und den Marmor nur vorzutäuschen.

Trotz allem gefällt das Innere durch eine rührende Wiederbelebung des Hellenismus, was in einem Theaterbau immer klug und richtig ist. Intensive Farben und optisch reizvolle Illusionen (insbesondere der Fußboden) beleben die Sinne. Die Räume vor dem Zuschauerraum entfalten so ein antikes und im besten Sinne idealistisches Ambiente, das den adligen und bourgeoisen Zeitgenossen kein weiteres Prunkfoyer vor Augen führte, sondern eine in demütigem Braun-Violett gehaltene Rückbesinnung auf die einfachen Ursprünge einer zeitlosen Theaterkultur.

The old painting has been renewed in the cloakrooms, as well. They are located directly beneath the graded amphitheater, which explains the slanted ceiling. The mirrors were renovated in the mid-1990s.

The renunciation of any external display of grandeur or splendor may explain the dark color scheme of the staircases leading up to the auditorium. It is a very muted violet, in the west the classic symbolic color of sorrow, humility and penitence. In the Easter week it adorns the Catholic churches and goes very well with every performance of PARSIFAL. Yet one should not fall prey to over-interpretation here: the brown-violet is simply a contrast to the predominant blaze of lights and gold in the traditional theater foyer.

In 1933 the entrances to the auditorium were shifted outward, and the whole foyer was expanded correspondingly. The dark doors are likewise not original. Their coffering recall antiquity, yet Brückwald intended another pattern and also implemented it (only one of the original doors, the one leading to the orchestra pit, has survived). It seems the restoration planners wanted to be even more Pompeian than the original. In accordance with new safety regulations, all of the doors are incidentally so-called panic doors, which can always be opened from the inside, so that although the usherettes in blue may look strict, Theodor Fontane's embarrassing experience (see page 168) can no longer occur today.

Summary

The entrance to the Königsbau is surprising: whereas the external facade appears to be in the style of the Renaissance and leads one to expect a similar interior design, a completely different style one might describe as neo-Pompeian is found. Even though both styles derive from antiquity, a striking breach of style is evident – in particular in relation to the interior of the Königsbau. Although such breaches are not unusual in history, they hardly support the idea of a consistent conception. It would have been easy to design the exterior of the building like the Pompeianum in Aschaffenburg, which would have made a clear aesthetic and programmatic statement. As it is, however, the modern neo-Renaissance of the years around 1870 was confronted with a fashion that, after the Biedermeier age, had long since become nostalgic, although it would have pleased King Ludwig I two generations beforehand. Adornment in the style of the neo-Renaissance, which uses a great deal of stucco, would presumably have been too expensive. It was considerably cheaper to just paint the walls in mock-antique style and to simply create an illusion of stonework and marble.

Despite everything, the interior is pleasing due to its stirring revival of Hellenism, which is always an intelligent and appropriate approach in a theater. The intense colors and optically attractive illusions (in particular those of the flooring) stimulate the senses. The rooms leading up to the auditorium therefore develop an ambient reminiscent of antiquity and (in the best sense) idealistic, that did not present its aristocratic and bourgeois contemporaries with yet another ornate foyer, but rather with a reminder in modest brown-violet of the simple origins of a timeless theatrical culture.

Die geschweifte Garderobe „duckt" sich unter das Amphitheater
The curved coatroom is "tucked" under the amphitheater

Die Büßerfarbe Braun-Violett beherrscht die (erneuerten) Holzkonstruktionen des Foyers und die neuen (Panik-)Türen
Brown-violet, the color of atonement, dominates the (restored) wooden constructions of the foyer and the new (panic) doors

Farbloses Foyer vor den Renovierungen der 1990er Jahre, Aufnahme von 1967
Drab foyer prior to renovations in the 1990s, photograph from 1967

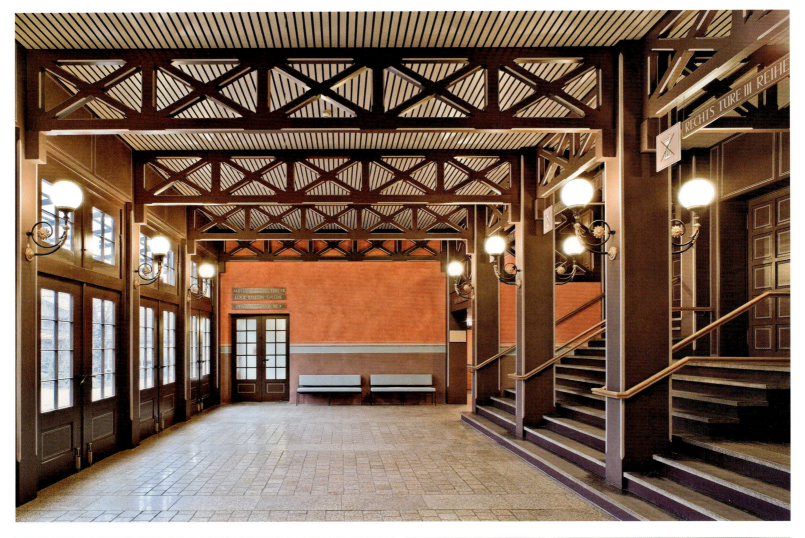

Hoffmanns Gibichungenhalle 1876. Hoffmann's Gibichung Hall, 1876.

Auch die innere Gestaltung des Foyers hat in seiner einfachen Konstruktion mit gefasten (abgekanteten), dunklen Holzbalken und soliden, kreuzverstrebten Bindern eine ländlich-rustikale Anmutung und lässt an die Tenne einer archaischen Wikingerscheune denken, was Besucher bei der Wahl ihrer Kopfbedeckung inspirieren kann.

The interior foyer design is likewise very simply constructed with bound (rounded off) dark beams and solid cross framing, giving it a rural-rustic feel like that of the threshing floor of an archaic Viking barn. This can be a source of inspiration for visitors in choosing their headdress.

Der Zuschauerraum

Eine völlige Schmucklosigkeit?

Wagner war zuallererst am Inneren seines Theaters interessiert. Es wird sich, wie er 1872 in seiner Rede zur Grundsteinlegung ankündigt, in *„allerdürftigstem Material"* und in einer *„völligen Schmucklosigkeit darbieten"*, die selbst die leichtesten *„Zierrathen vermissen"* lässt. Mit dieser Schmucklosigkeit beschreibt Wagner keineswegs nur die hölzernen Foyers, er meint das Innere des Zuschauersaals, der uns heute prächtig erscheint, damals jedoch als sehr schlicht empfunden wurde, wie ein französischer Zeitgenosse schildert: *„Der Zuschauerraum ist gedrückt, [...] das Innere ist von abstoßender Nacktheit und Einförmigkeit."*[1] Um dies zu verstehen, sei an das Markgräfliche Opernhaus zu Bayreuth und die Prachttheater des 19. Jahrhunderts erinnert.

Im Vergleich zum Rokoko und anderen Prunkstilen ist die Gestaltung des Bayreuther Zuschauersaals tatsächlich relativ schlicht, wie schon der Premierenbesucher Camille Saint-Saëns 1876 notierte: *„Man fühlt sich in einen der Kunst geweihten Tempel, nicht an eine der Zerstreuung und Schaulust dienende Stätte versetzt."*[2] Von einer *„völligen Schmucklosigkeit"* kann jedoch nicht die Rede sein. Die großen schlanken korinthischen Säulen sind in ihrer antiken Schönheit eigentlich nicht zu übersehen. Doch weder Wagner, der schon in Taormina von der Sonne geblendet war, noch Brückwald gehen auf die prächtigen Säulen und ihr mächtiges Gebälk im korinthischen Stil ein. Brückwald spricht lediglich abstrakt von einer *„Säulenstellung"*[3]. Semper dagegen hatte für seine Münchner Festspielhausprojekte ebenfalls korinthische Säulen vorgesehen und diese auch beim Namen benannt.

Die korinthische gilt als die schönste (und jüngste) Säulenordnung der antiken Architektur Griechenlands. Die Römer versuchten sie mit der kompositen Ordnung noch zu steigern, die im Historismus als prachtvollste Säulenordnung beliebt war. Brückwald wählte nicht die prächtigste, sondern die griechischste Säulenordnung – ein eindeutiges Bekenntnis zum Hellenismus und zur Blütezeit der griechischen Tragödie, die Wagner 1849 in seinem *„Kunstwerk der Zukunft"* einst feierte.

Auch theoretisch passt diese Ordnung in dieses Theater: Schon Vitruv hatte die korinthische Säule mit den Proportionen eines fraulichen Körpers verglichen, weshalb sie im Historismus des 19. Jahrhunderts für Gebäude empfohlen wurde, in dem das weibliche Element zur Geltung käme, also eher bei Theatern oder Museen als bei Kasernen, Maschinenfabriken oder Schlachthöfen. Wagner selbst hat in seiner letzten Schrift *„über das Weibliche im Menschlichen"* nachgedacht und an anderer Stelle die Musik als *„das weibliche Prinzip"* verstanden, *„das Dichterwerk als das männliche."*[4] Dorische oder toskanische Säulen wie am Außenbau galten dagegen als männliche Säulen.

Die runden Säulen des Zuschauersaals sind natürlich nicht aus Marmor, sondern aus Holz und Gips, aber geradezu klassisch ausgeführt: Sie stehen auf einer attischen Basis, sind etwa neun zu eins proportioniert, wie es Vitruv gefordert hatte, werden im unteren Drittel von einem Schaft umfangen, der die klassischen Kanneluren zeigt, die einst einem textilen Faltenwurf nachempfunden waren, und die Entasis als leichte Bauchung. Sie tragen ein relativ mächtiges Gebälk, doch ohne ornamentalen oder figurativen Fries, wie bei korinthischen Tempeln üblich. Dahinter stehen vierkantige Pfeiler, die ebenfalls korinthische Kapitelle tragen. Alle Säulen und Pfeiler sind original erhalten. In den 1990er Jahren wurde lediglich die Fassung und Vergoldung restauriert. Letztere war ursprünglich nur aus billiger Goldbronze und mit den Jahrzehnten stark gedunkelt, sodass der neue Glanz ab 1995 viele überraschte.

The auditorium

A complete lack of decoration?

Above all else, Wagner was interested in the interior of his theater. As he announced in his speech of 1872, during the cornerstone laying ceremony, it will be built using the *"humblest materials"* and display a *"complete lack of decoration,"* omitting even the simplest *"adornments."* With this lack of decoration, Wagner was by no means describing solely the wooden foyers. He was also referring to the interior of the auditorium, which seems to us today to be so magnificent, yet which in those days would have been regarded as very plain. As a French contemporary describes it: *"The auditorium is somber […] and the interior displays a repulsive bareness and uniformity."* In order to understand this, one need only recall the Margravial Opera House in Bayreuth and the splendid theaters of the 19th century.

In comparison to the Rococo and other stately styles, the design of the Bayreuth auditorium is indeed relatively plain as Camille Saint-Saëns noted after the premiere in 1876: *"One feels transposed into a temple devoted to art, not in a place providing entertainment and idle curiosity."* However this is by no means a *"complete lack of decoration."* The antique beauty of the tall slim Corinthian pillars cannot easily be overlooked. Nevertheless, neither Wagner, who had already been blinded by the sun in Taormina, nor Brückwald mention the magnificent pillars and their massive beams in Corinthian style. Brückwald speaks solely in an abstract manner, of *"pillar placement."* Semper, on the other hand, had also planned to use Corinthian pillars in his Festspielhaus project in Munich and had also mentioned them by name.

The Corinthian order of pillars is regarded as being the most beautiful (and most recent) of the ancient architecture of Greece. The Romans attempted to increase the compositional order, which was very popular in historicism as the most ornate pillar order. Brückwald chose an order of pillars that was not the most magnificent, but the most Greek – a distinct acknowledgement of Hellenism and of the pinnacle of Greek tragedy, which Wagner celebrated in his 1849 essay *"Artwork of the Future."*

This order fits this theater theoretically as well. Even Vitruvius compared the Corinthian pillars with the proportions of the female body, which is why in the historicism of the 19th century it was recommended for buildings in which the female element should be expressed, i. e. in theaters or museums rather than in military barracks, machine factories or slaughterhouses. Wagner himself reflected on this in his last essay *"On the Female in the Human"* and elsewhere identifies music as *"the female principle,"* and *"the poetic art as the male."* Dorian or Tuscan columns, such as those used in the exterior structure, were regarded as being "male" pillars.

The round columns of the auditorium are of course not made of marble, but of wood and plaster, but are almost classically finished: they stand on an Attic base, in proportions of about nine to one, as demanded by Vitruvius, are in the lower third enveloped by a shaft displaying classical flutes imitating the fall of textile folds, and have the entasis as a slight outward curve. They bear a relatively powerful entablature, yet without the ornamental or figurative frieze that is typical in Corinthian temples. Behind them are tetragonal pillars which likewise bear Corinthian capitals. All the columns and pillars are original. In the 1990s solely the frame and gilding were restored. The latter was originally only made from cheap gold-colored bronze and had darkened considerably with the decades, so that the new sheen of 1995 surprised a lot of people.

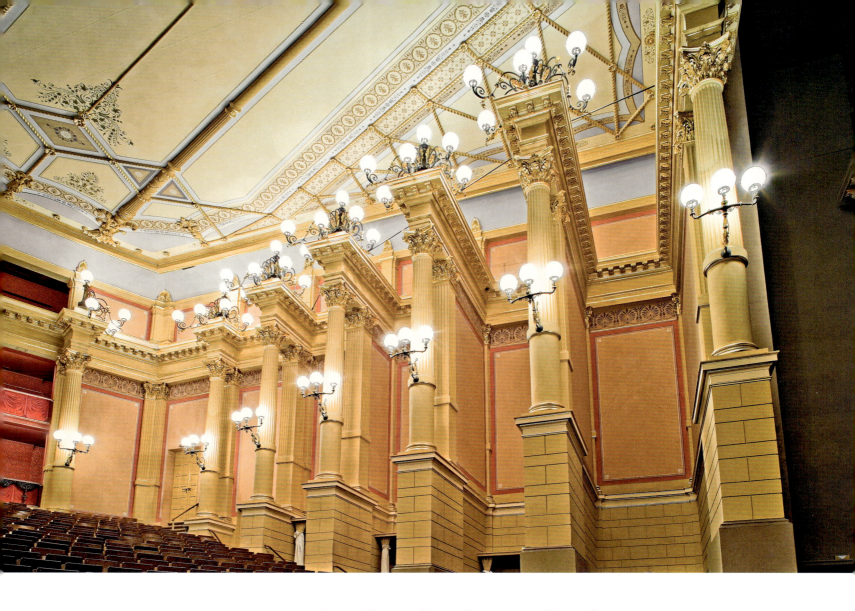

„In Taormina erfreuen die Säulen R. ganz besonders.
Bei der Heimfahrt bespricht er es, wie traumhaft es ist, derlei zu sehen,
wie es einen eigentlich gar nicht berühre."

"The columns in Taormina are especially appealing to R. During the return ride
he talks about how dreamlike it is to see things like that, how it actually
doesn't matter at all."

Cosima Wagner (3. April 1982)

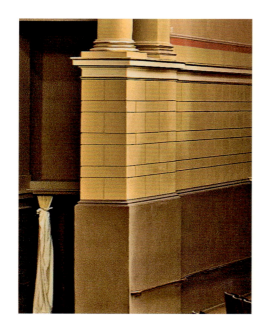

Schlanke korinthische Säulen mit neu vergoldeten Kapitellen, ein Stil aus der Blütezeit des griechischen Dramas
Thin Corinthian columns with new gilded capitals, a style typical at the height of the Greek drama

Ein weiteres ausgesprochen griechisches Zierelement, das zu den „leichten Zierrathen" gehört, ist ein Anthemion, das sich als aufgemaltes Band um den ganzen Raum rankt, bis zur Bühne. Wie im Foyer sind auch für den Zuschauerraum keine Originalpläne der tatsächlich ausgeführten Innenausstattung erhalten, doch hat sich diese Bemalung seit der Eröffnung des Hauses erhalten und konnte nach Originalbefunden restauriert werden.

Am Sonntagmorgen des 29. August 1874 notiert Cosima: „‚Du bist meine Lotos-Blume', sagt R. ‚Du bist die Palme und ich die Fichte', sagt er in der Frühe zu mir.‘"[1] Ob Wagner bei dieser Liebesbekundung womöglich ein Anthemion vor Augen hatte? Zumindest lässt dieser Satz an jenes antike Ornament denken, das mit seiner Verschlingung von stilisierten Palmblättern und Lotosblüten den Namen Anthemion trägt, nach dem griechischen Wort für „Blüte". Einst schmückten Anthemien als plastisch ausgeführte Antenkapitelle vornehmlich die verlängerten Wände der Cellawand, worin bekanntlich das Götterbild im ewigen Dunkel stand. In Bayreuth ziert ein Anthemion die Proszeniumswand, die damit – zumindest assoziativ – einen ebenfalls dunklen und von Mauern umschlossenen Bühnenraum (wo bisweilen auch so manche Götter stehen) zu einem Tempel macht.

Die Lotosblume galt schon den Ägyptern als heilig. Sie öffnet ihre Blüte bei Sonnenaufgang und schließt sie am Abend, sodass sie zum Symbol der lebensspendenden Sonne und der Liebe wurde. Letzteres verstärkt sich durch die in der Pflanze enthaltenen Alkaloide, die – wie die Musik Wagners (laut Thomas Mann) – eine narkotische Wirkung besitzen, ja sogar halluzinogen und erotisierend wirken können, was vermutlich so manches ekstatische Ritual inspiriert hat. Auch hier lassen sich Parallelen zum Festspielhaus erkennen.

Auch die immergrüne Palme galt als Lebens-, ihr radial gefächertes Blatt zudem als Lichtsymbol, das die alten Griechen unter anderem dem „Theatergott" Apoll weihten, sodass das Bayreuther Anthemion so zufällig nicht sein kann.

Palmetten finden sich als zierender Abschluss aller vertikalen Raumachsen des Zuschauersaals, die unter der Decke von Akroterien in fein ziseliertem Gips akzentuiert werden (hier vor und nach der Restaurierung 1995).

A further decorative element which is decidedly Greek and which belongs among the *"light adornments"* is an anthemion which winds around the whole room as a painted strip, right up to the stage. As in the case of the foyer, none of the original plans for the interior decoration of the auditorium have survived, although the paintwork here has survived ever since the opening of the building, so that it could be restored according to match the original findings.

On Sunday morning, August 29, 1874, Cosima recorded: *"You are my lotus flower,' R. said, 'You are the palm and I am the spruce,' he said to me in the morning."* When he made this declaration of love, was Wagner possibly having an other anthemion in mind? At least this sentence makes us think of that ancient decoration which with its entwinement of stylized palm leaves and lotus flowers bears the name of anthemion, after the Greek word for "flower." At one time, anthemions were used as sculpturally finished antecapitals to provide respectable decoration for the long walls of the cella wall, in which the image of the gods stood in eternal darkness. In Bayreuth, an anthemion decorates the wall of the proscenium, a likewise dark stage area surrounded by walls (where some gods have also stood on occasions) thus making it – at least associatively – a temple.

The lotus flower was regarded as holy even in ancient Egypt. It opens its blossoms at sunrise and closes them in the evening, so that they became a symbol of the life-giving sun and of love. The latter is enhanced by the alkaloids contained within the plant, which – like Wagner's music (according to Thomas Mann) – have a narcotic, even hallucinogenic and aphrodisiac effect, and which presumably must have inspired many an ecstatic ritual. Here, too, parallels to the Festspielhaus may be recognized.

The evergreen palm tree is also regarded as a symbol of life, its radially fanned leaf also being viewed as a symbol of light, which the ancient Greeks dedicated to (among others) Apollo, the God of the Theater, so that the Bayreuth anthemion cannot have been placed there wholly coincidentally.

Palmettes are used as a decorative conclusion of all the vertical spatial axes in the auditorium, which are accentuated under the ceiling by acroteria in finely chiseled plaster. (Here before and after the restoration work of 1995).

Anthemion-Fries nach der Restaurierung 1995
The anthemion frieze after the restoration of 1995

Palmetten akzentuieren alle Vertikalachsen, seit 1995 vergoldet
The palmettes accentuating all vertical axes have been gilded since 1995

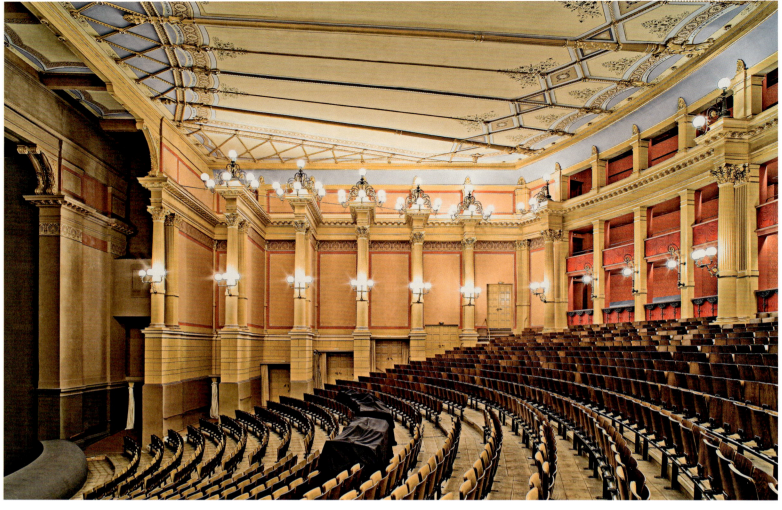

Der Zuschauerraum heute, aus akustischen Gründen ohne Vorhänge, mit rekonstruierten Brüstungsgittern an der Logenwand
The auditorium as it looks today without curtains, for acoustical reasons, and with reconstructed balustrade screens on the loge gallery

Die Logenrückwand besteht aus einer Kolonnadenwand, die im Rhythmus vier zu drei zu vier gegliedert ist und ein gebogenes Gebälk trägt. Auch die Brüstungen wurden bei den Sanierungen Mitte der 1990er Jahre aus akustischen Gründen leicht gekrümmt. Korinthische Säulen markieren die vertikalen Hauptachsen, dazwischen stehen einfache toskanische Pfeiler. Die symmetrische Mitte der Wand, wo in jedem älteren Theater eine Prunkloge für Könige und Fürsten prangt, wird hier nur minimal betont. Der Königsbau des Außenbaus findet keine repräsentative Fortsetzung im Innern! Die sogenannte Fürstenloge in Bayreuth umfasst die ganze Breite der Rückwand und kennt keine Hierarchie. Ursprünglich hatte Brückwald sie als hohe Loge gebaut und darüber eine mehr als halb so hohe „Künstlerloge". Siegfried Wagner sollte 1930 (nachdem die Weimarer Republik den Adel gänzlich entmachtet hatte) die Fürstenloge kappen und einen dritten Balkon mit sechsundneunzig neuen Plätzen als sogenannte Presseloge einziehen lassen. Das schwarze Loch im rot-goldenen Ambiente ist die 1934 in die Mitte des Balkons gebaute Rundfunkkabine.

The rear loges consist of a colonnaded wall divided up in a rhythm of four to three to four and bearing a curved entablature. The balustrades, too, were curved slightly for acoustical reasons during the restorations of the mid-1990s. Corinthian columns mark the main vertical axes, in between which are simple Tuscan pillars. The symmetrical center of the wall, where in every old theater a splendid box stood for kings and princes, is only minimally emphasized. The Königsbau of the exterior structure is not matched by any such representative continuation on the inside! The so-called Prince's Gallery in Bayreuth takes up the whole of the width of the rear wall and knows no hierarchy. Originally, Brückwald built it as a tall loge with an artists' gallery over half its height above it. In 1930 (after the Weimar Republic had wholly deprived the nobility of their political power) Siegfried Wagner capped the Prince's Gallery and installed a third dress circle with ninety-six new seats as the so-called press box. The black hole in the red-and-gold ambience is the radio cabin, which was built in the middle of the balcony in 1934.

Die Logenwand 1926 mit Original-Vorhängen, noch ohne „Presseloge", die 1930 eingebaut wurde[1]
The loge gallery in 1926 with original curtains, still without the "press box," which was added in 1930[1]

Zustand 1950er Jahre ohne Vorhänge, fehlende Brüstungsgitter
Condition in the 1950s without curtains and with missing balustrade screens

1930 verschwanden wohl auch die schon von Brückwald gezeichneten roten Vorhänge, die man aus akustischen Gründen bei der denkmalpflegerischen Rekonstruktion Mitte der 1990er Jahre nicht wieder eingesetzt hat. Stattdessen wurde nach Auskunft des zuständigen Architekten Helmut Jahn während der Restaurierungen eine ganz neue Idee geboren, die Vorhänge – wie einst in der illusionistischen Wandmalerei in Pompeji – auf die Brüstung zu malen.

Das war im Sinne eines konservierenden Denkmalschutzes nicht legitim, als kreative Zutat im Stil der restlichen Innendekoration aber durchaus passend. Das Motiv des leicht gerafften Vorhangs ist allerdings eher aus den Chören gotischer Kirchen (wie der Sainte-Chapelle in Paris) vertraut. Zusammen mit den antikisierenden Brüstungsgittern mag die antike Anmutung aber dominieren.

Rote Vorhänge im antiken Kontext finden sich übrigens auch in Wagners RIENZI, im zweiten Aufzug, dritte Szene: *„Die Nobili werden von den Senatoren, den Trabanten und den Lictoren in den hintern Teil des Saales geführt, vor welchem ein roter Vorhang zusammengezogen wird."*[1] Aus der stürmischen Studentenzeit Wagners im Vorfeld der 1848er Revolution ist eine amüsante Anekdote überliefert. Von einem starken *„Sittlichkeitsgefühl"* getrieben kam es zu einem *„Volkswutanfall"*, bei dem Wagner half, ein *„übelberufenes Etablissement"* zu verwüsten. Der ausgiebige *„Genuss geistiger Getränke"* führte jedoch zu einem Vollrausch. *„Ich erwachte des anderen Morgens wie aus einem wüsten Traume und musste mich erst an einer Trophäe, dem Fetzen eines roten Vorhanges, welchen ich als Zeichen meiner Heldentaten mit mir geführt hatte, daran erinnern, dass die Vorgänge dieser Nacht wirklich von mir erlebt worden seien."*[2]

Die meisten Brüstungsgitter aus Gusseisen sind vermutlich während der amerikanischen Ära nach 1945 verschwunden. Zwei fand man in den 1990er Jahren zufällig unter dem Fußboden der Sitzreihen des Zuschauerhauses, sodass die restlichen Brüstungen nachgegossen und vollständig vor der „Fürstenloge" eingesetzt werden konnten.

Rot ist auch die Wandbemalung in den Logen, keine Tapete, wie man auf den ersten Blick glauben könnte, sondern eine vom Maler aufgewalzte Ziererei oder Schablonenmalerei, die vermutlich auch 1930 verschwunden ist, fast schon verloren schien und 1995 anhand weniger verbliebener Befunde rekonstruiert werden konnte. Auch sie zeigt eine seit der griechischen Antike bekannte vegetabile Ornamentik.

Eine rote Tapete begleitete Wagner bei der Komposition von TRISTAN UND ISOLDE: *„Ich entschloss mich, dieses große Zimmer mit einer, wenn auch sehr ordinären, doch in vollständiges Dunkelrot gefärbten Tapete überziehen zu lassen: dies brachte zunächst viele Unruhe; doch schien es mir sie zu überstehen wohl der Mühe wert, wenn ich von dem Balkon aus mit allmählich immer größerem Behagen auf den wunderbaren Kanal hinabblickte und mir nun sagte, hier wollte ich den TRISTAN vollenden."*[3]

The red curtains drawn by Brückwald probably disappeared in 1930 and for acoustic reasons they were not reinstalled during the preservationist reconstruction in the mid-1990s. Instead, in accordance with the information supplied by Helmut Jahn, the architect in charge, a whole new idea was born in the course of the restoration, namely that of painting the curtains on the balustrade – as had once been done in the illusionistic wall paintings in Pompeii.

That was not legitimate in terms of the conservation measures stipulated for the preservation of historical monuments, even though it was thoroughly appropriate as a creative addition in the style of the rest of the interior decoration. However, the motif of the slightly draped curtain is more familiar from the choirs of Gothic churches (such as Sainte Chapelle in Paris). As with the balustrade screens, the tendency towards antiquity predominates.

Red curtains in the context of antiquity are incidentally also mentioned in Wagner's RIENZI, Act two, Scene three: *"The Nobili are led by the Senators, the Trabantes and the Lictors into the rear part of the hall, in front of which a red curtain is drawn."* An amusing anecdote has been passed down to us from Wagner's tempestuous days as a student in the run-up to the 1848 Revolution. Driven by a strong feeling of *"morality,"* there arose an *"outburst of popular anger,"* in which Wagner helped devastate a *"disreputable establishment."* However, extensive *"enjoyment of spirits"* led to a state of complete intoxication. *"I woke up the next morning as if out of a wild dream and only by means of the ragged pieces of a red curtain, a trophy which I had carried with me as a token of my heroic deeds, could I remember that I had really experienced the events of this night."*

Most of the balustrade screens made of cast iron presumably disappeared during the American era after 1945. Two of them were found by chance in the 1990s, under the floor of the rows of seats in the auditorium, so that the rest of the balustrades could be reproduced based on them and a complete set installed in front of the Prince's Gallery.

Red is also the color used for the wall paintwork in the loges. It is not wallpaper, as one might believe at first glance, but a rolled decoration or stencil painting executed by a painter, which presumably also vanished in 1930 and was presumed lost until it was reconstructed in 1995 on the basis of a few remaining finds. This too shows vegetative ornamentation going back to Greek antiquity.

Red wallpaper accompanied Wagner during his composition of TRISTAN UND ISOLDE: *"I decided to have this big room decorated with wallpaper that even if it was very vulgar, was nevertheless completely dark red. At first this caused much unrest, yet it seemed to me worthwhile to weather it out, and when I looked down with growing pleasure from the balcony at the wonderful canal I then said to myself: this is where I wanted to complete TRISTAN."*

Gusseisernes Brüstungsgitter, zum Teil nachgegossen und ergänzt mit aufgemalten Vorhängen, unhistorisch, aber stilecht
Cast iron balustrade screens, partly reproduced and completed with painted curtains – historically inaccurate but stylistically appropriate

Diverse Entwürfe für Brüstungsvorhänge, 1992
Various design ideas for the balustrade curtains from 1992

Rekonstruierte rote Bemalung der Logenrückwand (keine Tapete)
Reconstrued red painting on the rear wall of the loges (not wallpaper)

Das Zeltdach der Sommerbühne

Eine auffallend schöne Dekoration des Zuschauerhauses bietet die Decke. Sie wurde als eine der letzten Baumaßnahmen kurz vor Eröffnung der Festspiele am 13. August 1876 von den Hoftheatermalern Max und Gotthold Brückner aus Coburg geschaffen, die auch die Dekorationen des RINGS DES NIBELUNGEN nach Entwürfen des Malers Josef Hoffmann ausführten, wie auch 1882 die Dekoration der Uraufführung des PARSIFAL.

Noch am 26. April 1876 war die Deckenbemalung nicht fertig, wie Cosima berichtet: *„Die von den Herrn Brückner versprochene Decke ist nicht da, die Leinwand sei falsch gewesen!"*[1] Dieses Zitat belegt, dass es sich um keine echte Wandbemalung und kein Fresko handelt, sondern um eine applizierte Leinwand, die mit plastischem Schmuck aus Pappmaché reliefiert wurde. Laut Habel wurde sie ab dem 29. März begonnen und zwar im (bereits ab 1872 errichteten) Malersaal, um die schon auf Hochtouren laufenden Proben nicht zu stören. Zur Anbringung musste freilich ein Gerüst gebaut werden, wie auch 1995 zur Restaurierung. Noch am 16. Mai klagt ein ungeduldiger Wagner: *„Das Gerüste, noch immer im Theater, bringt R. zu heller Verzweifelung, die er dem Architekten Brückwald mitteilt; dieser entschuldigt sich demütigst und gut, der Bauführer Runckwitz dagegen ganz tückisch und roh."*[2] Am 24. Mai endlich: *„Das Gerüst ist abgenommen, erhabener Eindruck vom Zuschauerraum wie von der Bühne, gleich traumhaft; es stimmt wehmütig erhaben!"*[3]

Die Deckendekoration der Gebrüder Brückner entspricht einem im Theaterbau durchaus häufigen Motiv, der Simulation eines Zeltdachs. Das erinnert an den griechischen Ursprung des Theaters, das bekanntlich in freier Natur gelegen eine Zeltdachkonstruktion besaß, ein sogenanntes Velarium, was den Archäologen freilich lange unbekannt blieb, da die vergänglichen Materialien Holz und Leinwand keine 2000 Jahre überdauerten. Hinweise aus der Literatur und im Gemäuer der antiken Theater ließen jedoch solche Sonnen- und Regendächer vermuten, die dann rekonstruiert wurden. Das Renaissance-Theater in Vicenza zum Beispiel zeigt noch einen freien blauen Himmel als Deckenmalerei. Seit dem Klassizismus wusste man um solche Velarien, wie in dem – Wagner wohlbekannten – Goethe-Theater in Bad Lauchstädt (1802) heute noch zu sehen, wie auch im Prinzregententheater in München und vielen anderen Theatern des 19. Jahrhunderts.

Das Velarium in Bayreuth greift die Achsen der Logenwand auf und gliedert sich wie diese im Rhythmus vier zu drei zu vier. Es zeigt scheinbar echte Zeltstangen als Gerippe eines Segeltuchs, das an den Rändern kunstvoll mit scheinbar echten Seilen verspannt wird und sogar ein bisschen blauen Himmel freigibt, was jenes eingangs beschriebene „Open-Air-Feeling" anregen kann.

Ursprünglich wurden solche Velarien im alten Rom tatsächlich von echten Seeleuten aufgezogen, im Kolosseum sogar nur von erfahrenen Matrosen der in Neapel stationierten kaiserlichen Flotte. Vielleicht ließ sich ein Kritiker der ersten Aufführung des RHEINGOLD 1876 unbewusst vom Velarium inspirieren, als er diese

The tented roof of the summer stage

One conspicuously beautiful piece of decoration of the auditorium is located on the ceiling. It was one of the last building measures to be undertaken shortly before the festival opened on August 13, 1876 and was executed by the court theater painters Max and Gotthold Brückner from Coburg, who were also responsible for stage decorations for DER RING DES NIBELUNGEN based on designs by the painter Josef Hoffmann, and for decorations for the premiere of PARSIFAL in 1882.

By April 26, 1876 the ceiling frescoes had still not been completed, as Cosima reports: *"The ceiling promised by Messrs Brückner is not in place. They say the canvas was wrong!"* This quotation shows that it was not a genuine wall painting and not a fresco, but an applied canvas, displaying reliefs of sculpted decoration made from papier maché. According to Habel, the work was started on March 29 in the paint shop (already built in 1872), in order not to disrupt the rehearsals that were by then already well underway. Of course, in order to attach them it was necessary to build a scaffold, as was the case during the 1995 restorations. On May 16, an impatient Wagner complained: *"The scaffolding, still here in the theater, sends R. into complete despair, which he communicates to the architect Brückwald; the latter apologizes most humbly and well, the foreman Runckwitz, on the contrary, most insidiously and roughly."* On May 24 finally: *"The scaffolding has been taken down, sublime impression of the auditorium, as of the stage, quite marvelous; it makes one feel wistfully sublime!"*

The ceiling decoration by the Brückner brothers corresponds to a motif frequently encountered in theater buildings, the simulation of a tent roof. It reminds one of the Greek origins of the theater, which, as is now known, was played in the open air and had a tent roof construction, a so-called velarium. This fact remained unknown to archaeologists for a long time, since the transitory materials of wood and canvas naturally could not survive for 2000 years. However, evidence found in literature and in the walls of the theaters of antiquity indicates the existence of such roofs, which had afforded protection from the sun and the rain, and they were subsequently reconstructed.

The Renaissance theater in Vicenza, for example, still displays an open blue sky on its ceiling fresco. Since classicism one has known about such velaria, and they can still be seen today at the Goethe Theater in Bad Lauchstädt (1802) – well known to Wagner – or at the Prinzregententheater in Munich and in many other theaters from the 19th century.

The velarium in Bayreuth takes up the axes of the loge gallery and is likewise divided into a rhythm of four to three to four. It shows apparently real tent poles like the ribs of a canvas which has been artificially stretched by apparently genuine ropes at the edges and even discloses a bit of blue sky, stimulating that open-air feeling mentioned at the outset.

Originally, in ancient Rome, such velaria were actually spanned by seamen, in the Coliseum only by experienced sailors from the imperial fleet stationed at Naples. Perhaps a critic at the premiere of DAS RHEINGOLD in 1876 was unconsciously inspired by the velarium, when he wrote these unfriendly lines: *"Otherwise the same wavelike surging*

Aufwendige Restaurierungsarbeiten am Velarium, Aufnahme 1995
Painstaking restoration of velarium, photograph from 1995

Für entlegene Details steht Lilo Heuberger seit 1962 mit ihren Ferngläsern gerne zur Verfügung
Lilo Heuberger, since 1962, has opera glasses on hand for seeing distant details

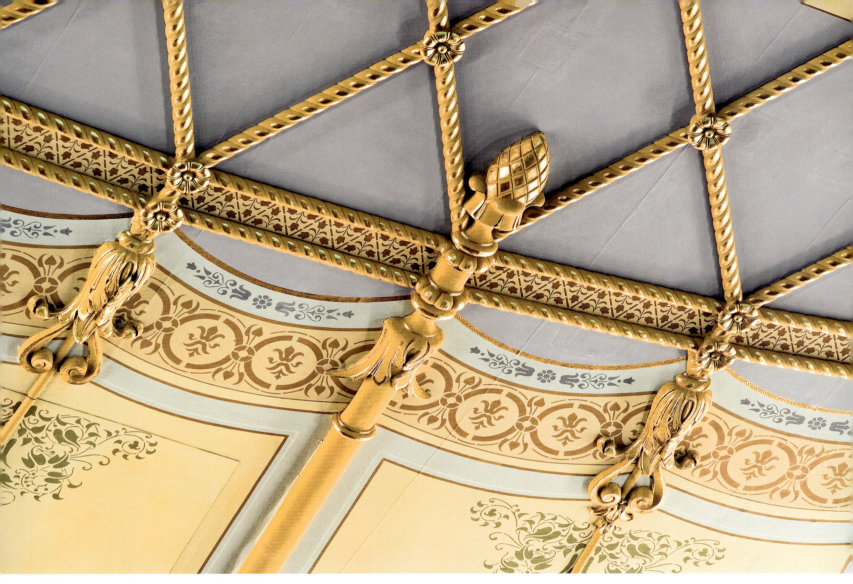

Gedrehte Seile aus Pappmaché, mit Rosetten, Pinienzapfen und Akanthusblättern verziert, „spannen" ein mit Arabesken dekoriertes „Zelttuch"
Twisted ropes made of papier maché decorated with rosettes, pine cones and acanthus leaves "stretch" a "canvas" roof decorated with arabesques

unfreundlichen Zeilen schrieb: „*Sonst geht durch die ganze Darstellung dasselbe Wogen und Drängen, das den Hörer und gerade den Aufmerksamsten zumeist, alsbald in einen der Seekrankheit ähnlichen Zustand versetzt, und jene peinliche Ermüdung und qualvolle Abspannung erzeugt, wie sie eben Wagners spätere Werke so vielfach hervorrufen.*"[1] Ein anderer schrieb schon 1872: „*So dick wie Schiffstaue müssen die Gehörnerven sein, will einer aus dem Lärm einer Wagnerschen Oper heil hervorgehen.*"[2]

Nimmt man sein Opernglas zur Hand, lassen sich schöne Details erkennen. Die Zeltstangen schließen mit Akanthusblättern ab, andere zusätzlich mit Pinienzapfen, Querverstrebungen sind mit Rosenblüten akzentuiert. Das ist nicht nur dekorativ, sondern entspricht einem Forderungskatalog des im Historismus einflussreichen Bauakademielehrers Karl Bötticher, der verlangte, dass man antike Zitate nicht willkürlich einsetzte, sondern stets mit einer Funktion in Verbindung zu bringen habe. Akanthusblätter waren nur tragenden Elementen zuzuordnen, Pinienzapfen als Spitze von Zeltstangen und Rosetten lediglich als angeheftete Bindeelemente. Das in zarten Blau-, Braun- und Ockertönen sehr klassizistisch anmutende Velarium zeigt neben den Stangen und Seilen viel dekorative Malerei, die ebenfalls den alten Griechen abgeschaut ist: stilisierte Blüten (oft Lotusblumen) in arabeskem Dekor.

runs through the whole performance, soon transporting the listener – particularly the most attentive one – to a state resembling seasickness and producing an embarrassing tiredness and tormented weariness which Wagner's later works so often arouse." Another wrote as early as 1872: "*The auditory nerves have to be as thick as a ship's ropes if one wishes to emerge safely from the noise of a Wagnerian opera.*"

Beautiful details can be made out with a little help of an opera glass. The tent poles conclude with acanthus leaves, others with additional pine cones and transverse struts are accentuated by rose blossoms. This is not only decorative, it also corresponds to a catalog of requirements drawn up by Karl Bötticher, the influential lecturer at the building academy, who demanded that one should not simply employ ancient references arbitrarily, but should constantly connect them to a function. Acanthus leaves could only be attributed to load-bearing elements, pine cones as the tips of tent poles and rosettes solely as applied connecting elements. The velarium, which is very classicistic in its gentle blues, browns and ochre tones, shows a great deal of decorative painting apart from the poles and ropes, and that too has been copied from the ancient Greeks: stylized blossoms (often lotus flowers) in arabesque decoration.

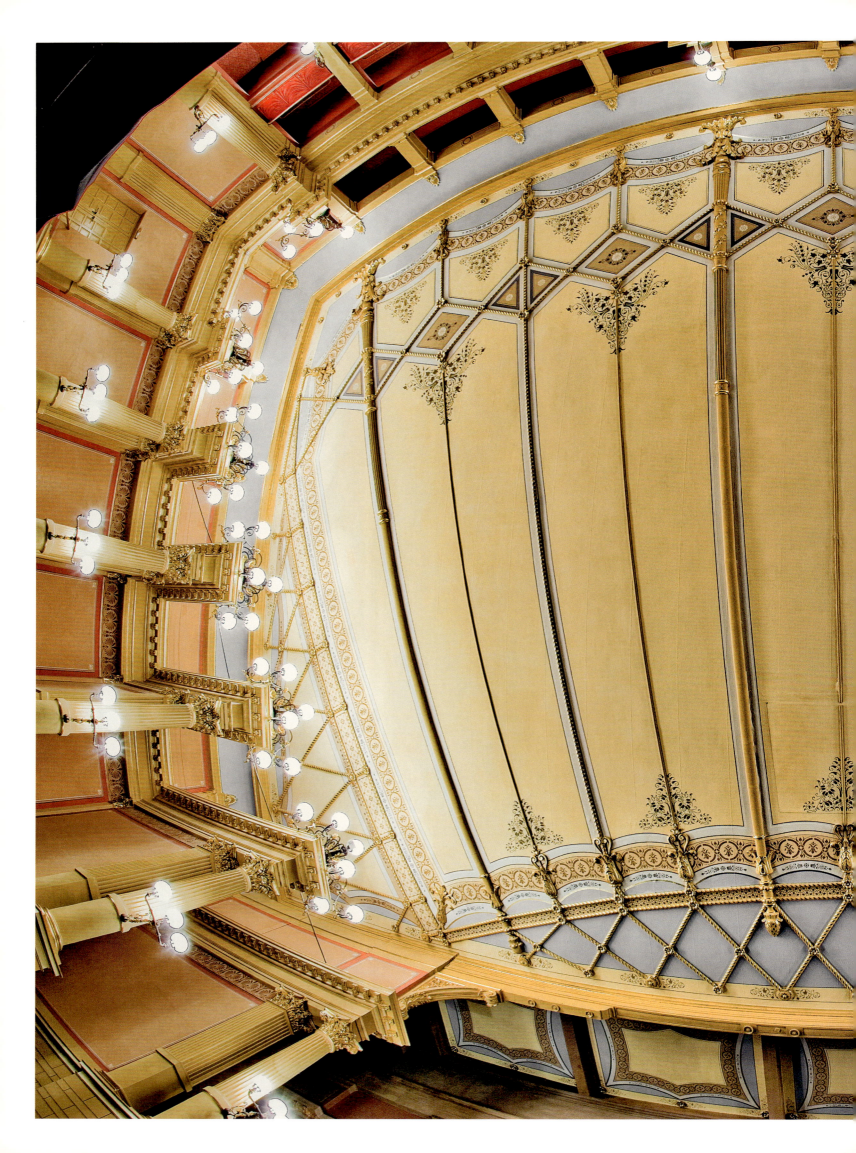

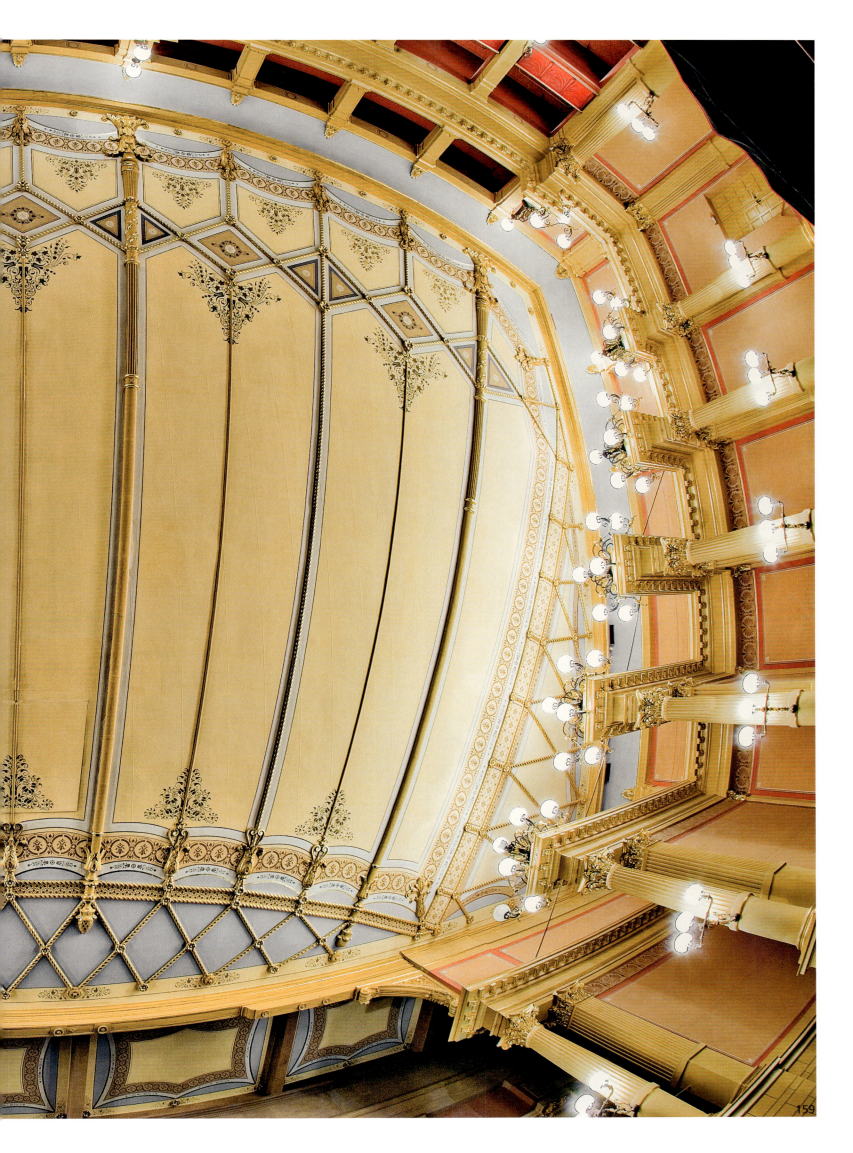

Vor der Bühne finden sich weitere kleinere Zeltdächer ohne Stützgerippe, die einfach wie Tücher aufgespannt scheinen. Auch hier leuchtet der blaue Himmel hindurch, als könnte die Sonne oder der Regen wirklich ins Festspielhaus dringen, wie es tatsächlich mehrfach geschah. Cosima notiert am 30. September 1875: „Besuch von Brandt und Brückners; ersterer sehr ungehalten über die Nachlässigkeit der Bauführung, es regnet herein"[1]; und sogar noch am 31. Mai 1876: „Abends im Theater, die meisten Musiker schon da, [...] Gewitter, es regnet herein durch das Pappdach!"[2] (die äußere Dachpappe). Das mag erklären, warum an dem Velarium immer schon viele Wasserflecken zu sehen waren und wie nötig die Restaurierungen in den 1990er Jahren waren. Das Pappmaché hatte erstaunlich gut gehalten. Es ist noch heute original, nur in neuer, nach historischen Befunden gestalteter Farbfassung.

In front of the stage there are other smaller awnings without supporting ribs, which simply seem to be spanned like fabric. Here, too, the blue sky shines through, as if the sun or the rain really could penetrate the Festspielhaus, as in fact did happen several times. Cosima notes on September 30, 1875: *"Visit from Brandt and the Brückners; the former very displeased about the negligence of the building supervisor, the rain is getting in"* and even on May 31, 1876: *"Evening in the theater, most of the musicians already here, [...] storm, the rain is getting in through the roof!"* (the outer roofing paper). That might explain why there were always so many watermarks on the velarium and how necessary it was to undertake the restoration work in the 1990s. The papier maché had held out astonishingly well. It is still original even today, only in a new color scheme, as dictated by historical findings.

„Die Decke sagt uns mit echt germanischer Treuherzigkeit, dass – wenn unser nordisches Klima uns schon das offene Amphitheater unter freiem Himmel verbietet – wir uns mit Bedauern in das Unvermeidliche eben fügen müssen."[3]

"The ceiling tells us with true Germanic innocence, that – if our Nordic climate denies us the open amphitheater under the sky – we unfortunately have to acquiesce to what is unavoidable."

Adolphe Appia (1902)

Abschattierte Farben ziehen den Blick in das Dunkel der Bühne Toned-down colors draw the eye toward the darkness of the stage

Beleuchtungsklappe vom Zuschauerraum und vom Dachstuhl aus gesehen, wohl Mitte der 1960er Jahre eingebaut, durchbricht sie die schöne Optik des Velariums
The lighting flap visible from the auditorium and the roof truss, likely built during the 1960s, interrupts the beautiful visual effect of the velarium

Nach der Modernisierung der Stromversorgung 1925 wurde 1926 auch die Beleuchtungsanlage erneuert, unter anderem durch eine neue Beleuchtungsloge in der Rückwand des Zuschauerraums. Auch in den Proszenien wurden Scheinwerfer angebracht. Damit manifestiert sich eine grundlegende Zäsur in der Geschichte der Bühnenästhetik der Festspiele, als der Sohn des Meisters den „mystischen Abgrund", der die Welt des Seins von der des Scheins trennte, übersprang, und das Bühnenlicht nicht mehr ausschließlich aus dem Bühnenraum kam. Siegfried Wagners Regiestil mit transparenten Schleiern erforderte diese Beleuchtungs- und Projektionstechnik.

In der Beleuchtungsklappe sitzt während den Vorstellungen meist ein Feuerwehrmann, allein mit den Fledermäusen, die hier leben sollen. Bisweilen gesellen sich Titurel oder das Waldvögelein zu ihm und singen, weil der Klang von hier oben im Zuschauerraum nicht lokalisierbar ist und ganz weltentrückt klingt.

After the modernization of the electricity supply in 1925, the lighting system was also renewed in 1926, including a new lighting box in the back wall of the auditorium. Spotlights were also set up in the proscenia. This represents a fundamental break in the history of the stage aesthetics of the festivals, as the maestro's son leaped over the *"mystical abyss"* dividing the world of being from that of appearance, no longer lighting the stage only from the stage area. Siegfried Wagner's style of directing with transparent veils demanded such lighting and projection technology.

In the lighting flap a fireman usually sits up here during the performances, along with the bats said to live here. Sometimes Titurel and the "Waldvogel" keep him company and sing, because the sound from up here cannot be localized in the auditorium and sounds otherworldly.

*Lustig im Leid
sing' ich von Liebe;
wonnig und weh'
web' ich mein Lied:
nur Sehnende kennen den Sinn!*

Der Waldvogel in SIEGFRIED, 2. Aufzug Act 2

Beleuchtungsklappe aus den 1960er Jahren vom Zuschauerraum und vom Dachstuhl aus gesehen
Lighting flap from the 1960s seen from the auditorium and the roof truss

Beleuchtungsloge in der Galerierückwand von 1926, darunter das Fenster der Rundfunkkabine
Lighting gallery in the rear loge from 1926, below that the window of the radio studio

Im Rahmen der Umbauten 1963 bis 1966 wurde weiterer Platz für die immer zahlreicher werdenden Beleuchtungskörper geschaffen. Da die Ansprüche des Publikums durch Fernsehen und Kino stetig wuchsen, musste auch die Beleuchtungsstärke in Bayreuth jedes Jahr um zehn Prozent wachsen, so Wolfgang Wagner. Offensichtlich fällt in die Zeit von Wolfgang Wagners erster RING-Inszenierung der Einbau der markanten Klappe im Velarium in der Zuschauerraummitte, was einen groben Eingriff in die filigrane Deckenarchitektur bedeutet und die illusionistische Wirkung des Zeltes – trotz tapetentürartiger Kaschierung – zerstört.

Fazit

Wagners Ankündigung in seiner Rede 1872, „*keine der überkommenen Ornamente zu verwenden*", wurde nicht eingelöst, vielleicht als eine Konzession an Brückwald, dem Wagner – wie zitiert – das (nachträgliche) Anbringen von „Zierrathen" erlaubt hatte. So wie man einem Koch das Würzen nicht verbieten kann, konnte man einem Architekten des 19. Jahrhunderts noch keine puristische Bauhaus-Gesinnung abverlangen. Für Maler-, Anstreicher- und Tüncherarbeiten wurden lediglich zehn Prozent der gesamten Baukosten verwendet, die Brückners erhielten für ihr Velarium lediglich 1440 Mark. Wer es Wagner Recht machen will, richte sein Opernglas ausschließlich auf die Bühne. Doch Brückwald und die Brückners handelten im Sinne Wagners, als sie seine Liebe zum alten Griechenland aufgriffen und den hellenistischen Charakter des Hauses mit korinthischen Säulen, Anthemien und Velarien, mit Lotosblüten und pompejanischer Scheinmalerei und Ornamentik unterstützten.

As part of the conversion work undertaken between 1963 and 1966, additional space was created for the ever increasing number of lighting elements. According to Wolfgang Wagner, since audience expectations were constantly growing due to television and cinema, the lighting power in Bayreuth also had to grow each year by ten per cent. It was evidently at the time of Wolfgang Wagner's first RING production that the distinctive flap was inserted into the velarium in the middle of the auditorium, which signified a brutal intervention in the filigree ceiling architecture, and destroyed the illusionistic effect of the tent – despite the wallpaper-like glue work.

Summary

Wagner's announcement in his speech of 1872 that he would "*not use any of the traditional forms of decoration,*" was not adhered to, perhaps as a concession to Brückwald, whom Wagner – as quoted – had given permission to add "adornments" afterward. Just as one cannot forbid a cook to use seasoning, so one could not yet demand a purist Bauhaus view from an architect in the 19th century. Only ten per cent of the whole building costs was spent on painting and whitewashing and the Brückners received only 1,440 marks for their velarium. Those who want to do Wagner justice should focus their opera glasses exclusively on the stage. Yet Brückwald and the Brückners were acting according to Wagner's wishes when they took up his love of ancient Greece and supported the Hellenistic character of the building with Corinthian pillars, anthemions and velaria, with lotus blossoms and Pompeian illusionistic painting and ornamentation.

Anordnung des antiken Amphitheaters

Eine der wichtigsten Anforderungen Wagners an ein ideales Theater war von Anfang an die „*Anordnung eines antiken Amphitheaters*" im Zuschauerhaus. Das Theater in Riga hatte er in diesem Sinne bewusst wahrgenommen, aber auch das Theater in Königsberg, das als ältestes Theaterhalbrund in Deutschland gilt (allerdings noch mit den von Wagner gehassten Logen). Wagner wusste um die Tradition der echten römischen Amphitheater, im Unterschied zu den griechischen (Semi-)Theatern, die den „*Göttern und Helden des Mythos*", „*den freien Tänzern und Sängern des heiligen Chores*" geweiht und gewidmet waren. In Rom dagegen mussten sich „*wilde Bestien, Löwen, Panther und Elefanten (...) im Amphitheater zerfleischen, um dem römischen Auge zu schmeicheln, Gladiatoren, zur Kraft und Geschicklichkeit erzogene Sklaven, mussten mit ihrem Todesröcheln das römische Ohr vergnügen.*"[1]

Stattdessen beschwor Wagner mit seinem Bayreuther (Amphi-) Theater die Tradition eines demokratischen Theaters, das vom 1848er Revolutionär Wagner noch als Symbol einer „*vorgeschichtlichen Urgemeinschaft*" verehrt wurde. „*In den weiten Räumen des griechischen Amphitheaters wohnte das ganze Volk den Vorstellungen bei; in unseren vornehmen Theatern faulenzt nur der vermögende Teil desselben.*"[2]

Diese politische Motivation des Amphitheaters als demokratisches Theater wurde immer wieder hervorgehoben. In diesem Sinne hätte Wagner freilich die Einrichtung einer „Fürstenloge" und den Bau des Königsbaus draußen unterlassen müssen. Die Architektur des Bayreuther Zuschauerhauses ist keine konsequent demokratische, allenfalls eine republikanische, die einen repräsentativen König und seine Fürsten hinter den eigentlichen Machthaber stellt: das Volk im Parkett.

Von diesen politischen und ideologischen Motivationen ist in der Rede Wagners zur Grundsteinlegung jedoch nichts mehr zu finden. Die Revolution war 1872 schon fast ein Vierteljahrhundert verraucht, und Wagner war nur noch an seiner Kunst interessiert. Sein Amphitheater hatte keine politischen, sondern primär funktionale Gründe, und zwar optische. So beschreibt Wagner in seiner Rede, dass der „*sogar überschrittene Halbkreise*" des griechischen Theaters um eine zentrale „*Orchestra*" angeordnet war. Letztere sei aber zugunsten einer „*in ihrer vollen Tiefe benutzten Szene* [Bühne]" gewichen, sodass die Zuschauer am Rande des Halbkreises keine gute Sicht mehr gehabt hätten. „*Demnach waren wir gänzlich den Gesetzen der Perspektive unterworfen, welchen gemäß die Reihen der Sitze sich mit dem Aufsteigen erweitern konnten, stets aber die gerade Richtung nach der Szene gewähren mussten.*"[3] In diesem Sinne ist der Bayreuther Zuschauerraum ein Hybride aus griechischem Halbrundtheater und neuzeitlichem Guckkastentheater.

Arrangement of an ancient amphitheater

Right from the beginning, one of Wagner's most important demands for his ideal theater was the *"design of an ancient amphitheater"* in the auditorium. This was how he had consciously perceived the theater in Riga, but also the theater in Königsberg, which was regarded as being the oldest semicircular theater in Germany (although still with the loges which Wagner so hated). Wagner was aware of the tradition of the true Roman amphitheater, as distinct from the Greek (semi-) theaters, which were devoted and dedicated to the *"Gods and heroes of myth," "the free dancers and singers of the sacred chorus."* In Rome, on the other hand, *"wild beasts, lions, panthers and elephants [...] had to tear each other to pieces in the amphitheater in order to flatter the Roman eye, while gladiators and slaves brought up for their strength and skill, had to please the Roman ear with their death rattle."*

Instead, Wagner's Bayreuth (amphi-)theater summoned up the tradition of a democratic theater, which Wagner, the revolutionary of 1848, still valued as a symbol of a *"prehistoric primordial society." "The whole population gathered for performances in the expansive space of the Greek amphitheater. Today, only the well-off portion of the population lazes around in our highbrow theaters."*

This political motivation of the amphitheater as a democratic theater was emphasized time and again. In this sense, Wagner would of course have had to desist from setting up a Prince's Gallery or adding on the Königsbau. The architecture of the Bayreuth auditorium is not consistently democratic, it is at most republican, placing a purely representative king and his princes behind the actual power possessors: the people in the parquet.

However, there is nothing about this political and ideological motivation to be found in Wagner's speech at the cornerstone laying ceremony. By 1872, the revolution had already cooled down after a quarter of a century and all Wagner was still interested was in his art. He chose the amphitheater not for political, but primarily for functional reasons, namely optical ones. Thus Wagner says in his speech that *"even the transcended semicircle"* of the Greek theater was arranged around a central *"orchestra."* Yet the latter had given way to a *"scene utilized to its full depth* [the stage]*,"* so that the spectator at the edge of the semicircle would no longer have a very good view. *"Accordingly, we were totally subject to the laws of perspective, which, depending on the seating row, could be extended by grade but we had to constantly maintain a direction facing towards the scene."* In this sense the Bayreuth auditorium is a hybrid of the Greek semicircular theater and the modern picture-frame theater.

Nor are the rising rows of seats a reference to the ancient Greeks, but rather solely born of the wish to create optimal viewing conditions. In this lies the reason for doing without the side loges, which had been typical of almost every theater up until then: *"The whole system of our tiers of loges was therefore excluded because its elevation, which begins*

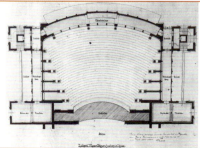

Der 1873 von Wagner edierte Holzschnitt Brückwalds zeigt den Zuschauersaal noch ohne Bestuhlung, Brüstungen und Deckengemälde, mit anderen Beleuchtungskörpern
Brückwald's 1873 woodcut edited by Wagner, shows the auditorium still without seating, balustrade and ceiling frescoes and with other lighting fixtures

Von Carl Runckwitz für Ludwig II. gezeichneter Grundriss (1876)
Ground plan drawn for Ludwig II by Carl Runckwitz (1876)

Auch die aufsteigenden Sitzreihen sind keine Reverenz an die alten Griechen, sondern allein aus dem Wunsch geboren, optimale Sichtverhältnisse zu schaffen. Hierin liegt der Grund für den Verzicht auf die seitlichen Logen, die bis dahin fast jedes Theater prägten: *„Das ganze System unserer Logenränge war daher ausgeschlossen, weil von ihr, sogleich an den Seitenwänden beginnenden, Erhöhung aus der Einblick in das Orchester nicht zu versperren gewesen wäre."*[1] Brückwald formuliert es noch deutlicher, *„dass die stets sich aufdrängende Sichtbarkeit der im Orchester ausübenden und sich abmühenden Musiker auf den Zuschauer störend und ablenkend wirkt, zumal wenn es sich bei einer dramatischen Aufführung gerade darum handelt, das Auge zur genauen Wahrnehmung der szenischen Darstellung zu fesseln"*[2].

Darüber hinaus wollte Wagner, wie er in seiner Schrift „Über Sänger und Schauspieler" schreibt, unbedingt die *„zu Logenreihen eingerichteten Stockwerke des Colisseums"* vermeiden, und verhindern, dass sein Theater *„zu dem glänzenden Versammlungssaale der unterhaltungslustigen reicheren Gesellschaft der Städte"* werde, *„in welchem das Publikum vor allem sich selbst zur Augenweide wird, und wo ‚die Damen, sich selbst und ihren Putz zum Besten gebend, ohne Gage mitspielen'"*[3].

Die gleichen Gedanken gelten für die hintere Logenwand. Hatte Wagner im „Kunstwerk der Zukunft" noch *„die Übereinanderschichtung der Stände"* kritisiert, spielt dieses politische Moment in Bayreuth kaum noch einer Rolle. Allerdings begrüßt er, dass sein (relativ niedriges) Zuschauerhaus den *„ärmeren Klassen der Bevölkerung"* keine *„Gepäcknetzplätze"*[4] anbiete. Am wichtigsten aber ist ihm, dass von keinem Platz, auch von der „Fürstenloge" nicht, in sein Orchester geschaut werden konnte. Nur den Freunden auf der Künstlergalerie darüber gestattete er solche Einblicke.

right at the side walls, would preclude closing off the view into the orchestra pit." Brückwald formulated it even more clearly, *"... that the constantly imposed visibility of the musicians working in the orchestra pit has a disturbing and distracting effect on the spectators, especially when, as in the case of a dramatic performance, it is precisely a matter of catching the eye so that it can exactly perceive the scenic presentation."*

Furthermore, as he writes in his essay "On singers and actors," Wagner definitely wanted to avoid the *"stories of the Coliseum organized into tiers of balcony loges"* and to prevent his theater from becoming a *"gleaming meeting hall for the wealthier class of society of the city in search of entertainment"* … *"in which the audience becomes a fest primarily for its own eyes,"* and where *"the ladies entertain and display themselves, joining in with the acting even without being paid for it."*

The same idea applies to the rear loges. Whereas Wagner still criticizes *"the overlayering of the classes"* in his essay "Artwork of the future," this political moment in Bayreuth hardly plays any role at all. Nevertheless, he applauds the fact that his (relatively low) auditorium does not offer the *"poorer classes of the population (…) luggage net seats."* His greatest concern is that none of the seats, not even those in the Prince's Gallery, allow a view into the orchestra pit. He only allows his friends in the artists' gallery such a view.

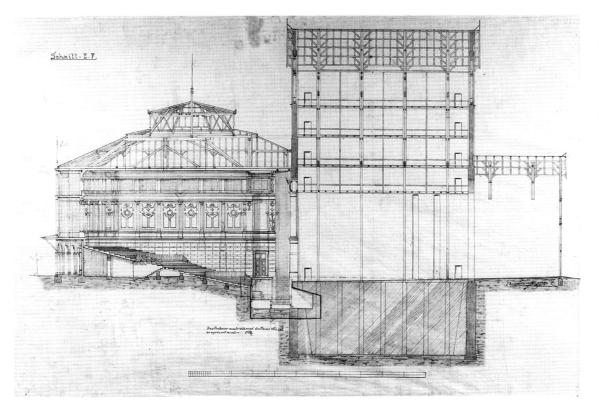

Der Längsschnitt von Otto Brückwald durch das Festspielhaus (1872): Das ansteigende Amphitheater ist nicht unterkellert und zeigt noch die ursprünglich vorgesehenen Treppen zwischen den Sitzreihen. Über dem Orchestergraben ist der freie Zugang zum offenen Dachstuhl und zur Lüftungslaterne erkennbar. An der Wand des Zuschauersaals ist noch die von Brückwald ursprünglich vorgesehene Dekoration der Interkolumnien mit Girlanden zu sehen.
Otto Brückwald's longitudinal cross-section of the Festspielhaus (1872): The graded amphitheater does not have a basement and still shows the originally planned steps between the seating rows. The clear access above the orchestra pit to the open roof truss and to the ventilation lantern is recognizable. The intercolumniation decorated with garlands Brückwald had originally planned is still visible on the wall of the auditorium.

Die Bestuhlung

Der demokratische beziehungsweise republikanische Geist des Bayreuther Theaters offenbart sich sehr anschaulich in der Bestuhlung des Zuschauerhauses, die für viele zu den bleibendsten Eindrücken der ganzen Festspiele gehört. Ursprünglich waren es 1345 hölzerne Klappstühle mit einem Strohgeflecht, die breiter waren als die 1943 Sitze heute: In Generalproben konnten – so Wolfgang Wagner – sogar drei Personen auf zwei Plätzen sitzen. Leider stiegen viele Besucher mit ihren Schuhen darauf, was das Geflecht zerstörte, weshalb viele Jahre lang schwarze Schonbezüge über die Sitze gestülpt wurden. 1968 wurde für kurze Zeit ein noch spartanischeres, noch schmaleres Gestühl aus Draht eingebaut, um noch mehr (zahlende) Gäste unterzubringen, ehe Ende der 1970er Jahre das heutige Holzgestühl mit schlichter Stoffbespannung eingesetzt wurde. Vom vergleichsweise komfortablen Originalstuhl finden sich heute noch an den Außenwänden ein, zwei Sitze für die blauen Mädchen sowie einige einsam und verlassen auf Dachstühlen und vergessenen Gängen der Nutzbauten.

Diese asketische Bestuhlung galt für alle Menschen gleich, zumindest im Parkett: ein demokratischer, fast kommunistischer Gedanke. Vielleicht kam Wagner die Idee dazu auf seiner Reise nach Wien in dem Jahre, als er sein revolutionäres „Kunstwerk der Zukunft" visionierte, *„... nachdem er in der österreichischen Eisenbahn die Höllenmarter der dritten Klasse überstanden hatte."*[1] Das sogenannte Wiener Geflecht der Urbestuhlung, ein Achteckgeflecht, war freilich eine Erfindung der Gebrüder Thonet aus Boppard, die damit zunächst Kaffeehausstühle bespannten.

Wagner zwang sein Publikum also in eine enge, harte Bestuhlung, er selbst dagegen *„konnte keine schwach gepolsterten Stühle lang vertragen"*[2]. Wagner litt an einem von ihm oft beklagten Unterleibsleiden, sodass er häufig über zu langes Sitzen schimpfte und das Problem sogar zu einem philosophischen erhob: *„Was könnten wir genießen, wenn wir nicht immer dem verfl. Sitzorgane uns zum Opfer brächten. Ach! Dieses Sitzwerkzeug ist der eigentliche wahre Gesetzgeber des ganzen zivilisierten Menschengeschlechtes."*[3]

Die heutigen Stühle in Bayreuth sind da nicht bequemer und die Stücke Wagners nicht kürzer geworden. Eine sehr neuzeitliche Kritik, die immer wieder das Büro der Festspiele schriftlich erreicht, zielt auf die zu niedrige Höhe der Rückenlehne, die die Damen exakt an einem gewissen Verschluss drücke. Eine Lösung des Problems ist in absehbarer Zweit nicht zu erwarten. Nach neuester Versammlungsstättenverordnung müssten neue Stühle wesentlich breiter ausfallen und jedem Gast Armlehnen gewähren, was wiederum weniger Plätze bedeuten würde und die begehrten Karten noch begehrter machte.

The seating

The democratic or republican spirit of Bayreuth Theater is revealed very clearly in the seating of the auditorium, which for many people is one of the most lasting impressions of the whole festival. There were originally 1,345 folding wooden chairs with a wickerwork straw seat, which were broader than the 1,943 seats that exist today. According to Wolfgang Wagner, as many as three people could sit on two seats at dress rehearsals. Unfortunately, many visitors stood on them with their shoes on, which destroyed the wickerwork, so that for many years black protective coverings were put over the seats. In 1968 even more Spartan and still narrower seats made of wire were installed for a short time, in order to accommodate still more (paying) guests. Toward the end of the 1970s today's wooden seats with a plain fabric covering were put in. One or two of the comparatively comfortable seats still exist today along the outside walls for the usherettes in blue, the so-called blue girls, as well as some solitary and neglected examples in the attics and forgotten corridors of the utility buildings.

This ascetic seating is the same for all people, a democratic, almost communist idea. Perhaps Wagner hit upon the idea during his journey to Vienna in the year in which he envisioned his revolutionary "Artwork of the Future" *"... after having survived the hellish torture of traveling third class in an Austrian train."* The so-called Viennese, octagonal, wickerwork of the original seats was of course an invention of the Thonet brothers from Boppard, who at first used it to cover coffeehouse seats.

Wagner therefore made his audience sit in narrow, hard chairs, although he himself was *"unable to bear any poorly cushioned chairs for long."* Wagner suffered from a complaint of the lower abdomen, about which he often complained, so that he frequently grumbled about having to remain seated for too long and even elevated the problem to one of philosophical status: *"How we could enjoy things if our damned buttocks didn't always demand a sacrifice of us. Oh! this seating instrument is the true lawmaker of the whole of civilized humankind."*

The seating used today in Bayreuth has not become more comfortable and Wagner's works have not become any shorter. A very modern criticism, which repeatedly reaches the office of the festivals in writing, aims at the low height of the back of the chair, which presses the ladies exactly at a certain fastener. A solution to the problem cannot be expected in the foreseeable future. In accordance with the latest regulations concerning public gathering places, new seats would have to be considerably broader and guarantee every guest arm rests, which on the other hand would mean fewer seats and would make the already highly sought after tickets even more sought after.

*„So sitzt er, sagt kein Wort,
auf hehrem Sitze, stumm und ernst ..."*

Waltraute in GÖTTERDÄMMERUNG

Einer der letzten erhaltenen, heiligen Originalsitze von 1876
One of the last surviving, holy original seats dating from 1876

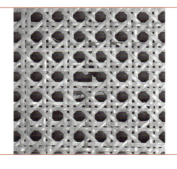

Wiener Geflecht der Originalbestuhlung
Vienna wickerwork of the original seats

Neue Bestuhlung 1968
New seating from 1968

Langes Sitzen war Wagner also suspekt und die physische Realität der Stühle eher ein Vehikel der Fantasie, wie eine Kindheitsanekdote berichtet: „R. erzählt mir, dass, wie er Kind war, er sich Pappenwolken machte und sie an Stühlen fest machte, Versuche anstellte darauf zu schweben und sich schändlich ärgerte, wenn es nicht ging."[1]

Vielen Menschen mag dieses Schweben in Bayreuth nicht gelingen. Viele leiden auch an der Tatsache, dass Brückwald seine ursprünglich geplanten Treppen in der Mitte nicht baute und jede Sitzreihe bei empfindlichen Menschenkindern Klaustrophobie und Korridoreffekte verursachen kann. Ein besonders prominenter Märtyrer war zum Beispiel Theodor Fontane bei einer Aufführung im Jahre 1889. In einem Brief schildert er, wie er vor der Vorstellung in einen Wolkenbruch geriet und mit hochgekrempelten Hosen hinein musste: „Fünfzehnhundert Menschen drin, jeder Platz besetzt. Mir wird so sonderbar. Alle Türen geschlossen. In diesem Augenblicke wird es stockduster. [...] Und nun geht ein Tubablasen los, als wären es die Posaunen des Letzten Gerichts. Mir wird immer sonderbarer, und als die Ouvertüre zu Ende geht, fühle ich deutlich: ‚Noch drei Minuten, und du fällst ohnmächtig oder tot vom Sitz.' Also wieder raus. Ich war der letzte gewesen, der sich an vierzig Personen vorbei bis auf seinen Platz, [...] durchgedrängt hatte [...] Und nun wieder ebenso zurück. Ich war halb ohnmächtig; [...] die Sache genierte mich aufs äußerste." Fontane wird entlassen, der Türhüter bekommt das Billett (zum Weiterverkauf) geschenkt und Fontane stiftet sein TRISTAN-Billett für den nächsten Tag einer „frommen Stiftung"[2].

Igor Strawinsky erlitt 1912 den PARSIFAL und berichtet: „Ich kroch ganz zusammen und rührte mich nicht. Nach einer Viertelstunde hielt ich es nicht mehr aus; meine Gliedmaßen waren mir eingeschlafen, ich musste eine andere Stellung einnehmen. Krach – schon geht's los! Mein Stuhl macht ein Geräusch, das mir hundert wütende Blicke einbringt. Ich krieche noch einmal ganz in mich zusammen, denke aber dabei nur noch an eines, nämlich an das Ende des Aktes, das meinen Qualen Einhalt gebieten wird. Schließlich kommt die Pause, und ich werde durch ein paar Würstchen und ein Bier belohnt. Kaum habe ich mir eine Zigarette angezündet, da ruft mich die Fanfare schon wieder zur Andacht auf. Noch ein Akt, den man über sich ergehen lassen muss! Und ich denke beharrlich an meine Zigarette, von der ich einen einzigen Zug zu rauchen vermochte! Auch diesen Akt erdulde ich. Dann sind wieder die Würstchen an der Reihe, wieder ein Bier, wieder die Fanfare, wieder die Andacht, wieder ein Akt – der letzte. Fertig!"[3]

Long periods of sitting was something Wagner himself distrusted and the physical reality of chairs tends to be a vehicle of fantasy, as a childhood anecdote records: "R. told me that when he was a child he made cardboard clouds and attached them to chairs, made attempts to float on them and became shamefully annoyed when he could not succeed in this."

Many people may not be able to attain this hovering in Bayreuth. Many also suffer from the fact that Brückwald did not build the staircase in the middle as he had originally planned and every row of seats can cause claustrophobia and corridor effects among more sensitive people. A particularly prominent martyr was, for example, Theodor Fontane, at a performance in 1889. In a letter he describes how he got caught in a cloudburst before the performance and had to go in with his trousers rolled up: "Fifteen hundred people inside and every seat taken. I felt so strange. All the doors closed. At that very moment it went completely dark. [...] And then the tubas started playing, as if they were the trumpets of the Last Judgment. I felt stranger and stranger, and when the overture came to an end, I distinctly felt: 'Another three minutes and you will faint or fall down dead from your seat.' So I went outside again. I had been the last one and had pushed my way past forty people to get to my seat, [...] I had to back the same way. I was half unconscious; [...] the situation embarrassed me in the extreme." Fontane was let out, the doorman was given the ticket (to sell it on to someone else) and Fontane donated his ticket for TRISTAN UND ISOLDE for the next day to a "pious foundation."

Igor Stravinsky suffered PARSIFAL in 1912 and reports: "I curled up inside myself and did not stir. After a quarter of an hour I couldn't stand it any longer; my limbs had gone to sleep, I had to take up another posture. Creak – it's starting already! My seat made a noise that brought me a hundred angry glances. I curl up inside myself once again, yet I am only thinking of one thing, namely of the end of the act, which will signify an end to my torment. Finally the intermission arrives and I am rewarded with a couple of sausages and a beer. No sooner do I light a cigarette when the fanfare summons me back to worship once more. Another act to which one has to submit! I think persistently about my cigarette, which I was only able to take one puff of! This act too I suffer through. Then once again it's time for sausages, time for beer, once again the fanfare, again the worship, another act – the last one. Finished!"

Einziger offizieller Rauchertreff
The only official meeting point for smokers

*„Ein sehr heitrer Augenblick ergibt sich daraus,
dass ich R. sage,
wenn er wohl eine Zigarette würde rauchen können;
in demselben Augenblick hatte er daran gedacht,
und ich kann ihm gleich eine reichen,
die er sehr heiter raucht."[4]*

*"A very funny moment arises
when I tell R.
if he were able to smoke a cigarette;
in the same moment he thinks
the same thing and asked me to for one,
which he very cheerfully smokes."*

Cosima Wagner, 9. Dezember 1879

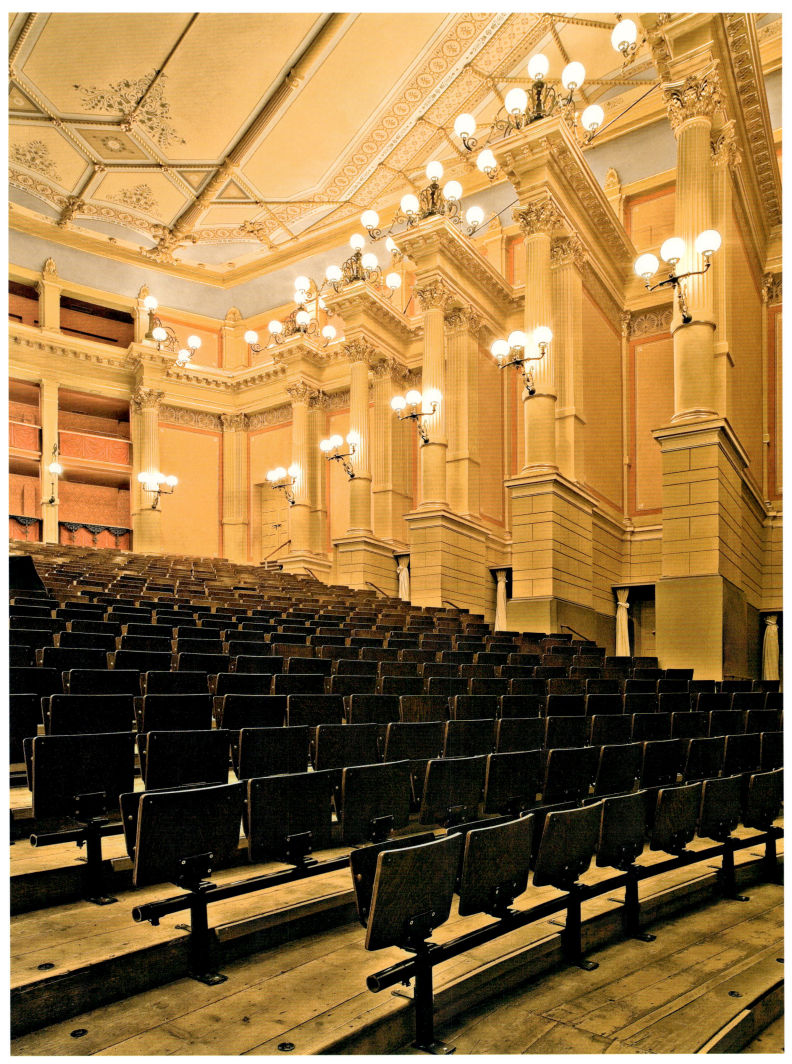
Die sogenannten Illusionswände mit optischer wie akustischer Funktion The so-called walls of illusion, which have an optical and an acoustic function

Die Illusionswände

"Wie Sphinxe reihen sich unten die Pfeiler aneinander, wie geheimnisvolle Gänge breiten sich die Seitenflügel aus."[1] So beschreibt Cosima die Scherwände, die den Zuschauerraum kulissenartig staffeln. Solche Wände finden sich in keinem anderen Theater und sind in der Tat geheimnisvoll. Sie sind aus Holz und Gips, original erhalten, und suggerieren in ihrem hohen Postament echtes Mauerwerk. Aufgesetzte Holzplatten erscheinen wie massive (teure) Steinquader mit tiefen Fugen. Es handelt sich – wie schon im Königsbau – um ein echtes Scheinmauerwerk, das der Kunstgeschichte als pompejanische „Inkrustation" bekannt ist, weil schon die Römer und Griechen vor knapp zweitausend Jahren den Maurer zu sparen und aus der Not eine ästhetische Tugend zu machen wussten. Dieses Detail unterstreicht den hellenistischen Charakter des Zuschauerraums und nicht nur die Sparsamkeit Wagners.

Der Wiener Architekt Camillo Sitte fertigte bereits 1873, nachdem er die Pläne des Festspielhauses gesehen hatte, unaufgefordert ein Gutachten an, in dem er große Bedenken formulierte und die Scherwände als *„Schallverzerrungsapparat"*[2] bezeichnete. Sitte hatte jedoch Unrecht. Man kann sich in Bayreuth über harte Stühle oder zu teure Bratwürste beschweren, doch über den Klang hat sich noch niemand mokiert, im Gegenteil, das Bayreuther Festspielhaus gilt als eines der akustisch besten Theater der Welt, nicht nur wegen der durch das versenkte Orchester subtil veredelten Klänge.

Das ganze Zuschauerhaus ist ein Resonanzkörper, aufgrund seiner konsequent aus Holz ausgeführten Architektur. Es war die aus Sparsamkeit und Geldnot gewählte Holzarchitektur, die letztlich die gute Akustik bewirkt. Das Parkett ist heute noch in seinen Originalplanken erhalten. Es ruht auf einem akustisch wirksamen Luftraum, wie der Längsschnitt von Brückwald zeigt. Darüber schwingen die dünne Holzdecke und der Luftraum des hölzernen Dachstuhls. Wolfgang Wagner erklärt die gute Akustik vor allem durch das gleiche Luftraumvolumen von Bühne und Zuschauersaal. Auch die Scherwände schwingen mit, wie die schlechtere Akustik im Münchner Prinzregententheater beweist, ein Nachbau des Bayreuther Festspielhauses, doch ohne dessen Scherwände.

Wagner hat schon vor dem Bau seines Theaters immer wieder von indirekten Klangerlebnissen geschwärmt, die der Musik ein besonderes Geheimnis verliehen. Sein Biograf Gregor-Dellin berichtet von seiner Zeit in der Ostra-Allee in Dresden, wo Wagner in den 1840er Jahren in der Nr. 6 wohnte: *„Nichts ließ sein Herz schneller schlagen als die geisterhaften Quintenklänge jenes Geigers, der hinter den Mauern eines Palais an der Dresdner Ostra-Allee sein Instrument stimmte. Das Grabesgähnen dieser leeren Klänge entzündete seine Phantasie."*[3] 1859 erzählte Wagner dem Musiker Felix Draeseke von seiner Zeit in Paris und den Konzerten im Conservatoire. Einmal sei er *„zu spät gekommen und habe in einem Raum warten müssen, der durch eine ziemlich hohe, aber nicht die Decke des Saales erreichende Schallwand vom Orchester getrennt gewesen sei. Die Wirkung des über diese Schallwand*

Walls of illusion

"The pillars stand next to each other in rows below like sphinxes, like mysterious corridors they open out their side wings." That is how Cosima describes the shear walls, which line the auditorium like a stage backdrop. Such walls are not found in any other theater and in fact really are mysterious. They are made of wood and plaster, are surviving originals and in their high plinth suggest real walls. Applied wooden panels appear like massive (and expensive) stone ashlars with deep joints. As was also the case with the Königsbau, it is a matter of genuine mock walls, a technique which is known in art history as Pompeian incrustation, because both the Romans and the Greeks had begun to save on the bricklayers some two thousand years ago and knew how to make an aesthetic virtue of a necessity. This detail underlines the Hellenistic character of the auditorium and not only Wagner's economy.

The Viennese architect Camillo Sitte produced an unrequested expert's opinion as early as 1873, after he had seen the plans for the Festspielhaus, about which he expressed great misgivings, describing the shear walls as *"sound distortion equipment."* However, Sitte was wrong. One may complain about the hard chairs in Bayreuth or about over-priced bratwurst, but no one has ever complained about the sound. On the contrary, the Bayreuth Festspielhaus is regarded as one of the best theaters in the world for its acoustics, not least on account of the sounds that are subtly refined by the sunken orchestra pit.

The consistently wooden finish of the architecture makes the whole auditorium a resonance box. The wooden architecture chosen for reasons of economy and lack of funds ended up producing the good acoustics. The original planks of the parquet survive to this day. It rests on an acoustically effective air space, as Brückwald's longitudinal cross-section shows. The thin wooden ceiling and the air space of the wooden roof structure vibrate as well. Wolfgang Wagner attributes the good acoustics primarily to the fact that the stage and the auditorium have the same volume of air space. The shear walls vibrate as well, as the poorer acoustics at the Munich Prinzregententheater show, having been constructed on the model of the Bayreuth Festspielhaus, yet without its shear walls.

Even before his theater was built, Wagner had repeatedly enthused about indirect sound experiences, which endow the music with a special secrecy. His biographer Gregor-Dellin reports from his time in Ostra-Allee in Dresden, where in the 1840s Wagner lived at no. 6: *"Nothing made his heart beat faster than the ghostly fifths of the violinist tuning his instrument behind the walls of a palace on Dresden's Ostra-Allee. The funerary yawns of these empty sounds enflamed his imagination."* In 1859 Wagner told the musician Felix Draeseke about his time in Paris and the concerts at the Conservatoire. Once he had *„arrived too late and had to wait in a room which was separated from the orchestra by a sound wall that was rather high but did not reach to the ceiling of the room. The effect of the sounds of the orchestra that came over this sound wall surprised him greatly and made him think of producing a similar effect in a theater that he himself might build."*

*„Das Prachtgemäuer prüfte ich selbst;
ob alles fest, forscht' ich genau ..."*

Loge in DAS RHEINGOLD

hinaufgeleiteten Orchesterklangs habe ihn im höchsten Maße überrascht, und das habe ihn auf den Gedanken gebracht, in einem dereinst zu bauenden Theater dem Orchester eine ähnliche Wirkung zu sichern."[1]

Diese Effekte werden vor allem durch das versenkte Orchester bewirkt, doch mögen die Scherwände in Bayreuth wie jene nicht an die Decke stoßenden Schallwände in Paris funktionieren. Doch aus diesen Gründen sind sie nicht errichtet worden. Der gute akustische Effekt war ein glücklicher Zufall. Sitte hätte auch Recht behalten können. Wagner erklärt in seiner Rede 1872 den wahren Grund für die Scherwände, der zunächst ein architektonisches Problem war. Durch den Grundriss des (Amphi-)Theaters war ein *„der Bühne zu sich verengendes Oblong"* entstanden, sodass *„sich uns überhaupt die Frage, was mit diesen [...] Seitenwänden anzufangen sei"* aufdrang, da die Außenwände rechtwinklig zum Bühnenhaus zulaufen, was Wagner als *„unerlässlich"* bezeichnet. So war auf beiden Seiten eine *„unschöne Winkelecke"*[2] entstanden, ein Dreieck im Grundriss.

Natürlich hätte man dem von Wagner formulierten Funktionalismus folgen können und auch die Außenwände schräg auf das Bühnenhaus zulaufen lassen – so wie die Südfassade den halbrunden Grundriss des (Amphi-)Theaters zeichnet. Doch das wollte man nicht, obwohl es eigentlich eine Kaschierung bedeutete, die Wagner an anderen Theatern an anderer Stelle seiner Rede kritisiert hatte. Vielleicht wäre der Dachstuhl auf einem konisch zulaufenden Gebäude zu teuer geworden, aber eigentlich ergibt das keine zwingende Begründung.

Der wahre Grund, diese Scherwände zu bauen und das Zuschauerhaus nach außen rechtwinklig abzuschließen, liegt woanders: nicht im Akustischen oder Architektonischen, sondern im Visuellen. Hierzu möge das Auge des Betrachters auf die vorderen Scherwände vorrücken, auf das sogenannte Proszenium. Dieser Bereich flankiert den unbestuhlten Raum zwischen Zuschauern und der eigentlichen Bühne.

These effects are created mainly by the sunken orchestra pit, yet the shear walls in Bayreuth may function in the same way as the sound wall that did not quite reach to the ceiling in Paris. Yet they were not constructed for these reasons. The good acoustical effect was a lucky coincidence. Sitte could have ended up being right. In his speech of 1872, Wagner explains the real reason for the shear walls, which initially presented an architectural problem. Through the ground plan of the (amphi-)theater an *"oblong narrowing towards the stage"* was created, so that we were faced with *"the question of what to do with these [...] lateral walls,"* since the outer walls ran at right angles to the stage house, which Wagner describes as *"indispensable."* This caused an *"unattractive angular corner"* seen as a triangle on the ground plan.

Naturally one could have followed the functionalism formulated by Wagner and also let the external walls run at an oblique angle to the stage house – just as the south facade describes the semicircular ground plan of the (amphi-)theater. Yet that was not what was wanted, although it actually amounts to a cover-up, which Wagner had criticized about other theaters in other places in his speech. Perhaps the roof structure on a conically shaped building would have become too expensive, at any rate there is no compelling reason.

The real reason for building these shear walls and to square off the auditorium to the outside lies elsewhere: Not in the acoustic or architectural realm, but in the visual realm. For this purpose, the eye of the beholder should look forward toward the front shear wall, toward the so-called proscenium. This area flanks the unseated space between spectators and the actual stage.

Grundriss von Brückwald 1872 mit den *„unschönen Winkelecken"*
Brückwald's 1872 ground plan with the "unseemly angular corners"

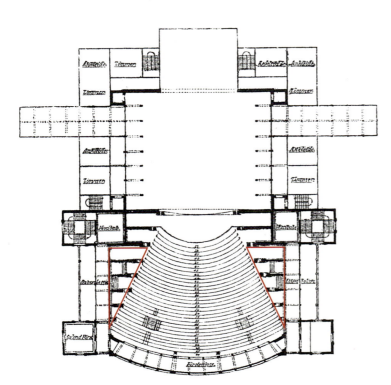

Brückwalds Holzschnitte (1873) mit Quer- und Längsschnitt durch den Zuschauerraum
Longitudinal cross-section by Otto Brückwald 1873

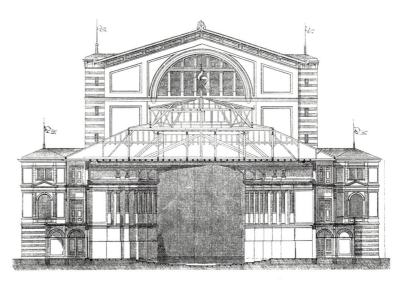

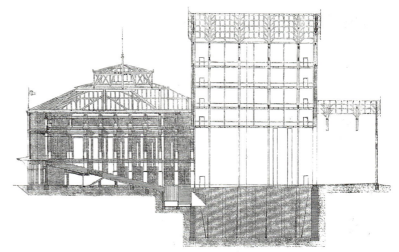

Die Scherwände setzen das Proszenium in den Zuschauerraum fort und erzeugen so eine perspektivische Sogwirkung
Aufnahme während der Probephase mit Regiepult und temporärer Gasse

The shear walls are a continuation of the proscenium into the auditorium and draw the audience in
Photograph during rehearsal phase with music stand for conductor and temporary aisle

Karlheinz Müller
Die Demokratisierung der Akustik

Zwischen 1850 und 1910 entstanden in Europa viele neue Theater und Konzerthäuser, die oft noch heute das Kulturleben der Städte prägen. Allerdings entstand nur ein einziges Haus, in dem fast alle zweitausend Besucher ideale akustische Bedingungen vorfinden sowie beste Sichtverhältnisse zur Bühne haben: das Festspielhaus Bayreuth. Richard Wagner realisierte hier seine frühe revolutionäre Idee, ein rangloses Volkstheater zu bauen. Die Demokratisierung der Akustik nahm ihren Lauf.

Der Grundriss des Zuschauerraums basiert auf einem Quadrat von 33 mal 33 Metern, wie Abbildung 1 zeigt. In dieses Quadrat schnitten Richard Wagner und sein Architekt Otto Brückwald einen amphitheatralisch ansteigenden Zuschauerraum, wobei die seitlichen Begrenzungen sich in einem Winkel von 45 Grad bei einer Bühnenöffnung von etwa 13 Metern aufspreizen. Die soffittenartig gemauerten Seitenwände im Saal begrenzen die Zuschauerfläche und fokussieren zusätzlich den Blick des Zuschauers auf die Bühne. Dadurch entstanden große Seitennischen, die wie Nachhallkammern wirken. Die klanglichen Qualitäten eines Musikraums können akustisch unter anderem mit den Nachhallzeiten beschrieben werden. Wie ausgeprägt diese sind, zeigt die Abbildung 2 in den Oktaven von 125 Hz bis 4 kHz für das voll besetzte Haus. Die vergleichsweise langen Nachhallzeiten von 1,3 bis 2,0 Sekunden kommen dem Orchester und den Sängern entgegen. Die Stimmen der Sänger und Sängerinnen erhalten eine voluminöse Fülle und die melodischen Linien mit dem Orchester einen klanglichen Zusammenhalt.

Während der Fußboden stark ansteigt, ist die Decke vollständig waagerecht und zur Auflockerung der strengen Geometrie mit bemalten Putzflächen gestaltet. Die Materialien des Zuschauerraums und der Bühne entsprechen durchaus der Bautradition in der zweiten Hälfte des 19. Jahrhunderts: ein aufgeständerter Holzfußboden auf massiven Fundamenten, dicke gemauerte Wände mit Putz und Gipsstrukturen bis hin zu Dekorationsteilen, die aus dem damals sehr populären Gips-Pappmaché hergestellt wurden. Auf den massiven Außenwänden ruhen die bis zu vier Meter hohen Holzbinder der Dachkonstruktion, an deren Unterseite direkt über Brettstrukturen die bereits erwähnte Saaldecke in Form einer zirka fünf Zentimeter dicken Putzschicht angebracht ist.

Die besondere Form, die Konstruktionen und die verwendeten Materialien prägen zusammen einen akustischen Raum, den es bis dahin für Opernhäuser nicht gegeben hat. Dieser Raum scheint die Töne förmlich zu tragen. Dies liegt auch an der einzigartigen Ankopplung der Bühne an den Zuschauerraum. Selbst bei unterschiedlichen Bühnensituationen ändern sich die Nachhallzeiten im Zuschauerraum kaum. Die Bühne ist mit speziellen Schall reflektierenden Wandelementen ausgestattet, die kontinuierlich den Klang des Orchesters und der Sänger aus dem Bühnenraum in den Zuschauerraum lenken. Diese Elemente müssen bei neuen Bühnenbildern den entsprechenden Szenen angepasst werden.

Nun zum Orchestergraben, der immer das Thema langer Diskussionen bei Musikliebhabern ist. Der Orchestergraben in Abbildung 3 entspricht im Grundriss noch dem Original aus dem Eröffnungsjahr 1876. Der Querschnitt und die Höhe des Orchestergrabens wurden jedoch vor vierzig Jahren erheblich verändert. Der sehr niedrige Bereich des Orchestergrabens unter der Bühne wurde auf über drei Meter Raumhöhe vergrößert. Dadurch entstand ein Orchesterraum, der zur gewünschten Lautstärkereduzierung für die Musiker führt, aber auch den Zusammenhang der einzelnen Orchesterstimmen wesentlich stärkt. Im Querschnitt der Abbildung 3 kann nachvollzogen werden, dass die Kopfhöhe der Musiker der ersten und zweiten Streicherpulte auf Höhe des Bühnenbodens liegt, der Kopf des Dirigenten befindet sich deutlich über dem Bühnenniveau. Der Dirigent und etwa die Hälfte

Karlheinz Müller
The democratization of acoustics

Many of the theaters and concert halls built in Europe between 1850 and 1910 still play a significant role in the cultural life of the cities in which they stand. But only one theater was built which gives all two thousand people in the audience ideal acoustics and an excellent view of the stage: the Bayreuth Festspielhaus. This theater embodies Richard Wagner's early revolutionary idea of building an egalitarian people's theater. The democratization of acoustics had begun.

The floor plan of the auditorium is a 33 x 33 meters square, as shown in Figure 1. Richard Wagner and his architect, Otto Brückwald, inserted a graded auditorium in the shape of an amphitheater into this space such that the outer edges fan out at a 45 degree angle with a stage width of approximately 13 meters. The fly-like solid side walls in the house limit what the spectator can see and direct the spectator's focus toward the stage. These lateral walls create large side niches, which act like echo chambers. One way to acoustically describe the tonal quality of a musical space is by measuring its reverberation period. Figure 2 illustrates how long these are in the octaves between 125 Hz and 4 Hz with a full house. The relatively long reverberation periods of 1.3 to 2.0 seconds are beneficial for the orchestra and the singers, giving the singers' voices a voluminous full sound and mixing their melodic lines with the orchestra.

Whereas the floor is strongly graded, the ceiling is completely horizontal and decorated in painted stucco areas to break up the rigid geometrical pattern. The materials used to build the auditorium and the stage are typical for the construction tradition in the second half of the 19th century: floor-mounted wooden parquet on massive foundations, thick masonry walls with stucco and plaster structures, and decorations made of papier maché, as was very popular at the time. The massive external walls support the up to four meters tall wooden framing of the roof construction. The bottom of this construction directly above the board structure is the five centimeters thick stucco layer forming the auditorium ceiling mentioned above.

Together, the unique shape, the construction and the materials used create an acoustic space such has had never before existed in opera houses. The space seems to literally carry the tones. This also has to do with the unique way the stage meets the auditorium. No matter what the situation on stage, the reverberation times in the auditorium hardly vary at all. The stage is equipped with special wall elements that reflect the sound and effectively direct the sound of the orchestra and the singers from the stage area out into the auditorium. These elements have to be adjusted for each scene of a new stage design.

A few words to the orchestra pit in the Bayreuth Festspielhaus, which is often the topic of long discussions among music aficionados. The orchestra pit illustrated in Figure 3 is how it originally looked for the grand opening in 1876. Around forty years ago, the orchestra pit's cross section and height were altered significantly. The very shallow part of the orchestra pit below the stage was enlarged by over 3 meters in height. That produces an orchestral space with the desired volume reduction for the instrumentalists, but also increases the unity of the individual sections of the orchestral lines. The cross section in Figure 3 makes it clear that the first and second violins' heads are level with the stage, while the conductor's head is clearly above stage level. This gives the conductor and around half of the orchestra close tonal contact with what is happening on stage. This is only true to a limited degree for the other half of the orchestra below the stage.

Since a large part of the orchestra sits quite high, Richard Wagner had a shell built before the Festspielhaus opened in 1876 to prevent the audience from seeing in. What was the purpose of this screen? The Bayreuth Festspielhaus was the first opera house in the world to perform its works with dimmed lights in the auditorium – but the instrumentalists' oil lamps continued to shine. It was typical through the beginning of the 20th century to light the auditorium (with candles)

Abbildung Illustration 1
Grundriss Plan

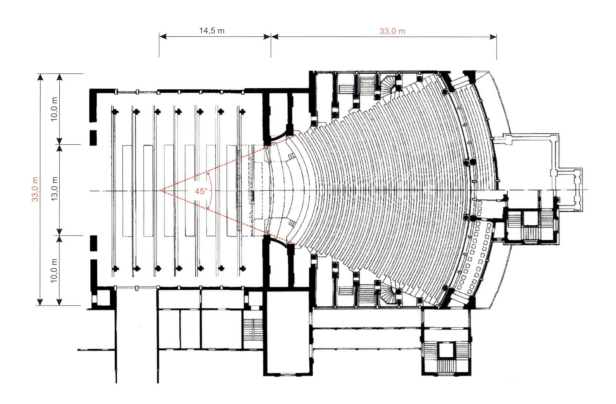

Abbildung Illustration 2
Zuschauerraum Auditorium

Nachhallzeit T_{60} (Musikbandbreite)
Reverberation T_{60} (octave band width)

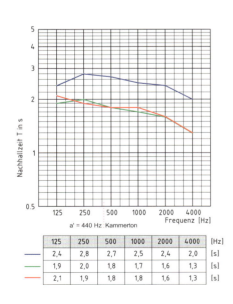

	125	250	500	1000	2000	4000	[Hz]
	2,4	2,8	2,7	2,5	2,4	2,0	[s]
	1,9	2,0	1,8	1,7	1,6	1,3	[s]
	2,1	1,9	1,8	1,8	1,6	1,3	[s]

— unbesetzt; mit Bestuhlung
  unoccupied; with chairs

— besetzt; Eiserner Vorhang geschlossen
  occupied; iron curtain closed

— besetzt; Eiserner Vorhang offen; Bühnenbild: Rheingold
  occupied; iron curtain opened; setting: Rheingold

Abbildung Illustration 3
Orchestergraben Orchestra Pit

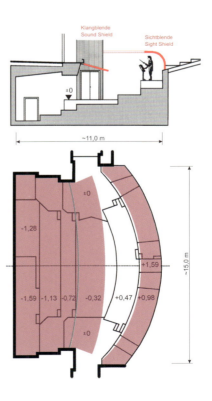

des Orchesters haben somit einen engen klanglichen Kontakt zum Bühnengeschehen. Für die andere Hälfte des Orchesters unter der Bühne gilt dies nur eingeschränkt.

Da ein großer Teil des Orchesters sehr weit oben sitzt, ließ Richard Wagner schon vor der Eröffnung des Festspielhauses 1876 eine Sichtblende zum Zuschauerraum anbringen. Warum diese Blende? Das Bayreuther Festspielhaus war das erste Opernhaus der Welt, das konsequent die Werke bei abgedunkeltem Zuschauerraum aufführte. Bis ins frühe 20. Jahrhundert hinein war es üblich, bei Opernaufführungen die Saalbeleuchtung (Kerzen) brennen zu lassen. Nicht so in Bayreuth mit seiner zu dieser Zeit einmaligen Gasbeleuchtung! Ein Kritiker schrieb damals: *"Jetzt spielt der Wahnsinnige auch noch bei verdunkeltem Raume."* So nahm das Schicksal des Orchestergrabens auch seinen besonderen akustischen Lauf. Da die erste Sichtblende den Streicherklang im Zuschauerraum dämpfte, ließ Richard Wagner bei den zweiten Bayreuther Festspielen 1882 eine zweite Schallblende an der Bühnenvorderkante anbringen. Damit konnte er dem starken Klang der Holz- und Blechbläser begegnen und ihn wieder in Balance mit den Streichern bringen. Durch die beiden Blenden können sicherlich einzelne Orchesterstimmen weniger Präsenz zeigen, dafür wird der Gesamtklang des Orchesters sehr gut gemischt und es steht für die Interpretationen viel Raum und Zeit zur Verfügung. Der große Dynamikbereich verbunden mit der langen Laufzeit der Töne wird oft als *"mystischer Klang von Bayreuth"* beschrieben.

Seit Inbetriebnahme des Festspielhauses im Jahre 1876 wurde immer wieder betont, welch ein differenziertes und ausgewogenes Zusammenspiel zwischen den Sängern und Sängerinnen auf der Bühne und dem großen Orchester möglich ist. Die baulichen Gegebenheiten helfen den Sängern, dass ihre Gesangspassagen durch den mächtigen Orchesterklang nicht überdeckt werden. In Abbildung 4 kann diese Wirkung beispielhaft an einem Zuhörerplatz in Saalmitte nachvollzogen werden. Bei identischer Lautstärke der Schallquelle sind die Bühnenpositionen außergewöhnlich lauter als Orchestergrabenpositionen, auch im Vergleich mit anderen Opernhäusern. Neben der sehr guten Direktschallversorgung des Publikums bei Gesangspassagen stützt der Raum auch die typischen Sängerformanten, das heißt, die charakteristischen Obertonbereiche zwischen 2500 Hz und 4000 Hz.

Richard Wagner ist es gelungen, einen akustisch neuen Klangraum für seine Musik zu schaffen. Seine großen Erfahrungen als Dirigent und Komponist haben in ihm die Idee eines neuen Festspielhauses aufkeimen lassen, die er konsequent verfolgte und mit dem Festspielhaus Bayreuth realisieren konnte. Alle Renovierungsschritte der letzten fünfzig Jahre wurden immer mit größter Vorsicht vorgenommen. So ist es gelungen, dass auch für die nächsten Jahrzehnte das Festspielhaus Bayreuth seine akustisch herausragende Rolle spielen kann.

during opera performances. But not in Bayreuth, where the auditorium was uniquely equipped with gas lights! A critic of the time wrote: *"Now the lunatic is even performing with a darkened auditorium."* And that's what led to the orchestra pit's special acoustical development. Since the original sight screen muted the sound of the strings in the auditorium, Richard Wagner had a second sound cover installed on the front edge of the stage to check the strong sound of the woodwinds and brass and bring them back into balance with the strings. As a result of the two covers, individual orchestral sections certainly have less presence, but the overall sound of the orchestra is very well mixed, giving plenty of time and space for interpretation. The large range of dynamics together with the long delay of the sound is often described as the *"mystical tone of Bayreuth."*

Ever since the first performances in the Festspielhaus in 1876, it has often been remarked how finely and in balance the singers on the stage are able to interact with the large orchestra. The physical structure helps the singers prevent their musical lines from being covered over by the powerful orchestral sound. Figure 4 illustrates the effect from the standpoint of a seat in the middle of the auditorium, as an example. A sound source of identical volume is uncommonly louder from the stage than from the orchestra. This is true compared with other opera houses as well. Not only is the audience supplied with excellent direct sound from the stage during vocal passages, but the space also supports typical singer formant frequencies, i.e., the characteristic overtones between 2,500 Hz and 4,000 Hz.

Richard Wagner successfully created a new acoustic space for his music. His extensive experience as a conductor and a composer generated the idea of a new festival theater, which he pursued diligently and was able to bring to fruition in the Festspielhaus Bayreuth. The renovations over the past fifty years have always been undertaken with the utmost care. As a result, the Bayreuth Festspielhaus will continue to play its acoustically exceptional role for decades to come.

Karlheinz Müller, langjähriger Mitarbeiter des Akustikbüros Müller-BBM in Planegg bei München, ist ständiger Berater der Bayreuther Festspiele, der Salzburger Festspiele und der Bregenzer Festspiele bei akustischen Fragen. Außerdem ist er Lehrbeauftragter und Professor an der Universität für Musik und darstellende Kunst in Wien. Er hat auch viele große Objekte akustisch geplant, unter anderem Festspielhaus Baden-Baden, Haus für Mozart Salzburg, Philharmonie Essen, Helmut List Halle Graz und Reichstag Berlin.

Karlheinz Müller, a veteran engineer at the accoustical consultancy Müller-BBM in Planegg near München, is a permanent acoustics advisor to the Bayreuth Festival, the Salzburg Festival, and the Bregenz Festival. He also holds a teaching post and is a professor at the Universität für Musik und darstellende Kunst in Vienna. He has also helped design the accoustics for many large objects, including the Baden-Baden Festspielhaus, the Haus für Mozart in Salzburg, the Philharmonie in Essen, the Helmut List Halle in Graz, and Reichstag Berlin.

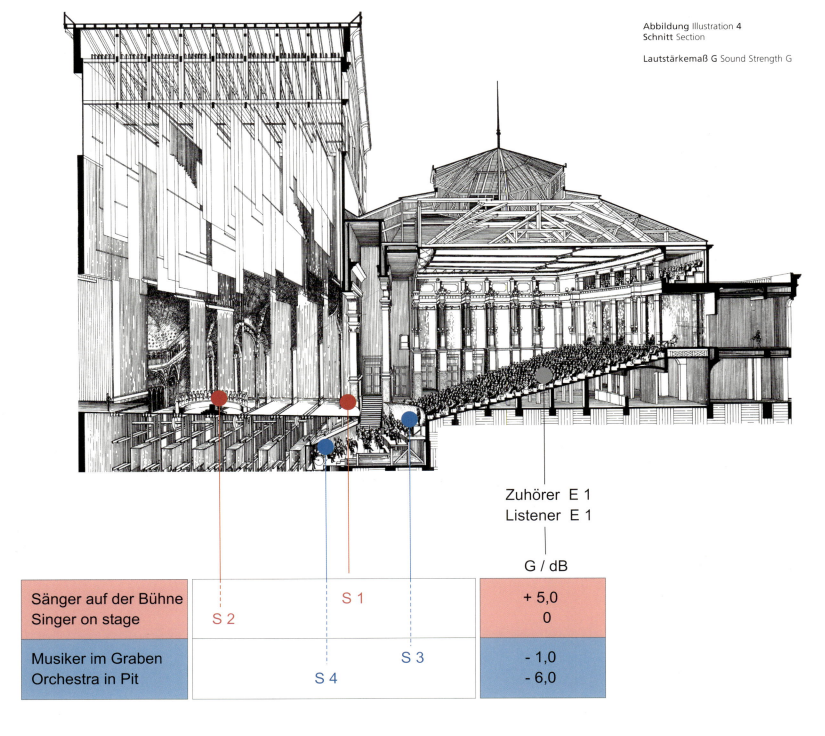

Abbildung Illustration 4
Schnitt Section

Lautstärkemaß G Sound Strength G

Zuhörer E 1
Listener E 1

				G / dB
Sänger auf der Bühne Singer on stage		S 1		+ 5,0
	S 2			0
Musiker im Graben Orchestra in Pit			S 3	− 1,0
		S 4		− 6,0

Der mystische Abgrund

Die Bühne in Bayreuth wird durch ein kragendes Flachgewölbe (oder ein flaches Kraggewölbe) eingefasst wie viele andere Theaterbühnen. Das war nicht neu, neu aber war eine dreifache Staffelung dieser Bühneneinfassung, die zusätzlich durch jeweils abschattierte Brauntöne optisch unterstrichen wurde und heute nach den Restaurierungen wieder deutlich ist. Diese dreifache Staffelung umfasst das eigentliche Proszenium, das in anderen älteren Theatern meist für Logen genutzt wird, in Bayreuth jedoch ein leerer Raum bleibt. Wagner selbst beschreibt in seiner 1872er Rede, wie diese Idee entstanden ist:

„Meine Forderung der Unsichtbarmachung des Orchesters gab dem Genie des berühmten Architekten [gemeint ist Semper], [...] sofort die Bestimmung des hieraus, zwischen dem Proszenium und den Sitzreihen des Publikums entstehenden, leeren Zwischenraumes ein: wir nannten ihn den ‚mystischen Abgrund', weil er die Realität von der Idealität zu trennen habe, und der Meister schloss ihn nach vorn durch ein erweitertes zweites Proszenium ab, aus dessen Wirkung [...] er sich alsbald die wundervolle Täuschung eines scheinbaren Fernerrückens der eigentlichen Szene zu versprechen hatte, welche darin besteht, dass der Zuschauer den szenischen Vorgang sich weit entrückt wähnt, ihn nun aber doch mit der Deutlichkeit der wirklichen Nähe wahrnimmt; woraus dann die fernere Täuschung erfolgt, dass ihm die auf der Szene auftretenden Personen in vergrößerter, übermenschlicher Gestalt erscheinen."[1]

Der so oft zitierte und gedeutete „mystische Abgrund" ist also nicht nur der Orchestergraben, sondern die ganze „Gasse" zwischen Zuschauerraum und Bühne inklusive Orchestergraben. Das war neu, das Prinzip jedoch alt. Schon immer hatte man die wechselnden Kulissen einer Theaterbühne nach hinten gestaffelt, um einen perspektivischen, tiefensuggestiven Effekt (die sogenannte Theaterperspektive) zu erzielen – in Bayreuth setzt sich dieses Prinzip aber auch nach vorne fort und wird zu einer ständigen architektonischen Kulisse mit besonderem optischen Effekt. Diesen beschreibt Wager selbst:

Der Zuschauer *„befindet sich jetzt, sobald er seinen Sitz eingenommen hat, recht eigentlich in einem ‚Theatron', d. h. einem Raume, der für nichts Anderes berechnet ist, als darin zu schauen, und zwar dorthin, wohin seine Stelle ihn weist. Zwischen ihm und dem zu erschauenden Bilde befindet sich nichts deutlich Wahrnehmbares, sondern nur eine, zwischen den beiden Proszenien durch architektonische Vermittlung gleichsam im Schweben erhaltene Entfernung, welche das durch sie ihm entrückte Bild in der Unnahbarkeit einer Traumerscheinung zeigt, während die aus dem ‚mystischen Abgrunde' geisterhaft erklingende Musik, gleich den, unter dem Sitze der Pythia dem heiligen Urschoße Gaias entsteigenden Dämpfen, ihn in jenen begeisterten Zustand des Hellsehens versetzt, in welchem das erschaute szenische Bild ihm jetzt zum wahrhaftigsten Abbilde des Lebens selbst wird."*[2]

Bisher war nur von einem doppelten Proszenium die Rede, wie es schon Semper ersonnen hatte. Die dritte Staffelung ist eine Erfindung von Carl Brandt, wie Wagner in seiner Rede betont, der „*auf den Gedanken gekommen [war], ein nochmals vorgerücktes und erweitertes drittes Proszenium einzuschalten*", um jene „*unschönen Winkelecken*" zu füllen. Doch damit nicht genug: „*Von der Vortrefflichkeit dieses Gedankens erfasst, gingen wir aber bald noch weiter, und mussten finden, dass wir der ganzen Idee der perspektivisch nach der Bühne zu sich verkürzenden Breite des Zuschauerraumes nur dann vollkommen entsprechen würden, wenn wir die Wiederholung des von der Bühne aus sich erweiternden Proszeniums auf dessen ganzen Raum, bis zu seinem Abschlusse durch die ihn krönende Galerie, ausdehnten, und somit das Publikum, auf jedem von ihm eingenommenen*

The mystical abyss

The stage in Bayreuth is framed by a protruding flat vault (or flat protruding vaulting), as are many other theater stages. That was nothing new, but what was new was a threefold staggering of this stage framework, which was optically underlined by respectively shaded brown tones and today, after the restoration work, has once again become more distinct. This threefold staggering comprises the actual proscenium, which in other older theaters was usually utilized for the loges, yet in Bayreuth remains an empty room. Wagner himself describes in his 1872 speech how this idea arose.

"My requirement that the orchestra should be concealed immediately gave the genius of the famous architect [i.e. Semper] [...] the idea of how to use the empty intermediate space that arose between the proscenium and the rows of audience seats. We called it the 'mystical abyss', because it was intended to divide reality from ideality and the master closed it off at the front by means of an extended second proscenium, with the promised effect [...] of the wonderful illusion of the actual scene apparently moving into the distance, created by the fact that the spectators believed the events on the stage to be far away from themselves, yet now perceived them in all the clarity of actual proximity; thus producing the subsequent illusion that the people entering onto the stage appeared to have taken enlarged, superhuman form."

The often quoted and interpreted "mystical abyss" therefore comprises not only the orchestra pit, but the whole 'alley' between the auditorium and the stage, including the orchestra pit. That was new, although the principle was old. One had always staggered the changing backdrops of a theater stage towards the back, in order to create a perspective effect that suggested depth (the so-called theater perspective) – yet in Bayreuth this principle is also continued toward the front as well, becoming a constant architectural set with a special optical effect. This is described by Wagner himself:

"As soon as they have taken their seats, (the spectators) *now find themselves well and truly in a 'theatron', i.e. a space which has been designed with no other purpose in mind than to look into it and namely toward that place which is indicated by their positions. Between the spectators and the image that they are looking at there is nothing distinctly perceptible, but only a distance that is kept in suspension, as it were, between the two proscenia by architectural mediation, a distance which endows the image that has been moved away from them with the inapproachability of a dream manifestation, while the ghostly sound of the music that emerges from the 'mystical abyss', like the vapors rising from under the seat of Pythia from the holy primordial womb of Gaia, transports them into that inspired state of clairvoyance in which the scenic image that they behold now becomes the truest image of life itself."*

So far, discussion had only revolved around a double proscenium, just as Semper had devised it. The third staggering was an invention of Carl Brandt, as Wagner pointed out in his speech, who *"had the idea that a third proscenium could be introduced that would be moved forwards and extended"* in order to fill those *"unseemly angular corners."* However, that was not the end of it: *"Consumed with the appropriateness of this idea, we soon went even further and had to discover that we could only completely achieve the whole idea of the perspective foreshortening the breadth of the auditorium from the stage outwards by expanding the repetition of the proscenium from the stage to its whole space, right up to its conclusion in the gallery that crowned it, and thus inserted the audience, in each of the seats that they occupy, into the proscenic perspective itself. For this purpose, a pillar arrangement was designed that corresponded to the initial proscenium but expanded upwards to form a limitation of the rows of seats, creating an illusion about the straight lateral walls lying behind them and between which the necessary flights of steps and access points were purposefully hidden."*

Platze, in die proszenische Perspektive selbst einfügten. Es ward hierzu eine dem Ausgangsproszenium entsprechende, nach oben sich erweiternde Säulenordnung als Begrenzung der Sitzreihen entworfen, welche über die dahinter liegenden geraden Seitenwände täuschte, und zwischen welcher die nötigen Stufentreppen und Zugänge sich zweckmäßig verbargen."[1]

Damit war, zählt man die Scherwände und die eigentlichen Proszenien zusammen, letztlich ein achtfaches Proszenium geschaffen, allein aus optischen, theatralischen Gründen, die eine optimal gesteigerte Suggestion des Bühnengeschehens auf den Betrachter besorgen sollte. Das erklärt endlich den Bau dieser merkwürdigen Scherwände, die zufälligerweise auch für eine gute Akustik sorgen und das griechische (Amphi-)Theater mit der neuzeitlichen „Guckkastenbühne" auf eine einzigartige und wahrhaft geniale Weise verbinden!

Der Vorhang

Die intelligente Kunst, das Auge subtil zu täuschen, ist eine typische Finesse der alten Griechen, die sich sehr geschickt der Optik des Auges anzupassen wussten, die eine organische und keine streng geometrische ist. Beim Bau ihrer Tempel erkannten sie zum Beispiel, dass die äußersten Säulen immer etwas schlanker schienen, weshalb diese einfach etwas kräftiger ausgeführt wurden. Die Griechen erfanden in ihrer Malerei die Luftperspektive und die illusionistische Wandmalerei, wie sie in Pompeji zu bewundern ist, wenn man sich die Täuschungen des Auges gefallen lässt.

In Bayreuth findet sich ein weiterer optischer Trick, den der Bühnenbildner Adolphe Appia 1902 beschreibt. Es handelt sich um einen von Wagner schon für die LOHENGRIN-Uraufführung (1850) erdachten, späterhin nach ihm benannten Vorhang (siehe auch Wagners Bühnenarchitektur), der sich wie die Linse einer Kamera in der Mitte weich zur Seite teilt und nicht einfach senkrecht nach oben oder waagerecht zur Seite gezogen wird: Sanft sollte das Auge des Zuschauers „hinaus gleiten in die Welt des Traumes"[2]. Er war in den Farben des Raumes, vermutlich Ockerbraun, gehalten und verschmolz so optisch mit der Architektur. Aber das war noch nicht alles: „Eine waagerechte Linie zog er [Wagner] unten, quer über den Vorhang", die beim Zuschauer den Eindruck hervor rief, „als bezeichne sie die Mannshöhe auf der Bühne."[3] Diese Linie wurde an den Proszeniumswänden durch ein kleines Gesims aufgegriffen. Während des Orchestervorspiels habe sich der Betrachter an diesen Maßstab gewöhnt, sodass bei Beginn der Vorstellung die auf der Bühne erscheinenden Darsteller nicht mehr mannshoch, sondern kleiner und damit entrückter erschienen, was die subtile Suggestion sensibel forcierte. Ob Wagner selbst oder Brandt oder ein anderer diese Idee entwickelte, ist in den Quellen nicht belegt. Der Originalvorhang war bis 1944 in Betrieb, es folgten andere Vorhänge ohne Wagnermechanik, die erst seit den 1990er Jahren von Wolfgang Wagner wieder eingebaut wurde. Die weiße Linie wurde leider übersehen und nicht wieder realisiert.

Fast wäre dieser ganze schöne „Budenzauber", die so subtil inszenierte Illusion in sich zusammengebrochen. Der Flachbogen des vordersten Proszeniums war mit den Jahren aus dem rechten Winkel geraten, der Zapfen, der zwei Balken miteinander verband, hatte sich gelockert. Man untersuchte die Auflage des doppelten Balkens und entdeckte mit Erschrecken, dass dieser nur eine handbreite Auflage besaß. Eine Schlamperei – wie schon die ungebrannten Ziegel im Fundament – doch ein Provisorium wird eben nicht für die Ewigkeit gebaut. Heute wird die ganze Konstruktion durch ein Stahlgerüst gesichert.

With that, if one counts the shear walls and the actual proscenia as one, an eightfold proscenium was finally created, solely for optical, theatrical reasons, in order to give the spectator an optimally enhanced suggestion of the events on the stage. That finally explains the construction of these remarkable shear walls, which coincidentally also provide good acoustics and also combine the Greek (amphi-)theater with the modern "picture-frame stage" in a unique and truly ingenious way!

The curtain

The intelligent art of subtly deceiving the eye is a typical refinement of the ancient Greeks, who knew how to very skillfully adapt to the optics of the eye, which are organic and not strictly geometrical. In building their temples they recognized, for example, that the outermost columns always looked as if they were somewhat slimmer, and therefore made them somewhat stouter. In their painting, the Greeks invented the bird's eye perspective as well as illusionistic wall painting, as can be admired in Pompeii, if one allows the deception of the eye to act.

Bayreuth offers a further optical illusion, as described by the stage designer Adolphe Appia in 1902, namely a curtain invented by Wagner for the LOHENGRIN premiere (1850), which was later named after him (see the chapter on Wagner's stage design), which slightly divides sideways in the middle like the lens of a camera and is not simply drawn vertically upwards or horizontally to the side. The spectator's eye should gently *"glide out into the world of the dream."* It had the same colors as the room, presumably ochre-brown, and thus merged optically with the architecture. But that was still not all: "He [Wagner] *drew a further horizontal line clear across the curtain,"* creating the impression among the audience that *"it represented the height of a human being on the stage."* This line was taken up in the walls of the proscenium by a small ledge. During the orchestral prelude the spectator would become accustomed to these dimensions, so that at the start of the performance the actors that came onto the stage no longer appeared to be the height of a human being, but smaller and thus farther away. This sensitively created a subtle suggestiveness. It is not documented whether it was Wagner himself or Brandt or someone else who actually developed this idea. The original curtain was in use until 1944, when it was followed by other curtains which did not rely on Wagnerian mechanics. Wolfgang Wagner only reinstalled a Wagnerian curtain in the 1990s. The white line was unfortunately overlooked and was not included.

All this beautiful "stage magic" and the ever-so-subtly produced illusion almost collapsed. Over the years, the flat arch of the front proscenium had lost its right angle and the pinecone that connected two of the beams together had become loose. The support of the double beam was investigated and it was discovered in horror that the support was only as wide as a hand. Negligence, certainly – like the unbaked brick in the foundations – yet, after all, a provisional theater is not built to last forever. Today the whole construction is supported by steel scaffolding.

Original-Bühnenvorhang (Aufnahme 1927) Original stage curtain (1927 photograph)
Dramatischer Befund von 1964 Dramatic findings dating from 1964

Die Beleuchtung

Zu dem von Wagner so fein ersonnenen Illusionstheater Bayreuth gehört ganz wesentlich auch die Beleuchtung des Zuschauerraums. Wagner hatte bewusst auf einen zentralen, „normalerweise" üblichen Kronleuchter verzichtet, der die unmittelbare Sicht auf die Bühne gestört hätte. Stattdessen wurden zahlreiche Kandelaber angebracht: *„Die Säulenstellungen selbst, um nicht zwecklos dazustehen, wurden als Träger der Beleuchtung benutzt"*[1], schreibt Otto Brückwald und deutet noch einmal an, dass diese Säulen architektonisch eigentlich überflüssig sind. Die zwölf korinthischen Säulen an den Seiten und die vier an der Rückwand tragen an ihrem Schaft jeweils einen Armleuchter mit drei Kugellampen und darüber einen mit sechs Kugeln. Die acht Armleuchter an den toskanischen Pfeiler an der Rückwand tragen jeweils nur eine Kugel. Zusammen spenden alle Lampen ein relativ warmes Licht im gelben Spektrum, das das Gold und die Ockerfarbe (giallo antico) an den Wänden harmonisch zur Geltung bringt.

Dabei handelte es sich ursprünglich um eine Gasbeleuchtung, die elektrische Glühbirne wurde erst 1879 erfunden und ab 1886 im Festspielhaus etabliert. Bis dahin sorgte die „Bayreuther Gasfabrik" für den Bedarf, wobei pro Vorstellung zirka 1350 Kubikmeter verbraucht wurden, was zwölfeinhalb Prozent der gesamten Produktion bedeutete, die sich 1882 auf neununddreißig Prozent steigerte, was den enormen Bedarf an Licht und die damals wie heute hohen „Nebenkosten" des Festspielhauses andeuten mag.

Die Originallampen wurden 1876 von der Augsburger Firma Riedinger geliefert und installiert. Stilistisch erinnern diese Armleuchter in ihrem geschnörkelten Rankenwerk mit Blümchen wiederum an antike Vorbilder, die schon im Biedermeier beliebt waren. Überhaupt lässt die Verwendung von Kandelabern wiederum an Pompeji denken, wo ein ganzer Dekorationsstil „Kandelaberstil" genannt wird: Auf die Wand gemalte zierliche Kandelaber umrahmen hier statt Säulen die illusionistischen Bildmotive.

Mitte der 1990er Jahre wurden die Lampen restauriert und teilweise vergoldet. Sie sind – nach Auskunft von Helmut Jahn – bis auf wenige Ergänzungen an der hinteren Logenwand (die Originale sind wie die Brüstungen um 1945 vermutlich als Souvenirs in die USA verschwunden) alle original. Lediglich die Glaskugeln wurden völlig neu angefertigt. Die alten Gläser waren durchsichtig und beleuchteten den Raum mit den neuen Glühlampen über hundert Jahre lang viel zu hell. Bei der Restaurierung entschied man sich deshalb für Milchglas, um den warmen Ton der Gasbeleuchtung des 19. Jahrhunderts nachzuempfinden.

Lassen wir uns in die Zeit der Uraufführung zurückversetzen. Gregor-Dellin schildert die Premiere am 13. August 1876. Zunächst stahl der angereiste Kaiser allen die Schau: *„Ein Beifallssturm brach los ‚wie ein gewaltiger Orkan', und der Kaiser verneigte sich nach allen Seiten. Dann ging, für viele überraschend, das Licht aus, man sah die Hand vor den Augen nicht."*[2] Das war eigentlich nicht so beabsichtigt und eine echte Premierenpanne.

Richard Wagner schildert in seinem „Rückblick auf die Bühnenfestspiele des Jahres 1876", wie es dazu gekommen war: *„Die Einrichtung für die Gasbeleuchtung des Zuschauerraumes war wirklich erst am Mittag der ersten Vorstellung des RHEINGOLDES soweit fertig geworden, dass überhaupt wenigstens beleuchtet werden konnte, wenn gleich eine Regulierung dieser Beleuchtung durch genaue Abmessung der verschiedenen Brennapparate noch nicht hatte vorgenommen werden können. Das Ergebnis hiervon war, dass [...] gegen unsern Willen im Zuschauerraume vollkommene Nacht ward, wo wir nur eine starke Dämpfung des Lichtes beabsichtigten."*[3]

Lighting

Another essential aspect of the illusionistic theater of Bayreuth so finely tuned by Wagner is the lighting of the auditorium. Wagner deliberately dispensed with central "normally" typical chandeliers, which would have disturbed the direct view of the stage. Instead numerous candelabras were installed: *"The pillars themselves were used as bearers of light fittings, so that they didn't stand there without a purpose,"* writes Otto Brückwald in 1904, again confirming that these columns were actually superfluous from an architectural point of view. The twelve Corinthian columns on the sides and the four at the rear wall each bear on their shafts a chandelier with three globe lamps and above that one with six globes. The eight chandeliers on the Tuscan pillars on the rear wall each bear only one globe. Together, all the lamps give out a relatively warm light in the yellow part of the spectrum, harmoniously enhancing the gold and the ochre color (giallo antico) on the walls.

Originally gas lighting was used, since the electric light bulb was only invented in 1879 and not installed in the Festspielhaus until 1886. Up until then, the "Bayreuth Gas Factory" delivered the requisite supplies, with approx. 1,350 cubic meter being needed for each performance, accounting for twelve and a half per cent of the whole production costs, rising to thirty-nine per cent by 1882, which indicates the enormous lighting needs of the Festspielhaus.

The original lamps were delivered and installed in 1876 by the Riedinger company from Augsburg. Stylistically, these chandeliers, with their adorning flourishes, embellishments and little flowers again recall antique models popular in the Biedermeier era. In general, the use of candelabras is reminiscent of Pompeii, where a whole style of decoration was known as the "candelabra style": decorative candelabras painted on the wall here provide the frames for the illusionistic pictorial motifs instead of columns.

In the mid 1990s the lamps were restored and partially gilded. They are – according to information provided by Helmut Jahn – all original, apart from a few additions on the rear balcony loges (the originals, like the balustrades, presumably disappeared as souvenirs to the USA around 1945). Only the glass globes were manufactured completely new. The old glass balls were transparent and illuminated the room with the new electric light bulbs far too brightly for more than hundred years. During the restoration work it was therefore decided in favor of milky glass, in order to recreate the warm tones of the gas lighting of the 19th century.

Let us imagine ourselves back in the time of the premiere. Gregor-Dellin describes the premiere on August 13, 1876. At first the Emperor stole the show when he arrived: *"Rapturous applause broke loose 'like a powerful hurricane,' and the Emperor bowed to all sides. Then, surprisingly for many people, the lights all went out and you couldn't see your hand in front of your face."* That was not actually intended and constitutes a true premiere mishap.

In his "Review of the 1876 stage festival" (1878), Richard Wagner describes how it happened: *"Only at midday on the day of the first performance of RHEINGOLD the equipment for the gas lighting in the auditorium was only ready to the extent that it could at least be turned on, since it had not yet been possible to regulate the lighting by carrying out an exact measurement of the various pieces of burning equipment. The result was that [...], against our will, it got pitch black in the auditorium, where we had actually only intended greatly subdued lighting."*

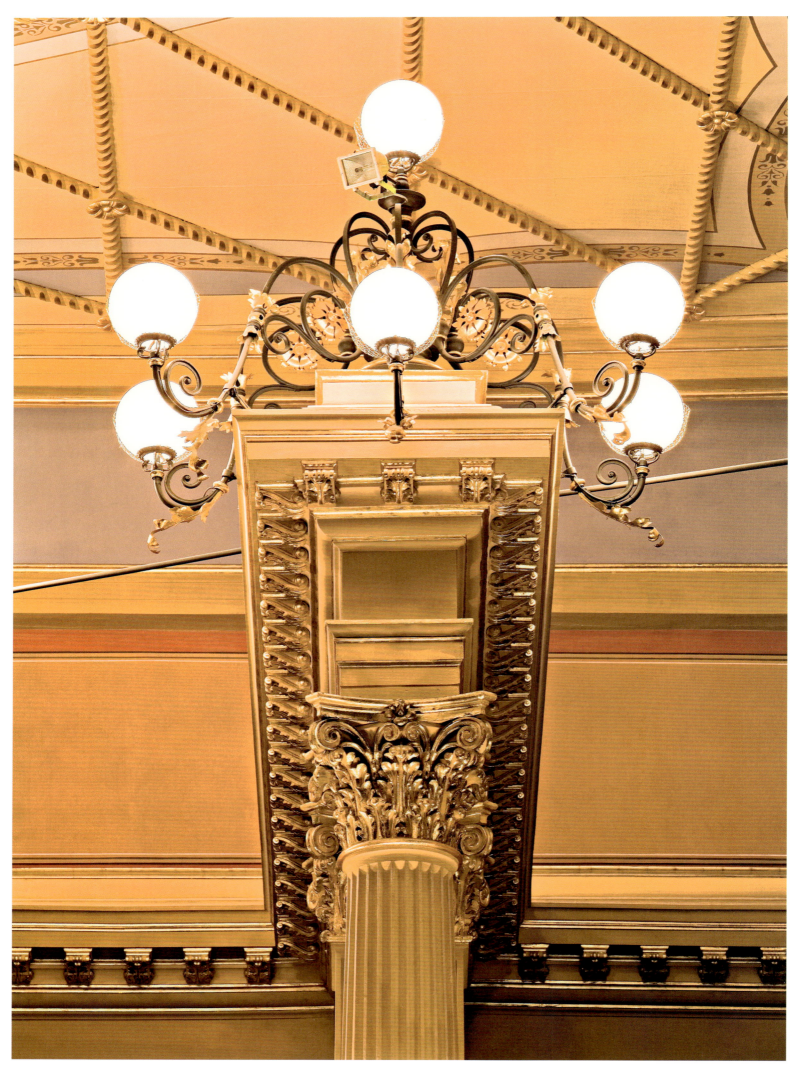

A certain subdued light was therefore desired and that was in fact achieved at later performances. Wagner did not want – as was usual at that time in all theaters – a brightly illuminated auditorium, so that the audience could read along with the libretto. Wagner himself confirmed the habit of those days, which we today only know from concert evenings, and in "My Life" he tells of a friend who had experienced a performance of TANNHÄUSER at the Lerchenfelder Sommertheater in Vienna and complained *"principally about the darkness of the theater, because it was impossible to read even a single word of the text"* and *"that it had rained a great deal inside."* After a performance of Handel's "Messiah" in London Wagner reported the *"lively participation of an audience that read along in the score."*

In this point, too, Wagner broke with every convention and even wrote down his thoughts in an instruction which he sent out to those involved in 1875/76. One from 1876 is called: "On the use of the libretto." In it, the maestro orders: *"In order to obtain the correct effect of the scenic image, the lighting in the auditorium has to be reduced to such an extent that it is impossible to read the libretto during the act. Therefore, if the clarity of the dramatic performance is still mistrusted, it is advised either to become acquainted with the whole text before the performance or to become familiar with parts of the same between the acts."*

That was no small matter to demand, since his texts were long and the poetry of DER RING DES NIBELUNGEN does not contain simple, easy-to-learn German. However, the 19th century was still not such a fast-living period and people took the time to make a thorough preliminary study of the text. That has become rather rare today. Nevertheless, even today, one sees a few festival guests sunk in a little, often yellow book before each act.

Richard Wagner's rather cruel demand derived from his wish that the audience should concentrate on the stage and the immediate experience. The darkness, which was controversially discussed all over Europe until well into the 20th century, has today become quite usual at every opera (since Bayreuth), and helps one to forget everyday life and to stride into the dream world. In this sense Wagner was anticipating the cinema and the products of the "dream factories" of the 20th century.

Of course, all that only works if one understands what is being sung. The poet and composer Wagner places great importance on that. In the famous "Final plea to my colleagues," an instruction to the singers for the day of the premiere, he writes: *"Clarity! The big notes come of their own accord; the little notes and their text are the most important."* Here Wagner relies on the architecture that he has invented, the sunken orchestra pit, which reduces the distance between the audience and the singers not only optically, but above all acoustically and through architecture seeks to provide the circumstances for a better understanding of the singers' texts.

Not only the singers, but also the visitors to the premiere of 1876 were challenged, more so than today, because everything was still new. The darkness irritated and even frightened many people: *"When you leave the bright sunlight of the summer afternoon, you have first of all to rely on your sense of touch in the dark room, which will lead you up the steps to the rows of seats. Only gradually does the eye grow accustomed the mysterious half-light. A sensation which comes closest to that of the respectful shudder is the first thing that is aroused by the view of this new world."*

A composer colleague rather lacking in understanding, Igor Stravinsky, experienced the beginning of PARSIFAL in 1912 (even before his desire for cigarettes and sausage) as follows: *"First of all, the whole atmosphere in the hall, the presentation and the setting seemed to me to be strangely gloomy. It was like being in a crematorium (and what is more in a very old one), where one has to be prepared to see the appearance of the gentleman dressed in black, who will make a solemn speech on the glorification of he who has passed away."*

Ein als Komponistenkollege recht unverständiger Igor Strawinsky erlebte den Beginn des PARSIFAL 1912 (noch vor seinem Gelüsten nach Zigaretten und Bratwurst) wie folgt: *„Zunächst kamen mir die ganze Stimmung im Saal, die Aufmachung und der Rahmen unheimlich düster vor. Es war wie ein Krematorium (und zudem noch ein sehr veraltetes), in dem man sich darauf gefasst machen musste, den schwarz gekleideten Herrn auftreten zu sehen, der die feierliche Rede zur Verherrlichung des Dahingegangenen zu halten hat."*[1]

Fazit

Der Zuschauersaal des Festspielhauses entspricht allen theoretischen Forderungen Wagners von 1849, 1865 und 1872. Er präsentiert sich als demokratisches (Amphi-)Theater, das aufgrund seiner Bestuhlung auch ein spartanisches Theater genannt werden darf. Die von Wagner so kritisierten Seitenlogen wurden tatsächlich nicht gebaut, stattdessen eine „republikanische" Fürstenloge ohne Betonung einer zentralen Herrscherloge, die der Königsbau der Außenfassade erwarten lässt. Doch nicht die Politik war für diese Raumkonzeption die Ursache, sondern der Wunsch nach einer optimalen Sicht für alle. Das gilt insbesondere für die Scherwände, die als eine Art achtfaches Proszenium den optischen Sog auf die Bühne verstärken. Die Tatsache, dass sie akustisch als Resonanzkörper nützlich sind, war nicht konzipiert, sondern das Glück des Mutigen. Das gilt auch für das versenkte Orchester, dessen guter Klang reiner Zufall war. Überhaupt dankt das Festspielhaus seine gute Akustik nicht genialen Raumkonzepten, sondern der Tatsache, dass die ganze Holzarchitektur nicht nur die billigste, sondern auch die akustisch beste war und ist.

Die ganze Konzeption des Zuschauerraums wurde – entgegen vieler Vorurteile – nicht von akustischen, sondern von optischen Überlegungen beherrscht. Hier spielt der „mystische Abgrund" als optische Schwelle zwischen Realität und der Fiktion auf der Bühne eine besondere Rolle, der als Luftraum rund um die Bühne zu verstehen ist und nicht als Orchestergraben. Letzterer ist ebenfalls primär aus optischen Gründen eingerichtet worden, um dem Bühnengeschehen eine größere Unmittelbarkeit und Illusionskraft zu geben. Darüber hinaus sollte er für eine bessere Verständlichkeit der Sänger sorgen.

Andere optische Effekte, wie die raffinierten Tricks des „Wagner-Vorhangs", sollten für ein optimales Illusionstheater sorgen, das im multimedialen 21. Jahrhundert natürlich kaum noch so subtil wahrgenommen werden kann. Eine solche – schon von den Griechen erfundene – Täuschung des Auges bietet vor allem die Decke mit einem fast realistisch anmutenden Sonnensegel aus Farbe und Pappmaché, das den Himmel des alten Arkadiens imaginiert.

Griechisch sind auch alle weiteren Dekorationen des insgesamt keineswegs so schmucklosen Raums, wie Wagner es 1872 angekündigt hatte. Korinthische Säulen mit goldenen Kapitellen markieren fast alle Vertikalachsen des Raums, die sich in der Horizontale mit korinthischem beziehungsweise toskanischem Gebälk und einem zierlichen Anthemion-Fries an den Wänden kreuzen. Pompejanisch sind das Scheinmauerwerk der Scherwände, die Scheinmalerei auf den Brüstungen, die Brüstungsgitter selbst und die Wandbemalung. Wie pompejanische Kandelaber erscheinen auch die Lampen, die sich bei der Premiere ungewollt völlig verdunkelten und so die Magie eines außergewöhnlichen Theatererlebnisses zu steigern wussten. Wenn sie leuchten, illuminieren die dem Charakter der alten Gasbeleuchtung nachempfundenen neuen Lampen ein insgesamt vorbildlich Mitte der 1990er Jahre nach Originalbefunden restauriertes Zuschauerhaus, das in seiner hellenistischen Anmutung und seiner goldgelb glänzenden Festlichkeit nicht nur außergewöhnliche Klangerlebnisse beherbergt, sondern selbst ein Kunstwerk Richard Wagners darstellt.

Summary

The Festspielhaus auditorium fulfills all of Wagner's theoretical requirements from 1849, 1865 and 1872. It has the characteristics of a democratic (amphi-)theater that could be called a Spartan theater based on its seating. The side loges Wagner so despised were not built, but instead a comparatively simple "republican" Prince's Gallery without the emphasis of a central monarchial gallery that the Königsbau would lead one to expect from the exterior. However, politics were not the reason for this conception of space, but rather the desire that everyone have optimal sightlines. That is especially true for the shear walls that function as a sort of eightfold proscenium to increase the optical draw toward the stage. The fact that they are acoustically useful as resonance bodies was not conceptualized, but rather the luck of the bold builder. That is also true for the sunken orchestra, which purely coincidentally has a good tone. The good acoustics of the Festspielhaus in general are not based on some ingenious spatial concept, but mostly on the fact that the wooden architecture was not only the least expensive, but rather also provided and still provides the best acoustics.

Contrary to many preconceptions, the entire concept of the auditorium was not driven by acoustic, but rather by optical considerations. The "mystical abyss" as an optical border between reality and the fiction on stage plays an especially important role. It should be understood as the airspace surrounding the stage rather than only the orchestra pit. The latter was also conceived primarily for optical reasons to make the action on the stage seem even more immediate and to strengthen its illusionary power. It was also designed to help make the singers easier to understand.

Other optical effects, such as the brilliant "Wagner curtain" trick, create an optimal theater of illusion that can hardly be appreciated in all their subtleties in the multimedial 21st century. One such optical illusion that the Greeks had already mastered is the ceiling with its nearly realistic tented roof made of paint and papier maché that imagines the sky of the old Arcadia.

Other decorations in the hardly unadorned hall (as Wagner had called it in 1872) are likewise borrowed from Greek tradition. Almost all vertical axes of the room are marked with Corinthian columns with golden capitals that are horizontally bound by Corinthian and Tuscan entablatures and a decorative Anthemion frieze along the walls. The mock stonework of the shear walls, the faux painting on the balustrades, the balustrade screens themselves and the wall paintwork are likewise all Pompeian. The lights also resemble Pompeian candelabras, and were inadvertently shut off completely during the premiere, heightening the magic of an extraordinary theater experience. The current lights were designed to capture the character of the old gas lighting. When they are lit, they reveal an auditorium restored in the middle of the 1990s in exemplary fashion based on original models, an auditorium with Hellenic spirit and a golden-yellow shining festiveness that offers not only an unusual tonal experience, but is in itself a work of art by Richard Wagner.

„Die Säulenstellungen selbst, um nicht zwecklos dazustehen, wurden als Träger der Beleuchtung benutzt."

"The pillars themselves were used as bearers of light fittings, so that they didn't stand there without a purpose."

Otto Brückwald

Das versenkte Orchester

Die Idee eines unter der Bühne versenkten und vor den Blicken des Publikums verborgenen Orchesters ist neben dem Amphitheater die wichtigste Anforderung Wagners an sein ideales Theater. Diese Vorgabe hatte bereits Semper für München zu beherzigen und nach ihm Brückwald, der *"die Hauptbedingungen des mir gestellten Bauprogramms hauptsächlich in der Herstellung eines unbedeckten unsichtbaren Orchesters sowie eines Zuschauerraumes für 1.500 Personen, welche einen vollständig freien Einblick über das Orchester nach der Bühne haben sollten"*[1] nennt.

Viel ist über das versenkte Orchester geschrieben und philosophiert worden. Man kann neben visuellen und akustischen Beweggründen auch über psychologische Motive nachdenken. Besonders interessant sind hier die ersten Erlebnisse, die Wagner mit Theaterarchitektur überhaupt machte. Sein Stiefvater, der Schauspieler Geyer, nahm schon den Siebenjährigen mit ins Theater, wo er in einer *"heimlichen Theaterloge mit ihrem Eingange über der Bühne"*[2] sehr unmittelbare Erlebnisse hatte. Auch bei der allerersten Aufführung eines seiner Werke, der B-Dur-Ouvertüre 1830 im Leipziger Theater, versteckte sich Wagner im Theater: *"Ich hatte unter großen Besorgnissen in einem Versteck der Probe beigewohnt"*, das er auch bei der Aufführung benutzte *"und in meiner Unsichtbarkeit recht zufrieden war."*[3] Später bei seinen ersten Erfolgen des RIENZI in Dresden schien es ihm eher peinlich zu sein, beim Applaus immer wieder vom Publikum vor den Vorhang gerufen zu werden. Behaglicher fühlte er sich in der Unsichtbarkeit, die er in Bayreuth schließlich sehr konsequent realisierte.

"Ich bin kein Musiker"[4], schrieb Wagner einmal in einem offenen Schreiben an Friedrich Schön in Worms (1882), kein "normaler" Musiker zumindest, sondern einer, der ein Gesamtkunstwerk schaffen wollte, weshalb das Orchester in den Dienst der Bühne rückte, auf dass die Musik mit der Dichtung und den Bildern auf der Bühne zu einer Einheit verschmolz. Um dieses Ideal in Bayreuth zu realisieren, musste Wagner allerdings kämpfen. Vom 6. September 1874 ist ein Brief an Carl Brandt erhalten: *"Ich kam gestern mit schwerem Herzen von der Besichtigung des Orchesterraumes zurück. Gott weiß, worin hier das Versehen liegt, durch welches dieser Raum unendlich enger ausgefallen ist, als ich es annahm; nur so viel ersehe ich, dass, wenn hier nicht die ausgiebigste Erweiterung bewerkstelligt wird, ich mit der Aufstellung meines Orchesters in gänzlich unlösbare Verlegenheiten geraten muss. Hier kann nichts helfen, als die äußerste Verschiebung des Orchesterraumes unter das Podium, mindestens bis über den ersten Kulissenpfeiler hinaus."*[5] Bauführer Runckwitz wurde mit der Lösung des Problems beauftragt. Er korrigierte den Bauplan, der ebenfalls erhalten ist, mit rotem Stift und der orthografisch etwas flüchtigen Anweisung: *"Das Orcheser muste während des Baues wie rot vergrösert werden."*

Doch damit nicht genug. Am 6. April 1875 schreibt Wagner an Carl Brandt: *"Ich war heute wieder im Theater, und muss [...] eingeste-*

The sunken orchestra

The idea of having the orchestra at a lower level than the stage and concealed from the view of the audience is, along with that of the amphitheater, Wagner's most important demand of his ideal theater. This stipulation had already been heeded by Semper in Munich and after him Brückwald, who writes: *"The main condition of the construction program entrusted to me was to produce an uncovered invisible orchestra as well as an auditorium for 1,500 people, all of whom should have a completely unobstructed view over the orchestra onto the stage."*

Much has been written and philosophized about the sunken orchestra. One can reflect not only upon the visual and acoustic motives but also the psychological ones. Of especial interest here are Wagner's very first experiences with theater architecture. His stepfather, the actor Geyer, once took the 7-year-old boy with him to the theater, where he had a very immediate experience of a *"secret theater loge, the entrance to which was reached over the stage."* In the case of the very first premiere of one of his own works, the B-Major Overture performed at the Leipzig theater in 1830, Wagner hid in the theater: *"I attended the rehearsal with great concern and in concealment"* – in fact he did the same at the premiere itself and *"was rather pleased with my invisibility."* Later, with his first success of the RIENZI in Dresden, he felt rather embarrassed to be called back in front of the curtain repeatedly by the audience for applause. He felt more comfortable when he was invisible and at Bayreuth he finally managed to achieve that in a very consistent way.

"I am not a musician," Wagner once wrote in an open letter to Friedrich Schön in Worms (1882), not a "normal" musician at any rate, but rather one who wanted to create a Gesamtkunstwerk, a total work of art, which is why the orchestra has been placed at the service of the stage, so that the music, the poetry and the images on the stage can merge into a unity. However, in order to be able to achieve this ideal in Bayreuth, Wagner had to struggle. A letter written to Carl Brandt on September 6, 1874 has come down to us: *"Yesterday I came back with a heavy heart from viewing the orchestra area. God knows where the mistake lies here, which has made this space endlessly narrower than I supposed it would be; I only desire this much: that if the most extensive expansion cannot be achieved, then I will be forced to set up my orchestra in a state of wholly inextricable embarrassment. Here nothing can help except the most extreme shifting of the orchestral area beneath the podium, at least out as far as beyond the first column of the backdrop."* The head of construction, Runckwitz, was entrusted with finding a solution to the problem. He corrected the building plan, which has also been preserved, in red pencil and jotted down the instruction: *"During the building work, the orchestra had to be enlarged as marked in red."*

Yet that was not all. On April 4, 1875 Wagner wrote to Carl Brandt: *"I was at the theater again today and had [...] to admit that the architect has utterly misbuilt my orchestra pit. I cannot accommodate my musicians in this space, it is impossible! There remains nothing for it but to remove two rows of seats from the auditorium (which is of no import), and then take down the wall and move it further back."* A few

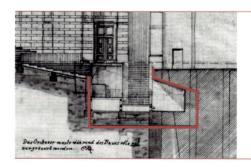

Unter die Bühne vergrößerter Orchestergraben (während des Baus)
Enlargement of the orchestra pit under the stage (during the construction work)

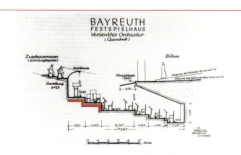

In den Zuschauerraum vergrößerter Orchestergraben
The enlarged orchestra pit in the auditorium

DIE FEEN werden wie andere Frühwerke Wagners nicht in Bayreuth gespielt
Like other early works, DIE FEEN is not performed in Bayreuth

Blick in den Orchestergraben kurz vor der Vorstellung WALKÜRE 2006
View into the orchestra pit just before the performance of WALKÜRE in 2006

hen, dass der Architekt mein Orchester gänzlich verbaut hat. In diesen Raum bringe ich meine Musiker nicht unter, es ist unmöglich! Es wird nichts übrig bleiben, als 2 Sitzreihen vom Zuschauerraum hinweg zu nehmen (was nichts ausmacht), demnach die Mauer wegzunehmen und zurück zu verlegen."[1] Immerhin gingen so einige Dutzend verkäuflicher Plätze verloren, zugunsten des Dirigenten und der Streicher, die zwei Stufenreihen gewannen.

Dieser Umbau wurde laut Habel nach dem 27. Mai ausgeführt, sodass die Proben im Juli im Theater beginnen konnten. Am 24. Juli erklangen erstmals die Rheintöchter von der Bühne und am 1. August nahm das Orchester in seinem Abgrund seine Arbeit auf. Wagner war mit der Akustik sehr zufrieden: *"Das ist es, was ich wollte; jetzt klingen die Blechinstrumente nicht mehr so roh."*[2] Die „Deutsche Rundschau" lobt 1876, *„dass ein zweites Theater in Betreff des Stimm- und Orchesterklanges, sowie in der Vermischung beider (!) diesem gleich – nicht existiert."*[3] Schon bei dem Gesang der Rheintöchter im Juli war Wagner über die „*Klangwirkung des Hauses*"[4], wie Kietz berichtet, sehr zufrieden. Sein akustisch überaus riskantes Konzept war tatsächlich aufgegangen (und sollte sogar noch verbessert werden).

1967/68 wurde der Orchestergraben saniert, wobei der ganze Raum aus Brandschutzgründen zur Bühne hin mit Beton abgeschlossen werden musste. Der durch diesen Umbau um zirka vierzig Kubikmeter vergrößerte Orchestergraben blieb innen mit Holz verkleidet, sodass der Mythos eines durch und durch hölzernen Resonanzraums weiterleben konnte.

Eigene Erfahrungen bestätigen die einzigartige Akustik des Hauses. Man scheint mitten in einer Musik zu sitzen, deren

dozen sellable seats were lost in favor of the director and the string section, who gained two rows of steps.

According to Habel, this alteration was implemented after May 27, so that the rehearsals could begin at the theater in July. On July 24, the daughters of the Rhine were first heard on the stage and on August 1 the orchestra started work in its abyss. Wagner was greatly satisfied with the acoustics: *"This is what I wanted; now the brass instruments do not sound so raw."* In 1876 the "Deutsche Rundschau" praised the fact *"that no other theater like this exists with regard to the sound of the voice and the orchestra, or in a combination of the two (!)."* As Kietz reports, Wagner was very content with the *"sound effects of the building"* even upon hearing the daughters of the Rhine sing in July. His acoustically highly risky concept had in fact turned out to be a success (and would even be improved).

In 1967/68 the orchestra pit was modernized and the whole space had to be closed up with concrete for reasons of fire prevention. As a result of this alteration the orchestra pit was enlarged by approximately forty cubic meter and was paneled with wood, so that the myth of a resonance space made completely of wood could continue to live on.

Personal experiences confirm the unique acoustics of the building. It feels like sitting in the midst of music, the intensity of which was achieved because one never heard the orchestra as loud as it was playing, yet perceived the sound just as intensively. Or, to put it another way, a horn which can play one loud note without being loud sounds more intensive than a horn which has to continuously make an effort to play quietly in an open pit. This effect is particularly noticeable in the contrast between orchestral music and stage music – for example in the use of the stage trumpets after the LOHENGRIN prelude, when the curtain opens.

Beim Einbau eines neuen Lüftungssystems 1990/91 wurde die von Wagner zurückversetzte Backsteinwand des Orchestergrabens wieder sichtbar
During the installation of a new ventilation system in 1990/91 the brick wall of the orchestra pit which Wagner moved further back, could once again be seen

Neue, brandsichere Rückwand des Orchestergrabens zur Unterbühne
New fireproof back wall between the orchestra pit and the sub-stage on the right

Intensität dadurch erreicht wird, dass man das Orchester nie so laut hört, wie es spielt, den Klang aber genauso intensiv wahrnimmt. Anders gesagt: Ein Horn, das einen lauten Ton blasen kann, ohne laut zu sein, klingt intensiver als ein Horn, das sich bei offenen Gräben dauernd bemühen muss, leise zu spielen. Besonders nimmt man diesen Effekt beim Kontrast zwischen Orchestermusik und Bühnenmusik wahr – zum Beispiel beim Einsatz der Bühnentrompeten nach dem LOHENGRIN-Vorspiel, wenn sich der Vorhang öffnet.

Sehr subtil erklingen in Bayreuth die Anfangstöne. Den ersten Ton, den man beim RHEINGOLD vernimmt, ist ein Ton, den es eigentlich gar nicht gibt. Es ist das tiefe Es in den Kontrabässen. Da die Saiten der Kontrabässe aber normalerweise mit dem tiefen E gestimmt sind, müssen die Musiker kurzfristig um einen halben Ton „umstimmen".

Es ist überhaupt interessant, wie Wagner in vielen Werken gleich zu Beginn den Zuschauer in seiner Wahrnehmung irritiert, ihn von seinem inneren und vom Alltag geprägten Rhythmus abholt und in eine andere Welt von akustischem Raum und Zeit entführt. Ob das der unmerklich-unwirkliche Beginn des RHEINGOLD, ob es der synkopisch verschobene Beginn des PARSIFAL ist, ob es die Fermaten und die durch die Intervallstruktur der ersten Töne des TRISTAN-Vorspiels fast zwangsläufigen Rubati sind – man kann nicht wirklich „mitzählen" und man fängt an, seinen inneren Rhythmus aufzugeben und dem Alltag zu entschweben.

Am 14. Juli 1876, also ein Monat vor der Eröffnung der Festspiele, wurde zusätzlich eine konkav gewölbte Sichtblende (Muschel) eingebaut, nicht aus akustischen Gründen, sondern wegen des Streulichts der „Leselampen" (ursprünglich beschirmte Fettöllampen) im Orchestergraben, das die perfekte Illusion gestört hätte. Die nach außen ringförmige Wulst ist heute noch original erhalten, innen schwarz gestrichen, um ebenfalls Streulicht zu absorbieren. 1882 wurde die Abdeckung von der Bühne her hinzugefügt. Immer wieder haben Dirigenten versucht, mit einer anderen Sitzordnung (Karajan) oder Veränderungen dieser Abdeckungen (Solti) zu experimentieren. Zurzeit ist die konvexe Wölbung der Sichtblende durch dünne Platten geschlossen. Diese Details machen den experimentellen Charakter des Bayreuther Festspielhauses deutlich.

In Bayreuth the sound of the initial note is very subtle. The first note that one hears in DAS RHEINGOLD is a note that doesn't actually exist. It is a low E-flat in the double basses. However, since the strings of the double basses are normally tuned to a low E, the musicians have to briefly "retune" by a half a tone.

It is interesting how Wagner confuses the spectators' perception right at the beginning of many of his works, taking them away from the rhythm of what is typical for their inner and everyday world and abducting them into another world of acoustic space and time. Whether it is the imperceptible and unreal start of DAS RHEINGOLD, the syncopically transposed start of PARSIFAL, or the pauses and the almost compelling rubati caused by the interval structure of the first notes of the prelude to TRISTAN – one cannot really "keep count" and begins to give up one's own inner rhythm and drift away from everyday life.

On July 14, 1876, i.e. one month before the opening of the festival, a concave arched screen (shell) was additionally installed, not for acoustic reasons, but rather on account of the scattered light of the "reading lamps" (originally shaded oil lamps) in the orchestra pit, which would have destroyed the perfect illusion. The bulge, which is ring-shaped toward the outside, is today preserved as an original, painted black on the inside, in order to also be able to absorb scattered light. In 1882 the covering from the stage side was added. Conductors have repeatedly attempted to experiment with a different seating arrangement (Karajan) or by making changes to this covering (Solti). At present, the convex vaulting of the screen is closed off with thin plates. These details clearly demonstrate the experimental character of the Bayreuth Festspielhaus.

„Nicht präludieren. Piano pianissimo – dann gelingt alles."

"Don't prelude. Piano pianissimo – then everything will work."

Letzte Bitte Wagners an das Orchester (am 13. August 1876)[1]
Wagner's last request to the orchestra on August 13, 1876

Ein Teil der Porträts aller seit 1876 in Bayreuth tätigen Dirigenten im Gang vom Orchesterraum zur Kantine
Some of the portraits of all the conductors who have conducted in Bayreuth since 1876 in the corridor from the orchestra space to the canteen

Souffleusen-/Souffleurkasten, rechts Leiter zu demselben
Prompting box, on the right the ladder to it

1882 ließ Wagner kurz vor der Uraufführung des PARSIFAL zusätzlich eine hölzerne Schallblende zur Bühnenseite hin einbauen, die das Orchester nach oben hin fast völlig verbirgt
In 1882, shortly before the premiere of PARSIFAL, Wagner had an additional wooden sound screen built toward the stage, which almost completely concealed the orchestra from above

Der Kaiser höchstpersönlich ließ sich 1876 von Wagner den Orchestergraben zeigen, „um, wie er scherzend sagte, auch den Ort kennen zu lernen, wo ‚seine Hofmusiker schwitzen müssten'"[1]. Dies geschieht fast jeden Sommer seit einhundertdreißig Jahren tatsächlich, weshalb die Musiker ihre Unsichtbarkeit für leichte und legere Bekleidung nutzen. Nur die wenigsten Instrumente (Bratschen und Celli) haben Luft nach oben; die Violinen sitzen unter der muschelförmigen Abdeckung vor der ersten Zuschauerreihe. Die anderen Instrumente sitzen unter der Abdeckung vor dem Proszenium oder unter der Bühne. Man hört von der Bühne kaum etwas und es ist schrecklich laut.

Für mehr Armfreiheit der zweiten Geigen hat Wolfgang Wagner, selbst gelernter Musiker, gar die halbe Wand unter der „Muschel" um zirka 20 Zentimeter ausweiten lassen. Die Geigen sitzen in Bayreuth anders als sonst üblich: erste Geigen rechts, zweite Geigen links, damit durch die Haltung der Musiker der Klang der ersten Geigen ungehindert auf die Bühne und nicht in die Abdeckung geht. Eine weitere Kuriosität ist das „Klarinettengitter", wo Wolfgang Wagner eine Stufe herausbrechen und durch ein Gitter ersetzen ließ, damit die Klarinetten nicht gegen eine Stufe spielen, sondern der Ton ungehindert nach oben entweichen kann.

Wann weiß das unsichtbare Orchester in seinem dunklen Abgrund eigentlich, wann die Vorstellung beginnen soll? Alle schauen auf den Dirigenten und dieser auf eine Art Ampel, die mit dem Licht im Zuschauerraum gekoppelt ist, sodass Dirigent und Musiker wissen, wie die Situation in der Oberwelt ist. Wenn hier langsam das Licht verlöscht, leuchten kurz vor dem Einsatz nochmals zwei rote „Alarmleuchten" an der vorderen Seite des Dirigentenpults auf, damit auch der ganz hinten und unten sitzende Musiker weiß, dass es jetzt Ernst wird.

In 1876, even the Emperor personally had Wagner show him the orchestra pit, *"in order, as he jokingly said, to be able to know the place where 'his court musicians have to sweat.'"* This has been going on for almost every summer for one hundred and thirty years, which is why the musicians take advantage of their invisibility to be able to wear light and casual clothes. Only very few instrument (violas and celli) have any space upwards; the violins sit under the shell-shaped covering in front of the first row of spectators. The other instruments sit under the covering in front of the proscenium or beneath the stage. Not only can one hardly hear anything from the stage, but it is also terribly loud.

To allow the second violin more arm movement, Wolfgang Wagner, himself a trained musician, had half the wall under the "shell" extended by approximately twenty centimeters. In Bayreuth the violins sit differently than usual: first violin right, second violin left, so that through the posture of the musicians the sound of the 1st violin goes unimpeded onto the stage and not into the covering. A further curiosity is the "clarinet screen," where Wolfgang Wagner had one step broken out and replaced by a screen, so that the clarinets do not play against a step but the sound can escape unhindered upwards.

When does the invisible orchestra in its dark abyss actually know when the performance should start? Everyone looks at the conductor and he looks at a kind of traffic light, which is connected to the light in the auditorium, so that the conductor and the musicians know what the situation is in the world above them. When here the light gradually goes out, two red "alarm lamps" light up briefly before the start on the front side of the conductor's desk, so that those musicians sitting right at the back and underneath also know that things are getting serious.

Podest, Pult und Stuhl des Dirigenten. Berühmt ist die Klappe von 1882, über die Wagner vom Zuschauerraum aus Kontakt zum Dirigenten aufnehmen konnte. Bald sorgten Telefone für eine interne Kommunikation. Eine Ampel im Graben signalisiert dem Orchester den Beginn der Vorstellung. Für frische Luft sorgen Belüftungsdüsen im Podest des Dirigenten.
Conductor's platform, desk and chair. The famous flap of 1882, through which Wagner could contact the conductor from the auditorium. Telephones soon made internal communication more easily possible. A traffic light in the pit informs the orchestra about the start of the performance. Ventilation boxes in the conductor's platform provide fresh air.

Das sogenannte Klarinettengitter im Boden des Orchestergrabens
The so-called "clarinet screen" in the floor of the orchestra pit

Mehr Armfreiheit für die zweiten Geigen durch eine nachträglich „ausgebeulte" Wand
The wall was later "curved out" to give the 2nd violins more arm freedom

Zugang zum Orchestergraben hinter der ersten Proszeniumswand
Access to the orchestra pit behind the first proscenium wall

Originaltür von 1876 zum Graben mit Sanitätertrage
Original door to pit from 1876 with medical stretcher

Pierre Boulez
"Ein einzigartiges Objekt und Modell"

Pierre Boulez
"A unique object and a model"

Siegfried Wagner hat einmal geschrieben: „Der Dirigent spielt in Bayreuth die 2. Rolle ..." Fühlt man sich – als Dirigent wie als Musiker – zurückgesetzt, weil man in einem abgedeckten Orchestergraben sitzt beziehungsweise dirigiert, oder spielt man nicht auch eventuell freier, weil unbeobachtet?
Ja sicher. Es gibt einen Vorteil und einen Nachteil. Vorteil: Man fühlt sich lockerer. Nachteil: Die Musiker glauben, sie werden nicht gehört. Vor allem jene Kollegen, die ganz unten spielen, also Posaunen und Blech. Für sie ist sehr schwer, da sie während der Vorstellung keinen der Sänger hören können. Und daher denken viele in umgekehrter Richtung: Wenn ich die Sänger oben nicht höre, hört man mich oben im Publikum – oder auf der Bühne – auch nicht. Und das ist natürlich vollkommen falsch, weil die Akustik in Bayreuth im Gegenteil sehr viel unterstützt und trägt. Der Beginn von RHEINGOLD zum Beispiel ist ja vom ersten piano-Ton überall in voller Deutlichkeit zu hören. Kurz: Die Musiker glauben, wenn sie nicht gesehen werden, hört man sie auch nicht. Es gibt ein psychologisches Phänomen ähnlicher Art: In der Dunkelheit der Nacht sprechen Sie automatisch lauter.

Sie haben einmal geschrieben, dass „die Haupteigenschaft seines [Bayreuths] akustischen Raumes darin besteht, Deutlichkeit und Verschmelzung miteinander zu paaren". Aber ist der abgedeckte Orchestergraben nicht ein Problem für die Kommunikation zwischen Sängern und Musikern?
Komischerweise ist der Dirigent der Einzige, der diese Verbindung herstellen kann. Ich stehe zum Beispiel immer, wenn ich dirigiere; und von der Position des Dirigenten in Bayreuth sieht man alles, was man sehen muss. Ich mache auch sehr wenige körperliche Bewegungen und versuche in meiner Gestik sparsam zu sein. Aber ich sehe ganz genau auch die weit entfernt sitzenden Musiker und bemerke ihre Konzentration und Reaktionen. Man hat einen falschen Eindruck, wenn man denkt, der Dirigent sitzt da unten weit ab vom Geschehen. Das braucht ein bisschen Zeit, bis man sich an diese Verhältnisse gewöhnt hat; aber dann kann man mit der Akustik spielen und experimentieren.

Jeder Orchestergraben – auch wenn er offen ist – hat seine eigene Akustik, die mit der des eigentlichen Theaterraums, und zwar Bühne und Zuschauerraum, in ein Verhältnis gebracht werden muss. Wie beurteilen Sie diese Extremsituation in Bayreuth?
Diese Situation ist gar nicht problematisch, sondern im Gegenteil, sie hilft bei einer für mich wesentlichen Problematik: Sehen Sie, man hat immer über mich gesagt, das ist „transparent" und manchmal auch, es ist zu „dünn" und so weiter, aber ich habe es eben gern, wenn die Sänger nicht dauernd brüllen müssen und überhaupt dauernd laut singen. Diese schlechte Gewohnheit führt ja zu einer völlig monotonen Ausdrucksweise beziehungsweise zeugt von einem andauernden Mangel an Ausdruck überhaupt.

Für den RING ist das Theater gebaut worden. Haben dann die Architektur beziehungsweise die Erfahrungen des RING von 1876

Siegfried Wagner once wrote: "The conductor plays a supporting role in Bayreuth…" As a conductor and musician, do you feel neglected sitting and conducting in a covered orchestra pit, or are you freed up because you are not being observed?
Yes, of course. It has advantages and disadvantages. The advantage: you feel more relaxed. The disadvantage: the instrumentalists think the audience can't hear them. Especially players seated way down at the bottom, trombones and brass. It is difficult for them because they can't hear any of the singers during the performance. So many of them conclude that if they can't hear the singers on the stage, the audience – or the singers on the stage – can't hear them either. And of course that is completely erroneous. The opposite is true. The acoustics at Bayreuth support and carry the sound. For example, the beginning of DAS RHEINGOLD is clearly audible from everywhere from the very first piano tone. In short, the musicians believe that if they can't be seen, they can't be heard either. There's a similar psychological phenomenon where you automatically talk louder in the darkness of night.

You once wrote that "the main feature of its [Bayreuth's] acoustical space is that it combines clarity and blending." But doesn't the covered orchestra pit make it difficult for the singers and the instrumentalists to communicate?
Strangely enough, the conductor is the only person who can achieve this connection. For example, I always conduct standing up, and from the vantage point of the conductor in Bayreuth, you can see everything you need to see. I do not make a lot of physical gestures and try to keep them to a minimum. But I can see the musicians very well, even those sitting far away from me, and notice their concentration and reactions. It's wrong to think that the conductor sits down there far removed from the action. It takes a little while to get used to these conditions, but then you can play and experiment with the acoustics.

Every orchestra pit – even if it is open – has its own acoustics that have to be adapted to the actual theater space, the stage and the auditorium. What is your opinion of this extreme situation in Bayreuth?
This situation is not at all problematic. On the contrary, it helps me overcome a key difficulty: You see, people have always called my tone "transparent," and sometimes too "thin", etc. But I like it when the singers don't have to shout or even just sing forte all the time. This bad habit leads to completely monotonous expression or demonstrates a long-term lack of expression in the first place.

The theater was built for DER RING DES NIBELUNEN. Did the architecture or the experiences from the 1876 performance of DER RING influence how Wagner composed PARSIFAL? Put another way, did the architecture of the Bayreuth Festspielhaus leave an imprint on PARSIFAL?
Yes absolutely. Wagner was more careful when he composed PARSIFAL. After the experiences with DER RING, and especially a few passages in DIE GÖTTERDÄMMERUNG he was much more careful in PARSIFAL about balancing the orchestra with the singers. Take for example the big scene between 'Kundry' and 'Parsifal' in Act 2. He said he wanted the orchestra to be a cothurn for the singers. Like what the actors have

die Komposition des PARSIFAL beeinflusst? Anders gefragt: Ist die Architektur des Bayreuther Festspielhauses an der Partitur des PARSIFAL ablesbar?

Ja absolut. Wagner war beim PARSIFAL vorsichtiger. Nach den Erfahrungen des RING – vor allem bei einigen Stellen der GÖTTERDÄMMERUNG – war er beim PARSIFAL viel behutsamer, was die Behandlung des Orchesters im Verhältnis zu den Singstimmen betrifft. Gerade in der großen Szene zwischen „Kundry" und „Parsifal" im zweiten Aufzug. Er hat auch gesagt, ich möchte, dass das Orchester für die Sänger wie ein Kothurn ist. Wie im griechischen Theater unter den Schuhen der Schauspieler. Es geht darum, den Sänger hervorzuheben, nicht ihn zu töten!

Gibt es eine Schallverzögerung zwischen Orchestergraben, Bühne und Zuschauerraum? Man liest immer wieder von dem Phänomen, der Schall brauche eine gewisse Zeit vom Graben auf die Bühne und von dort – vermischt – in den Zuschauerraum. Wie bewältigt man diese großen akustischen Entfernungen? Oder anders gefragt: Muss man in Bayreuth anders dirigieren als anderswo auf der Welt?

Also man darf nicht nachgeben. Wenn die Sänger oder Chöre ganz hinten sind, entspricht das etwa einer Sechstelsekunde, die der Klang länger braucht, um nach vorne zu kommen. Diese Sechstelsekunde hört man natürlich. Wesentlich ist – und das ist immer das Erste, was ich sage: Nie auf den Ton warten, bis man ihn hört, sondern immer optisch mit dem Schlag singen – egal, was man als Sänger selbst auf irgendeiner Position der Bühne hört. Das klingt etwas technisch, aber es funktioniert. Es gab ja 1876 oder 1882 und noch später keine elektronischen Übertragungen des Dirigenten oder des Orchesters auf die Bühne. Weder akustisch mit Lautsprechern noch optisch mit Monitoren. Das heißt, man hat entweder durch kleine Löcher auf den Dirigenten geschaut oder man musste eben auf den Toneinsatz warten – sobald man ihn gehört hat. Und das multipliziert sich ja. Der eine wartet, der andere wartet und so weiter. Vielleicht sind deshalb die Aufführungen von 1882 bis vor dem Krieg immer langsamer geworden ...

Haben Sie Bayreuth und das Festspielhaus schon gekannt, bevor Sie dort selbst inszeniert haben?

Nein. Ich habe das Haus in derselben Zeit für mich entdeckt, als ich dort 1966 den PARSIFAL gemacht habe. In diesem Jahr habe ich natürlich auch andere Vorstellungen und Proben gehört. Wieland Wagner hat mich gewarnt, dass es viele Dirigentenkollegen gegeben hätte, die mit den akustischen Verhältnissen nicht fertig geworden wären.

Beeinflusst das im Hinterkopf stets präsente Gebäude, also die Wirkung des Ortes und die Architektur selbst, ein musikalisches Konzept? Hatten Sie als Dirigent mit der vorhandenen Architektur für sich die Möglichkeiten gesehen, dort etwas zu machen, was Sie woanders nicht machen konnten?

Als ich das erste Mal nach Bayreuth gekommen bin, hat mich Wolf-Siegfried Wagner, der Sohn von Wieland Wagner, am Flughafen abgeholt. Es war schon später am Tag, also keine Probe mehr, und er fragte mich, ob ich vor dem Hotel noch erst das Theater sehen wollte. Ich sagte, ja natürlich. Und ich kam in den Graben und stand vor einer Skulptur Richard Wagners – einer Raumskulptur.

Wagner hat kurz vor der Uraufführung des RING an die Künstler geschrieben: „Deutlichkeit! Die kleinen Noten und ihr Text sind das wichtigste." Wie schafft man nun – trotz der Abdeckung über dem Graben und dem großen Proszenium, also einer sehr großen Entfernung der Sänger zum Publikum – die erforderliche Dichte und Präsenz?

Georg Solti, der gleich nach mir 1983 den RING dirigiert hat, hat mich einmal gefragt, wie das mit dem Mischklang und dem Verhältnis zwischen Bühne und Graben sei, wonach man sich also orientieren kann. Ich habe einen Vergleich zu Hilfe geholt: Wenn under their shoes in Greek theater. It's about accentuating the singers, not killing them!

Is there a sound delay between the orchestra pit, the stage and the auditorium? You often read about the phenomenon that the sound needs time to rise up out of the pit onto the stage and then from there – mixed – into the auditorium. How can you overcome this large acoustical distance? Put another way: do you have to conduct differently in Bayreuth than anywhere else in the world?

You can't let up. If the singers or the chorus are far upstage, it takes the sound about one sixth of a second longer to travel. Naturally you can hear this one sixth of a second. The important thing – and that's always the first thing I say: never wait to hear the tone, but rather sing when you see the beat optically – no matter what you hear as a singer from any position on stage. That sounds a bit technical, but it works. The conductor and the orchestra weren't electronically conveyed onto the stage in 1876 or in 1882 or even later. Neither acoustically with speakers nor optically with monitors. That meant you had to look through tiny holes to see the conductor or you had to wait to hear the entrance – if you could hear it at all. And that all adds up. One person waits, the other person waits, etc. Maybe that's why the performances got slower and slower from 1882 until before the war…

Did you know Bayreuth and the Festspielhaus before you first conducted there yourself?

No. I discovered the theater for myself during the same time I conducted PARSIFAL there for the first time in 1966. Naturally I heard other performances and rehearsals there that year. Wieland Wagner had warned me that many other conductors couldn't come to grips with the acoustic conditions.

Does having the building in the back of your mind, the effect of the location and the architecture itself influence your musical concept? Did the architecture inspire you as a conductor to do something there that you couldn't do somewhere else?

The first time I came to Bayreuth, Wolf-Siegfried Wagner, Wieland Wagner's son, picked me up at the airport. It was already late in the day, so there were no more rehearsals that day. He asked me if I wanted to see the theater before he brought me to the hotel. I entered the pit and stood facing a sculpture of Richard Wagner – a spatial sculpture.

Shortly before the premiere of DER RING, Wagner wrote a note to the artists that said: "Clarity! The little notes and their text are the most important." How do you create the required density and presence – despite the cover over the pit and the large proscenium, the large distance between the singers and the audience?

Georg Solti, who directed DER RING right after me in 1983, once asked me about mixing the sound and about the relationship between the stage and the pit – what you have to go on. In responding, I drew a comparison: If you're swimming on your back with your ears under water and you can't hear a thing, the orchestra is too loud. If your ears are all the way out of the water, the orchestra is too soft. If the water is right in the middle and you have the impression that the singers are just a little too weak, then it's wonderful. That was my experience, in any case. – That reminds me of my first stage orchestra rehearsal for PARSIFAL. At the end of the first scene, the trombones from the stage music have a big crescendo that I didn't hear. I was shocked, wondering why I didn't hear it from my position. But I had conducted too fast and the musicians weren't yet in position on stage … for once it wasn't the acoustics at all!

Does Wagner's vision really work, even though the theater was actually built "blindly" for the premiere of DER RING? That is, is the Bayreuth Festspielhaus a "good" theater by modern standards?

At the time it was built, it was a coincidence and at the same time not a coincidence. You know that the Bayreuth Festspielhaus was "copied" to build the Prinzregententheater in Munich, and that it didn't work there. I don't know why. Maybe stone and marble were used in Munich and were the wrong materials. It had to be cheap in Bayreuth, and what is there plenty of here in the Fichtelgebirge? – Wood! Wood is more alive and resonant.

Sie im Wasser auf dem Rücken schwimmen und die Ohren sind unter Wasser und Sie hören gar nichts, dann ist das Orchester zu laut. Wenn Sie die Ohren ganz aus dem Wasser haben, dann ist das Orchester zu leise. Wenn Sie das Wasser gerade in der Mitte und den Eindruck haben, die Sänger sind nur ein bisschen schwach, dann ist es wunderbar. Das war jedenfalls meine Erfahrung. – Ich erinnere mich in diesem Zusammenhang an meine erste Bühnenorchesterprobe des PARSIFAL. Am Ende des ersten Aufzugs gibt es die Posaunen der Bühnenmusik mit einem großen crescendo, das ich nicht gehört habe. Ich war sehr erschrocken, da ich dachte, warum höre ich das hier auf meiner Position nicht. Aber ich war nur zu schnell mit meinem Dirigat und die Musiker waren noch nicht auf ihren Plätzen auf der Bühne angekommen ... Das war also ausnahmsweise gar nicht die Akustik!

Funktioniert Wagners Vision tatsächlich, obwohl das Theater ja eigentlich „blind" auf die Uraufführung des RING hin gebaut wurde? Ist das Bayreuther Festspielhaus nach heutigen Anforderungen also ein „gutes" Theater?
In der Zeit, als es gebaut wurde, war das Zufall und gleichzeitig nicht Zufall. Sie wissen, dass das Bayreuther Festspielhaus im Prinzregententheater in München „nachgebaut" wurde, und dort hat es nicht funktioniert. Ich weiß nicht warum, vielleicht hat man in München mit Stein und Marmor falsches Material benutzt. In Bayreuth musste das billig sein, und was gibt es hier im Fichtelgebirge? – Holz! Das ist lebendiger und klingt.

Wo stößt die Immobilie an ihre Grenzen? Oder anders gefragt, was könnte man verbessern, nach – mit Unterbrechungen – fast vierzig Jahren Arbeit dort, sechsundneunzig Vorstellungen und Ihren internationalen Erfahrungen?
Nein, nichts. Es ist jetzt ein einzigartiges Objekt und ein Modell.

Sehen Sie eine Chance oder Tendenz für die weitere künstlerische Entwicklung Bayreuths in der Frage oder Forderung nach einem historischen Instrumentarium (also nach Instrumenten aus der Mitte des 19. Jahrhunderts) verbunden mit vibratolosem Spiel und so weiter, also nach all dem, was man unter dem Begriff „historische Aufführungspraxis" subsumieren könnte?
Ich kann das für die Barockmusik nachvollziehen. Aber ich bin gegen diesen Historizismus beziehungsweise „Hysterizismus". Warum: Man spricht zum Beispiel in Frankreich viel über Berlioz. Man will zurück zu den Instrumenten der Jahre der Uraufführung der „Symphonie phantastique" 1830. Aber als Berlioz selbst dreißig Jahre später dieses Werk wieder aufgeführt hat, hat er selbstverständlich zu den neuesten Instrumenten gegriffen. Viele ältere Instrumente – Naturhörner und andere – konnten vieles nicht ausführen und man war froh, endlich chromatische Hörner zu haben. Auch Beethoven war froh, wenn er ein modernes Klavier hatte. Das Problem der historischen Authentizität über das Instrumentarium zu lösen ist eine Phantasmagorie, die nichts mit der Realität zu tun hat, eine Purifizierung – wie bei Violet Le Duc –, die nichts bringt. Im Französischen gibt es den Satz, „sei nicht goethischer als Goethe"...

Where does the theater run into limits? Put differently, what could be improved in your opinion after nearly forty years of working there (with interruptions), ninety-six performances and your international experiences?
No, nothing. It is a unique object and a model just the way it is.

Do you see an opportunity or a tendency for Bayreuth's further artistic development regarding or in support of historic instrumentation (that is, instruments from the middle of the 19th century) combined with playing sans vibrato, and everything else that could be included under the term "historical performance practice?"
I can see the advantages for Baroque music. But I am against this historicism, or "hystericism." Why? For example, in France there's a lot of talk about Berlioz. People want to go back to the instruments used for the premiere of the "Symphonie Phantastique" in 1830. But when Berlioz himself performed this work 30 years later, he naturally made use of the most modern instruments. Many older instruments – natural horns and such – weren't capable of playing everything, and it was good to finally have chromatic horns. Beethoven was also happy to have a modern piano. Solving historical authenticity by using old instruments is a phantasmagoria and has nothing to do with reality, a purification – like with Violet Le Duc – that isn't worth the effort. In French we have the saying "Don't be more Goethey than Goethe."

You are not only one of the most important composers and conductors in the music world. A question to the Director of IRCAM: Why didn't Bayreuth have any consequences in theater architecture?
I don't know and I can't explain it. Back in the day, I spoke with the steering committee for the new Opéra Bastille in Paris. There were no musicians on this board and as vice president I was asked to advise the commission. I proposed building a flexible orchestra pit. Of course not like in Bayreuth, where everything is permanently installed and immoveable, but rather incrementally horizontally mobile with variable covers in different zones, depending on the instrumental groupings – something like the landing flaps on an airplane. This would not have been difficult to solve technically. It was really a missed opportunity! – In 1875, the same year that the Opéra Garnier opened in Paris, the Festspielhaus in Bayreuth was ready for rehearsals. In Paris, a theater had been built in the tradition of the grand imperial theaters, and in Bayreuth a completely novel building – with a brand new concept. Paris became the model for most new theaters built in the 19th century in Europe, and therefore for the world. Bayreuth, on the contrary, remained completely isolated. To this day, I don't understand that. I don't want to embarrass architects, but I have the impression that they rarely go to the opera. If they have to build a theater, they often have no idea about the specific problems. So they take an existing model and make it a little bit more modern – but the concept is exactly the same as it has been for two hundred, three hundred years! Basically a big Baroque theater.

Wagner built his Festspielhaus based on two basic biographical experiences: he had experienced the perfect production conditions in the Paris Opera on the one hand and the desolate conditions in the German repertory theater on the other. Today even "provincial" theaters work seriously, rehearse long and perform works in historical-critical editions.

Sie sind nicht nur als Komponist und Dirigent eine der bedeutendsten Persönlichkeiten der Musikwelt. Aber noch eine Frage an den Direktor des IRCAM: Warum hat Bayreuth keine Konsequenzen in der Theaterarchitektur gezeitigt?
Ich weiß es nicht und es mir auch unerklärlich. Ich war seinerzeit in der Beratungskommission für den Neubau der Opéra Bastille in Paris. Man hatte in diesem Gremium keinen Musiker und ich sollte als Vizepräsident die Kommission beraten. Ich habe vorgeschlagen, einen Orchestergraben zu konstruieren, der flexibel ist. Natürlich nicht wie in Bayreuth, wo alles fest installiert und unbeweglich ist, sondern mobil, stufenweise in der Horizontalen fahrbar und die Abdeckungen in verschiedenen Feldern veränderbar je nach den Instrumentgruppen – also etwa wie bei den Landeklappen von Flugzeugen. Man hätte das mit den technischen Möglichkeiten problemlos machen können. Es war wirklich eine verpasste Gelegenheit! – 1875, im selben Jahr, als in Paris die Opéra Garnier eröffnet wurde, war auch das Festspielhaus in Bayreuth bereits für die Proben fertig. Dort in Paris war ein Theater in der Tradition der großen Hoftheater entstanden, und hier in Bayreuth ein vollkommen neuartiger Bau – vor allem mit neuem Konzept. Paris wurde Vorbild für die meisten Theaterneubauten des 19. Jahrhunderts in Europa und damit für die Welt, Bayreuth hingegen blieb vollkommen isoliert. Das ist mir bis heute ein Rätsel geblieben. Ich will die Architekten ja nicht blamieren, aber ich habe den Eindruck, sie gehen selten in die Oper. Wenn sie dann ein Theater bauen müssen, haben sie oft keine Ahnung von den spezifischen Problemen. Also nehmen sie ein Modell, das schon da ist, das macht man ein bisschen moderner – aber als Konzept ist das genau dasselbe wie seit zweihundert, dreihundert Jahren! Im Grunde ein größeres Barocktheater.

Wagner baute sein Festspielhaus aufgrund zweier grundlegender biografischer Erfahrungen: Zum einen kannte er die perfekten Produktionsbedingungen an der Pariser Oper und zum anderen die desolaten Zustände im deutschen Repertoirebetrieb. Heute wird doch auch in der „Provinz" seriös gearbeitet, recht lange geprobt, die Werke in historisch-kritischen Ausgaben aufgeführt. Der RING ist heute problemlos an den großen, aber auch an mittleren Häusern respektabel realisierbar. Man versucht den Intentionen des Autors mit der Betreuung von einem Heer von Dramaturgen möglichst nahe zu kommen und sie zu respektieren. Ist Bayreuth nicht überflüssig geworden?
Nein. Für mich muss und wird das ein Modell bleiben. Zwar konzipiert von *einem* Komponisten für *seine* Stücke. Aber das Konzept ist richtig. Was man jetzt braucht – nach mehr als hundert Jahren dazwischen –, ist ein Diskussion über Materialien, also darüber, wie man heute bauen kann. Man müsste mit Architekten wie Frank O. Gehry sprechen, der eine heutige Form finden müsste, die interessant wäre. Und man braucht Architekten, die etwas von Musik verstehen!

Das Gespräch führte Markus Kiesel.

It is not a problem for any large or even medium-sized theater to put on a respectable performance of DER RING. A veritable army of dramaturges help us satisfy and respect the author's intention as nearly as possible. Hasn't Bayreuth become superfluous?
No. In my mind, it must and will remain a model. Granted, conceptualized by *one* composer for *his* works. But the concept works. What we need now – now that over a hundred years have passed – is to have a discussion about materials, that is, about how it is possible to build today. Architects like Frank O. Gehry should be called on to find a modern form that is interesting. We need architects who know something about music!

Conversation with Markus Kiesel.

Pierre Boulez wurde am 26. März 1925 in Montbrison (Loire) geboren. Er studierte unter anderem bei Olivier Messiaen und René Leibowitz. 1954 gelang ihm der Durchbruch als Komponist, gleichzeitig hatte er Erfolge als Dirigent. Ab 1978 widmete sich Pierre Boulez überwiegend seiner Arbeit im „Institut de Recherche et de Coordination Acoustique/Musique" (IRCAM) im Pariser Centre Pompidou, ist Präsident des von ihm gegründeten L'Ensemble intercontemporain, eines der besten Orchester für zeitgenössische Musik. Dreimal dirigierte er in Bayreuth spektakuläre Inszenierungen, den PARSIFAL von Wieland Wagner 1966 bis 1970, den „Jahrhundert"-RING von Patrice Chéreau 1976 bis 1980 sowie 2004 und 2005 den PARSIFAL von Christoph Schlingensief. Pierre Boulez gehört zu den wichtigsten Gestalten des zeitgenössischen Musikgeschehens.

Pierre Boulez was born on March 26, 1925 in Montbrison (Loire). He studied under Olivier Messiaen and René Leibowitz. In 1954 he witnessed his breakthrough as a composer and had big success as a conductor. From 1978 on, Boulez dedicated himself largely to the "Institut de Recherche et de Coordination Acoustique/Musique" (IRCAM) in the Centre Pompidou in Paris and is president of L'Ensemble intercontemporain, which he had founded and which is one of the leading orchestras for modern music. He directed three spectacular productions in Bayreuth: Wieland Wagner's PARSIFAL from 1966 to 1970, Patrice Chéreau's "Centennial" RING from 1976 to 1980, and Christoph Schlingensief's PARSIFAL in 2004 and 2005. Pierre Boulez is one of the most important figures in the modern music scene.

Eiserner Vorhang zum Zuschauerraum
Iron curtain facing auditorium

Die Bühne

Die Bühnentechnik

In Fragen der Bühnentechnik und allen anderen technischen Realitäten eines Theaters war Wagner kaum kundig und reflektiert, sodass sich in seinen Schriften darüber kaum etwas findet. So wie Wagner beim Bau seines Theaters von den Architekten und Bauführern Brückwald und Runckwitz abhängig war, hieß sein Mann für die Bühnentechnik Carl Brandt, den Wagner in seinem Rückblick von 1878 als einen *"ebenso energischen als einsichtigen und erfinderischen Mann"* beschreibt, welcher *"meine Hauptstütze bei der Durchführung meines ganzen Planes ward."*[1] Brandts Aufgabe war es, *"eine Bühneneinrichtung von vollendetster Zweckmäßigkeit für die Ausführung der kompliziertesten szenischen Vorgänge"* einzurichten und dafür Sorge zu tragen, dass die *"Dekorationen in wahrhaft künstlerischer Absicht"*[2] ausgeführt werden. Wie das geschehen sollte, überließ er Brandt, denn Technik an sich war Wagner eher suspekt; sie war ihm ausschließlich Mittel zum Zweck, seine Visionen zu ermöglichen. *"Wagner schwärmt im Idealen. Alles Reale liegt ihm zu fern"*[3], klagte Carl Brandt.

Die wichtigste Forderung Wagners war, dass alle Technik am Ende unsichtbar blieb. Denn sein ganzes Theater war auf eine perfekte Illusion angelegt, weshalb für den Zuschauer alle *"Fäden, Schnüre, Leisten und Bretter der Theaterdekorationen"*[4] verborgen bleiben mussten, im gleichen Maße wie das Orchester. Diese geisterhafte Bühnentechnik war für Wagner ein Teil des Gesamtkunstwerks, der Synergie aller Kräfte: *"Nur bei genauer Kenntnis des ganzen dichterischen Gegenstandes, und nach einem sorgfältigen Vernehmen mit dem Regisseur, und selbst dem Kapellmeister, über dessen Darstellung kann es dem Dekorationsmaler und Maschinisten gelingen, die Bühne so herzurichten, wie es erforderlich ist."*[5]

Das alles klingt wieder sehr utopisch, doch was Wagner von Brandt in Bayreuth forderte, ging über den Rahmen des technisch Bekannten nicht hinaus – erstaunlicherweise. Als Gewährsmann lässt sich Otto Brückwald zitieren: *"Die Bühne, deren Dimensionen und Einrichtungen durch den Großherzoglichen Darmstädtischen Hoftheater Maschinenmeister Carl Brandt für diese Aufführung speziell entworfen waren, hat in seiner Ober- und Untermaschinerie anderen großen und neueren Theatern gegenüber keine wesentlich anderen Einrichtungen aufzuweisen."*[6]

Lediglich die Anhäufung der bühnentechnischen Effekte war ungewöhnlich. Viel ist darüber geschrieben worden, dass diese Möglichkeiten nicht ausgereicht hätten, Wagners poetische Visionen zu realisieren und seiner eigenen Fantasie gerecht zu werden. So war Wagner nach der großen RHEINGOLD-Premiere am 13. August 1876 nicht glücklich: Die Vollendung der Architektur wird mit keinem Wort als feierlicher oder erlösender Moment gewürdigt. Wagner war nahezu ausschließlich an der Inszenierung seines Gesamtkunstwerks auf der Bühne interessiert, und von dieser war er enttäuscht!

Cosima, die seit dem 7. August in ihrem Tagebuch geschwiegen hatte, berichtet vom 13. August: *"Erste RHEINGOLD-Aufführung mit vollständigem Unstern, Betz* [Sänger des Wotan] *verliert den Ring, läuft zweimal in die Kulissen während des Fluches, ein Arbeiter zieht den Prospekt zu früh bei der ersten Verwandlung heraus und man sieht die Leute in Hemdärmeln da stehn und die Hinterwand des Theaters, alle Sänger befangen etc. etc. – Jeder kehrt seinerseits heim, R. zuerst sehr verstimmt, heitert nach und nach auf …"*[7] Nachdem die ersten Festspiele verrauscht waren, flohen die Wagners nach Italien in den Urlaub. Hier wurde resümiert: *"Vielfache Gedanken an vollständiges Aufgeben der Festspiele und Verschwinden."* Am 9. September schreibt Cosima:

The stage

Stage technology

Wagner was hardly knowledgeable and reflective in questions of stage technology and all the other technical matters of the theater, so there is hardly any mention about such matters in his writings. Just as Wagner was dependent upon the architect and building supervisor Brückwald and Runckwitz when building the theater, his stage technology point person was Carl Brandt, whom Wagner describes in his review of 1878 as an *"equally energetic, reasonable and inventive man,"* who is *"my main support in implementing my whole plan."* Brandt's task was to set up *"stage equipment with great intent for implementing the most complicated scenic processes"* and making sure that the *"decorations are set up with a truly artistic intention."* He left it up to Brandt how that should be done, since Wagner was rather suspicious of technical matters as such; they were for him simply a means to an end, of putting his visions into practice. *"Wagner gets carried away by ideals. Everything real is too distant,"* complained Carl Brandt.

Wagner's most important demand was that all the technical matters should remain invisible at the end. After all, his whole theater was based on a perfect illusion, which is why all the *"strings, ropes, frames and boards of the theater decoration"* had to remain hidden, to the same extent as the orchestra. This ghostlike stagecraft was for Wagner part of the Gesamtkunstwerk, the synergy of all powers: *"Only with exact knowledge of the whole poetic object, and after a careful discussion with the stage director, and even with the musical director, about the presentation, can the decorative painter and technicians manage to set up the stage in the way that is required."*

That all sounds very utopian once again, yet what Wagner demanded from Brandt in Bayreuth did not overstep the bounds of what was technically known – astonishingly enough. Otto Brückwald (1904) can vie for this statement's truth: *"The stage, its dimensions and equipment were specially designed for this performance by the Grandducal Darmstadt Court Theater Stage Technician Carl Brandt. The upper and lower machinery contains essentially no different equipment to that of other large and new theaters."*

Only the accumulation of stage technology effects was unusual. Much has been written about how these possibilities would not have been sufficient to implement Wagner's poetic visions and to do justice to his own imagination. Thus Wagner was not happy after the great DAS RHEINGOLD premiere on August 13, 1876. He didn't utter a word to honor the completion of the architecture as a ceremonious or redeeming moment. Instead, Wagner was almost exclusively interested in the production of his own Gesamtkunstwerk on stage, and it disappointed him!

Cosima, who had maintained silence in her diary since August 7, reported on August 13: *"First performance of Rheingold complete with unlucky star, Betz* [the singer of Wotan] *loses the ring, twice runs into the backdrop while on the run, a worker takes the prospect out too early at the first transformation and one sees the people with their sleeves rolled up stand by the rear wall of the theater, all singers are embarrassed etc. etc. – Everyone goes home, R. at first very out of sorts, gradually becomes more and more merry…"* After the first festival had sped by, the Wagners went to Italy on holiday. Cosima summarizes: *"Many thoughts about completely giving up the festival and disappearing."* On September 9, Cosima writes: *"Costumes, decorations, everything will have to be checked for the repetition. R. is very sad and says that he wants to die!"*

It is understandable that Wagner suffered a depression after all his recent superhuman efforts, yet the stage technology was by no means as unprofessional as Wagner's disappointment might lead one to believe – on the contrary. In his letter to Feustel on April 12, 1872 Wagner noted in telegram style on *"Machinery and Decoration"*: *"Everything in*

Blick in die Unterbühne mit Maschinerie für die Hubpodien. Blaue Farbe markiert die Maschinentechnik, Grün die Konstruktion, Braun die Hydraulik, Gelb die Sicherheit und Rot den Brandschutz.
View below the stage with hydraulic equipment. The machinery is marked in blue, the construction in green, the hydraulics in brown, safety equipment in yellow and fire protection in red.

„Kostüme, Dekorationen, alles muss für die Wiederholung wieder vorgenommen werden. R. ist sehr traurig, sagt, er möchte sterben!"[1]

Eine Depression Wagners nach all den übermenschlichen Anstrengungen der letzten Zeit ist verständlich, doch die Bühnentechnik war keineswegs so dilettantisch, wie Wagners Enttäuschung glauben lässt – im Gegenteil. In seinem Brief an Feustel vom 12. April 1872 hatte Wagner für „Maschinerie und Decoration" im Telegrammstil notiert: *„Alles auf das ideale, innere Kunstwerk Bezügliche – ganz vollkommen. Hier nichts sparen: Alles wie für lange Dauer berechnet, nichts Provisorisches."*[2] So baute Brandt eine damals sehr moderne und professionelle Technik ein, wie er sie von seinen eigenen Arbeiten für die Münchner Hofoper (1866/69) und das Berliner Victoria-Theater (1859 bis 1861) kannte, die zum Teil erstaunlich lange in Betrieb blieb und damit ihre Qualität bewies.[3]

Bei Brandts Bühneneinrichtung handelte sich um eine der damals üblichen Holzkonstruktionen mit Kulissengassen, Freifahrten und Kassettenversenkungen, wobei alle Mechanik noch von Muskelkraft bewegt werden musste. Die Obermaschinerie erlaubte eine Bogen-Prospekt-Dekoration, die schon an anderen Theatern die barocke Soffitten-Kulissenbühne abgelöst hatte und eine stärkere perspektivische Tiefenwirkung erlaubte. Die einzige Besonderheit bestand darin, dass sie nicht in ein bestehendes Gebäude eingebaut, sondern das Gebäude geradezu um die Bühne herum konzipiert wurde. Der Vorteil lag somit in einer großen Einheitlichkeit der Einzelteile; die Bühne war – so würde man heute sagen – genormt.

Originale Pläne für die Einrichtung der Bühnentechnik existieren leider keine mehr, aber 1916 wurden wegen eines feuerpolizeilichen Gutachtens neue Pläne gezeichnet, die eine weitgehende Bestandsaufnahme des Zustands von 1876/1882 abbilden. Die Bühne hatte demnach zwischen den Umfassungsmauern eine Breite von achtundzwanzig Metern und eine Tiefe von dreiundzwanzig Metern, womit sie etwa im Mittelmaß der damaligen Bühnen zwischen Paris und Wien lag. Insgesamt sieben Gassen besaßen eine Breite von jeweils fast drei Metern, der Boden eine Neigung von drei Grad (wie heute noch), die sich auf der Hinterbühne fortsetzte. Die Portalbreite betrug dreizehn Meter, die Portalhöhe zwölf Meter, der Schnürboden war siebzehn Meter hoch, die Unterbühne zehn Meter tief. Zusätzlich zur fest installierten Maschinerie gab es einen zwölf Meter breiten und vierzehn Meter langen Bühnenwagen (bis 1924 in Betrieb).

In der Unterbühne befanden sich je Gassenpfeiler drei Freifahrtschlitze mit den entsprechenden vierzehn Paar Freifahrtwagen. In den Gassen eins bis sechs existierte je eine Versenkungsöffnung von dreizehn Metern für Tisch- und Kassettenversenkungen. 1933 bis 1936 und seit 2005 wurde und wird diese Untermaschinerie stetig erneuert.

Die Obermaschinerie bestand aus fünfzig Gardinenzügen (je sechs pro Gasse), sechs Panoramazügen, vierzehn Beleuchtungszügen, vierundzwanzig Soffittenzügen, einem Auffahrtsstuhl, Donner-, Wind-, Einschlagmaschinen. Diese Einrichtungen wurden 1907/08 mit Einführung eines kleinen und eines großen Rundhorizonts ergänzt, 1932 bis 1935 auch für die Hinterbühne. Diese alte hölzerne Obermaschinerie wurde erst 1963 bis 1966 im Zug der Generalsanierung des Gebäudes ersetzt.

Man baute in den 1960er Jahren im Bühnenturm eine Stahlkonstruktion ein, wodurch die Verschiebung der seitlichen Bühnenwände um drei Meter (jetzt einunddreißig Meter breit, dreiundzwanzig Meter tief und sechsundzwanzig Meter hoch) notwendig wurde. Danach konnte der Einbau eines neuen Schnür- und Rollenbodens, des berühmten doppelten „Bayreuther Schnürbodens", erfolgen, der eine getrennte Steuerung von Punktzügen (oben) und den Parallelzügen (unten) erlaubt.

connection with the ideal inner artwork – absolutely perfect. This is not the place for thrift. Calculate everything to last a long time, nothing provisional." Thus Brandt installed very modern and professional technical equipment for the time, as he did for his own work for the Munich Court Opera (1866/69) and the Berlin Victoria Theater (1859-61), which in part remained in use for an astonishingly long time, thereby proving their quality.

Brandt's stage equipment was a wooden construction, which was quite common at the time, complete with backdrop legs, tracks and trap doors, all requiring manual operation. The equipment in the flies made cut-cloth decorations possible, which other theaters were already using in place of the Baroque chariot-and-pole system because it created a stronger depth perspective. The stage's sole unique feature was that it was not built into an existing building, but rather the building was designed around the stage. This had the advantage that there was greater unity among the individual parts. The stage was – as we would say today – standardized.

Unfortunately the original plans for the stage technology equipment no longer exist, but in 1916 new plans were drawn up at a fire safety expert's request that provide an extensive record of the inventory from 1876/1882. According to these plans, the stage was twenty-eight meters wide and twenty-three meters deep between the surrounding walls, midsize in the range of the stages at that time between Paris and Vienna. A total of seven wings were nearly three meters wide each, the floor was at a three degree incline (and still is today), which continued back beyond the stage. The proscenium was thirteen meters wide and twelve meters tall, the flies were seventeen meters high, and the substage was ten meters deep. In addition to the permanently installed machinery, there was a twelve-meter-wide and fourteen-meter-long wagon (in use until 1924).

For each alley pillar in the understage there were three free journey sledges with the corresponding fourteen pairs of free journey vehicles. There was a thirteen meter stage trap opening in the alleys for table and box stage traps. This under-stage machinery was overhauled between 1933 and 1936 and has been under construction again since 2005.

The upper machinery consisted of fifty curtain winches (six per wing), six panorama fly bars, fourteen lighting bars, twenty-four border bars, a lift mechanism, and thunder, wind and lightning machines. This equipment was supplemented in 1907/08 by a small and a large cyclorama, and with another for upstage between 1932 and 1935. These pieces of old wooden stage fly equipment were replaced in the course of the general modernization of the building between 1963 and 1966.

In the 1960s a steel construction was built in the stage tower, which made it necessary to move the side stage walls out by three meters (now thirty-one-meter-wide, twenty-three-meter-deep and twenty-six-meter-high). Later, a new fly gallery and grid were installed, creating the famous double "Bayreuth rigging loft," which allows the point lifts (above) and the parallel fly bars (below) to be controlled separately.

Since Bayreuth has no wing stages, the equipment above and below the stage is of decisive importance. To this day these systems are always kept up-to-date. Bayreuth is a world leader in terms of its heavy duty (expensive) and technically complex point lifts, which can be individually controlled to accurately move and guide loads that weigh tons.

In addition to the general stage technology, work-specific equipment has been permanently installed as part of the stage architecture, e.g., the shift decoration from 1882 for the scene shift in Act 1 and Act 3 of PARSIFAL which was only replaced in 1934 by new decorations by Alfred Roller. As early as 1886 Friedrich Kranich, Senior, developed a new swimming device for the daughters of the Rhine, which 40 other theaters soon adopted. In 1925 Siegfried Wagner, whose own plays were incidentally not performed in his father's theater, purchased three new large stage wagons which could be combined with one another as well

Der berühmte doppelte „Bayreuther Schnürboden"
The famous double "Bayreuth flies"

Da Bayreuth keine Seitenbühnen besitzt, ist die Ausstattung der Ober- und Untermaschinerie von ausschlaggebender Bedeutung. Bis heute werden diese Anlagen immer auf den neuesten Stand der Technik gebracht. Gerade bei der Ausstattung mit (den teuren) und technisch aufwendigen leistungsfähigen Punktzügen, die tonnenschwere Lasten individuell, punktgenau und steuerbar bewegen können, ist Bayreuth weltweit führend.

Zusätzlich zu der allgemeinen Bühnentechnik gab und gibt es werkspezifische Besonderheiten, die fest in die Bühnenarchitektur eingebaut werden, wie zum Beispiel die Wandeldekoration von 1882 für die Verwandlungen im ersten und dritten Aufzug PARSIFAL, die erst 1934 mit den neuen Dekorationen von Alfred Roller abgelöst wurde. Schon 1886 entwickelte man eine neue Schwimmeinrichtung für die Rheintöchter durch Friedrich Kranich sen., die an vierzig Theatern übernommen wurde. 1925 schaffte Siegfried Wagner, dessen eigene Stücke übrigens nicht im Theater seines Vaters aufgeführt wurden, drei neue, miteinander kombinierbare große und sechs weitere kleinere Bühnenwagen für seinen neuen RING an; hierfür wurde die Erweiterung der Hinterbühne notwendig (siehe Kapitel „Architektonische Zukunftsmusik").

Auch in neuerer Zeit werden Sonderanfertigungen der Bühnentechnik übernommen und später wiederverwendet. So der Hydroantrieb der drehbaren Schwebebühne aus dem RING von 1983, der später für das FLIEGENDE-HOLLÄNDER-Haus von 1990 zum Einsatz kam, die eingebauten drehbaren konzentrischen Ring-Scheiben (TANNHÄUSER 1985), das RHEINGOLD-Karussell (1994), oder die aufwendige Mechanik aus dem LOHENGRIN von 1999 und zuletzt eine mobile Drehscheibe aus dem PARSIFAL von 2004. Für die MEISTERSINGER 2007 wurden in die Unterbühne zusätzliche Hydroantriebe für extreme Lasten eingebaut, die auch in Zukunft nützlich sein werden.

Eine Kuriosität ist eine Bühnenkonstruktion aus dem RING von 1983, die nach einer halbstündigen Probephase verworfen wurde und dann als Überdachung im Kantinengarten doch noch eine sinnvolle Verwendung fand – die „Peter Hall-Hall".

as six further small ones for his new RING. These purchases made it necessary to extend the backstage (see the chapter "Architectural dreams of the future").

In recent times, too, special technologies have been installed and later re-used. For example the hydro-drive of the revolving suspended stage from DER RING DES NIBELUNGEN of 1983, was later used for the DER FLIEGENDE HOLLÄNDER house in 1990, the installed revolving concentric Ring disc (1985 TANNHÄUSER), the carousel from DAS RHEINGOLD (1994), or the complex mechanics from LOHENGRIN in 1999 and finally a mobile revolving disc from PARSIFAL in 2004. For DIE MEISTERSINGER in 2007, additional hydro-drives were built into the understage for extreme loads, which could also be of use in the future.

One curiosity is a stage construction for the 1983 RING, which was abandoned after a 30-minute test phase, and then ended up serving a useful purpose after all by being used as a roof covering in the canteen garden – the "Peter Hall Hall."

Der von Wagner geforderte dreifache Bühnenraum auf einen Blick: Unterbühne, Bühnenportal und Schnürboden
Wagner's required triple stage space at a glance: substage, main stage and flies

„Peter Hall-Hall"

Parallel- und Punktzüge bei der technischen Einrichtung eines Bühnenbilds („Walkürenfelsen")
Parallel and point hoists in the equipment for a stage set ("Waküre cliffs")

Maximaler Durchblick bei geöffneten Eisernen Vorhängen von der Probebühne III. über Hinter- und Hauptbühne bis zum Zuschauerraum auf die Logenrückwand. Die Dekoration links stammt aus dem 2. Aufzug WALKÜRE von Tankred Dorsts RING-Inszenierung von 2006 (der „Friedhof der Geschichte").
Maximum view through open iron curtain from Rehearsal Stage III looking through backstage, main stage, the auditorium through to the rear loges. Parts of decoration from Act 2 of WALKÜRE from Tankred Dorst's 2006 RING staging (the "burial ground of history").

Die Bühnenbeleuchtung

Ein wesentlicher Illusionsfaktor eines Theaters ist die Beleuchtung der Bühne. Im Theater Dessau hatte Wagner einmal eine Aufführung von Glucks „Orpheus" als eine „*vollkommenere Gesamtleistung aller szenischen Mittel*" erlebt, wobei auch die Beleuchtung „*zu jener idealen Täuschung bei[trug], die uns wie in ein dämmerndes Wähnen, in ein Wahrträumen des nie Erlebten einschließt*"[1]. Auch hier hoffte Wagner für Bayreuth auf besondere Wunderwerke seines Technikers Brandt.

Cosimas Tagebücher belegen, dass in Bayreuth Beleuchtungsfragen häufig Thema waren, ohne Näheres darüber zu verlieren. Sie waren dem Illusionskünstler Wagner aber unverkennbar wichtig. Noch Wochen nach der Uraufführung träumte Wagner in Italien am 21. Oktober 1876, dass der SIEGFRIED aufgeführt würde und dass „*etwas Unrichtiges auf der Bühne*" geschehe: „,Brandt, die Beleuchtung geht ein', mit diesen Worten sei er aufgewacht!"[2]

In einem Brief an König Ludwig macht Wagner schon in den 1860er Jahren Vorschläge für das von Semper für München geplante Projekt, wo er von der „*Erfindung von Beleuchtungs-Vorrichtungen*" spricht, „*durch welche die szenischen Dekorationen zu wirklich malerisch-künstlerischer Bedeutung erhoben würden*"[3]. In einem anderen Brief an Ludwig fordert er ganz praktisch vom Maschinisten eine Beleuchtung am ersten Proszenium, welche durch „*Gardinen (aus bemaltem Holze)*" versteckt werden und beweglich sein müsse, "*um beliebig gehoben und gesenkt werden zu können. Auch ist ein horizontales Gasrohr mit vielen Gasöffnungen am obersten Rande der Orchestra anzubringen [...]. Auch hinter den senkrechten Wänden des ersten Proszeniums sind aufrechte Gasröhren mit Flammen anzubringen, um so von allen Seiten Licht zu bekommen.*"[4]

Von solchen Erfindungen war in Bayreuth keine Rede mehr. Die Beleuchtungsausstattung hielt sich im Rahmen damals üblicher Theater, auch wenn zeitgenössische Berichte etwas ganz Außerordentliches entdeckt haben wollen. In jeder der sechs Gassen hing eine Soffittenbeleuchtung mit je einhundertzwanzig Brennern für Oberlicht, für das Seitenlicht stand in jeder Gasse ein fünf Meter hoher Beleuchtungsapparat mit acht Doppelbrennern. Die Schlagschatten dieser Seitenbeleuchtung wurden durch ein zusätzliches Fußrampenlicht weggeleuchtet. Das Verdunkeln geschah durch Verringerung der Gasmenge, sie wurde „auf Sicht" reguliert, wobei gleichzeitig die insgesamt dreitausendsechsundsechzig offenen Flammen wegen einer immer gegenwärtigen Brandgefahr überwacht wurden. Die Beleuchtungsapparate waren für den Zuschauer (nicht wie in anderen Theatern) tatsächlich unsichtbar, sodass sogar der kritische Eduard Hanslick lobte, „*dass weder Seiten- noch Fußlampen sichtbar werden*" und die hell erleuchtete Bühne „*wie ein farbenglänzendes Bild in einem dunkle Rahmen*"[5] wirkte. Ab 1886 wurde das Haus nach und nach auf Elektrizität umgestellt, 1895/96 – zum neuen RING – auch die Bühnenbeleuchtung. Nach zahlreichen Erneuerungen zählt die Bühnenbeleuchtung des Bayreuther Festspielhauses heute zu den leistungsstärksten der Welt.

Seit den Inszenierungen Siegfried Wagners in den 1920er Jahren verlangte ein neuer Regiestil immer mehr Licht auf der Bühne. Den Strom dafür gewann man von Anfang an selbst – mittels einer eigenen Dampfmaschine, einem sogenannten Lokomobil. 1906 fiel bei einer TRISTAN-Aufführung der Strom für fünf Minuten aus, doch das Orchester spielte mit Streichholzlicht, die Sänger sangen ungerührt weiter, das (ohnehin an ein mystisches Dunkel gewöhnte) Publikum blieb ruhig. Erst 1933 wurde das Haus – zunächst für eine Teilversorgung – ans öffentliche Stromnetz angeschlossen. 1952 wurden alle elektrischen Einrichtungen grunderneuert und die Eigenversorgung ganz aufgegeben, die Lokomobile in den Ruhestand geschickt.

Stage lighting

An essential element of the illusion created in the theater is provided by the stage lighting. Wagner once experienced a performance of Gluck's "Orpheus" at the Dessau Theater as one of the "more perfect overall achievements of all the scenic means," with the lighting also "contributing to that ideal deception, which includes a dawning imagination and the dream-come-true of something never before experienced before." Here too Wagner hoped special miracles from his technician Brandt for Bayreuth.

Cosima's diaries record that lighting questions were frequently the subject of discussions in Bayreuth, without going into specific detail. They were unmistakably important to Wagner, the artist of illusion. Even weeks after the premiere Wagner dreamt in Italy on October 21, 1876, that SIEGFRIED was being performed and that *"something not quite right was happening on stage…'Brandt, the lighting is breaking down', with these words he woke up!"*

In a letter to King Ludwig in the 1860s, Wagner makes proposals for the project planned by Semper for Munich, where he speaks of the *"invention of lighting equipment [...] that will elevate the scenic decoration to truly visual and artistic significance."* In another letter to Ludwig he expresses the practical demand that the technicians provide lighting for the first proscenium which should be hidden by *"curtains (made of painted wood)"* and have to be mobile *"in order to be raised and lowered as desired. A horizontal gas pipe with many gas openings should also be fitted at the uppermost edge of the orchestra [...]. Upright gas pipes with flames should also be fitted behind the vertical walls of the first proscenium, in order to have light from all sides."*

There was no longer any talk of such inventions in Bayreuth. The lighting equipment was kept within the normal range for theaters at that time, even if contemporary reports believed that they had discovered something extraordinary. In every one of the six alleys hung ceiling light fittings each with one hundred and twenty burners to provide light from above, for side light there was a 5m high lighting fixture with eight double burners in every alleys. The heavy shadows of this side lighting were illuminated away by an additional footlight. The dimming occurred through reducing the amount of gas, so that it was regulated *"by eye,"* with the total of 3,066 open flames being monitored as an ever-present fire hazard. The lighting equipment was (unlike in other theaters) actually invisible for the spectators, so that even the highly critical Eduard Hanslick praised the fact *"that neither the side lamps nor the footlamps were visible"* and the brightly lit stage looked *"like a shining colored picture in a dark frame."* From 1886 on the house was converted to electricity, and in 1895/96 – for the new RING – the stage lighting was, too. After numerous renovations the stage lighting of the Bayreuth Festspielhaus is today one of the most powerful in the world.

Ever since the productions by Siegfried Wagner in the 1920s a new style of direction has always demanded more and more light on the stage. The electricity for it was at first self-produced by means of the theater's own steam engine, a so-called locomobile. In 1906 the electricity was off for 5 min. during a performance of TRISTAN UND ISOLDE, yet the orchestra played on by the light of matches, the singers sang on unperturbed and the audience (accustomed anyway to a mystical darkness) remained quite calm. It was not until 1933 that the building was connected to the electricity grid – at first only with a partial supply. In 1952 the entire electrical equipment was thoroughly renovated, the in-house generator finally dispensed with and the locomobile sent into retirement.

Heute garantiert ein Notstromaggregat im Maschinenhaus die Versorgung, sodass man bei Stromausfall des öffentlichen Netzes nicht fünf Minuten, sondern nur maximal fünf Sekunden im Dunkeln bleibt. Bei starker Beanspruchung des öffentlichen Netzes – zum Beispiel in der Weihnachtszeit – greift die Stadt Bayreuth gerne auf diesen Diesel, übrigens ein echter U-Boot-Motor, zurück.

Wagner selbst interessierte sich für die Elektrizität nicht als Künstler, sondern als alter Sozialist. Er hoffte, dass diese bei Eisenbahn und Industrie bewirke, *„die Kohlenarbeiter zu vermindern"*[1]. Am 25. Oktober 1878 notiert Cosima: *„R. lässt sich von Herrn Kellermann die Elektrizität auseinandersetzen und empfindet immer weniger Neigung für die Beschäftigung mit Naturwissenschaft."*[2]

Today an emergency generator in the technical building guarantees a supply, so that in the event of a power cut in the electricity network darkness does not last 5 minutes, but rather only a maximum of five seconds. In the case of a stronger demand on the public grid – e.g. at Christmas time – the city of Bayreuth gladly avails itself of the diesel-run submarine engine, incidentally a genuine model.

Wagner himself was interested in electricity, not as an artist but as an old socialist. He hoped that it would have the effect of *"reducing the number of coal miners working on the railways and in industry"*. On October 25, 1878 Cosima noted: *"R. is being instructed on electricity by Mr. Kellermann and is less and less interested in natural sciences."*

Arbeitsgalerie der Beleuchtung Working gallery for lighting

Kabelstand für Beleuchtungskörper Cable storage for lights

U-Boot-Motor als Notstromaggregat
Submarine motor serves as an emergency generator

Arbeitsplatz des Beleuchters mit Farbfiltern und Taschenlampe
Lighting designer's workstation with color filters and flashlights

Der Brandschutz

Unzählige Theater sind im Laufe der Geschichte abgebrannt, als Kerzen oder offene Gasflammen für die Beleuchtung sorgten, aber auch heute, wo alte Elektroleitungen den gleichen Effekt haben können. Wagner selbst war hier ein gebranntes Kind. Vom Revolutionsjahr 1848 in Dresden berichtet er in „Mein Leben" über den Brand des alten Opernhauses, wo er *„vor wenigen Wochen noch die letzte Aufführung der Neunten Symphonie dirigiert hatte"*. *„Von je [...] war die Feuergefährlichkeit dieses mit Holz und Leinwand angefüllten, seinerzeit nur provisorisch errichteten Gebäudes der schreckende Gegenstand der Befürchtung von Feuersgefahr gewesen."*[1] Am 10. Dezember 1881, zwei Tage nach der großen Brandkatastrophe am Ring-Theater in Wien mit 400 Toten, offenbart Wagner erneut den alten Revolutionär: *„Das nichtsnutzigste Volk säße in einem solchen Opertheater; wenn in einer Kohlengrube arme Arbeiter verschüttet würden, das ergriffe und empöre ihn, aber solch ein Fall berühre ihn kaum."*[2]

Sein schwarzer Humor reizte Wagner, seinen Bühnentechniker Brandt gerne „Theaterbrand" zu nennen. Fast hätte sein Kollege Runckwitz das ganze Theater am Eröffnungstage abgefackelt. Dieser hatte *„Tausende von Tonschalen auf dem First des Hauses rundherum aufstellen lassen"*, doch die Arbeiter versuchten das Feuer mit allzu viel Terpentin anzufeuern, *„und als die Festbeleuchtung begann, sahen die Festgäste zu ihrem Entsetzen [...] ein Feuer, das mit jedem Augenblick bösartiger wurde. Brennendes Terpentin floss überall an den Fassaden herab, [...] wohin man sah, die Gäste standen in Schrecken umher, und es sah aus, als wolle eine Panik ausbrechen [...]."*[3]

Wagner selbst spielte schon bei Probenbeginn am 2. August 1875 etwas mit dem Feuer. Er saß *„nahe dem Orchestergraben an ein[em] Tischchen. [...] Darauf stand eine Petroleumlampe. Hans Richter dirigierte, und Wagner bewegte sich dabei so heftig mit Armen und Beinen, das man befürchten musste, Tisch, Kiste und Lampe würden umstürzen und alles in Flammen aufgehen, weshalb Karl Brandt den Tisch nach der ersten Probe am Fußboden befestigte. So im Zentrum des Festspielhauses sitzend, ein Energie-Bündel, aus dem die Funken auf die Mitwirkenden übersprangen, hat ihn Adolf von Menzel in einer Kreidezeichnung festgehalten."*[4]

Beim Baugenehmigungsverfahren schreibt der Gutachter des Stadtbaurats am 29. April 1873 lediglich, dass das Bayreuther Festspielhaus *„technischerseits nicht beanstandet"* werde, da trotz des provisorischen Riegelfachs immerhin *„Treppenhäuser und ein großer Teil des Zuschauerraums massiv"* seien. Er forderte nur von den Treppen nach § 47 Absatz 4 der Bauordnung, *„dass dieselben aus unverbrennbarem Material herzustellen sind"*.[5] Erst am 18. Februar 1882 erfolgte eine offizielle Feuersicherheitsprüfung. Hier wurden die isolierte Lage des Hauses als günstig konstatiert (apropos Scheunenviertel), ausreichende Fluchtwege, eiserne Beleuchtungsapparate, ein Blitzableiter auf dem Dach und das Fehlen einer Heizung. Als Feuerlöschvorrichtungen werden zwei achtundzwanzig Meter über der Bühne befindliche, sechseinhalb Kubikmeter Wasser fassende Tanks (in den nördlichen Bühnentürmen) genannt.

Diese Tanks waren mit einem Röhrennetz verbunden, das sich über den ganzen Bühnenraum ausbreitete und zudem an die städtische Hochdruckwasserleitung durch Hydranten angeschlossen war, die von der „freiwilligen Turnerfeuerwehr Bayreuth" bedient wurden. Da das Festspielhaus bis heute einen eigenen Brunnen (Zisterne) besitzt, konnte das Röhrennetz mittels einer Dampfpumpe mit eigenem Hügelquellwasser gefüllt werden. Einst sorgte dieser Brunnen auch für den Bühnendampf, heute dient er nur noch als Bühnenabfluss, wie im RHEINGOLD 1983 und dem LOHENGRIN 1987.

Fire protection

Numerous theaters have burnt down in the course of history, when candles or naked gas flames used to provide the source of light, but even today it happens when old electric wiring can have the same effect. Wagner himself was once burned in this respect. In "My Life" he writes about the fire in the old Opera House in the year of the 1848 Revolution in Dresden where *"just a few weeks before [I] had conducted the last performance of the Ninth Symphony."* *"That this building filled with wood and canvas and at the time only provisionally erected could catch fire [...] was always a terrible source of fear."* On December 10, 1881, two days after the great fire catastrophe at the Ring Theater in Vienna, when 400 people died, Wagner once again showed that he was still the old revolutionary: *"The most good-for-nothing people would have been sitting in such an opera theater; when poor workers had been buried alive in a coal mine that affected him and infuriated him, but such a case hardly makes him flinch."*

Wagner's black humor made him like to call his stage technician named Brandt "Theaterbrand" (theater blaze). His colleague Runckwitz had almost burnt down the whole theater on the day of the grand opening. He had *"put up thousands of clay dishes all round the ridge of the roof the building,"* yet the workers tried to get the fire started with far too much turpentine *"and as the festival lighting began, the festival guests saw to their horror [...] a fire which was growing more and more threatening with every moment. Burning turpentine was flowing everywhere [...] wherever one looked, the guests were standing around in fear and it looked as if panic would break out."*

Wagner himself played with fire at the start of rehearsals on August 2, 1875. He was sitting *"near the orchestra pit at a table. [...] On it was standing a petroleum lamp. Hans Richter was conducting and Wagner was moving his arms and legs about so violently that people were afraid he would knock over the table, the box and the lamp and send everything up in flames, which is why, after the first rehearsal, Karl Brandt attached the table to the floor. That is how Adolf von Menzel recorded him in a chalk drawing, sitting in the center of the Festspielhaus, a bundle of energy from whom sparks flew across to his colleagues."*

On April 29, 1873, during the application process for a building permit, the expert from the municipal building authorities recorded only that *"from the technical point of view there were no objections"* to the Bayreuth Festspielhaus because despite the provisional timber structure the *"staircases and a great part of the auditorium were massive."* He only requested that the stairs, according to § 47 paragraph 4 of the building code, *"should also be made of non-inflammable material."* It was not until February 18, 1882 that was there an official fire safety check. It was regarded as favorable that the building was in an isolated location, that there were sufficient fire exits, iron lighting fixtures, a lightning rod on the roof and the lack of any heating. Two 6 1/2 cubic meter water tanks 28 meter above the stage (in the northern stage tower) were identified as fire extinguishing equipment.

These tanks were connected to a pipe network which extended over the whole stage area and in addition was connected to the municipal high-pressure water pipes via hydrants operated by the "Bayreuth Voluntary Fire Department." Since the Festspielhaus to this day owns its own well (cistern), the network of pipes could be filled with its own mountain

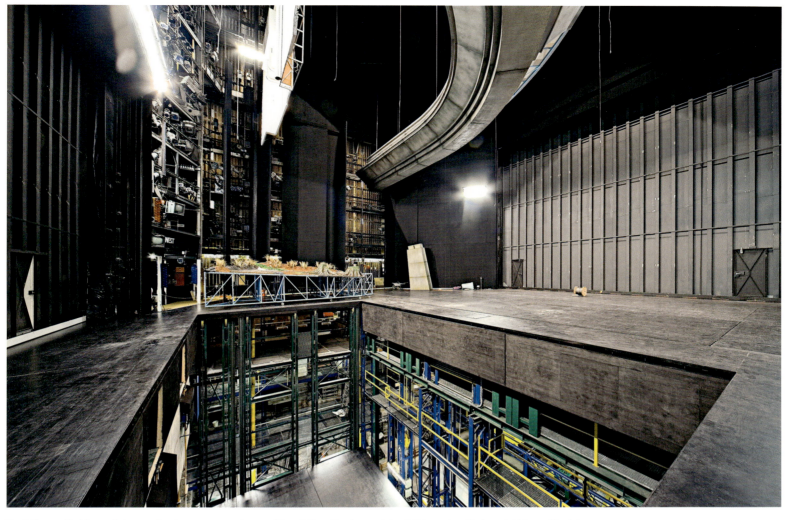

Zwei Eiserne Vorhänge, links zum Zuschauerraum, rechts zur Hinterbühne Two iron curtains, left toward auditorium, right toward backstage

Ein Eiserner Vorhang war bei jener ersten Brandschutzprüfung 1882 nicht vorhanden und wurde als nicht nötig angesehen: Insgesamt biete das *„ganze Theater hinsichtlich der Sicherheit für das darin verkehrende Personal und Publikum das beruhigende Bild eines Musterbaus"*[1], der sich bei vollbesetztem Hause in eineinhalb Minuten entleeren lasse, wie es bei der Hauptprobe zum zweiten Aufzug der GÖTTERDÄMMERUNG 1876 tatsächlich geprobt wurde.

Die Sanierungsarbeiten seit den 1960er Jahren, insbesondere der Austausch der Holzarchitektur, hatten vor allem brandschutztechnische Gründe. Mittlerweile wurden (1914 und 1974) auch zwei Eiserne Vorhänge eingebaut, einer zur Bühne hin, der andere zur Hinterbühne. Heute sorgt zusätzlich eine Sprinkleranlage mit zirka zweitausend Brandmeldern für die nötige Sicherheit sowie das ungebrochene Engagement der Freiwilligen Feuerwehr Bayreuth, die bei jeder Vorstellung mit bis zu neun Mann anwesend ist (vielleicht ein Tipp für alle, die keine Karten bekommen).

water by means of a steam pump. At a time, this well was used to create steam on the stage, today it only still serves as a stage drain, as was the case in DAS RHEINGOLD 1983 and LOHENGRIN 1987.

An iron curtain was not in place at the time of the first fire safety check in 1882 and was not considered necessary. All in all the *"whole theater created the calming image of a model building with regard to safety for the staff working there and for the public,"* since the fully occupied house could be emptied within 1 1/2 minutes, which was actually tested in a full rehearsal of Act 2 of the DIE GÖTTERDÄMMERUNG in 1887. The modernization work that has been going on since the 1960s, in particular the replacement of the wooden framing, had above all fire precautionary reasons. In the meantime, (1914 and 1974) two iron curtains were installed, one towards the stage the other towards the backstage. Today, there is also a sprinkler system with approx. 2,000 fire alarms providing safety, as well as the unbroken commitment of the Bayreuth Voluntary Fire Department, which provides up to nine firemen at every performance (perhaps a tip for people who don't have tickets).

Zeichnung von Adolf von Menzel: Richard Wagner mit Petroliumlampe bei den Proben zum RING 1875
Drawing by Adolf von Menzel: Richard Wagner with petrolium lamp during RING rehearsals in 1875

Wassertank der Sprinkleranlage Sprinkler system water tank

Hauseigene Zisterne unter dem Gitter In-house cisterns below the grate

Löschwagen der Bayreuther Feuerwehr Bayreuth fire brigade firetruck

Harry Kupfer
Man geht herum, man ist inspiriert und bekommt Ideen

<u>Haben Sie Bayreuth und das Festspielhaus schon gekannt, bevor Sie dort selbst inszeniert haben?</u>
Ja. Das war noch zu meiner Studienzeit in den 50er Jahren mit der Jeunesse musicale. Da habe ich meine ersten Vorstellungen in Bayreuth gesehen, TRISTAN, MEISTERSINGER und PARSIFAL. Das waren ganz große Erlebnisse!

<u>Sie hatten also ein Bild vor sich, als der Auftrag kam, in Bayreuth zu arbeiten; Sie wussten, was auf Sie zukam?</u>
Ich war zum „Jahrhundert"-RING von Chéreau eingeladen worden. Kurze Zeit darauf kam das Telegramm aus Bayreuth, ob ich nicht den HOLLÄNDER machen könnte. Aber dieser Druck, zur Zeit des Chéreau-RINGS! Als ich Wolfgang Wagner dann mein Konzept erläutert hatte, sagte er nur, „*na dann auf den nächsten Skandal!*"

<u>Beeinflusst das im Hinterkopf stets präsente Gebäude, also die Wirkung des Ortes und die Architektur selbst, ein Konzept oder seine Entstehung?</u>
Das ist ein bisschen schwierig. Als ich das erste Mal in Bayreuth war, hat mich die Mystik dort durchaus gefangen genommen. Natürlich zunächst die Akustik des Zuschauerraumes, wo man ganz anders hört; anders als zum Beispiel in Berlin. Das war ein großes Hörerlebnis. Später, wenn man dort arbeitet, muss man die Ästhetik von der theatralischen Praxis trennen, die der Raum oder das Gebäude bietet. Über die Ästhetik lässt sich streiten, darüber muss man eigentlich nicht diskutieren, das ist so zeitgebunden und bei allen Veränderungen ist es das, was es ist. Und wer den Stil mag, und wer ihn nicht mag – ich mag ihn zum Beispiel überhaupt nicht. Für mich ist das eine fürchterliche Fabrikhalle von außen. Aber die Zweckmäßigkeit des Baus hat mich dann doch mehr überzeugt, als ich dort gearbeitet habe: Das verdeckte Orchester hat mich schon am Anfang beeindruckt, aber dann vor allen Dingen, was die Bühne leisten kann. Das ist ja zunächst nicht so Richard Wagners Verdienst, sondern vor allem das Verdienst derjenigen, die nach ihm kamen und dort unentwegt geändert haben. Vor allen Dingen Wolfgang Wagner, der die modernste Technik eingebaut hat. Wir hatten wirklich die modernste Beleuchtungsanlage, die es auf der Welt überhaupt gab. Das Wort „es geht nicht", gab es nicht. Ich zeigte dem damaligen Technischen Direktor (Walter Huneke) zusammen mit unserem Bühnenbildner Peter Sykora, wie wir uns die Verwandlungen vorstellen: So müssen die Wände aufgehen, so muss das versinken, und das muss alles wie im Mysterium sein und man darf überhaupt nicht merken, dass das eigentlich Technik ist ... Eigentlich haben wir gedacht, er schmeißt uns raus. Irgendwann hab ich ihn dann gefragt, „*ja geht das überhaupt?*" Er antwortete: „*Ich bin hier der Ingenieur, das muss Sie überhaupt nicht interessieren. Sie erklären mir, was Sie wollen und ich mach das.*" Und es ist unglaublich geworden.

<u>Daraus ergibt sich eine nächste Frage: Ist das Bayreuther Festspielhaus nach heutigen Anforderungen also ein „gutes" Theater?</u>

Harry Kupfer
You walk around and it's totally inspiring, you get ideas

<u>Did you know Bayreuth and the Festspielhaus before you directed there yourself?</u>
Yes, that was when I was a student in the 1950s with Jeunesse musicale. That's when I saw my first performances in Bayreuth, TRISTAN, MEISTERSINGER and PARSIFAL. Those were unforgettable experiences.

<u>So you already had an image in your mind when you were invited to work in Bayreuth; you knew what to expect?</u>
I had been invited to Chéreau's centennial staging of DER RING DES NIBELUNGEN. Little later a telegram from Bayreuth arrived asking whether I could do DER FLIEGENDE HOLLÄNDER. But the pressure, right as Chéreau was doing DER RING! When I talked to Wolfgang Wagner through my concept he only said, "*well, it's on to the next scandal!*"

<u>Does having the building in the back of your mind, the effect of the location, and the architecture itself influence your musical concept or how it develops?</u>
That's a bit difficult. The first time I was in Bayreuth the mystique really took hold of me there. At first, of course, the acoustics of the auditorium, where you hear totally differently than in Berlin. It was an amazing listening experience in Bayreuth. When I later worked there, I had to divide the aesthetic from the theatrical practice that the space or the building has to offer. The aesthetic is a point of contention, it's not really worth discussing. It's so time-dependent and throughout all the changes, it is what it is. And whether you like the style or not is secondary – I don't like it at all, for example. In my eyes, the exterior looks like a horrible factory. But the building's functionality convinced me more when I worked there: the covered orchestra, that impressed me right from the beginning, but then especially what the stage is capable of. That isn't primarily Richard Wagner's doing, but rather is thanks to all of those who came after him and changed things all the time. Especially Wolfgang Wagner, who installed the most modern equipment. We really had the most modern lights in the world. The word "impossible" did not exist. Once our stage designer Peter Sykora and I went to the technical director (Walter Huneke) to explain how we envisioned the transformation. We showed him how the walls had to lift up, this had to sink, and it all had to be mysterious, without the audience even realizing that technology was at work ... actually, we thought he was going to throw us out. At one point I asked him "*is that even possible?*" He answered: "*I'm the engineer here. That is none of your concern. You tell me what you want, and I do it.*" And it turned out incredible.

<u>That leads to the next question: Is the Bayreuth Festspielhaus a "good" theater by modern standards?</u>
Yes, it is. It at started with Wagner himself when he seized on the original idea of the antique theater, which is democratic, over the imperial theater. It was one of a kind in the world. The way the auditorium creates community: everyone can hear well, everyone can see well, everyone is privy to everything happening on the stage. Of course, that's an innovation that has to do with Wagner's overall concept, which is mystical. He built the theater to reflect his emotional

Ja, das ist es. Das geht schon bei Wagner selbst los, dass er den ursprünglichen Gedanken des antiken Theaters, der ja ein demokratischer ist, dem Hoftheater entgegengesetzt hat. Das war einmalig auf der Welt. Die Art, wie der Zuschauerraum eine Gemeinschaft stiftet: Man kann überall gut hören, man kann überall gut sehen, man kriegt alles mit. Das ist natürlich eine Erfindung, die etwas mit dem Gesamtkonzept Wagners zu tun hat, das ja ein mystisches ist. Von seinem Gefühlsverständnis, dass man nicht „denkend" im Theater sitzt, sondern emotional überrumpelt werden muss, hat er den Bau untergeordnet. Und was da entstanden ist, das ist grandios. Aber auch, wie sich das alles weiterentwickelt hat, was in der Vergangenheit immer wieder gemacht wurde, schon zur Zeit von Cosima und Siegfried Wagner, und wie das in den Generationen immer weitergegangen ist. In Bayreuth kann man ja fast das ganze Theater umbauen, wenn man das braucht. Beim RING standen wir vor dem Problem, wie man zum Beispiel die ganzen Versenkungen und Hubmöglichkeiten lautlos hinbekommt, dass das eben nicht quiekt und quatscht; und das geht an keinem anderen Haus in dieser Qualität. Eventuell vielleicht noch – ich muss sagen, das ist eigentlich ein Witz! – beim Musicaltheater, wenn also alle Technik für einen längeren Zeitraum fest installiert ist.

Stichwort, der Zuschauer muss überrumpelt werden: Wagner hatte ja ganz spezielle Vorstellungen von dem Verhältnis Bühne – Zuschauerraum. Der Fokus mit dem doppelten Proszenium, das den Zuschauer auf die Bühne „heransaugt" ...
... ja auch schon wie sich der Vorhang wie eine Linse öffnet ...

Sie würden also sagen, dass Wagners Vision tatsächlich funktioniert, obwohl das Theater ja eigentlich „blind" auf die Uraufführung des RING hin gebaut wurde?
Es funktioniert in seinem Sinne! Wenn man ein Brechtianer ist und damit ein Gegner eines solchen Theaters, findet man das natürlich furchtbar. Aber in dem Sinne, wie er sich Theater vorstellte, also als totale emotionale Überrumpelung, Beeinflussung und Programmierung, ist das total geglückt.

Und wo stößt die Immobilie an ihre Grenzen? Oder anders gefragt, was könnte man verbessern, nach über zehn Jahren Arbeit dort und Ihren internationalen Erfahrungen?
Da fällt mir nichts ein! Natürlich muss man den Raum zunächst zur Kenntnis nehmen: Es gibt keine Seitenbühnen, aber dafür Tiefe; Drehbühne kann man einbauen; mit oben und unten, also Schnürboden und Unterbühne, kann man alles machen. Wenn's notwendig ist, kann man den ganzen Bühnenboden rausreißen und baut eine Maschine ein, wenn man will. Und da geht man herum und man ist inspiriert, bekommt Ideen. Das ist nicht hemmend, sondern motivierend.

Das führt zu der Frage nach einer anderen Besonderheit der Architektur. Wagner baut ja an den „griechischen" Zuschauerraum eine Guckkastenbühne des 19. Jahrhunderts. Eigentlich müsste das Theaterspiel nach antikem Vorbild ja in der „orchestra" stattfinden, da ist nun aber der Orchestergraben und das Proszenium. Ist die gefundene Lösung nicht doch ein Nachteil für die Sichtlinien? Es gibt zwar die Preisstaffelungen für die Außenplätze, aber wie geht man als Regisseur damit um?
Zu der Zeit, als das Theater gebaut wurde, war es ja so, dass man nur vorne gespielt hat. Bei meiner Inszenierung des RING gab es zwar gewaltige Auftrittsmöglichkeiten von hinten, aber die Hauptszenen haben doch alle vorne gespielt, und zwar ohne dass man das gemerkt hätte. Es war natürlich ein ausgewogenes Prinzip zwischen Tiefe und Nähe, von hinten und vorne. Im Grunde genommen war es nicht anders als bei der alten Kulissenbühne, wo man vorne gespielt hat, während man hinter einem Zwischenvorhang schon etwas anderes aufgebaut hat. Hier aber hatte ich die Möglichkeit, in Dimensionen zu schaffen, die man nirgendwo hat. Und wenn ein paar Plätze auf der Seite erst drei Sekunden später sehen, dass da jemand von hinten kommt, kann man das nicht

understanding that you don't sit in the theater "thinking," but rather that you have to be overwhelmed by emotions. The result is magnificent. But also the way it all developed from there, what was repeatedly done in the past, even by Cosima and Siegfried Wagner, and how that has been passed on through the generations. In Bayreuth you can rebuild practically the entire theater if you need to. When we did DER RING we faced the challenge of lowering and raising things without a sound, without squeaking and squawking. There is no other theater that can achieve that as well. Perhaps also – though I must say this is a joke! – in musical theater, where the equipment is permanently installed for a longer period of time.

Key phrase: the audience has to be overwhelmed: Wagner had a unique vision of the relationship between the stage and the audience. The focus with the double proscenium that "draws" the audience onto the stage ...
... Yes, and also the way the curtain opens like a lens ...

So, would you say that Wagner's vision really works, even though the theater was actually built "blindly" for the premiere of DER RING?
It works in its own way! If you're a Brechtian and therefore opposed to such theater, you'll think it's horrible, of course. But considering Wagner's vision of what theater is supposed to do, that is, emotionally completely overwhelm, influence and program, it works great!

Where does the theater run into limits? Put differently, what could be improved in your opinion after nearly ten years of working there and your international experiences?
I can't think of a thing! Of course first you have to get a feel for the space. There are no side stages, but there's depth. You can put in a revolving stage, and if you use the space above and below with the flies and the sub-stage, you can do anything. If you need to, you can tear out the entire stage floor and put in a machine, if you desire. You walk around and it's totally inspiring, you get ideas. It's not inhibiting, it's motivating.

That leads to the question of the unique architecture. Wagner built a proscenium stage from the 19th century onto the "Greek" auditorium. According to the antique model, the performance should take place in the "orchestra," but the orchestra pit and the proscenium are there now. Does the solution Wagner found cause problems with sight lines? The seats on the sides are less expensive, but how does a director deal with that?
When the theater was built, the action always took place downstage. In my staging of DER RING, there were great opportunities to enter from upstage, but the main scenes all took place downstage, without anyone noticing. There was, of course, a balanced principle between depth and closeness, between upstage and downstage. Basically it was no different than from the traditional stage with backdrops, where the scene would be taking place downstage while the next set was being set up upstage behind a curtain. But I had the chance to create in dimensions unavailable anywhere else. And if it takes three seconds longer for a few people sitting on the edge to see someone approaching from upstage, there's nothing that can be done about that. Everyone in the audience still had the impression that the space extended without limit, no matter where they were sitting.

Shortly before the premiere of DER RING, Wagner wrote a note to the artists that said "Clarity! The little notes and their text are the most important." How do you create emotional density and presence despite the wide double proscenium, the segmented arch-shaped orchestra pit, the cover over the pit, and the zone with the huge prompt-box, that is, the very large distance between the singers and the audience?
That's a question of lighting or the principles of lighting. The light seems to "scoop" the singers forward. The amazing thing about the theater is that despite two prosceniums and a large orchestra pit, indeed perhaps because it is hidden, you still get the impression that the scene is coming at you. It's a mystery to me how that effect was created. So old Wagner and his architects did some very good thinking about how to create that magic.

ändern. Jeder Zuschauer hatte ja trotzdem die Vorstellung – und zwar von allen Plätzen –, dass der Raum unendlich weitergeht.

Wagner hat kurz vor der Uraufführung des RING an die Künstler geschrieben: „Deutlichkeit! Die kleinen Noten und Text sind das wichtigste." Wie schafft man nun – trotz des breiten doppelten Proszeniums, des segmentbogenartigen Orchestergrabens, der Abdeckung über dem Graben, dann der Zone mit dem riesigen Souffleurkasten, also einer sehr großen Entfernung der Sänger zum Publikum – dennoch die emotionale Dichte und Präsenz?
Das ist eine Frage des Lichtes, beziehungsweise des Lichtprinzips. Das Licht „schaufelt" den Sänger geradezu nach vorne. Das ist das Wunder des Baus, dass trotz der zwei Proszenien trotz des großen Orchesterraums – ja schon, weil es eben verdeckt ist – man doch den Eindruck hat, das Bild kommt auf einen zu. Das ist für mich ein Mysterium, wie das geschafft ist. Also da waren schon sehr gute Überlegungen beim alten Wagner und bei seinen Architekten dabei, wie man da zaubert.

Sie haben das Stichwort „Akustik" genannt. Wenn man im Orchestergraben sitzt, wähnt man sich ja eher im Maschinenraum eines Ozeanriesen; es ist heiß, ungeheuer laut und von der Bühne hört man dort gar nichts. Ist dies wirklich so toll oder schadet das nicht eher der Korrespondenz zwischen Sängern und Musikern?
Das ist nicht der Fall und es schadet nichts, denn der Sänger kann innerlich mitsingen, weil er die Orchesterstimmen kennt und umgekehrt. Die Leute, die dort singen und spielen, sind so gut studiert. Sie haben vorher die Orchesterproben in einem gemeinsamen Proberaum gehabt, kennen daher den Orchesterpart ganz genau. Und sie haben den ungeheuren Vorteil, dass sie wissen, dass sie in jedem Fall nicht tot gemacht werden. Sie können den Mut haben, wirklich piano zu singen, und vorausgesetzt, dass sie eine entsprechende Technik haben, singen sie sogar verständlich. Sie können sich singend textverständlich ausdrücken.

Sie sind also der Meinung, Bayreuth ist nicht überflüssig?
Nein, es ist ganz wichtig! Wenn Bayreuth in dem Sinne weiter arbeitet wie das in den 70er und 80er Jahren war. Ich habe bis 1992 da gearbeitet und alle Produktionen, die dort stattfanden, wurde exzellent behandelt, beobachtet und gepflegt. Schlamperei war einfach undenkbar.

Beherrscht die Atmosphäre und die Bedeutung des Hauses einen Künstler oder dient sie ihm und seiner Arbeit?
Das Haus selbst nicht. Die Atmosphäre von Kritik und Publikum während der Festspiele selbst ist hingegen ein glatter Horror. Dass man überall belästigt wird, keine Privatsphäre mehr hat, das hab ich nicht so gerne gehabt. Die Probenzeit ist wunderbar – die Festspiele selbst der Horror.

Sagen Sie noch etwas zum Begriff „Werkstatt Bayreuth" und wie die Produktionen in den Jahren der Aufführungen betreut werden.
Regisseure sind doch immer, zumal wenn sie an einem Haus zusammen sind, Konkurrenten; man grüßt sich und lügt sich die Hucke voll. Das ist in Bayreuth nicht der Fall gewesen. Da saß man mit Patrice Chéreau und Götz Friedrich zusammen an einem Tisch, jeder erzählte von seinen Proben und war interessiert daran, dass man gegenseitig auf die Proben kam. Das alles ist das Verdienst von Wolfgang Wagner. Er hat solch blödsinnige Konkurrenzen nicht zugelassen. Bei Problemen saß man dann eben zusammen am Tisch, und es wurde ausgerechnet und sortiert. Den Satz, „das geht nicht", gab es auch hier nicht. Es wurde von Wolfgang Wagner immer versucht, ein Problem zu lösen.

Man hört ja immer wieder viel über die Akustik und die Abdeckung des Orchesters; man könnte doch mal, und man müsste doch ...
... was die alles da ausprobiert haben! Deckel ab, Deckel halb ab und hier und da ab. Dann sitzen immer die Gurus unten und hören die Flöhe husten. Da wird geraunt, es könnte ja dies sein

You mentioned the keyword "acoustics." If you are sitting in the orchestra pit, you feel more like you're in the engine room of an ocean liner; it's hot, incredibly loud and you can't hear a thing from the stage. Is that really so great, or does it perhaps get in the way of the communication between the singers and the instrumentalists?
That is the case but it doesn't get in the way. The singers can sing along in their heads because they know the orchestral parts and the other way around. The musicians who sing and play there are very well prepared. They have had joint orchestral rehearsals in a common rehearsal hall and they know the orchestral music precisely. And they have the enormous advantage of knowing that they will certainly not be drowned out. They can dare to sing truly piano and, assuming they have good technique, you can even understand them. They can use the text to express themselves while singing.

So you don't think Bayreuth has become superfluous?
No, it's totally important! If Bayreuth continues to work along these lines like it did in the 1970s and 1980s. I worked there until 1992 and every production that took place there was treated, monitored and supported. Sloppiness was simply unthinkable.

Do the atmosphere and the importance of the theater have power over an artist, or do they serve him and his work?
The theater itself doesn't. The atmosphere of critics and the audience during the festivals, however, is horrific. But I didn't like being nagged everywhere and not having any privacy. The rehearsal period is wonderful – the festivals themselves are a nightmare.

Say a few words about "Bayreuth workshop" and how the productions were supported during the years of performance.
Typically, when directors come together in a theater, they are competitors. They greet and lie up and down to each other's faces. It wasn't like that in Bayreuth. You'd sit there at a table with Patrice Chéreau and Götz Friedrich and everyone talked about their rehearsals and was interested in attending the others' rehearsals. Wolfgang Wagner is to thank for that. He did not accept such senseless competition. If you have problems you'd sit together at the table and calculate and sort things out. The sentence "That's impossible," wasn't in our vocabulary either. Wolfgang Wagner always tried to solve the problem.

You hear a lot about the acoustics and the orchestra cover; sometime they could, they should really ...
... the things they have tried! Cover off, cover half off and here and there off. Then the gurus sat around and imagined they heard this or that. They would murmur, it could be this, it could be that, and then they would say *"yes!"* Then they would have one rehearsal with it and one rehearsal without it and then Wolfgang Wagner would say dryly: *"That's no good! Put the cover on! It never bothered my grandfather."* And then suddenly all the gurus agreed completely again that that was the ultimate wisdom. It was all rather humorous. Why should you do that? The Bayreuth theater was built to meet Wagner's needs for his main works. Not for the early works. But ideal for DER RING and PARSIFAL. Compromises are always important in a certain direction. But that's always Bayreuth anyway. Why should you change the sound of the orchestra? If you want to hear it differently, you can hear it – worse – in any other theater in the world.

und das sein und dann sagen sie, „ja jetzt!" Dann machen sie eine Probe mit und eine ohne, und dann kommt Wolfgang Wagner mit seiner Nüchternheit und sagt, „das ist nichts! – Deckel zu! Meinen Großvater hat das nicht gestört, also." Und dann waren die Gurus auch alle sofort wieder einverstanden, dass das der Weisheit letzter Schluss war. Das war alles eher komisch. Warum sollte man das tun? Das Bayreuther Haus ist nach den Angaben Wagners für die Hauptwerke gemacht. Nicht für die frühen. Für RING und PARSIFAL ideal! Kompromisse sind natürlich immer nach einer Richtung notwendig. Aber trotzdem ist das immer Bayreuth. Warum soll man den Orchesterklang verändern? Wenn man das anders hören will, kann man das ja an jedem anderen Theater der Welt – schlechter – hören.

Und architektonisch? Kommt man nicht in die Versuchung, dieses oder jenes umgebaut, vergrößert oder verändert haben zu wollen?
Nein gar nicht. Weil ja nach allem, was ich dort gesehen habe, die Möglichkeiten, die man in der eigenen Fantasie haben könnte, noch gar nicht ausgeschöpft sind. Mit dem Raum kann man noch so viel, viel mehr machen, jetzt durch bestimmte technische Möglichkeiten, Lichtwände, Video und so weiter. Man muss ja keine Wand rausbrechen. Das hätte ja auch immer akustische Konsequenzen. Da weiß man vorher nicht, was dann passieren würde. – Als ich den zweiten Aufzug GÖTTERDÄMMERUNG geprobt habe, kam Norbert Balatsch, der Chordirektor, zu mir und sagte, es sei ein ehernes Gesetz und ein Geheimnis, über eine bestimmte Linie – genau zwischen erstem und zweitem Portal – zu gehen. Dann bricht der Chorklang auseinander, die Chorgruppen, die vorne stehen, sind isoliert von denen, die hinten stehen. Diesen Meter verletzt man nicht ungestraft. Es gibt eben Eigengesetzlichkeiten dieses Raumes, und die muss man berücksichtigen. Das war eine der wichtigsten Erfahrungen für mich, da sind Grenzen gesetzt, da verselbständigen sich Dinge, um den Klang zu stützen. Das gilt auch für Materialien: In Bayreuth werden beim Bau der Dekorationen alle Materialien geprüft; ob reflektierende, zu sehr reflektierende, dämpfende und so weiter. Das sind wichtige Fragen, die für die Akustik ausschlaggebend sind.

Was haben Sie aus Bayreuth nach Ihrem FLIEGENDEN HOLLÄNDER und nach dem RING mitgenommen, was hat Harry Kupfer von Bayreuth gelernt?
Ich würde sagen, vor allem den Ensemblegeist, der dort wirklich das A und O für eine gelungene Produktion war. Man kommt zusammen aus aller Herren Länder, aber nach maximal drei Tagen ist man ein Ensemble. Das ist an vielen anderen Theatern verloren gegangen. Wie so etwas stattfindet mit einem Theaterleiter à la Wolfgang Wagner und seinem Apparat drumrum, der wirklich – wie auch Felsenstein das formuliert hat – nur dazu da ist, dass auf der Bühne das Richtige stattfindet. Es ist niemand wichtiger als die Bühne. Das habe ich mitgenommen. – Man kann nicht im Detail sagen, was man da aus Bayreuth mitnimmt; es ist das gesamte: So muss Theater eigentlich sein! So muss ein Theater geführt werden!! So ein Ethos muss ein Theater haben!!!

Das Gespräch führte Markus Kiesel.

And architecturally? Weren't you be tempted to have this or that built differently, expanded or changed?
No, not at all. Because after everything I have seen there, the possibilities existing in your own fantasies are no where near exhausted. There is so very much more that can still be done in that space now, exploring certain technical possibilities, walls of light, video, etc. There's no need to break out a wall. That will always have acoustic consequences. You don't know ahead of time what's going to happen. When I was rehearsing the second act of GÖTTERDÄMMERUNG Norbert Balatsch, the chorus director, told me about an ironclad rule and a secret about crossing a certain line – precisely between the first and the second portal. If you do, the chorus falls apart. The chorus groups standing in front are isolated from those standing at the back. Crossing over that one meter will always have consequences. The space has its own rules, and they have to be followed. That was one of the most important experiences for me. There are limits, and things take on their own dynamic to support the sound. That's true for materials, too: When decorations are built for Bayreuth, all materials are tested to determine whether they are reflective, too reflective, absorptive, etc. Those are important questions that are critical for the acoustics.

What did you take away from Bayreuth after putting on DER FLIEGENDE HOLLÄNDER and DER RING DES NIBELUNGEN? What did Harry Kupfer learn from Bayreuth?
I would say especially the spirit of ensemble, that is the be-all and end-all for a successful production at Bayreuth. You come together from all over the world, but after at most three days, you are an ensemble. That has been lost in many other theaters. The way that happens with a theater director à la Wolfgang Wagner and his supporting apparatus, someone who is truly there – as Felsenstein put it – for the sole reason of making sure the right thing is happening on stage. No one is more important than the stage. I learned that. – You can't say what exactly you take away from Bayreuth. It's the whole thing: That's the way a theater should really be! That's the way a theater should be run!! That's the kind of ethos a theater needs to have!!!

Conversation with Markus Kiesel.

Harry Kupfer wurde am 12. August 1935 in Berlin geboren, studierte Theaterwissenschaft in Leipzig und inszenierte 1958 in Halle an der Saale mit Antonín Dvoráks „Rusalka" seine erste Oper. Er war Oberspielleiter der Oper von Stralsund, dann in Karl-Marx-Stadt. Es folgten Engagements als Operndirektor in Weimar und Dresden, bis er 1981 Chefregisseur der Komischen Oper Berlin wurde, an der er bis 2002 als einer profiliertesten Opernregisseure Europas arbeitete. Neben der Arbeit in Berlin gastierte er überall in Europa, in den USA und Australien. Sein Werkverzeichnis umfasst 190 Arbeiten. Für die Bayreuther Festspiele erarbeitete er 1978 eine spektakuläre Interpretation des FLIEGENDEN HOLLÄNDER und 1988 des RING DES NIBELUNGEN. Harry Kupfer ist Mitglied der Akademie der Künste in Berlin, der Freien Akademie der Künste in Hamburg und Professor an der Berliner Musikhochschule.

Harry Kupfer was born on August 12, 1935 in Berlin and studied theater in Leipzig. In 1958 he directed his first opera, "Rusalka" by Antonín Dvorák. He was Principal Director of the Stralsund Oper and Karl-Marx-Stadt. Thereafter, he had engagements as Opera Director in Weimar and Dresden and was named Principal Director of the Komische Oper Berlin in 1981, where he earned recognition as one of the most distinguished opera directors in Europe. Along side his work in Berlin, he held guest positions all over Europe, the USA and Australia. Kupfer developed spectacular interpretations of "Der Fliegende Holländer" for the 1978 Bayreuth Festival and "Der Ring des Nibelungen" in 1988. Harry Kupfer is a member of the Akademie der Künste in Berlin, the Freie Akademie in Hamburg, and is a professor in the Berlin Musikhochschule.

Blick in die Probebühne I., noch mit Probemarkierungen (auf dem Boden) von Wolfgang Wagners RING-Inszenierung 1970
View of Rehearsal Stage I with rehearsal markings (on the floor) remaining from Wolfgang Wagner's 1970 RING staging

Biografien

Markus Kiesel studierte Musikwissenschaft, Kunstgeschichte und Germanistik in Heidelberg und Architekturgeschichte in den USA. 1992 Promotion zum Dr. phil. über das Instrumentalwerk Siegfried Wagners. Regieassistent und Dramaturg in Freiburg und Kassel, Chefdisponent und Betriebsdirektor an den Opern in Frankfurt am Main, Cottbus, Dortmund und Wiesbaden. Lehraufträge und Vorträge an den Universitäten von Heidelberg, Bochum, Saarbrücken, Amiens. Seit 2005 Kaufmännischer Direktor der Ludwigsburger Schlossfestspiele / Internationale Festspiele Baden-Württemberg.

Joachim Mildner arbeitete nach einer kaufmännischen Ausbildung als Regieassistent am Opernhaus des Staatstheaters Kassel (Der Ring des Nibelungen, Parsifal), und studierte Graphic Design, Kunst und Architektur an der HbK Kassel, der HdK Berlin und der Cooper Union in New York. Master of Fine Art 1993, seither selbständig. Designer zahlreicher Bücher und Kataloge im Bereich Kunst und Architektur.

Hannelore Ostfeld studierte Betriebswirtschaft in Wuppertal, Englisch und Französisch in Köln (Dipl.-Übersetzerin). Redakteurin beim Wirtschaftsmagazin „Capital" (Ressort Kultur und Reisen). Langjährige leitende Redakteurin des Wirtschaftsmagazins „impulse" als Chefin vom Dienst. Seit 1998 freie Journalistin im Bereich Kultur, Reisen, Architektur und Existenzgründung. Lektorin zahlreicher Buchveröffentlichungen und Ausstellungskataloge in den Bereichen Architektur und Wirtschaft.

Dietmar Schuth studierte Kunstgeschichte und Germanistik in Heidelberg sowie Archäologie und Theaterwissenschaft in Wien. 1995 Promotion über die „Farbe Blau" in Heidelberg. Seit 2001 Künstlerischer Leiter des Kunstvereins Worms und seit 2005 auch des Kunstvereins Schwetzingen. Daneben künstlerischer Berater bei diversen Theaterproduktionen in Kiel und Wiesbaden sowie Forschungen zur Architektur des 19. Jahrhunderts in Worms und Heidelberg, Arbeit an einem Architekturführer „Hässliches Heidelberg".

Jens Willebrand studierte Fotografie an der Fachhochschule Dortmund, Diplom 1987. Seit 1984 eigenes Studio in Köln, spezialisiert auf Architektur- und Interieur-Fotografie. Auftraggeber: neben Nicholas Grimshaw, Norman Foster zahlreiche andere Architekturbüros, Unternehmen und Zeitschriften.

K. Scott Witmer studierte Musikwissenschaft und Gesang an der University of Richmond, Übersetzungswissenschaft an der Universität Wien und Germanistik an der University of Texas in Austin. Stipendiat der Freien Universität Berlin. Tätigkeit als Dozent/Museumsführer für die Gesellschaft für Staatsgeschichte in Minnesota. Heute arbeitet er als Editor/Übersetzer in Düsseldorf und New York.

Biographies

Markus Kiesel studied music history, art history and German literature in Heidelberg and architectural history in the USA. His 1992 PhD thesis was on Siegfried Wagner's instrumental works. Stage assistant and dramaturge in Freiburg and Kassel, organizational and operational manager of the operas in Frankfurt/Main, Cottbus, Dortmund and Wiesbaden. Guest university lectureships in Heidelberg, Bochum, Saarbrücken and Amiens. Business director of the Ludwigsburg Schloss-Festival / International Festival in Baden-Württemberg since 2005.

Joachim Mildner studied business and was a stage assistant in the opera house of the Staatstheater in Kassel (Der Ring des Nibelungen, Parsifal). He studied graphic design, art and architecture at the HbK in Kassel, at the KbK in Berlin, and at Cooper Union in New York. MFA in 1993, freelancing since then. Designed numerous art and architecture books and catalogs.

Hannelore Ostfeld studied business administration in Wuppertal, English and French in Cologne (diploma in translation). Editor of the business magazine "Capital" (culture and travel sections). Was principal editor of the business magazine "impulse" for many years. Freelance journalist for culture, travel, architecture and start-up business ventures. Has proofred many book publications and exhibit catalogs (on architecture and business).

Dietmar Schuth studied art history and German literature in Heidelberg and archeology and dramatics in Vienna. His 1995 PhD dissertation was about the color blue in Heidelberg. He has been artistic director of the Worms Kunstverein since 2001 and of the Schwetzingen Kunstverein since 2005. Artistic advisor for many theater productions in Kiel and Wiesbaden and research in 19th century architecture in Worms and Heidelberg. Works on the architectural guide „Ugly Heidelberg."

Jens Willebrand studied photography at the Fachhochschule Dortmund, diploma 1987. Has run an independent studio in Cologne since 1984 specializing in architectural and interior photography. Clients include Nicholas Grimshaw, Norman Foster and numerous other architectural offices, firms and magazines.

K. Scott Witmer studied music history/theory and voice performance at the University of Richmond, translation studies at the Universität Wien and German studies at the University of Texas at Austin. He held a fellowship at the Freie Universität Berlin and worked as a lecturer/museum guide for the Minnesota Historical Society. He currently works as an editor/translator in Düsseldorf and New York.

Einführung:
S. 16: (1) Habel, Heinrich: Festspielhaus und Wahnfried, geplante und ausgeführte Bauten Richard Wagners. München (Prestel), 1985, im Folgenden: [HH], 323-488, hier 393.
S. 18: (1) vgl. Fontane, Theodor: Brief an Karl Zöllner (1889) und: Strawinsky, Igor: Parsifal 1912. In: Barth, Herbert (Hg.): Der Festspielhügel, Richard Wagners Werk in Bayreuth. München (dtv), 1976 [Barth], 74 ff u. 116 ff.
S. 19: (1) zit. n. Carl Friedrich Glasenapp: Das Leben Richard Wagners, in sechs Büchern dargestellt, 6 Bde, 4. Aufl. Leipzig (Breitkopf & Härtel), 1905 [CFG], 4, 424.

Wagner und die Architektur:
S. 20: (1) Wagner, Richard: Mein Leben. Hg. v. Martin Gregor-Dellin. München (List) 1963 [RW ML]; Alle historischen Zitate sind im Folgenden orthographisch behutsam aktualisiert. (2) siehe: Bauer, Oswald Georg: Habent sua fata et imagines. In: Das Festspielbuch 2006, hg. v. Wolfgang Wagner, 14-64;
S. 22: (1) Im Folgenden sind alle Zitate Richard Wagners, wenn nicht anders angegeben, aus: Wagner, Richard: Sämtliche Schriften und Dichtungen. Volksausgabe, Bände 1–12 und 16. Leipzig (Breitkopf & Härtel), o. J. (1911); [RW SuD], hier 1, 267 (2) RW ML 231 (3) RW SuD 2, 79 (4) RW ML 626 f (5) RW SuD 7, 57 (6) RW SuD 7, 57 (7) RW SuD 16, 70 (Szenische Vorschriften für die Aufführungen des „Lohengrin" in Weimar 1850).
S. 24: (1) RW SuD 7, 191 (2) Wagner, Richard: Sämtliche Briefe (1842 – 1862). Hg. im Auftrage der Richard-Wagner-Stiftung Bayreuth, Leipzig (Deutscher Verlag für Musik ab 1983) bzw. Wiesbaden, Leipzig, Paris (Breitkopf & Härtel ab 2000), 14 Bände, [RW SB], hier 13, 338 (3) RW SuD 10, 324 (4) RW SuD 10, 350 (5) Wagner, Cosima: Die Tagebücher. Editiert und kommentiert von Martin Gregor-Dellin und Dietrich Mack, 2 Bde. München (Piper) 1976/77 [CT], hier 2, 1213.
S. 25: (1) CFG 6, 119 (2) Richard Wagners Briefwechsel mit B. Schott's Söhne. Hg. v. Wilhelm Altmann. Leipzig (Breitkopf & Härtel), 1911, 18 ff.
S. 26: (1) Wagner, Richard: Das Braune Buch. Tagebuchaufzeichnungen 1865 – 1882. Vorgelegt und kommentiert v. Joachim Bergfeld. Zürich (Atlantis), 1975, [BB] 83 (2) RW ML 93 (3) RW ML 98 (4) RW ML 591.
S. 27: (1) RW SB 2, 101 f (2) Gregor-Dellin, Martin: Richard Wagner. Sein Leben – Sein Werk – Sein Jahrhundert. München (Piper), 1980 [MGD], Erster Teil: 1821 – 1849, 374 (3) CT 2, 443.
S. 30: (1) RW ML 13 (2) RW ML 14 (3) RW ML 23 (4) RW SB 7, 288.
S. 31: (1) RW ML 430 (2) CT 2, 592 (3) RW ML 237 (4) RW ML 697 ff.
S. 32: (1) RW ML 171 (2) RW ML 707 (3) Weißheimer, Wendelin: Erlebnisse mit Richard Wagner, Franz Liszt und vielen anderen Zeitgenossen. Stuttgart und Leipzig (Deutsche Verlagsanstalt), 1898, 145; (4) König Ludwig II. und Richard Wagner: Briefwechsel, 5 Bde. Karlsruhe (G. Braun), 1936 [RW LII], 2, 224 (5) RW SuD 8, 55 ff („Deutsche Kunst und Politik").
S. 34: (1) RW SuD 12, 372.
S. 35: (1) RW LII 3, 230 (2) RW SB 10, 388 (3) CFG 6, 691 (4) CFG 6, 382 (5) CT 2, 933 (6„) RW SuD 16, 67.
S. 36: (1) RW SuD 3, 29 (2) CT 1, 506 (3) CT 2, 500 ff (4) CT 2, 1108 (5) CT 2, 1039 (6) CT 1, 1013.
S. 38: (1) CFG 6, 540 (2) RW SuD 9, 84; (3) RW ML 274 (4) RW SuD 12, 195.
S. 39: (1) RW ML 15 (2) RW SuD 9, 332 (3) RW ML 674 (4) CT 1, 902
(5) RW ML 94.
S. 40: (1) RW SB 1, 169 (2) RW SuD 9, 119 (3) RW SuD 3, 128 (4) ebd. (5) RW SuD 10, 120.
S. 42: (1) CFG 1, 91 (2) RW SuD 8, 36 (3) RW SuD 10, 41 (4) RW SB 3, 295 (5) RW SB 11, 401.
S. 43: (1) CT 1, 1002 (2) CT 2, 61 (3) RW SuD 3, 24.
S. 44: (1) Mack in CT 2, 16 und CT 2, 167 (2) CFG 6, 579 (3) CT 2, 922 (4) RW SuD 12, 121.

Visionen eines idealen Theaters:
S. 46: (1) RW SuD 3, 123-129; „Eine Kapitulation": RW SuD 9, 5.
S. 51: (1) RW ML 354 (2) RW SB 3, 425 (3) zit. n. MGD 316 (4) RW SuD 3, 111.
S. 52: (1) RW SuD 6, 273 ff.
S. 54: (1) HH 23-320 (2) RW LII 2, 125 (3) BB 83.
S. 55: (1) HH 325 (2) CT 1, 379 (3) ebd.; zu Neumanns Plan HH 337.

Das Bayreuther Festspielhaus:
S. 56: (1) HH 329; im Folgenden vgl.: HH 323-388 (2) HH 330 (3) HH 334 (4) HH 335.
S. 58: (1) Richard Wagner an Emil Heckel. Zur Entstehungsgeschichte der Bühnenfestspiele in Bayreuth, hg. v. Karl Heckel, Leipzig (Breitkopf & Härtel), (1899) 1912, 74 (2) RW LII 29 (3) RW SuD 12, 375 (4) CT 1, 1011 (5) CT 1, 715 (6) CT 1, 726 (7) CT 1, 727 (8) zit. n. HH 330.
S. 59: (1) ML 198 (2) RW ML 549 (3) RW ML11.
S. 62: (1) zit. n. HH 326 (2) siehe Thomas Strobel: historismusarchiv.net (3)
zit. n. HH 341 (4) vgl. Strobel a.a.O.
S. 63: (1) Strobel a.a.O. (2) aus: Tappert, Wilhelm (Hg.): Wörterbuch der Unhöflichkeiten. Richard Wagner im Spiegel der Kritik. München (dtv), 1967, [Tappert] 51 (3) RW SuD 9, 325 (4) CFG 4, 424 (5) CT 1, 522.
S. 64: (1) RW SuD 9, 342 ff (2) Wagner, Richard: Bayreuther Briefe (1871-1883). 2. Aufl. Leipzig (Breitkopf & Härtel) (1907) 1912 , 78 [BayB] (3) zit. n. HH 341 (4) zit. n. HH 351.
S. 66: (1) zit. n. HH 349 (2) zit. n. HH 343 (3) CT 1, 524.
S. 68: (1) Zitate oben: RW SuD 9, 341; CT 1, 662.
S. 70: (1) Das Bühnenfestspielhaus zu Bayreuth. RW SuD 9, 322 ff.
S. 71: (1) RW LII 2, 167.
S. 72: (1) Kietz, Gustav Adolf: Richard Wagner in den Jahren 1842 – 1849 und 1873 – 1875, Dresden 1905, 224 f (2) Briefwechsel zwischen Cosima Wagner und Ernst zu Hohenlohe-Langenburg. Stuttgart (Cotta), 1937, 111 (31.1.1895).
S. 75: (1) RW ML 663 (2) Nietzsche und Wagner, Stationen einer epochalen Begegnung. Hg. v. Dieter Borchmeyer und Jörg Salaquarda. Bd 1, Briefwechsel. Frankfurt am Main (Insel), 1994, 163 (3) CT 1, 1085 und CFG 6, 499 ff (4) HH 345 (5) RW an Mannheim, zit. n. HH 332 (6) CT 1, 580 (7) Kiez 202.
S. 76: (1) Kiez 183 und zit. n. HH 355 (2) CT 1, 758 (3) BayB 79f (4) CT 1, 616 (5) CT 1, 703 f.
S. 78: (1) CT 1, 711 f (2) RW SuD 12, 380 (3) RW SuD 12, 378.
S. 81: (1) CT 1, 733 (2) CT 1, 734 (3) CT 1, 880 (4) CT 1, 731 f (5) zit. n. HH 357 (6) ebd. (7) Brückwald, Otto: Das Bühnenfestspielhaus zu Bayreuth. In: Deutsche Bauzeitung, Nr. 1. Berlin, 1875 [OB 1875] 1 f.
S. 84: (1) Kietz 203 (2) CT 1, 741 (3) CT 1, 705 (4) CT 1, 693 (5) CT 1, 865 (6) CT 1, 808 (7) CT 2, 401 (8) Schletterer, H. M.: Richard Wagners Bühnenfestspiel. In: Tappert 45; „Und draußen auf einem Hügel...", Tappert 83.

Der Außenbau:
S. 88: (1) RW LII 1, 110 (2) CFG 5, 268 ff (3) MGD 717 (4) Tappert 96 (5) ebd. 52 (6) CT 2, 222 (7) RW ML 25 (8) CT 1, 786.
S. 92: (1) CT 1, 660.
S. 99: Richard Wagner an seine Künstler. Zweiter Band der „Bayreuther Briefe", Hg. v. Erich Kloss, 3. Aufl. Leipzig (Breitkopf & Härtel), (1910) 1912, 181.
S. 100: (1) zit. n. HH 25 (2) CT 2, 785 und RW SuD 8, 202 (3) RW SuD 2, 231 (4) HH 377 f (5) CT 1, 768.
S. 102: (1) RW SuD 9, 343.
S. 105: (1) OB 1875.
S. 106: (1) MGD, 791 (2) gemeint ist die Schrift „Über Polychromie und ihren Ursprung", 1851: CT 1, 398 (3) CT 2, 143.
S. 108: (1) Barth 77 f (2) CFG 6, 445 (3) RW SuD 12, 412.
S. 109: (1) CFG 3, 136.
S. 112: (1) CT 1, 1014.
S. 114: (1) CT 2, 571 (2) CT 1, 318.
S. 115: (1) Richard Wagner an Eliza Wille. 15 Briefe des Meisters nebst Erinnerungen und Erläuterungen von Eliza Wille. 2. Aufl. Hg. v. Wolfgang Golther. Leipzig (Breitkopf & Härtel), (1908) 1912, 11 (2) RW LII 1, 72 (3) Wolfgang Wagner im Gespräch am 28.11.1907.
S. 116: (1) RW SuD 3, 125 (2) CT 1, 157.
S. 120: (1) OB 1875 (2) RW SuD 3, 339.
S. 121: (1) CT 1, 477 (2) CT 2, 1031 (3) CT 2, 1041.
S. 123: (1) CT 2, 562 (2) CT 1, 815.
S. 125: (1) RW LII 3, 205 (2) ebd.
S. 127: (1) HH 395 (2) CT 2, 1011 (3) CT 2, 1025 (4) Alberti, Leon Battista: Zehn Bücher über die Baukunst. Ins Deutsche übertragen von Max Theuer, Wien/Leipzig, 1912, Darmstadt, 1975.
S. 130: (1) zit. n. CFG 2, 468.
S. 131: (1) CT 2, 169 (2) CT 1, 1006 (3) CT 1, 998 (4) CT 1, 799 (5) RW SuD 6, 277 (6) Tschaikowsky, Peter Iljitsch: Erinnerungen an Bayreuth. In: Barth 39 ff (7) ebd. „Bayreuth is Germany": CFG 5, 285.
S. 133: (1) Richard Wagner an Mathilde Wesendonck. Tagebuchblätter und Briefe 1853 – 1871, 42. Aufl. Leipzig (Breitkopf & Härtel), (1908), 9.
S. 134: (1) RW SuD 6, 275 ff (2) RW SuD 6, 277 (3) CFG 4, 404.
S. 135: (1) RW SuD 12, 397.
S. 136: (1) RW SuD 6, 276 (2) Richard Wagner an Emil Heckel. Zur Entstehungsgeschichte der Bühnenfestspiele in Bayreuth, hg. v. Karl Heckel, Leipzig (Breitkopf & Härtel), (1899) 1912, 50 (3) siehe Barth 39 ff (4) Romain Rolland, 1891 in Barth 75.
S. 138: (1) in Barth 89 (2) CFG 5, 202 (3) CFG 5, 300 (4) CFG 6, 620 (5) OB 1875.

Der Innenbau:
S. 143: (1) zit. n. HH 370.
S. 144: (1) RW SuD 16, 18 f (2) CFG 5, 132 (3) CT 1, 279.
S. 150: (1) in Tappert 96 (2) Saint-Saëns, Camille: Bayreuth und „Der Ring des Nibelungen". In: Barth 44 ff (3) OB 1875 und HH 638 (4) RW SuD 10, 167.
S. 153: (1) CT 1, 848.
S. 154: (1) Einer von Richard Wagner befürworteten Idee von Angelo Neumann folgend, vgl. N., A.: Erinnerungen an Richard Wagner. Leipzig (L. Staackmann), 1907, 259
S. 155: (1) RW SuD 1,59 (2) RW M 48 (3) RW ML 587.
S. 156: (1) CT 1, 982 (2) CT 1, 988 (3) ebd.
S. 157: (1) Schletterer, H. M. in Tappert 101 (2) Puschmann in Tappert 97.
S. 160: (1) CT 1, 938 (2) CT 1, 988 (3) Appia, Adolphe: Über das Bayreuther Festspielhaus. (1902) In: Barth 99 ff.
S. 164: (1) RW SuD 3, 13 (2) RW SuD 3, 24 (3) RW SuD 9, 336.
S. 165: (1) RW SuD 9, 336 (2) OB 1875 (3) RW SuD 9, 196 (4) RW SuD 3, 160.
S. 167: (1) RW SB 6, 608 (2) RW LII 1, 66 (3) RW SB 4, 344.
S. 168: (1) CT 1, 397 (2) Fontane, Theodor: Brief an Karl Zöllner. In: Barth 74 (2) Strawinsky, Igor: Parsifal. In: Barth 116 ff (4) CT 2, 459.
S. 170: (1) CT 1, 768 (2) zit. n. HH 358 (3) MGD 52.
S. 171: (1) MGD 147 (2) RW SuD 9, 339.
S. 179: (1) RW SuD 16, 160.
S. 181: (1) RW SuD 9, 337 (2) ebd.
S. 182: (1) RW SuD 9, 339 (2) Appia, Adolphe: Über den Saal des Bayreuther Festspielhauses. Eine technische Betrachtung. In: Die Gesellschaft, Münchner Halbmonatsschrift, 18. Jg 1902, 198-204, zit. n. HH 649 f. (3) ebd.
S. 183: (1) Brückwald, Otto: Zur Baugeschichte des Bayreuther Festspielhauses. In: Musikalisches Wochenblatt, 35. Jg. Leipzig 1904, Nr. 31-33 [OB 1904], o.S. Zur Bühnentechnik und Beleuchtung vgl.: Baumann, Carl-Friedrich: Bühnentechnik im Festspielhaus Bayreuth. München (Prestel), 1980 [Baumann], (3) MGD, 718 (4) Wagner, Richard: „Rückblick auf die Bühnenfestspiele des Jahres 1876" (1878), RW SuD 10, 111.
S. 185: (1) RW ML 559 (2) MGD 401 (3) RW SuD 16, 160 (4) ebd. (5) CFG 5, 268.
S. 186: (1) Strawinsky, in Barth 116.
S. 190: (1) OB 1904 o.S. (2) RW ML 6 (3) RW ML 60 (4) in einem offenen Schreiben an Friedrich Schön in Worms (1882), RW SuD 10, 292 (5) BayB 180.
S. 191: (1) BayB 209 f (2) CFG 5, 199 (3) zit. n. HH 366 (4) HH 365.
S. 192: (1) RW SuD 16, 161.
S. 194: (1) CFG 5, 291.
S. 204: (1) Diese Darstellung folgt im Wesentlichen Baumann (2) RW SuD 10, 110 (3) CFB 13 (4) RW SuD 6, 275 f (5) RW SuD 5,149 (6) OB 1904 (7) CT 1, 998.
S. 206: (1) CT 1, 1008 und 1002 (2) BayB 79.
S. 212: (1) RW SuD 9, 286 (2) CT 1, 1009 (3) RW SuD 8, 131 (4) RW LII 1, 82 (5) zit. n. Baumann 206.
S. 213: (1) CT 2, 605 (2) CT 2, 210.
S. 214: (1) RW ML 413 (2) CT 2, 845 (3) zit. n. HH 373 (4) MGD 688 (5) zit. n. HH 350.
S. 215: (1) Baumann 286.

Weitere Literatur:
Bauer, Oswald-Georg: Richard Wagner geht ins Theater. Bayreuth (Bayreuther Festspiele), 1996
Bayreuther Festspiele, die Idee – das Haus – die Aufführungen. Hg. v. Wolfgang Wagner. Bayreuth, 2003
„Dort stehe es, auf dem lieblichen Hügel", Baugeschichte des Bayreuther Festspielhauses. Katalog der Ausstellung der Bayreuther Festspiele und der Bayerischen Vereinsbank 1994. München, 1994
Gregor-Dellin, Martin: Richard Wagner, eine Biographie in Bildern. München (Piper), 1982; ds: Wagner-Chronik. München, Kassel, u.a. (dtv, Bärenreiter), 1983
Hamann, Brigitte: Die Familie Wagner. Reinbek bei Hamburg (rororo), 2005
Karbaum, Michael: Studien zur Geschichte der Bayreuther Festspiele. Regensburg (Gustav Bosse), 1976
Kiesel, Markus: Le séjour à Paris de Richard Wagner en 1839 – 1842, La Juive de Halévy et la constitution du drame musical. In: Richard Wagner: Points des départ et aboutissements, Anfangs- und Endpunkte. Hsg. von Danielle Buschinger u.a. Amiens (Presses du Centre d'Etudes Médiévales, Université de Picardie Jules Verne), 2002: ds: Studien zur Instrumentalmusik Siegfried Wagners. Frankfurt u.a. (Peter Lang), 1994
Kranich, Friedrich: Bühnentechnik der Gegenwart, 2 Bände. München (Oldenbourg), 1929, 1933
Mack, Dietrich und Voss, Egon (Hsg): Richard Wagner, Leben und Werk in Daten und Bildern. Frankfurt (Insel), 1978
Neumann, Angelo: Erinnerungen an Richard Wagner. Leipzig (L. Staackmann), 1907
Nietzsche und Wagner, Stationen einer epochalen Begegnung. Hsg. v. Dieter Borchmeyer und Jörg Salaquarda. Band 1, Briefwechsel. Frankfurt am Main (Insel), 1994
Der Ring, Bayreuth 1976 – 1980. Pierre Boulez u.a. Vorw. Wolfgang Wagner. Unter Mitarbeit von Sylvie Nussac. Berlin u Hamburg (Kristall), 1980
Schuth, Dietmar: Die Farbe Blau, Versuch einer Charakteristik. Münster (Lit), 1995; ds: Blaues Wunder blauer Berge. In: Der Berg, Ausstellungskatalog Kunstverein Heidelberg. Hsg. v. Hans Gercke. Heidelberg (Kehrer), o.J. [2002]
Wagner, Friedelind und Cooper, Page: The Heritage of Fire. New York and London (Harper & Brothers), o.J. [1946]
Wagner, Siegfried. Erinnerungen. Stuttgart (J. Engelhorns Nachf.), 1923
Wagner. Wolfgang: Lebensakte. München (Albrecht Knaus) 1994

Bildnachweis:
Jens Willebrand sowie Nationalarchiv der Richard-Wagner-Stiftung Bayreuth; Bildarchiv der Bayreuther Festspiele, Bautagebücher der Bayreuther Festspiele; Stadtarchiv Bayreuth; Bayerische Verwaltung der staatlichen Schlösser, Gärten und Seen; Deutsches Theater Museum München; Joachim Mildner; Dietmar Schuth.

„… ‚und nachdem ich das unsichtbare Orchester geschaffen, möchte ich auch das unsichtbare Theater erfinden! – Und das unhörbare Orchester', fügt er hinzu, das kummervolle Sinnen mit Humor beschließend."

"'… and once I've created the invisible orchestra, I also want to invent the invisible theater! – And the inaudible orchestra,' he added, rounding out the worried pondering with humor."

Cosima Wagner (23. September 1878)